OPTIONS
ESSENTIAL CONCEPTS AND TRADING STRATEGIES

Second Edition

OPTIONS
ESSENTIAL CONCEPTS AND TRADING STRATEGIES

Second Edition

Edited by The Options Institute:
The Educational Division of the Chicago Board Options Exchange

McGraw-Hill

New York San Francisco Washington, D.C. Auckland Bogota
Caracas Lisbon London Madrid Mexico City Milan
Montreal New Delhi San Juan Singapore Sydney Tokyo Toronto

McGraw-Hill

A Division of The McGraw-Hill Companies

Library of Congress Cataloging-in-Publication Data

Options : essential concepts and trading strategies / edited by The
    Options Institute, the Educational Division of the Chicago Options
    Exchange. —2nd ed.
      p.   cm.
    Includes index.
    ISBN 0-7863-0272-0
    1. Options (Finance)   I. Options Institute (Chicago Board Options
    Exchange)
    HG6024.A3065 1995
    332.63'228—dc20   94–18529

Printed in the United States of America
      6 7 8 9 0   BP   1 0 9 8

PREFACE

This text represents the efforts of many authors, most of whom have taught in The Options Institute. Its authors include professors and traders, option instructors and strategists. As such, the book provides information on the options market and options trading that is practical and, hopefully, easily understood.

Over the many years that The Options Institute has been educating people about option concepts and strategies, its goal has been to provide a practical, comprehensible approach to using options. The philosophy used in the classroom has carried over to this book.

The book is organized in three parts: Essential Concepts, Trading Strategies, and Real-Time Applications. An introduction to these main parts, Chapter 1, presents an entertaining and informative history of options.

The Essential Concepts part begins with Fundamentals of Options and skips the mathematics that often confuse rather than clarify. Instead, the reader finds a general discussion of option pricing theory, including usable concepts regarding the change in an option's price relative to stock price movement, passage of time, and changes in implied volatility.

This section also presents options strategies, giving the range of considerations for selecting a strategy, such as the effect of time and the optimal price movement of the underlying security, as well as taking a look at equivalent positions. The last chapter in this section describes new options products, such as longer-term options (LEAPS®), and covers strategies involving these.

Part 2, Trading Strategies, discusses subjective elements and practical considerations for individual investors, institutional investors, and floor traders. Individual investors can learn practical uses of equity options including the most important considerations in strategy selection and the most common pitfalls to be avoided. Institutional investors are shown how options can be used on a portfolio basis to manage risk, to increase income, and to benefit properly from leverage. In addition to exploring index options strategies, the section covers controversial options strategies (such as selling equity puts and buying out-of-the-money calls), and it describes how they can be appropriate and profitable for the professional money manager.

The chapter entitled "The Business of Market Making" gives the reader a close look at the method by which floor traders earn their living. The myths that floor trading is akin to gambling and that floor traders profit on every trade may well disappear after an examination of this low profit-per-transaction business. While not designed as a "how-to manual", this chapter does explain the trader's method of operation. Then it develops the conclusion that by providing the market with liquidity and by taking only the spread between bid and ask, the floor trader is not in competition with the off-floor trader.

Part 3, Real Time Applications, gives applications and results. The chapter entitled "Using Option Market Information to Make Stock Market Decisions" takes a look at three indicators: the put-call ratio, the options premium level, and the level of implied volatility. It discusses how this information has been used to make stock market predictions.

The "Institutional Case Studies" chapter presents two actual cases in contrasting investing environments. The first case study covers the use of option strategies for risk management from the portfolio manager's perspective. The second case discusses the issues involved when an investment trust seeks to gain approval from their trustees to allow investment in derivative securities. These real situations give the reader the opportunity to apply theory to practice.

Finally, a glossary of industry jargon is included as a reference for interested readers.

ACKNOWLEDGMENTS

Anyone who has participated in writing a book for publication knows the many hours invested by numerous people to reach the production date. In addition to our many heartfelt thanks to our authors, we thank the numerous members and staff who helped make this effort successful.

ABOUT THE AUTHORS

J. Marc Allaire (Chapter 5, New Product Strategies) is a staff instructor with The Options Institute. Mr. Allaire teaches classes on options strategies, futures, and portfolio management to stock brokers and professional money managers.

Mr. Allaire holds an undergraduate degree from the University of Ottawa and a master of business administration degree from McGill University in Montréal.

Prior to joining the Chicago Board Options Exchange, Mr. Allaire was vice president and options manager with Richardson Greenshields of Canada Limited. His primary focus was on the retail side of the business where he concentrated on broker education, strategy development, and sales support. Mr. Allaire also has traded futures and options for a regional brokerage firm in Montréal and had responsibility for options marketing for the Montréal Exchange.

James B. Bittman (Chapter 2, Fundamentals of Options, Chapter 3, Volatility Explained, and Chapter 7, Institutional Uses of Options) has over 10 years' experience as a floor trader, both at the Chicago Board Options Exchange trading equity options and at the Chicago Board of Trade trading options on financial futures and options on agricultural futures.

As a regular instructor at The Options Institute, Mr. Bittman teaches options to stock brokers and professional money managers from the United States and Europe.

Mr. Bittman holds a bachelor of arts from Amherst College and a masters of business administration degree from Harvard University.

Riva Aidus Hémond (Chapter 1, History of Options) is the director of retail marketing with the Chicago Board Options Exchange. Her responsibilities include the development of marketing materials and educational programs for retail brokers and individual investors on basic and advanced option strategies. Ms. Hémond also teaches the History of Options session in the Chicago Board Options Exchange's New Member Orientation program for new traders.

Prior to joining the Chicago Board Options Exchange, Ms. Hémond started an options department at Baker, Watts & Co., a regional brokerage firm in Baltimore, Maryland. She also has worked with Dean Witter, Merrill Lynch, and E.F. Hutton.

Ms. Hémond has a bachelor of arts degree from Goucher College in Maryland.

Elliot Katz (Chapter 4, Option Strategies: Analysis and Selection) is in sales management with a major Wall Street firm. Prior to that, Mr. Katz was an instructor with The Options Institute, and was involved with teaching options strategy to retail brokers and professional money managers.

Mr. Katz has been the options strategist for Tucker, Anthony and R.L. Day where he developed and recommended option strategies for retail and institutional clients.

Also, Mr. Katz holds a bachelor of science in computer science from State University of New York at Stony Brook.

Harrison Roth (Chapter 6, Option Strategies for the Small Investor) had been involved with options for more than 10 years when the Chicago Board Options Exchange started listed options trading. During his nine years with Drexel Burnham Lambert, he wrote several options reports which became widely known and respected. These include *Trading Put Options, Trading Index Options,* and *The Future of Derivative Products.* He wrote the text for two options videotapes, *Conservative Use of Options* and *Index Options,* as well as writing the text for an audiotape on options buying and writing.

Mr. Roth, a recognized option authority, is quoted frequently in *Barron's, Forbes, Investor's Business Daily,* and other publications. He makes liberal use of computers and says he is most proud of his work in pioneering "custom-made" options computer programs for account executives.

Currently, Mr. Roth is first vice president, senior options strategist for Cowen & Company. He is the author of *LEAPS®* (Irwin Professional Publishing).

Anthony J. Saliba (Chapter 8, The Business of Market Making) is the general partner of Saliba and Company as well as Chairman and chief executive officer of International Trading Institute. In addition, Mr.

Saliba is a member of the Chicago Board Options Exchange, the Chicago Board of Trade, the Chicago Mercantile Exchange, the New York Stock Exchange, and the Chicago Stock Exchange.

Mr. Saliba began his career as a market maker at the Teledyne trading post. He developed his own trading system, which made him one of the most active individual traders on the Chicago Board Options Exchange. Mr. Saliba served on the board of directors of the Chicago Board Options Exchange from 1987 to 1989.

Mr. Saliba now directs the International Trading Institute, which conducts high performance trading simulations for traders worldwide on market dynamics. Also, Mr. Saliba is on the Executive Advisory Board of the Stuart School of Business in Chicago.

Mr. Saliba attended Indiana University where he received a bachelor of science in accounting in 1977.

Gary L. Trennepohl (Chapter 10, Institutional Case Studies) is the Peters Professor of Banking and Finance, and the Interim Dean of the College of Business Administration and Graduate School of Business at Texas A&M University. He regularly serves as a consultant to pension funds, endowments, and corporations about investment management and employee benefits programs. Professor Trennepohl also is an instructor in The Options Institute, teaching the institutional investor case study. A seminar leader in executive development programs, he frequently conducts seminars for business journalists about financial analysis and current developments in financial markets.

During the past three years, Professor Trennepohl has helped faculties at universities in the middle Europe and the former Soviet Republics to develop courses in financial markets and investment management. He has lectured about corporate and investment management in Russia, Germany, France, China, and Australia. Part of his current responsibilities include developing contacts and completing operating agreements between Texas A&M and foreign universities.

Professor Trennepohl has coauthored two texts, *Investment Management* (1993), and *An Introduction to Financial Management* (1984). His research about investment management and portfolio strategies using options has been published in the *Journal of Financial and Quantitative Analysis, Journal of Financial Research, Financial Management,* and other professional journals. He has been an officer in several professional associations, and currently is serving as president of the 11,000 member *Financial Management Association.* In 1968, Professor

Trennepohl graduated from the University of Tulsa with a B.S. degree in economics, and he received his Ph.D. in finance from Texas Tech University in 1976.

C. R. (Sonny) Tucker (Chapter 10, Institutional Case Studies) is the director of investment planning for Shell Oil Company. He joined the Shell Pension Trust in February 1990 as the director of investment planning and deputy administrator. Mr. Tucker is primarily responsible for determining overall investment strategy, tactical asset allocation, investment research, currencies, domestic and international index funds, and private investments.

Prior to his current assignment, Mr. Tucker spent 23 years in various Shell Oil Company financial and operational responsibilities, which included general operating manager, Pecten, Syria; treasurer, Shell Offshore Inc., and assistant general auditor, Shell Oil Company.

Mr. Tucker received his B.A. in finance from the University of Arkansas in 1966 and is a member of the Houston Chapter of the Financial Executives Institute.

James W. Yates, Jr. (Chapter 9, Using Option Market Information to Make Stock Market Decisions) is president of DYR Associates of Vienna, Virginia, an investment research and consulting firm specializing in listed options. He is the creator of The Options Strategy Spectrum, a visual presentation of the relationship of option strategies.

DYR Associates provides daily option research to a number of institutions and brokerage firms. Among the products developed by DYR are The Institutional Options Writers Index, a gauge of option strategy performance, and The Option Phase Chart, a measure of volatility expectations contained in the market. DYR's philosophy is that the listed option market provides a superior risk management tool that can be of significant value when used with fundamental research.

As a consultant, Mr. Yates helped develop The Options Institute; he teaches at many courses sponsored by the Institute.

CONTENTS

PART 3
REAL TIME APPLICATIONS

CHAPTER 1

HISTORY OF OPTIONS

Many people tend to associate options with speculation. Yet options evolved as a way to help manage business risk, not as a vehicle for speculation. An option is simply a contract to buy or sell an asset at some time in the future. Options were used by individuals trading goods as a method of ensuring that there would be a market for their goods at a specified price when the goods were available for sale.

OPTIONS TRADING BEGAN CENTURIES AGO

Although many people perceive options as a recent innovation, options have been traded for centuries. In fact, many trace the use of options back to 3500 BC, when the Phoenicians and Romans traded contracts with terms similar to options on the delivery of goods transported on their ships.

Probably the earliest record of options dates back to ancient Greece and the philosopher Thales. Using his knowledge of astrology, Thales studied the stars and predicted a great olive harvest in the coming spring. There generally was little bidding activity for olive presses among the farmers. So, Thales negotiated prices in the winter, with little competition from the farmers, for the option (or the choice) to use the olive presses the following spring. Thales' forecast was correct and he was able to exercise his option and rent the use of the olive presses to neighboring farmers at a considerable profit.

OPTIONS TRADING IN INDUSTRIAL EUROPE

Perhaps the most often cited example of the historical significance of options occurred in Holland during the tulip craze in the 17th century. During the tulip craze, contracts on tulip bulbs were actively traded by tulip dealers and tulip farmers. Dealers and farmers traded contracts for the option to buy or sell a particular type of tulip bulb at a specified price by some future date as a way to hedge against a poor tulip bulb harvest.

1

Tulip dealers bought call options to guarantee them the right to purchase a supply of bulbs at a stated price, in case bulb prices rose substantially. Tulip growers bought put options as insurance that they could sell their bulbs at a stated price after the harvest.

A secondary market in tulip contracts evolved, and speculators began trading contracts based on price fluctuations, rather than manage the business risk of a poor harvest. Tulip bulb prices skyrocketed, and many members of the public began using their savings to speculate.

Soon afterward the Dutch economy collapsed, partly because of speculators who refused to honor their obligations under the contracts. The government tried to force people to uphold the contracts, but many never did. Not surprisingly, options developed a terrible reputation throughout Holland and Europe.[1]

Options rose again in popularity in England about 50 years later. In 1711, the South Sea Company was granted a trading monopoly in exchange for assuming some of the government's debts. Prices for the company's stock rose to unrealistic levels, from £130 to £1,000 in 1720, as the public clamored to buy stock in a company with a trading monopoly in the profitable South Seas.

The directors of the South Sea Company then realized that company profits could not support the current stock price, and some directors began selling their stock. This news led to a frenzy of stock selling and the stock price plummeted to £150 pounds.

At that time option trading was unregulated; such trading had allowed the public to speculate on stock prices by entering into contracts for the right to buy or sell South Sea's stock at a certain price at a future date. When the price plummeted, many speculators could not fulfill their obligations. As a result, options trading was declared illegal, although options trading did continue on a smaller scale.

OPTIONS TRADING IN THE UNITED STATES

As in Europe, options were traded by individuals in private transactions in the United States. However, after the creation of what would become the New York Stock Exchange in the 1790s, investors began thinking

---

[1] Charles Mackay, L.L.D., *Extraordinary Popular Delusions and the Madness of Crowds*, first published in 1841 (New York: Farrar, Straus and Giroux, 1932), p. 95.

about forming an organized exchange on which to trade options. During this time, Wall Street firms attempted to develop option trading, a business new to the United States. Seeking to avoid the option debacles faced in Europe, firms published suggestions for trading, such as the ideas listed below by Turnbridge and Company.

> *If you think stocks are going down, secure a Put; or you can obtain a Call and sell the stocks against it.*
>
> *If you think stocks are going up, secure a Call; or you can obtain a Put, and buy stock against it.*[2]
>
> *No Liability—There is no liability, or risk, beyond the amount paid for the privilege.*[3]

Many of these suggestions recommended in 1875 are still applicable in today's market. Their application is easier because options are now listed on exchanges and investors have access to more information, including historical and implied volatility data.

In the late 1800s put and call options began trading in an over-the-counter market. Russell Sage, one of the great railroad speculators of his day, is referred to by many as "the grandfather of options." Sage developed a system of puts and calls known as *conversions* and *reverse conversions*; this trading system is still used today. (For a complete discussion, see Chapter 8.)

Basically, Sage found that a relationship could be established between the stock price, the option price, and the interest rate. This concept, *conversion*, provides a way to price options and thus to convert calls into puts and vice versa. Sage and other traders used and still use this concept to add liquidity to the market for options. A reverse conversion strategy, developed and used by Sage, is outlined below (and described in more detail in subsequent chapters).

When investors wanted to borrow from Sage, Sage loaned money to them in exchange for stock. Thus, Sage was *long stock*.

Sage then bought a put option; this allowed him to sell the stock back to the investor at the purchase price at a later time. This is a *long put* position.

---

[2] Herbert J. Filer, *Understanding Put and Call Options* (New York: Crown Publishers, 1959), p. 92.

[3] Ibid.

Sage also sold the investor a call option on the same stock. By initiating this position, known as a *short call* position, Sage took on the obligation to sell the stock back to the investor (upon option exercise). The option premium was calculated to permit Sage to earn the maximum rate of return that the market would bear.

This is known as a *conversion*: Long stock + Long put + Short call = Conversion.

Despite the activities of Turnbridge and Sage, the options market remained very small through the early 1900s. Options still had a negative connotation because investors used them for speculative purposes in unregulated markets, which resulted in losses for many investors.

ABUSE IN THE 1900s

Unfortunately, the reputation of options as an investment tool did not improve in the 1900s when some abusive practices in the financial markets were unchecked. One such practice was the opening of what are referred to as *bucket shops*. Bucket shops charged a small premium (typically $1 per share) to carry a speculator's stock position for a short period of time. If the underlying stock declined below a certain level, the bucket shop would sell him out. In other words, an investor gave the bucket shop owner the right to take possession of his position if the stock dropped below a certain price.

Public perception of options declined further in the 1920s when brokers were granted options on certain securities in exchange for an agreement to recommend these stocks to their customers. Small investors were the main target for these manipulative schemes, and many lost great sums of money. Due to these abuses of options, the fate of options as an investment vehicle was uncertain.

Another unsavory practice occuring at this time was *option pools*. Option pools purchased stock by acquiring options directly from major stockholders of the company, including directors, banks, and the company itself. The options could be exercised at the discretion of the pool manager. If the pool manager could control the stock price enough to make it rise above the contract price, the option pool could earn a substantial profit. In one case, pool managers were able to obtain options to buy 20 percent of an oil company's stock at 30. Before the agreement was signed, the stock was trading at 28. The day that the pool managers signed the agreement, the stock opened at 32 and rose to 35 3/4 at the close. The option pool was able to exercise its options to purchase the stock for 30 and then sell the stock in the open market (at market prices) for a net profit of more than $2 million. Option dealers began following the moves of the pools, trading stock based on whether the pools were buying or selling a specific stock. "If you knew which pool was going to move which stock in the next two days, you could do well."[4]

CREATION OF THE SECURITIES AND EXCHANGE COMMISSION

Following the stock market crash in 1929, Congressional hearings were held to determine how to regulate the securities industry and hopefully prevent market crashes in the future. These hearings resulted in the formation of the Securities and Exchange Commission (SEC).

Many of the option pools had folded following the 1929 stock market crash. After the SEC was created, it began to review the options business and the manipulative schemes of the 1920s. The fate of the options market appeared dismal.

In an attempt to save the options industry, Herbert Filer, a put/call dealer and author of *Understanding Put and Call Options*, was asked to testify before Congress about the positive uses of options. In his book, Filer recalled how, during the hearing, he was seated among 300 onlookers as a bill concerning the options market was read. The bill stated that ". . . not knowing the difference between good and bad options, for the matter of convenience, we [Congress] strike them all out".[5]

Congress had judged the option business by the option pool stock offerings, not public offerings, and concluded that all options trading was manipulative.[6] In response, Filer explained to the Congressional committee the difference between "the options in which [put-call dealers] deal which are primarily offered openly and sold for a consideration,

---

[4] Ibid.

[5] Ibid.

[6] The Statutes at Large of the USA Vol. XLVIII edited, printed, and published by authority of Congress, Part I, June 6, 1934, C404, 48 statute 881, Washington, DC., 1934.

and the manipulative options secretly given, for no fee, but for manipulative purposes."[7]

Congress was concerned about the number of options that expire worthless. The committee assumed that worthless options meant that public investors were losing considerable amounts of money from option speculation. The committee asked Filer, "If only 12 1/2 percent are exercised, then the other 87 1/2 percent of the people who bought options have thrown money away?" Filer replied, "No sir. If you insured your house against fire and it didn't burn down you would not say that you had thrown away your insurance premium."[8]

The committee was looking at options only from the speculative side. As explained above, options were originally developed for the purpose of insurance or hedging. Options provide an investor the means to speculate or to insure. A put option gives the holder the right to sell the underlying security at a specified price within a certain period of time no matter how low the underlying security may decline.

Filer was successful in his argument, convincing the committee that options have economic value. The options business was saved but with certain restrictions. The Investment Securities Act of 1934, which created the SEC, gave the SEC the power to regulate options. The SEC still regulates the options industry today. The SEC has concluded that not all option trading is manipulative and that properly used, options are a valuable investment tool.

THE OPTIONS MARKET BEFORE THE CBOE

Until April 26, 1973, when the Chicago Board Options Exchange opened its doors, options were only traded over the counter. During this period a put/call dealer would advertise each morning in *The Wall Street Journal*, showing the options that were being offered that day (see Figure 1–1). An investor who wanted to purchase or sell an option would telephone a put/call dealer.

Options did not have standardized terms as they do today. For example, options did not have standardized expiration dates, rather they expired on a date a specified number of days from the transaction

---

[7] Filer, p. 79
[8] Ibid.

FIGURE 1–1
The Advertising or Offering of Special Options

These special options are offered for resale. Quotations for regular 60 day, 90 day or 6 month contracts can be had on request.

SPECIAL CALL OPTIONS

Per 100 Shares (Plus Tax)
Per 100 Shares Plus Tax

Jones & Laughlin	71⅝	Aug. 21	$850.00
Union Pacific	36⅛	July 27	275.00
Philco	31⅞	Aug. 31	375.00
Raytheon	56	July 30	575.00
American Motors	37⅜	Dec. 7	625.00
Lee Rubber	26¾	Aug. 31	250.00
General Motors	52⅛	Aug. 18	275.00
Admiral	25⅛	July 20	200.00
Western Airlines	36¼	Aug. 25	200.00
Trans World Airlines	22¼	Dec. 9	375.00
Rayonier	27	Aug. 24	200.00
U. S. Rubber	65½	Sept. 4	575.00
Reynolds Tobacco	52⅝	Aug. 24	225.00
John Morrell	28	July 22	225.00
Amer. Stand. Radiator	16½	Nov. 17	237.50
Gen'l Prec. Eqpmt.	38⅞	Aug. 31	325.00
Amer. Steel Fdry.	64	July 27	400.00
Cudahy Packing	13¾	Nov. 30	225.00
Diners' Club	35¼	July 23	400.00
Crane Co.	44.30	Aug. 31	400.00

Subject to prior sale or price change
Ask for Booklet on How to Use Options

Filer, Schmidt & Co.
MEMBERS PUT & CALL BROKERS & DEALERS ASSN. INC.
120 Broadway, N. Y. 5 BA 7-6100

Orders for these options may be placed through your stock broker

Special Put Options

PER 100 SHARES

U. S. Steel	95½	Dec. 8	$700.00
Miami Copper	45	Nov. 30	425.00
Kaiser Aluminum	51⅛	Sep. 1	375.00
International Silver	44½	Dec. 2	425.00
N.Y. Central RR Co.	30⅛	Aug. 28	425.00
Siegler Corp.	35	Aug 31	375.00
Raytheon	56	July 30	475.00
American Motors	37⅜	Dec. 7	525.00
Chrysler	72	July 27	675.00
Chance Vought	36	July 27	425.00
Beech Aircraft	40	July 20	425.00
Sperry Rand	28⅛	Aug. 25	325.00
Boeing Airplane Co.	37⅝	Dec. 2	400.00
Revlon	58	July 23	525.00
Minneapolis Moline	25¼	Aug. 25	250.00
Great Atlantic & Pac	43¼	Dec. 2	375.00
Harris Intertype	51¼	Aug 17	600.00
Gillette	51⅞	July 20	475.00
Tri Continental wts	28⅞	Nov. 24	300.00
Anaconda	68	5/31/60	875.00

Subject to Price Change & Prior Sale
ASK FOR BOOKLET ON HOW TO USE OPTIONS

Filer, Schmidt & Co.
MEMBERS PUT & CALL BROKERS & DEALERS ASSN. INC.
120 Broadway, New York 5 BArclay 7-6100

These advertisements offer special options. The one on the left is from *The New York Times* and the one on the right is from *The Wall Street Journal*, both of the June 2, 1959, issues.

Source Herbert Filer *Understanding Put and Call Options* (New York Crown Publishers 1959)

date. And the option exercise price would often be the current market price of the underlying stock when the option was executed. Therefore, it was unusual for two investors to have options with the same terms. What would happen if an investor wanted to close the position prior to expiration? Without much of a secondary market, the investor would need to go back to the person with whom he or she originally traded (usually the put/call dealer). The option prices quoted by the put/call dealers to investors who wanted to close their positions often reflected this monopoly.

Grain Traders Expand into Option Trading

In 1968, the U.S. economy was suffering one of the worst bear markets in history. Volume in the commodity futures market declined drastically. Responding to the Chicago Board of Trade's need to expand business and to increase volume, a special committee was appointed to explore the feasibility of a forward securities contract based on commodity futures. Although not common knowledge, in 1935 the Chicago Board of Trade received its registration from the SEC as a stock exchange. This meant the Chicago Board of Trade could trade securities, not just grain futures. A consulting firm hired in 1969 to study the feasibility of a stock options exchange concluded that the idea had great potential.

After reviewing the Chicago Board of Trade's proposal and finding that "the proposed options exchange does not appear to be inconsistent with relevant statutory requirements," the new exchange—the Chicago Board Options Exchange—began as an SEC pilot program with call options on 16 stocks.

Standardization of Option Contracts

The proposal that created the CBOE also contained a suggestion for creating an intermediary organization to standardize and clear option contracts. This organization is now known as the Options Clearing Corporation (OCC). The OCC is a corporation owned by the exchanges that trade listed stock options; it guarantees all option contracts.

Also, option contracts now have standardized terms so investors can trade them in the market. For example, the proposal recommended a standard expiration day. Expiration day was determined to be the Saturday after the third Friday of the month; this is when all options in the series would expire. All underlying stocks were assigned a quarterly expiration cycle. For example, IBM is on the January cycle. This means that originally all IBM options expired in either January, April, July, or October. Only three consecutive option expirations were available at any time. The expirations have now evolved to the two most current months and additional months from the quarterly cycle.

The strike (or exercise) price is the price at which an option buyer or seller has agreed to buy or sell the underlying security. Strike prices are standardized with intervals of 5 and 10 points. Stocks that trade at $25 or less are given strikes 2 1/2 points apart because 5 points is too great a percentage of the underlying.

Prior to standardization, an option would usually have an expiration date that was a number of days from the actual trade date; the strike price often would be the market price of the stock at the time of the transaction. Thus, an individual would find himself to be the only one with an option with that particular strike price and expiration, making it difficult, if not impossible, to trade the option.

Another reason for creating the Options Clearing Corporation was the need for a central organization to guarantee option clearance and settlement. Centralized option clearing allows investors the comfort of knowing that their trades will be exercised and matched. The OCC guarantees option trades; it was recently given an AAA rating by Standard & Poor's Corporation. The OCC also gives buyers and sellers the opportunity to close their positions with an offsetting trade in an open market. They no longer need to approach the person with whom they made the original trade, as in the old system with put/call dealers.

This open market, known as an *open outcry system*, is a group of market makers who are required to make a two-sided market (a bid and an offer) in all option series. Also, there is a maximum on the width of the markets (i.e., the difference between the bid and the offer) depending on the premium (i.e., the price) of the option.

THE CHICAGO BOARD OPTIONS EXCHANGE ARISES FROM HUMBLE BEGINNINGS

When the CBOE opened on April 26, 1973, in a small smokers lounge off the main floor of the Chicago Board of Trade, its success was far from certain. Some questioned the wisdom of launching a new securities exchange in the midst of one of the worst bear markets on record. Others wondered how "grain traders in Chicago" could successfully market a new trading instrument that the established New York exchanges had deemed too complex for the investment public.

The doubters soon were silenced. Both individual investors and, later, institutional investors flocked to the fledgling market—to a point where today the CBOE is the second largest securities market in the United States and the largest options market in the world.

The CBOE revolutionized option trading by providing secondary markets for option contracts and guaranteeing option trades. A few other statistics illustrate the Exchange's progress. Seats that sold for $10,000 when trading began have sold for as high as $465,000. The CBOE opened its doors in 1973 trading *only* calls on 16 stocks.

FIGURE 1–2
CBOE Annual Volume (in millions)

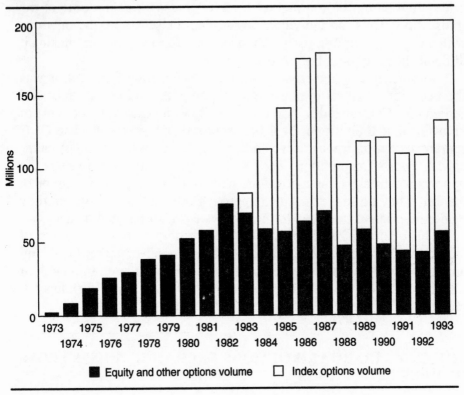

By 1975, options were becoming popular, and other exchanges realized the potential opportunity. The American Stock Exchange and what is now the Philadelphia Stock Exchange began trading options and were soon joined by the Pacific Stock Exchange and the New York Stock Exchange. Exchanges in Montreal, Toronto, and Sydney also began listing options. Today options trade at over 50 exchanges in 38 countries around the world.

A few years after opening with call options, the CBOE began trading put options. This, in part, led the SEC to impose a moratorium on option market expansion, as it wanted an opportunity to step back and review an industry that was growing much faster than anticipated. The review resulted in significant improvements in customer protection, such as revised sales practice procedures. Satisfied with revised procedures implemented by the CBOE and other exchanges, the SEC lifted the moratorium in 1980. The CBOE responded to the lifting of the moratorium by increasing the number of options listed on the Exchange from 95 to 120.

INDEX OPTIONS

Ten years after the CBOE opened its doors, another revolution occurred in the options business with the introduction of index options. The Chicago Board Options Exchange began trading cash-settled options on the Standard & Poor's 100 Index (ticker symbol OEX). 4,827 contracts on the OEX traded that first day, and the popularity of the OEX option product continues to grow. OEX options are the most actively traded index option, with an average daily volume of 253,091 contracts in 1993.

Due to the success of options on the S&P 100, other exchanges began listing options on broad-based indices (i.e., indices with stocks from many different industries). The American Stock Exchange followed with listed options on the Major Market Index, and the New York Stock Exchange listed options on the NYSE Composite Index. The Chicago Board Options Exchange also added options on the Standard & Poor's 500® Index (ticker symbol SPX). Both SPX and OEX have been very successful products, helping the CBOE to achieve 92 percent of the trading market in all index options.

Later that year, the option exchanges began listing options on narrow-based indices. Narrow-based indices are indices composed of stocks from the same industry. In the past few years, many narrow-sector indices have begun trading. For example, some of the industries represented by index options include: biotech, retail, computer software, pharmaceutical, insurance, banking, gold and silver, and gaming.

During the 1980s, the option exchanges continued to introduce new products, including options on new indices, currency options, and bond options as well as adding options on more stocks. Currently, there are options trading on over 1,200 stocks.

LEAPS® OR LONGER-DATED OPTIONS

In the late 1980s, in response to a desire on the part of public investors for options expiring further out in time, Long-term Equity AnticiPation Securities® (known as LEAPS) began trading on the CBOE. LEAPS are long-term options; puts and calls are available with expiration dates up to three years in the future.

The trademark LEAPS was developed by the CBOE; now four of the five U.S. option exchanges list LEAPS. The New York Stock Exchange refers to the long-term options listed on their exchange as "Longer-dated Options". Regardless of what they are called, long-term options are options that expire up to three years in the future.

When LEAPS first began trading, the option terms were completely unstandardized. However, requests from member trading firms and public investors led the industry to standardize the terms of LEAPS options. Equity LEAPS all expire in January and are initially brought out with three strike prices: at-the-money, 20 percent in-the-money, and 20 percent out-of-the-money. Strike prices are added as the stock price moves up or down.

LEAPS give investors more choices with options. For instance, investors can purchase a call option that expires up to three years in the future. Options can thus be used as a true alternative to stock, or as long-term protection or insurance against a stock price decline. LEAPS are one of the most successful products listed by the option exchanges. The number of stocks that list LEAPS is constantly expanding; currently there are LEAPS on over 150 stocks. And LEAPS are traded on index options as well. For consistency, all LEAPS index options expire in the month of December.

CONCLUSION

The CBOE continually seeks to respond to the needs of its customers—retail firms, institutional investors, and the public—by introducing new products and refining trading support systems.

For example, in response to a need to hedge against changing interest rates, the CBOE introduced interest rate options in 1989. These were different from the original bond options in two basic respects: the original bond options were based on the current bond yield not on the price of the bond, and account executives were not required to carry any additional license to trade the product. These bond options have been replaced with three separate interest rate options based on the most recently auctioned 13-week, 5-year, 10-year, and 30-year Treasury securities.

As the world marketplace expands, so will the options markets. Product innovations will not stop with index options and interest rate options. The derivatives market is still evolving as investors seek new ways to manage the risk in their stock portfolios.

No one, of course, can predict where these changes will lead—just as no one could predict in the 1970s how successful the CBOE would be by the 1990s. But the future looks bright for investors who now understand options and options strategies. As an investor, whether you are looking to hedge a portfolio or take a position based on an opinion of a particular stock, business sector, or the market in general, over the long-term or short-term, there is an option strategy to meet your investment objectives.

PART 1

ESSENTIAL CONCEPTS

CHAPTER 2

FUNDAMENTALS OF OPTIONS

Options are derivative instruments. This means that an option's value and its trading characteristics are tied to the asset that underlies the option. It is this essential defining characteristic that makes options valuable to the knowledgeable investor. A major advantage of options is their versatility. They can be used in accordance with a wide variety of investment strategies. As a result, any investor who understands when and how to use options in pursuit of his or her individual financial objectives can enjoy a clear advantage over other investors. The investor will have an effective means of managing the risk inherent in any investment program. In most investment situations, understanding options gives the investor a wider range of investment choices.

The asset on which the option is traded might be a stock, an equity index, a futures contract, a Treasury security, or another type of security. Although the discussion and examples within this chapter are centered on stock options, the concepts and pricing theories also apply to other kinds of underlying assets.

Whatever the underlying asset, the pricing of an option is commonly thought to be an esoteric and difficult task, certainly not something to be attempted by the mathematically unsophisticated person. At one level, this perception is true—advanced mathematics for the pricing of options have been evident in the past and continue to be utilized. The Black-Scholes option-pricing model, for example, was first developed with stochastic calculus and differential equations. What these techniques are and their manner of application need not concern us here. The important point is that options pricing can generally be explained using a conceptual approach rather than a highly technical mathematical approach. The discussion of options pricing that follows is directed toward the options investor who seeks an explanation at the intermediate level in accessible terms.

This chapter explains option pricing theory in four steps. First, puts, calls, and related terms are defined. Second, the five elements of an option's theoretical value are explained in a general fashion. Third, each of these elements is examined in greater depth. Fourth, and finally, the concept of *put-call parity* ties together many of this chapter's concepts.

SOME DEFINITIONS

Option

An *option* on an underlying asset is either the right to buy the asset (a *call* option) or the right to sell the asset (a *put* option) at some predetermined price and within some predetermined time in the future.

The key feature here is that the owner of an option has a right, not an obligation. If the owner of the option does not exercise this right prior to the predetermined time, then the option and the opportunity to exercise it cease to exist.

The seller of an option, however, is obligated to fulfill the requirements of the option if the option is exercised. In the case of a call option on stock, the seller has sold the right to buy that stock. The seller of the call option is therefore obligated to sell the stock to the call option owner if the option is exercised. In the case of a put option on a stock, the seller of the put option has sold the right to sell that stock. The seller of the put option is therefore obligated to buy the stock from the put option owner if the option is exercised.

Strike Price and Expiration Date

The predetermined price of the option is known as its *strike price*. When a call option is exercised, the call owner pays the amount of the strike price in exchange for receiving the underlying stock. When a put option is exercised, the put owner receives the amount of the strike price in exchange for delivering the underlying stock. The date after which the option ceases to exist is the *expiration date*. For example, the XYZ SEP 50 call option is the right to buy the stock XYZ at the price of $50 per share until the expiration date in September.

Listed options have clearly defined rules establishing strike prices, contract sizes, and expiration dates. Although rules may vary slightly from exchange to exchange, listed stock options generally have strike prices at intervals of $2.50 from a stock price of $5 to $25. Between stock prices of $25 and $200, option strike prices are generally set at intervals of $5. Above stock prices of $200, strike price intervals are $10.

Stock options in the United States are denominated in quantities of 100 shares each or one round lot of stock. If the XYZ SEP 50 call option in the previous example was quoted at $3, its actual cost would be $300. This is because the $3 quoted price represents the cost on a per-share basis, but the call option contract covers 100 shares. Thus, 100 shares times $3 per share equals the cost of $300.

Expiration Rules

Listed stock options in the United States technically expire on the Saturday following the third Friday of the expiration month. Exceptions are made when legal holidays fall on the Friday or Saturday in question. The Saturday expiration, however, is irrelevant to nonexchange members. The Saturday expiration exists so that brokerage houses and exchange members will have the morning after the last trading day to resolve any errors.

Customers of brokerage firms must concern themselves with two procedures in regard to expiration. First, brokerage firm customers must be aware of their firm's specific rules regarding the deadline for notification for exercise. Second, brokerage firm customers must be aware of the rules for automatic exercise. A call option will be automatically exercised if the stock's last trade in its primary market on expiration Friday is $0.75 or more above the strike price unless the customer has given specific instructions not to exercise. A put option will be automatically exercised if the stock's last trade on expiration Friday is $0.75 or more below the exercise price. Many firms have a final notification deadline of 4:00 PM EST on the expiration Friday, but this rule varies from firm to firm.

While listed stock options have fairly consistent specifications, listed futures options differ considerably in contract specifications, strike prices, the unit value of price movements, and expiration dates. This is so because the specifications of futures contracts themselves vary. Whereas stock prices are dollar-dominated in 100 share lots and stock option prices move accordingly, a futures contract on corn at the Chicago Board of Trade covers 5,000 bushels, and a futures contract on No. 2 heating oil at the New York Mercantile Exchange covers 42,000 gallons. Even futures contracts on the same underlying asset can vary: the Japanese yen futures contract at the Chicago Mercantile Exchange covers 12,500,000 yen, and the yen contract at the MidAmerica Commodity Exchange covers 6,250,000 yen. As a result of these differences, the futures options trader must be familiar with all the terms of a contract before trading. A trader who does not do this first usually learns very fast, but, unfortunately, it can be an expensive process.

American-Style Options
An *American-style* option has a right (not an obligation) that may be exercised at some predetermined price *at any time until the expiration date*. Sometimes these are referred to as *American* options.

European-Style Options
A *European-style* option has a right that may be exercised *only on the expiration date* of the option. Sometimes these are referred to as *European* options.

   The difference between European-style options and American-style options has nothing to do with geography! The distinguishing feature is the right of early exercise that exists with American options and does not exist with European options. Until the CBOE introduced European options on the S&P 500 Index on July 1, 1983, the distinction was not particularly important to investors in options markets since only American-style options had been listed; since then, several other European-style options have been listed.

   For the purpose of this discussion, the early exercise feature of American options as it relates to pricing theory need not be considered in detail. It is sufficient to point out that the early exercise privilege of American options is a feature that sometimes has value. As a result, American options sometimes have a higher theoretical value than do European options. With this one distinction in mind, the following discussion of option pricing theory applies to both American and European options.

Price and Strike Price

The relationship of the stock's price to the option's strike price determines whether the option is referred to as in-the-money, at-the-money, or out-of-the-money.

A call option is *in-the-money* when the stock price is above the strike price. A call option is *at-the-money* when the stock price is at the strike price. And a call option is *out-of-the-money* when the stock price is below the strike price. For example, with a stock price of $50, the $45 call is an in-the-money call option, because the call option strike price is below the current market price of the stock. The $50 call is at-the-money, and the $55 call is out-of-the-money.

For a put option, the in-the-money and out-of-the-money designations are opposite those of call options. This is because put options increase in price as the price of the underlying stock decreases.

A put option is *in-the-money* when the stock price is below the strike price. A put option is *at-the-money* when the stock price is at the strike price. And a put option is *out-of-the-money* when the stock price is above the strike price. For example, with a stock price at $50, the $55 put is in-the-money, because the stock price is below the put option's strike price. The $50 put is at-the-money, and the $45 put is out-of-the-money.

Intrinsic Value and Time Value

The price of an option may consist of intrinsic value, time value, or a combination of both. *Intrinsic value* is the in-the-money portion of an option's price. *Time value* is the portion of an option's price that is in excess of the intrinsic value.

If the stock price is above the strike price of a call option, then the stock price minus the strike price represents the intrinsic value of the call option. For example, if the stock price is $53, then the $50 call option has an intrinsic value of $3. Any value above $3 that the market places on this option is time value. Time value exists because the market realizes that the stock may decline below $50, and the stock owner may suffer a loss greater than $3—possibly as much as $53! Because this risk exists, the call option purchaser should be willing to pay more than $3 for the $50 call option since he does not have the same risk if the stock price declines below $50. The call option buyer's risk is limited to the premium paid for the option. The premium paid above $3 for the option—the time value—measures in some sense the market's estimate of the likelihood of the stock price declining below $50. The call buyer who pays $4 for the $50 call option is paying an extra $1 for protection against a stock price decline below $50. If the stock price rises, the call buyer participates in the price rise. The $1 time value paid for the option is the price of the insurance policy against losing money if the stock price were to decline below $50.

For put options, intrinsic value equals strike price minus stock price because put options are in-the-money when the stock price is below the strike price.

> **Example:** If the stock price is $53, then the $55 put option has an intrinsic value of the $2. Any value above $2 that the market places on this put option is time value.

An out-of-the-money option consists entirely of time value. By definition, the price of an out-of-the-money option has no in-the-money portion; consequently, it has no intrinsic value.

The concepts of intrinsic value and time value for call and put options are illustrated in Figure 2–1.

FIGURE 2–1
Intrinsic Value and Time Value

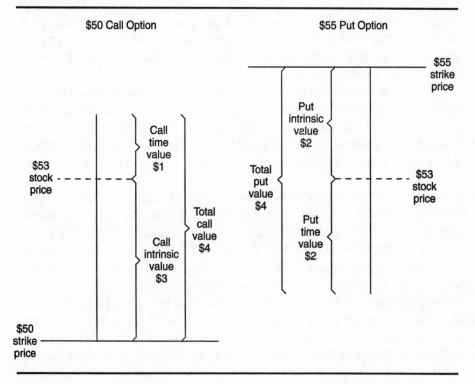

Parity

An option is trading at *parity* with the stock if it is in-the-money and has no time value. This situation exists when the stock price minus the strike price (for call options) equals the option price. For example, if the $50 call option were trading at $3 when the stock was at $53, then it would be *trading at parity*. In-the-money options, especially deep-in-the-money options, tend to trade at parity when only a few days remain until expiration. This happens when the market perceives that the option is almost certain to be exercised. The logic for this is simple. Since it is only a matter of time until the option is exercised and becomes stock, the option price trades in step with the stock price until exercise occurs.

OPTION PRICE TABLES INTRODUCED

Traditional profit and loss diagrams as presented in Chapter 4 illustrate an option strategy's risk profile *at expiration*. In this chapter, the focus is on how option prices behave prior to expiration, and the important factors that affect an option's theoretical value will be explained. To begin, Table 2–1 shows theoretical call option prices for a $50 call at various times prior to expiration with the underlying stock at different prices. Table 2–2 shows the same information for put options. These tables reveal important characteristics of option price behavior.

First, it should be observed that with the stock at $50 at any time prior to expiration, the call price is greater than the put price. At stock prices other than $50, the call's time value is greater than the put's time value. The reason for this relates to the interest component in call prices, which is discussed later in this chapter under interest rates and put-call parity.

Second, it should be observed that at any time prior to expiration, a $1 move in the underlying stock price will result in an option price change of less than $1. The name of option price change per unit of stock price change is called *delta*, and it is discussed later in this chapter, but it is important to note that option price changes per unit of change in the underlying is not constant over changes in stock price or over time.

Third, it should be observed that option prices decline with the passage of time. Time decay is, perhaps, the best known aspect about option prices, but there are some misconceptions about time decay. They are discussed thoroughly later in this chapter.

TABLE 2–1
$50 Call—Theoretical Values

Stock Price ($)	91 Days	84 Days	77 Days	70 Days	63 Days	56 Days	49 Days	42 Days	35 Days	28 Days	21 Days	14 Days	7 Days	Expiration
$55	6 1/2	6 3/8	6 1/4	6 1/8	6	5 7/8	5 3/4	5 5/8	5 1/2	5 3/8	5 1/4	5 1/8	5	5
54	5 3/4	5 5/8	5 1/2	5 3/8	5 1/4	5 1/8	5	4 7/8	4 5/8	4 1/2	4 3/8	4 1/4	4 1/8	4
53	5	4 7/8	4 3/4	4 5/8	4 1/2	4 3/8	4 1/4	4	3 7/8	3 5/8	3 1/2	3 1/4	3 1/8	3
52	4 3/8	4 1/4	4 1/8	4	3 7/8	3 5/8	3 1/2	3 3/8	3 1/8	3	2 3/4	2 1/2	2 1/4	2
51	3 3/4	3 5/8	3 1/2	3 3/8	3 1/4	3	2 7/8	2 5/8	2 1/2	2 1/4	2	1 3/4	1 1/2	1
50	3 1/8	3	2 7/8	2 3/4	2 5/8	2 7/16	2 1/4	2 1/16	1 15/16	1 3/4	1 1/2	1 1/4	7/8	0
49	2 5/8	2 1/2	2 3/8	2 1/4	2 1/8	1 15/16	1 3/4	1 5/8	1 7/16	1 1/4	1	3/4	7/16	0
48	2 3/16	2 1/16	1 15/16	1 3/4	1 5/8	1 1/2	1 3/8	1 3/16	1	13/16	5/8	7/16	3/16	0
47	1 3/4	1 5/8	1 1/2	1 3/8	1 1/4	1 1/8	1	7/8	3/4	9/16	3/8	1/4	1/16	0
46	1 3/8	1 1/4	1 3/16	1 1/16	15/16	7/8	3/4	5/8	1/2	3/8	1/4	1/8	0	0
45	1 1/8	1	7/8	13/16	11/16	5/8	1/2	3/8	5/16	3/16	1/8	1/16	0	0

TABLE 2–2
$50 Put—Theoretical Values

Stock Price ($)	91 Days	84 Days	77 Days	70 Days	63 Days	56 Days	49 Days	42 Days	35 Days	28 Days	21 Days	14 Days	7 Days	Expiration
$55	1 1/8	1 1/16	15/16	7/8	3/4	11/16	9/16	7/16	3/8	1/4	1/8	1/16	0	0
54	1 3/8	1 1/4	1 3/16	1 1/16	1	7/8	3/4	5/8	1/2	3/8	1/4	1/8	0	0
53	1 11/16	1 9/16	1 7/16	1 3/8	1 1/4	1 1/8	1	7/8	3/4	9/16	7/16	1/4	1/16	0
52	2	1 7/8	1 3/4	1 11/16	1 9/16	1 7/16	1 5/16	1 1/8	1	13/16	5/8	7/16	3/16	0
51	2 3/8	2 1/4	2 1/8	2 1/16	1 15/16	1 3/4	1 5/8	1 1/2	1 3/8	1 3/16	15/16	3/4	7/16	0
50	2 13/16	2 11/16	2 9/16	2 7/16	2 5/16	2 3/16	2 1/16	1 15/16	1 3/4	1 9/16	1 3/8	1 1/8	13/16	0
49	3 1/4	3 1/8	3	2 15/16	2 13/16	2 11/16	2 9/16	2 7/16	2 1/4	2 1/8	1 15/16	1 11/16	1 3/8	1
48	3 7/8	3 3/4	3 5/8	3 1/2	3 3/8	3 1/4	3 1/8	3	2 7/8	2 3/4	2 1/2	2 3/8	2 1/8	2
47	4 1/2	4 3/8	4 1/4	4 1/8	4	3 7/8	3 3/4	3 5/8	3 1/2	3 3/8	3 1/4	3 1/8	3	3
46	5	4 7/8	4 7/8	4 3/4	4 3/4	4 5/8	4 1/2	4 3/8	4 1/4	4 1/4	4 1/8	4	4	4
45	5 3/4	5 5/8	5 5/8	5 1/2	5 3/8	5 3/8	5 1/4	5 1/4	5 1/8	5 1/8	5	5	5	5

ELEMENTS OF AN OPTION'S VALUE

The five components of an option's theoretical value are:

1. Price of the underlying asset.
2. Strike price of the option.
3. Time remaining until the expiration date.
4. Prevailing interest rates.
5. Volatility of the underlying asset.

(As a reminder, the following discussion centers on stock options, but the concepts apply to all types of options.)

FIGURE 2–2
$50 Call at Various Stock Prices

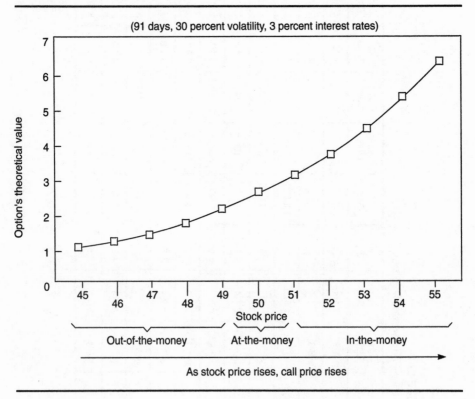

Option Price Relative to Stock Price

Column 2 in Table 2–1 shows theoretical values of a $50 call 91 days prior to expiration. As the stock rises from $45 to $46, the theoretical option value rises from 1 1/8 to 1 3/8. As the stock rises from $50 to $51, the theoretical option value rises from 3 1/8 to 3 3/4. And as the stock rises from $54 to $55, the theoretical option value rises from 5 3/4 to 6 1/2. The information in this column is presented in the line graph in Figure 2–2. As can be seen, as the underlying stock price rises, the theoretical value of the call rises in a nonlinear fashion at an increasing rate.

As illustrated by the brackets under the graph in Figure 2–2, a call option is in-the-money when the stock price is above the option's strike

FIGURE 2–3
$50 Put at Various Stock Prices

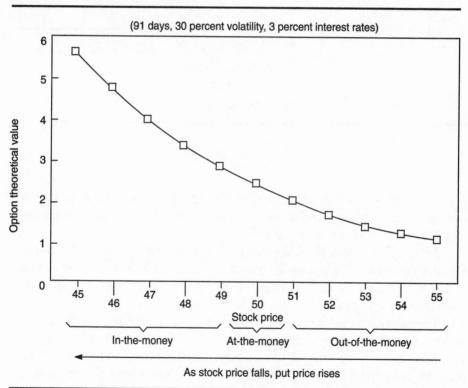

FIGURE 2–4
Effect of Time—At-the-Money

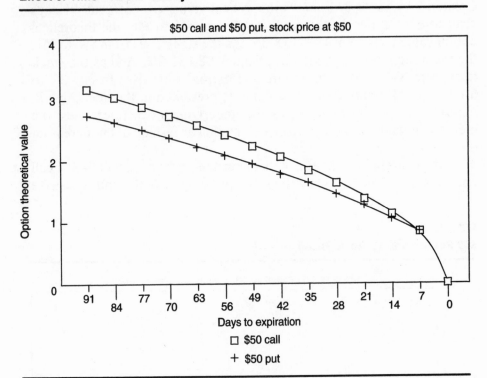

price. A call option is at-the-money when the stock price is at the option's strike price. And a call option is out-of-the-money when the stock price is below the strike price.

Figure 2–3 shows the information from column 2 in Table 2–2—Put Option Theoretical Values—in line-graph form. The conclusion is that as the underlying stock falls in price, the put option's theoretical value rises in a nonlinear fashion at an increasing rate.

The brackets under the graph in Figure 2–3 illustrate that the designations of in-the-money and out-of-the-money for put options are opposite those for call options. A put option is in-the-money when the stock price is below the strike price, and a put option is out-of-the-money when the stock price is above the strike price.

FIGURE 2–5
Effect of Time—Out-of-the-Money

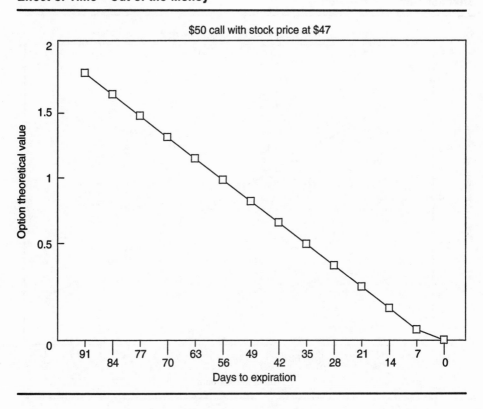

Option Price Relative to Time

Looking across any row in Table 2–1 illustrates how option prices change with the passage of time. The *time decay* factor in option prices is well known, but there are some misconceptions about how time affects option values.

Figure 2–4 illustrates in line-graph form the call option prices in row 6 of Table 2–1 and the put option prices in row 6 of Table 2–2. With the stock price at $50, the $50 call declines in value from 3 1/8 to 0 over the 91 days to expiration, and the $50 put declines from 2 13/16 to 0. The important observation is that time decay for at-the-money options does not occur in a linear manner. During the week from 91 days to 84

FIGURE 2–6
Effect of Time—In-the-Money

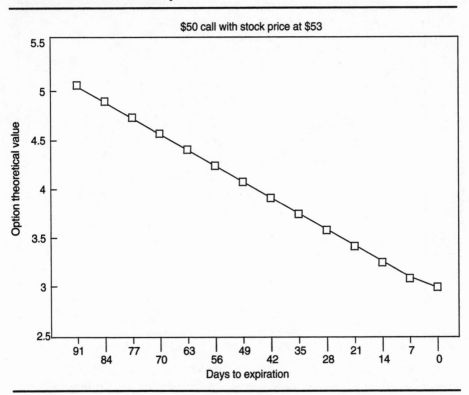

days before expiration, the $50 call declines by 1/8 from 3 1/8 to 3. During the week 63 days to 56 days, the $50 call declines by 3/16 from 2 5/8 to 2 7/16. From 28 days to 21 days, the decline is 1/4 from 1 3/4 to 1 1/2, and the last week, the decline is 7/8 from 7/8 to 0.

Time decay for in-the-money and out-of-the-money options, however, is closer to being linear. To illustrate this concept, Figure 2–5 shows how the $50 call declines in value with the stock price at $47, and Figure 2–6 shows how the $50 call declines in value with the stock price at $53. With the stock price at $53, the stock is above the strike price and, therefore, the total option price of $5 at 91 days prior to expiration consists of $3 of intrinsic value and $2 of time value. It must be remembered that only the time value decreases with the passage of time. Consequently, with the stock price $53, the $50 call will decline in value

FIGURE 2–7
$50 Call at Various Times Prior to Expiration

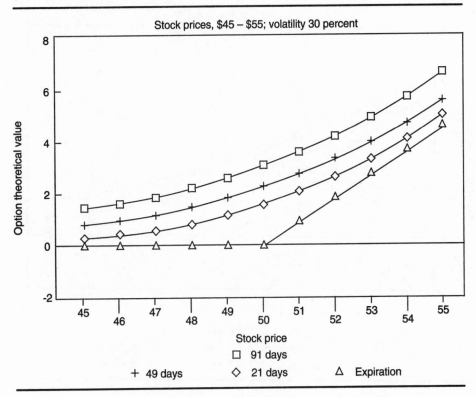

Stock prices, $45 – $55; volatility 30 percent

Option theoretical value

Stock price
□ 91 days
+ 49 days   ◇ 21 days   △ Expiration

from $5 at 91 days prior to expiration to $3 at expiration—a price equal
to its intrinsic value.

Time decay for put options is similar to time decay for call options.
Out-of-the-money and in-the-money options decay in a more linear
fashion than do at-the-money puts.

Figure 2–7 consists of the information in Table 2–1, column 2 ($50
call prices 91 days prior to expiration), the prices in column 8 (49 days
prior to expiration), column 12 (21 days), and column 15 (expiration).
Together, these lines show how call option prices decay over time so
that at the expiration date there is no time value in the option's price,
and the result is the *hockey-stick* diagram at expiration, which is familiar
to many traders of options. Figure 2–8 presents similar time information
for put options.

FIGURE 2–8
$50 Put at Various Times Prior to Expiration

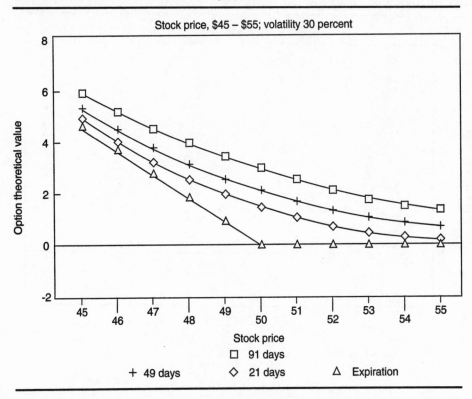

A frequently asked question about options is, "Why does the passage of time affect at-the-money options in a nonlinear fashion?" After all, insurance premiums are almost linear; for example, a one-year house insurance policy costs half of a two-year policy. The answer is that option values are related to the square root of time. Although this sounds esoteric, the relationship is quite simple. If a 30-day at-the-money option has a value of $1, the 60-day option (having twice as much time until expiration) has a value of approximately $1 \times \sqrt{2}$ or $1 \times 1.414 = 1.414$.

This important concept about the nonlinear impact of time on option prices should give pause to those option traders who resolutely believe in buying only front-month options. Considering time decay alone, option buyers should prefer to buy longer-term options. After all, it is cheaper to buy one six-month option for approximately $2.45 (1 $\times$

FIGURE 2–9
Effect of Interest Rates

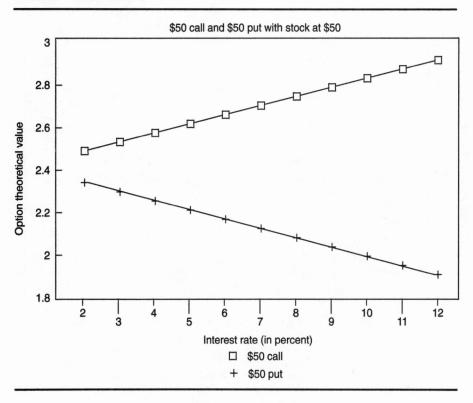

$\sqrt{6}$) than it is to buy six 1-month options at $1 each. Conversely, with all else equal, option sellers should have a preference to sell shorter-term options since there is more profit to be made by selling six one-month options than one six-month option. Of course, in the real world, all else is rarely equal. Transaction costs have an impact, and option traders must balance the impact of these real world considerations versus the theoretical.

Interest Rates

The effect of changes in interest rates is most easily understood after having read the section of this chapter concerning put-call parity, in which the arbitrage relationship between options and stock is explained.

FIGURE 2–10
Effect of Volatility—At-the-Money

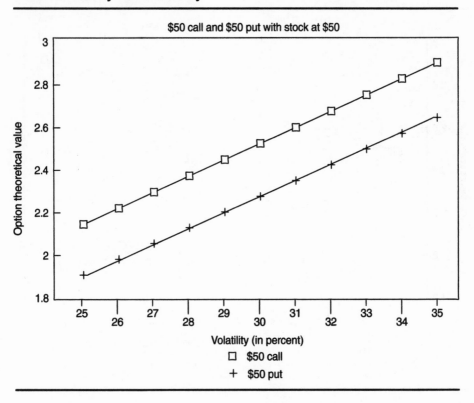

At this point, it is sufficient to be aware of two points that are illustrated in Figure 2–9.

The first point revealed in Figure 2–9, which is surprising to many option traders, is that rising interest rates cause call prices to rise and put prices to decline. The second point is that the effect of changes in interest rates is small. The figure shows that a rise in interest rates from 2 percent to 12 percent causes call prices to rise from 2 1/2 to 2 7/8 and put prices to decline from 2 3/8 to 1 7/8. Both of these points will be explained more fully in the section on put-call parity.

Option Prices and Volatility

Volatility is discussed in depth in the next chapter. This discussion touches on the major points of how changes in volatility affect option prices. The relationship between volatility and option prices is a direct

FIGURE 2–11
Effect of Volatility—Out-of-the-Money

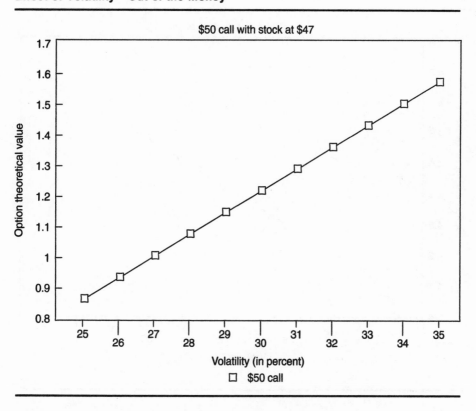

$50 call with stock at $47

Option theoretical value (y-axis)

Volatility (in percent) (x-axis)

□ $50 call

one—as the volatility percentage increases, so do option prices. Since volatility refers to the price movement of the underlying stock, higher volatility means that greater movement is likely, and greater movement justifies higher option prices.

Figures 2–10, 2–11, and 2–12 show that the relationship between volatility changes and option prices is nearly linear, but that it is a different line for in-the-money options, at-the-money options, and out-of-the-money options.

Figure 2–10 shows that the effect of changes in volatility is linear for both puts and calls and that the difference between the two remains constant when volatility changes. The constant difference is the result of the interest component as discussed above. Figures 2–11 and 2–12 show the effect of changes in volatility on in-the-money and out-of-the-money calls. While the effect is nearly linear, it should be noted that the slope of the lines is different.

FIGURE 2–12
Effect of Volatility—In-the-Money

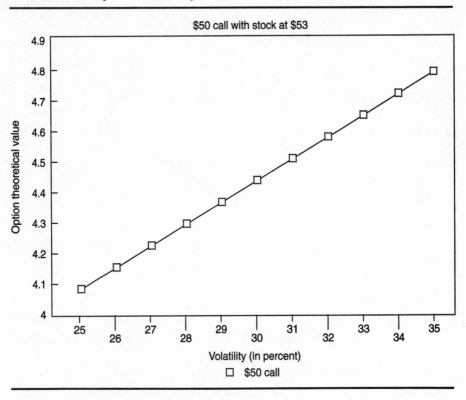

It must be remembered that option prices are based on the expected volatility of the underlying stock. Mathematically, volatility is nondirectional. If the market expects greater fluctuation in a stock's price, then the fluctuation could be up or down. Consequently, when higher volatility is expected, both call prices and put prices rise.

With an increase in expected volatility, at-the-money options will increase in price more than out-of-the-money options because of how price movements are distributed according to probability theory. Mathematically, a $50 stock always has a greater probability of moving at least $1 than of moving $6. This explains why at-the-money options have higher prices than out-of-the-money options.

Implied Volatility
Implied volatility is the volatility percentage that justifies an option's price. Consequently, the price at which an option is trading tells what

volatility level in the stock is implied by the option price. For the professional floor trader who trades a large number of options and who manages large open positions, differences between actual stock price volatility and implied volatility of options may have a significant impact. For the off-floor user of options, however, differences in implied volatility and recent actual volatility rarely are significant. For the off-floor trader, other factors such as stock selection, timing of price movements, and desired rates of return are the most important considerations.

Volatility—the Unknown Factor

Of the five components of an option's theoretical value, the stock price, strike price, time until expiration, and prevailing interest rates are readily observable. It is only the volatility of the underlying stock that is unknown.[1] Thus one can conclude that an option's theoretical value is ultimately subjective because the selection of a volatility estimate is subjective. After all, it is the future volatility of a stock that determines an option's true value and the future volatility, of course, cannot be known. These and other concepts about volatility will be developed further in the next chapter.

THE SECOND LEVEL OF UNDERSTANDING

Now that the five elements of an option's theoretical value have been introduced, the second step is to understand how a change in each element affects the theoretical value of an option. The questions we address are:

1. Given that changes in option values are not constant with stock price changes, how can changes in option values be measured?
2. How does option price decay change with the passage of time?
3. How do changes in volatility affect option values?

Typically, this is the point where advanced mathematics takes the forefront. This discussion, however, will continue to emphasize concepts. The successful user of options should be aware of the components of option price changes, just as he should be aware of the five

---

[1] Chapter 8 revisits these factors as they pertain to longer-dated options.

elements of value, but a detailed knowledge of the mathematics is not required.

The Effect of Stock Price Change—Delta

During the discussion above under the heading "Option Price Relative to Stock Price," it was stated that "As the underlying stock price rises, the theoretical value of the call rises in a nonlinear fashion at an increasing rate." What happens is, at first, the option price rise is only a small fraction of the stock price rise. This fraction increases as the stock price rises. When the stock is significantly above the strike price, then the option price movement approaches 100 percent of the stock price movement. It is this "fraction of the stock price movement" that is known as the option's *delta*.

As an example, assume that the underlying stock rises $1 and the option price rises $0.25. In this case, the delta of the option is .25—the option moved 25 percent of the stock price movement.

Delta, however is not static. The delta of an option changes as the option goes from being an out-of-the-money option to an in-the-money option. The price of an out-of-the-money option changes by a small percentage of the stock price change. The price of an at-the-money option changes by approximately 50 percent of the stock price change. As an option becomes more and more in-the-money, its delta rises and gradually approaches 1.00 or 100 percent. This means that the price of a deep-in-the-money option moves dollar for dollar with the stock price movement. The concept of delta is demonstrated in Table 2–3.

Although the arrow in Table 2–3 points to an instance where the delta equals exactly the option price change for a $1 price rise or fall in the stock, any reader with a calculator can quickly ascertain that the relationship between other option price changes and the corresponding delta are not as exact. This situation occurs because the delta is a theoretical measure designed for a very small stock price movement, not a full dollar move. For the mathematically sophisticated, there are many books that go into this concept in depth.

A graphical representation of how deltas change with stock price changes is presented in Figure 2–13. As the top half of the graph illustrates, call option deltas are positive and increase as the stock price rises. This is consistent with Table 2–3.

Put options, however, have negative deltas, because put options decrease in value as stock prices rise. This is represented by the

TABLE 2–3
Delta of Call Option

		$50 Call Option	
	Volatility: 35%	Days to expiration: 90	
Stock Price	Theoretical Value	Delta	
$56	7 1/4	.78	
55	6 1/2	.75	←————— The .75 delta
54	5 3/4	.71	implies a .75
53	5 1/8	.68	value change if
52	4 1/2	.64	the stock price
51	3 7/8	.60	rises or falls
50	3 1/4	.54	by $1.
49	2 3/4	.50	
48	2 3/8	.46	
47	2 3/16	.41	
46	1 7/8	.36	
45	1 7/16	.32	
44	1 3/16	.27	

bottom half of Figure 2–13. Referring back to Figure 2–3, the $50 put option increases in price at an increasing rate as the stock price moves from $55 down to $45. Consequently, when the stock moves from $55 to $54, the put option increases only slightly in price and at this point has a small negative delta. Subsequently, when the stock price moves from $46 to $45, the option price change is a much larger percentage of the $1 price change in the stock. At this point, the put option has a much larger negative delta.

Another method of illustrating the concept of how delta changes with stock price changes is in Figure 2–14. This shows delta on the vertical axis and stock price on the horizontal axis. Call deltas are shown on the top half of the graph, and put deltas are shown on the bottom. The concept is the same as that in Figure 2–13: as stock prices rise, call deltas rise from 0 to 1.00, and put deltas fall from −1.00 to 0.

The delta is important to the user of options because it gives a current estimate of the expected value of an option price change. "Current" is the key word. Too often, option traders think only of what will happen on the date of expiration. Such focus, however, is limiting.

As an example, assume that you expect XYZ, which is currently at $50, to rally when its earnings are released next week. Rather than buy the stock, you buy the $50 call option to limit your risk in the event the

FIGURE 2–13
Delta: Change in Option Price per 1 Unit Change in Stock

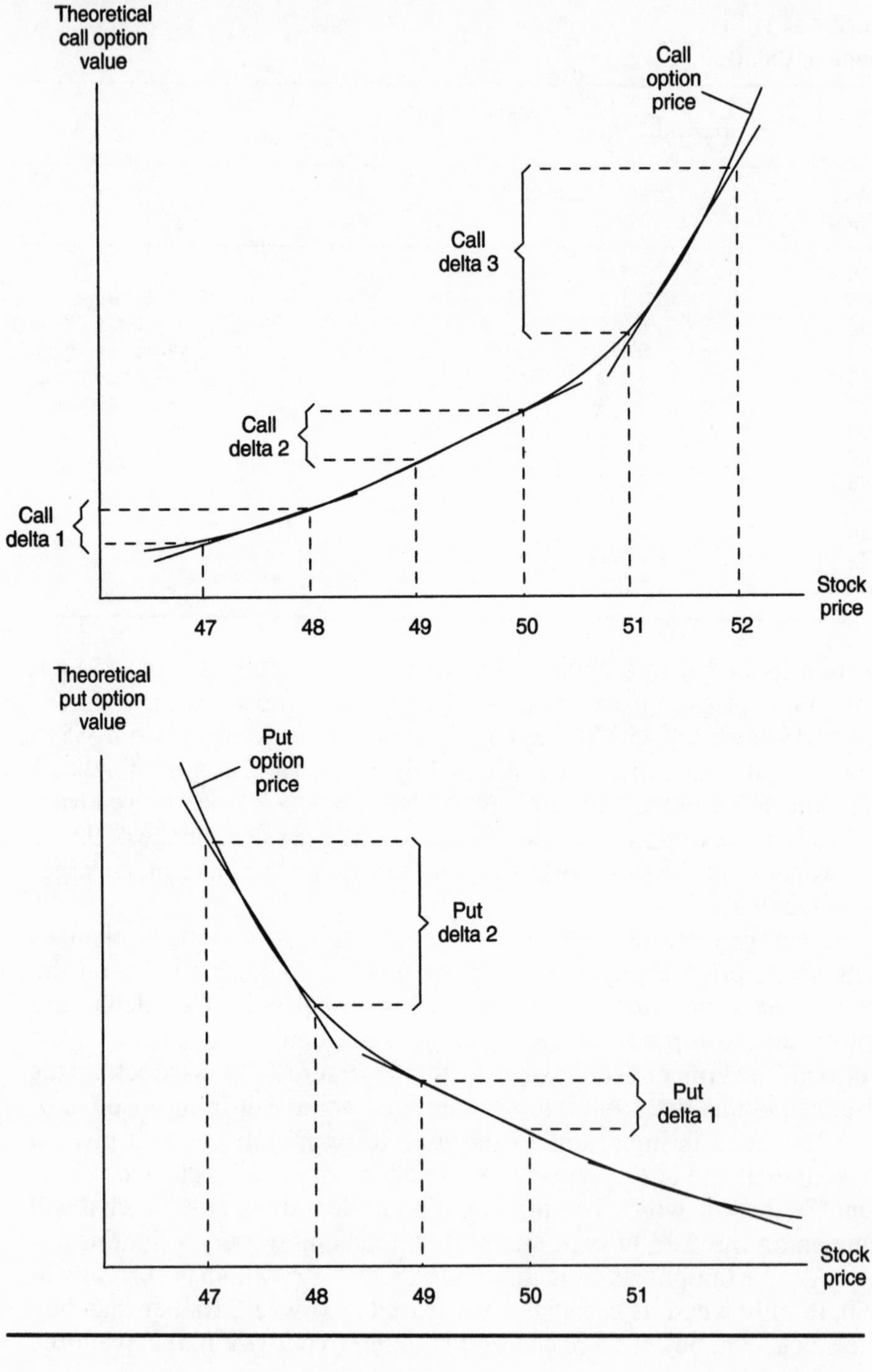

Theoretical call option value

Call option price

Call delta 3

Call delta 2

Call delta 1

Stock price

47   48   49   50   51   52

Theoretical put option value

Put option price

Put delta 2

Put delta 1

Stock price

47   48   49   50   51

FIGURE 2–14
Effect of Stock Price on Call and Put Deltas[2]

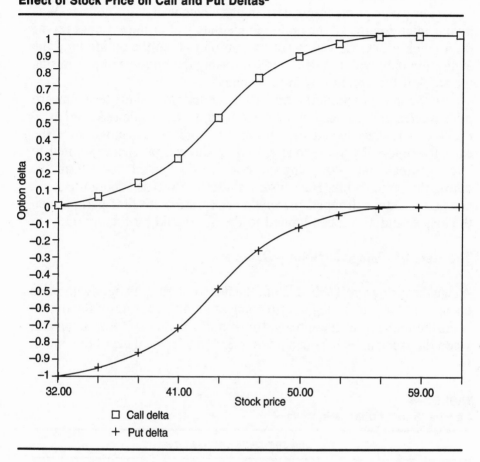

earnings report is unfavorable. For this example, assume that the $50 call option is trading at $2, its delta is .50, and that the stock moves up $1. With a delta of .50 and a stock move of $1, the option can be expected to move by .50 to $2.50, for a profit of .50. The analysis, at expiration, however, yields completely different results. With the stock at $51 on the date of expiration, the $50 call option is worth $1. Since the option was purchased for $2, the result is a loss of $1. This is quite a

---

[2] Figures 2–14 through 2–19 in this chapter were produced using The Options Analyst, a set of Lotus 1–2–3 spreadsheets produced by Fin Calc, Inc., Chicago, Illinois.

different result from the profit of $.50 realized on the movement of the stock and the option at the time of the earnings release.

Your trading time frame determines which analysis is correct. Was it your intention to sell the option immediately after the earnings report for a quick profit? Or was it your intention to hold the option until the expiration date with the desire of exercising the option and purchasing the stock if the option was in-the-money?

In the first situation, the trader was counting on short-term upward price movement. The call purchase limited the downside risk, and a .50 profit was realized when the option was sold on the move after the earnings report. In the second situation, the call purchaser wanted to buy the stock, but was using the option as a limited risk alternative during the option's life. Had this purchaser been wrong about the stock and had the stock dropped sharply in price during this time period, then the loss would have been limited to the $2.00 paid for the option.

The Rate of Change in Delta—Gamma

As can be seen from Table 2–3 on, the delta not only changes with price changes of the underlying, it also changes at different rates if the option is in-the-money, at-the-money, or out-of-the-money. For example, when the stock moved from a price of $50 to $51, the delta of the option

TABLE 2–4
Gamma: Rate of Change in Delta

Stock Price	$50 Call and Delta and Gamma		
	91 Days	Delta	Gamma
$55	6.5153	0.7941	0.0319
54	5.7574	0.7579	0.0362
53	5.0397	0.7177	0.0402
52	4.3660	0.6737	0.0440
51	3.7398	0.6262	0.0475
50	3.1640	0.5758	0.0504
49	2.6411	0.5229	0.0529
48	2.1724	0.4687	0.0542
47	1.7585	0.4139	0.0548
46	1.3989	0.3596	0.0543
45	1.0919	0.3070	0.0526

FIGURE 2–15
Effect of Stock Price on $50 Call Gammas

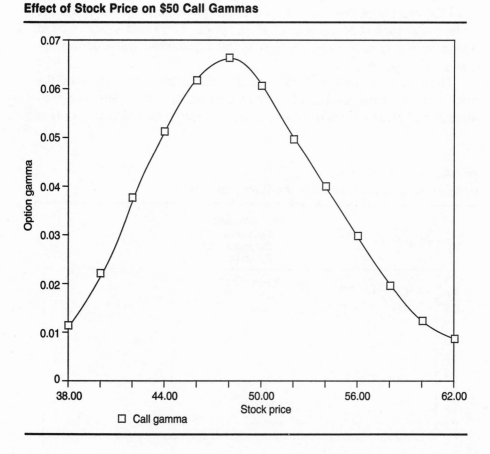

changed from .54 to .60—a .06 change. However, when the stock rose from $55 to $56, the delta rose from .75 to .78—a .03 change. These rates of change in delta are called *gamma*. By adding a third column to Table 2–3, as in Table 2–4, we can see gamma and how it changes.

In order to demonstrate the concept of gamma clearly, it is necessary to go out at least three decimal points. Such refinements are relevant primarily to professional traders who carry large numbers of options in their portfolios. The typical individual investor should be careful not to place too much emphasis on this concept. For the typical individual investor, stock selection and market forecasting are, by far, the most important concerns. Another way to illustrate how gamma changes is in Figure 2–15.

Figure 2–15 shows that gammas are greatest when the underlying stock is slightly below the option's strike price and smaller when the underlying stock is at a higher or lower price. The exact stock price at which option gammas are greatest is the discounted value of the option's strike price.

Gamma is a sophisticated concept (the second derivative of the price line). Gamma has little importance to the nonprofessional or non-market maker who does not carry large and frequently changing option

FIGURE 2–16
Delta's Change over Time for In-the-Money Options

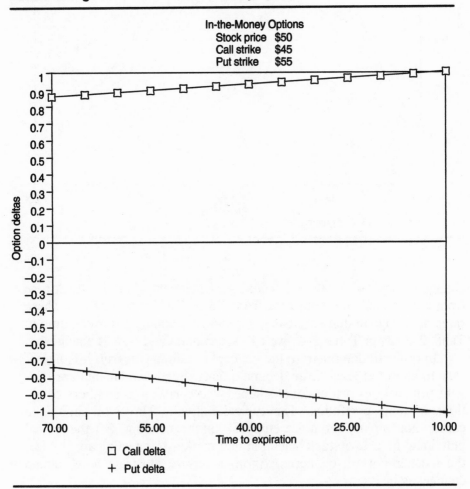

positions. This concept is used in determining the rate at which an option position changes. Professional traders with large option positions (several hundred long options and short options and thousands of shares of stock—long or short) frequently try to balance their long options against their short options with a goal of being *delta neutral*. This means that their long deltas equal their short deltas. The gamma of the position tells the professional trader how quickly the total position becomes long or short—how fast his long deltas get longer versus his short deltas

FIGURE 2–17
Delta's Change over Time for Out-of-the-Money Options

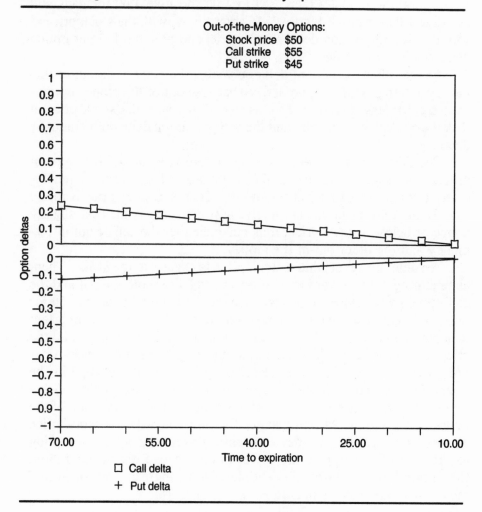

getting shorter. Again, this concept is relevant primarily to the professional option trader.

How Deltas Change with Time

As time progresses toward the expiration date, the delta of an option changes differently depending on whether an option is at-the-money, in-the-money, or out-of-the-money.

In-the-money options are exercised at expiration. This means that over the time period approaching expiration, the delta of an in-the-money option gradually increases to 1.00 (positive 1.00 for calls and negative 1.00 for puts). Figure 2–16 shows how, with the stock price at $50, the $45 call option delta rises to 1.00 and how the $55 put option delta declines to −1.00.

At the other extreme of delta behavior, the delta of an out-of-the-money option gradually approaches 0 because out-of-the-money options expire worthless. Figure 2–17 illustrates how, with the stock price at $50, the $55 call option delta and the $45 put option delta both gradually decrease to 0.

The delta for an at-the-money option presents an interesting theoretical discussion. The discussion is theoretical because, in reality, rarely is an option exactly at-the-money. That is, a stock price is rarely exactly at a strike price. Normally, a stock price is at least slightly above or below a strike price, thus making either the call or put in-the-money and the other out-of-the-money.

Assume, however, that a stock price is exactly at the strike. Then, as time progresses toward expiration, the delta for both the put and the call remain very close to .50 (positive .50 for call and negative .50 for puts). While this, at first, may be difficult to comprehend, it is important to separate in one's mind the effect of time on total option price and the effect of time on delta. The total option price gradually decreases over time, but regardless of the total option price, a 1 unit change in the underlying security will cause about a 1/2 unit change in the at-the-money option. This remains true at any time right up to the point of the option's expiration. At the instant of expiration, with the stock price exactly at the strike, the delta instantly drops to zero as the option expires worthless. But, in theory, even one second before expiration, the option has a delta of .50. The delta hovering near .50 for at-the-money puts and calls is illustrated in Figure 2–18.

FIGURE 2–18
Delta's Change over Time for At-the-Money Options

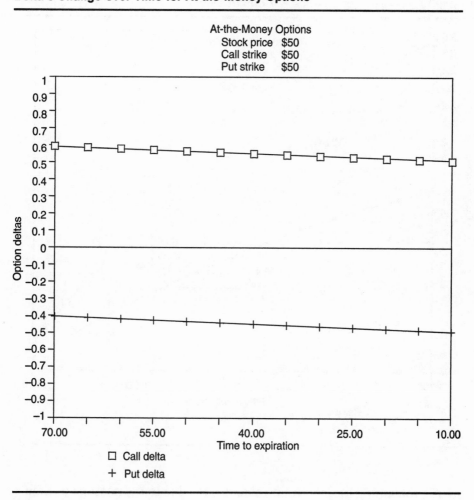

Delta's change over time is important primarily to the professional trader. An in-depth examination is not within the scope of this book.

Time Decay—Theta

Theta is the rate at which an option price erodes per unit of time. As was seen in tables 2–1 and 2–2 and Figure 2–4, the price of an at-the-money option decays at an increasing rate. During half of an at-the-money

FIGURE 2–19
Theta: Decrease in Option Price per Unit of Time

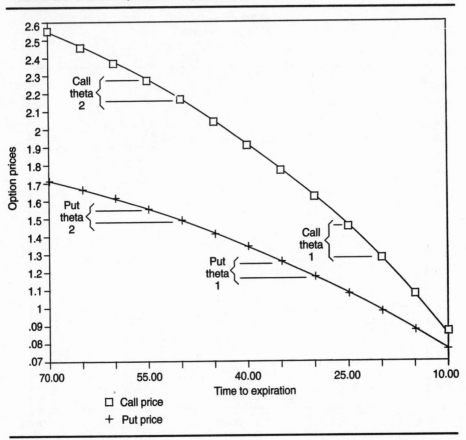

option's remaining life, the time value erodes due to the passage of time by approximately 33 percent. The concept of theta is illustrated in Figure 2–19.

Although theta is a sophisticated mathematical concept (it is the first derivative (slope) of the time line in Figure 2–4), it is valuable to all users of options.

For speculators, theta is useful in planning the duration of trades. If a speculator plans to trade out of a purchased option before expiration, then knowledge of time decay helps in deciding when to sell an option. The trader would balance time decay against the delta effect on the option from expected movements in the underlying stock price.

Professional traders use theta as another balancing tool to manage large positions of long and short options.

Changes in Volatility—Vega

The *vega* of an option is the change in an option's value that results from a change in volatility. Vegas are expressed in dollar terms. For example, if a 1 percent change in implied volatility causes a $.25 change in the option's value, then the option is said to have a vega of .25.

The vega is mathematically similar to the delta and theta in that it is a first derivative. As can be seen from figures 2–10, 2–11, and 2–12, the relationship of volatility to option price is nearly linear. However, the linear relationship for in-the-money, at-the-money, and out-of-the-money options is different for each. The implication is that vega does not change much unless the underlying stock moves considerably in relation to the option's strike price. Again, this is a concept that is most relevant to the professional trader.

THE PUT–CALL PARITY RELATIONSHIP

We have just completed a discussion of the theoretical elements of option value and how changes in each of the elements affect that value. Now our discussion shifts focus—from theoretical value to relative value.

Users of options need some assurance that they are, in some sense, paying a fair price for an option. Traders of stock have the same concern. Fundamental analysis or technical analysis are generally tools used by stock traders to address this concern. In the options market, fair prices are the result of an interplay of participants and a concept known as *put–call parity*. As will be demonstrated, there exists an exact relationship between the prices of calls and puts with the same strike price and expiration and the underlying stock.

Put–call parity is the pricing relationship concept that keeps option prices in line with each other and the underlying stock.

Put–call parity is explained in four steps. First, the maximum risk of a simple stock and option position is defined. Second, it is demonstrated how the use of a second option can eliminate this risk. Third, the role that arbitrage plays in making the market function is discussed.

Fourth, real world factors such as dividends, cost of money, and time are factored into the put–call parity relationship.

Step 1: Consider the following stock and option position:

	Per Share	Total
Long 100 share XYZ	Cost $52	$5,200
Long 1 $50 XYZ put	Cost $3	$ 300

Question: What is the maximum risk of this combined position? For this introductory example, we are assuming no commissions, no dividends, and zero interest rates.

To answer this question, consider what would happen at various stock prices on the expiration date. At a stock price of $50, for example, the put option would be exercised and the stock would be sold at $50 for a $2 loss per share, or $200. Adding the $300 cost of the put option to the $200 loss on the stock results in a total loss of $500. Similarly, at any stock price from $50 down to $0 a $500 loss would result.

If the stock were to close between $50 and $52 on the option expiration date, the put option would expire worthless for a loss of $300. The per-share loss on the stock, however, would be less than $2, thus making the entire loss less than $500. At $52, of course, the stock position would break even and the total loss would equal $300.00, the cost of the put option.

At prices above $52, the stock position would show a profit, but that profit would be reduced by the cost of the put option. The breakeven stock price on this combined position would be $55, which is where the $300 profit on the long stock would equal the $300 cost of the put option. Above $55, the combined position shows a total profit because the profit on the long stock exceeds the cost of the put option. Figure 2–20 illustrates the range of profit/loss outcomes at various stock prices at the time of option expiration.

From the above discussion and Figure 2–20, it is clear that the maximum possible loss from the combined position of long stock and long put described above is $500.

Step 2 is eliminating the risk of the long stock and long put position. A second option position—writing a $50 XYZ call at $500—is now added to the original combined position. The new position is as follows:

FIGURE 2–20
Long Stock and Long Put

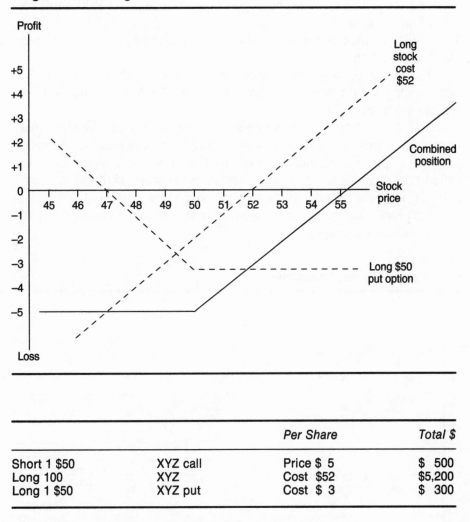

		Per Share	Total $
Short 1 $50	XYZ call	Price $ 5	$ 500
Long 100	XYZ	Cost $52	$5,200
Long 1 $50	XYZ put	Cost $ 3	$ 300

What is the maximum risk of this position?

Again, consider the outcome at various stock prices on the date of option expiration. At $50 or below, the $500 loss on the long stock and long put position is offset by the $500 received from selling the call option. The result is exactly breakeven.

At any price above $50, the put will expire worthless for a $300 loss, but the long stock and short call combination will result in a $300 profit. This is so because at a stock price above $50, the call will be exercised and the stock will be sold at $50 for $200 loss. The $500 received for selling the call, however, is kept. Thus, the $500 profit on the call is reduced by the $200 loss on the stock for a total net profit of $300. This, again, exactly equals the cost of the put option that expired worthless with the stock price above $50.

Net result: At any stock price, the three-way call option–put option–stock position described above achieves breakeven. This is illustrated by Figure 2–21.

Step 3 is arbitrage. The three-sided option-stock combination just described is the basis for how professional traders operate in the marketplace to provide liquidity to other participants. Professional traders, called arbitrageurs, are constantly active in the stock and options markets, looking for opportunities to buy stock, buy puts, and sell calls. Their goal, of course, is to make a profit, not to break even as described in the previous example.

FIGURE 2–21
Long Stock, Long Put, Short Call

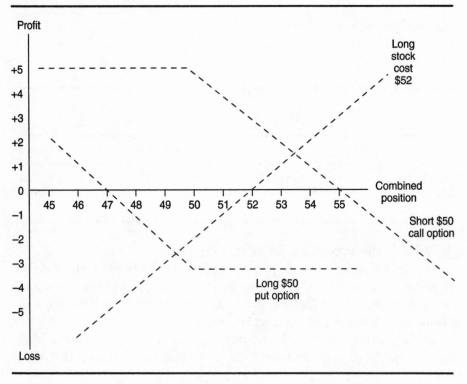

In the previous example, with the stock at $52, the $50 call at $5, and the $50 put at $3, the market is said to be *in line* or *at parity*. Professional traders are constantly seeking opportunities where they can sell the call option above $5 or buy the put option below $3. These competitive pressures will maintain prices at or near the option's fair value.

The price is *fair* because the process of arbitrage keeps all prices in line with each other, thus maintaining market equilibrium or parity between calls, puts, and stocks.

For example, if an imbalance of call-buying orders raised call prices, then professional traders would rush to increase their bids for put options. Bidding higher for puts would presumably entice more put sellers into the market. With the increased availability of puts (at the higher prices), the arbitrageurs would be able to buy puts, buy stock, and thus sell the calls being bid for at a higher price.

After this series of transactions occurred, both put and call prices would be higher than previously, but still fair. The new prices are fair because they would be in line with each other under the new market conditions.

Similarly, in another example, if a large order to sell puts at lower prices entered the market, then professional traders would compete against each other to offer call options at lower prices so that they could complete the three-sided option-stock position profitably. After these transactions occurred, both puts and calls would be lower in price than previously. Nevertheless, the prices would still be in line or at parity with each other under the new market conditions.

It should be clear from the preceding discussion that competition between professional traders causes put and call prices to rise and fall together. This concept should put to rest some misconceptions about the options markets expressed in typical statements such as "calls are overpriced" or "puts are cheap." Because of put–call parity, both puts and calls may be at a relatively high price level, or they may both be at a relatively low price level. But, barring transitory distortions, it is impossible for one to be "overpriced" or "expensive" relative to the other.

INFLUENCE OF REAL WORLD FACTORS

In the simple three-way example used above, it was assumed that there were no dividends, no cost of money, and no early exercise. In the real world, these factors affect option prices.

Dividends

Reviewing the basic 3-way position of long stock, long put, and short call, we now ask: How would this position be affected if the stock paid a $1 dividend?

Without the dividend, the position at the stated prices broke even. The presence of a $1 dividend, therefore, would imply a $1 profit. But what would competitors in the marketplace do when they saw the opportunity to make a $1 profit? Some professional traders or arbitrageurs would be willing to settle for a smaller profit, say 75 cents. Consequently, they would be willing to pay 25 cents more for the put or the stock or sell the call for 25 cents less. Other professional traders would be satisfied with only a 40-cent profit, and their bidding and offering would raise put prices and lower call prices.

Competition in the marketplace would thus raise put prices or lower call prices (or a combination of both) until the basic three-sided stock and option position was back to breakeven. The conclusion to be drawn is that the presence of dividends has the effect of raising put prices and lowering call prices.

Cost of Money

The cost of money is an important consideration for all investors because investment performance is measured against the benchmark riskless investment, usually the short-term Treasury bill. It is no different for the professional option trader who must borrow money to finance large stock and option holdings and who seeks a return to cover those costs and earn a profit.

To illustrate how the cost of money affects option prices, consider the following example and ask this question: At what price must the $50 call option be sold to make this position break even?

	Per Share	Total $
Short 1 $50 call option	Price ?	?
Long 100 XYZ	Cost $50	$5,000.00
Long 1 $50 put option	Cost $ 3	$ 300.00
9 percent prevailing cost of money		
90 days until option expiration		

The answer to this question is reasoned through as follows:

In 90 days, this three-way position will turn into $50 cash per share because either the stock will be above $50 and an assignment notice will be received for the short $50 call, or the stock will be below $50 and the put will be exercised. In either case, the stock is sold and $50 cash for each share is received. Thus, the question becomes: How much should be invested today to earn 9 percent (annually) if $50 per share will be received in 90 days? Since 90 days is one-fourth of a year, we expect to earn 9 percent $\times$ 1/4 = 2.25 percent on this three-sided position. Consequently, we must invest 50 $\times$ (1 $-$ .0225) = 48.875 or $48 7/8 per share. Therefore, the call should be sold for $1 1/8 more than the put, or $4 1/8; and the final position looks like this:

	Per Share	Total
Short 1 $50 call option	Price $4 1/8	$ 412.50
Long 1 share XYZ	Cost $50	$5,000.00
Long 1 $50 put option	Cost $3	$ 300.00
Total invested	$48 7/8	$4,887.50

$48 7/8 + ($48 7/8 $\times$ 9% $\times$ [1/4 of 1 year]) = $50 at option expiration.

Interest Rates

From the above example, if interest rates rise while the stock price, put price, and days until option expiration remain constant, then the call price must rise by the amount of the increased interest cost. This is the necessary result because the cost of carrying the position will increase and the call must be sold for a greater amount to cover that increased cost of carry.

The effect of interest rates on put prices is exactly opposite: as interest rates rise, put prices decline. This can be demonstrated by reasoning through what must happen to put prices when interest rates rise but the other elements (stock price, call price, and days until expiration) remain constant.

Rising interest rates result in an increased cost of carry. To compensate for the higher cost, either the revenue of the position must increase, or the cost of the position must decrease. Because the call price (the revenue side) is assumed to be unchanged, the cost of the position must be reduced. Since the stock price is assumed to be constant, only the put price is left to be reduced to compensate for the increase in cost of carry.

From these examples, it should be clear that the put–call parity relationship will hold at all times. Changes in supply or demand factors for any one or more of the parts of the equation will result in professional traders raising their bids or lowering their offers for other parts of the equation. Consequently, the interaction of different market participants, including competition among professional traders, will result in call, put, and stock prices that are in line with each other, or fair.

SUMMARY

The purpose of this chapter has been to introduce several fundamental concepts about call and put options and the rational nature of option prices. American-style options give the owner a right that may be exercised at any time prior to expiration, and European-style options involve rights that may be exercised only at expiration. Option prices have two components: intrinsic value and time value. In-the-money, at-the-money, and out-of-the-money are designations that refer to the relationship of the current price of the underlying to the option strike price.

The theoretical value of an option depends on five factors: the price of the underlying asset, the strike price of the option, the time remaining to expiration, prevailing cost of carry (interest rates and dividends), and the volatility of the underlying asset. Option values will change by less than the price change of the underlying asset; the ratio of this price change is called delta. Deltas of at-the-money options are approximately .50 regardless of the time to expiration. In-the-money options have deltas greater than 0.50, and they increase to 1.00 as expiration approaches. Deltas of out-of-the-money options are less than .50 and decrease toward 0 as expiration approaches. A unit of time decay in an option price is called theta. Time decay for at-the-money options is nonlinear, but in-the-money and out-of-the-money options decay in a nearly linear fashion. Volatility is the unknown element in calculating an option's theoretical value; as a result, the calculation of an option's theoretical value is, ultimately, subjective.

Advanced pricing concepts such as how deltas change, how theta changes, and how changes in volatility affect option prices are important primarily to professional option traders who manage large option positions of both long and short options. The typical individual investor and portfolio manager should be most concerned with market prediction, stock selection, and risk management. Options are a valuable investment tool because they offer investors a wider range of risk profiles from which to choose.

CHAPTER 3

VOLATILITY EXPLAINED

INTRODUCTION

Volatility is the most used and least understood word in the options business. To most people, the term volatility has an intuitive definition that relates to price movement, and this intuition is correct. On an annual basis, it can be said that a stock that had a 12-month high of $120 and a 12-month low of $80 was more volatile than a stock that traded between $105 and $95. Over a shorter term, it can be said that a stock with an average daily trading range (high price to low price) of $5 is more volatile than another stock that has an average daily trading range of $2 (assuming the average underlying price of both stocks is the same).

Examination of historical stock price movements shows that individual stocks go through periods of high volatility and low volatility. There are many possible explanations for these variations in stock price volatility. One explanation might be general economic factors affecting an industry group of stocks; another might be specific developments for the specific stock. A third possibility could be the psychological state of investors. Regardless of the cause, investors must be aware that the volatility characteristics of a stock can change dramatically at any point in the future.

Another factor that adds to the confusion regarding volatility is that there are four words commonly used in conjunction with volatility. These four words are historical, future, expected, and implied. But what is the concept of volatility that is relevant to the option user? The purpose of the following discussion is to explain when and how each of these four words is used properly. First, we illustrate in a simple example how the historical volatility of a stock is calculated. Second, in conceptual terms, we show how volatility and changes in volatility affect option values. Third, we discuss what expected volatility and implied volatility mean and what overvalued and undervalued mean and how all the confusing terms associated with volatility can be used properly.

HISTORICAL VOLATILITY

Historical volatility is a measure of actual stock price movement that occurred during a period of time in the past. Specifically, stock price volatility is the annualized standard deviation of a stock's daily returns. A simplified example presented in Table 3–1 illustrates the concept.

Columns 1 and 3 in Table 3–1 show closing prices of two stocks for 10 days. While the prices of both Stock A and Stock B start the 10-day period at $51 and end at $51 1/2, Stock B has larger price changes every day. Columns 2 and 4 show the daily returns. A daily return is calculated by dividing the daily price change by the starting price. Consequently, from day 1 to day 2, Stock A rose by 1/2, which was a daily return of positive 0.98 percent on the starting price of $51. From day 7 to day 8, Stock B moved down by 3/8, which was a daily return of negative 0.72 percent on the starting price of $52 1/8.

The standard deviation of these daily returns is calculated and annualized, and the result is the 10-day historical volatility presented at the bottom of Columns 2 and 4. As expected, Stock B is shown to have the higher volatility because it experienced greater price fluctuations on very nearly the same base price. It should be noted that there is nothing special about the 10-day period. Historical volatility can be calculated for any time period. The mathematics of calculating standard deviations

TABLE 3–1
Calculation of Historical Volatility

	Stock A		Stock B	
	Daily Close	Daily Return	Daily Close	Daily Return
Day 1	$51		$51	
Day 2	$51 1/2	0.0098	$51 3/4	0.0147
Day 3	$50 5/8	−0.0170	$50 3/8	−0.0266
Day 4	$50 7/8	0.0049	$50 3/4	0.0074
Day 5	$51 5/8	0.0147	$52 1/4	0.0296
Day 6	$51 3/8	−0.0048	$51 3/4	−0.0096
Day 7	$51 5/8	0.0049	$52 1/8	0.00725
Day 8	$51 1/2	−0.0024	$51 3/4	−0.0072
Day 9	$51 3/8	−0.0024	$51 1/4	−0.0097
Day 10	$51 1/2	0.0024	$51 1/2	0.0049
10-day historical volatility (annualized standard deviation)		13.9%		24.7%

is beyond the scope of this book. For an extensive mathematical treatment of volatility, there are a number of references available; for example, books on options by Cox and Rubinstein, Jarrow and Rudd, Hull, and Natenburg.

Now that it has been illustrated how the historical volatility of a stock price is calculated, the following discussion presents volatility in a nontechnical way, as a concept that can be understood and used in making investment and trading decisions with options.

VOLATILITY AND OPTION VALUE—A CONCEPTUAL APPROACH

To begin a discussion of volatility, consider the simplistic world presented in Figure 3–1 in which a stock with a starting price of 100 has only two possible outcomes at option expiration: 99 or 101. In this simplistic case, time to expiration is not considered. With the stock price starting at 100 and only being able to rise one point to 101 or fall one point to 99, the stock price has a one point volatility—a one-point movement without regard to direction. The ending value of the 100 call depends on the ending stock price. If the stock price rises to 101, the 100 call will have a value of 1. If the stock declines to 99, the 100 call will expire unexercised and be worth 0. Knowing the possible final prices for the stock and the probability that each might occur, it is possible to calculate expected values for both the stock price and the 100 call.

Expected value is a statistical concept that means the weighted average outcome. The assumption is that the event is repeated a large

FIGURE 3–1
Expected Value Calculations (One-Point Volatility, One Time Period, Starting Price 100)

		Probability	Expected Stock Price	Expected Value of 100 Call
	101	50%	.50 × 101	.50 × 1.00
100				
	99	50%	.50 × 99	.50 × –0–
		Total	100	.50

number of times so that each possible outcome occurs in accordance with its statistical probability.

In Figure 3–1, there is a 50 percent chance the stock will rise to 101 and a 50 percent chance it will fall to 99. Consequently, the weighted average outcome, or the expected stock price, is 100. The calculation is shown in Figure 3–1 and is as follows:

$$\text{Expected value of stock price} = (50\% \times 101) + (50\% \times 99)$$
$$= (.50 \times 101) + (.50 \times 99)$$
$$= 50.5 + 49.5 = 100$$

Calculating the expected value for the 100 call is accomplished through a similar process. With the stock at a final price of 101, the 100 call is worth 1. With the stock at a final price of 99, the 100 call expires unexercised with a value of 0. Consequently, given a 50 percent probability the 100 call will have a value of 1 and a 50 percent probability it will have a value of 0, the weighted average, or expected value, is 0.50. The calculation is shown in Figure 3–1 and is as follows:

$$\text{Expected value of 100 call option} = (50\% \times 1) + (50\% \times 0)$$
$$= (.50 \times 1) + (.50 \times 0)$$
$$= .50 + 0 = .50$$

CHANGING THE VOLATILITY

The above exercise raises the following question: If the magnitude of the up or down movement is changed, what happens to the expected values?

In Figure 3–2, we assume the stock price, starting at 100, can either rise to 102 or fall to 98. The volatility—movement without regard to direction—has been increased to two points from one point. Figure 3–2 shows the expected value calculation for the stock price is still 100. Although this answer may surprise some readers, the stock has a 50 percent probability of ending at 102 and a 50 percent probability of ending at 98. As a result, the expected value of the stock is 100 (the calculation is shown in Figure 3–2), the same as in the previous case even though the volatility was lower.

In the second case, however, the larger volatility of the underlying stock, results in a different expected value for the 100 call. At a final stock price of 102, the 100 call has a value of 2. At a final stock price of

FIGURE 3–2
Expected Value Calculations (Two-Point Volatility, One Time Period,
Starting Price 100)

	Probability	Expected Stock Price	Expected Value of 100 Call
102	50%	.50 × 102	.50 × 2.00
98	50%	.50 × 98	.50 × –0–
Totals		100	1.00

98, the 100 call will expire unexercised and have a value of 0. Since there is a 50 percent chance of either outcome occurring, the expected value of the 100 call in this situation is 1. The calculation is shown in Figure 3–2.

An Analogy to Volatility

There are two differences between the two situations just described in Figures 3–1 and 3–2. First, there is a different size of the up or down movement—the volatility. The two-point movement example can be said to be more volatile than the one-point movement example. The second difference is the expected value for the 100 call: 0.50 versus 1.00. But it is important to note that there is no difference in the expected value for the underlying stock; both cases had an expected stock price of 100.

   This leads to the first important concept about volatility: *an increase in volatility increases the expected value of the 100 call, but does not affect the expected value of the underlying stock.* Although presented in simplified form, this is a general conclusion that holds true in the more sophisticated world of higher mathematics.

A More Advanced Example

The previous example was extremely simplistic in that it assumed only two possible outcomes in one time period. In the real world, of course, many outcomes are possible, and more than one time period exists. Although it is impossible to replicate reality, it is possible to carry the

FIGURE 3–3
Expanding the Binomial Process to Two Periods
(One-Point Volatility, Two Time Periods, and Probabilities
of Final Outcomes)

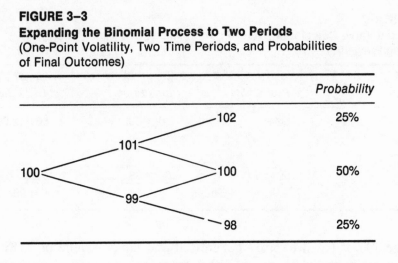

	Probability
102	25%
100	50%
98	25%

single time period example forward to more time periods so that more outcomes can be generated. The purpose of doing this is to illustrate some important concepts of option price behavior.

The examples just reviewed are one-time-period examples. Figure 3–3 illustrates how a two-time-period example is created, and Figure 3–4 illustrates a three-time-period example. This is called the *binomial process* because in each time period, there are only two possible out-

FIGURE 3–4
Expanding the Binomial Process to Three Periods (One-Point Volatility,
Three Time Periods, and Probabilities of Final Outcomes)

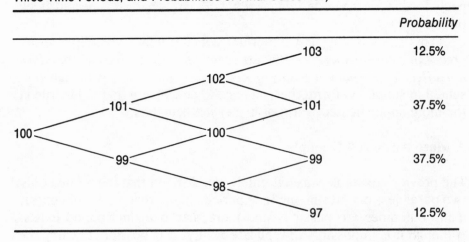

	Probability
103	12.5%
101	37.5%
99	37.5%
97	12.5%

comes. As additional periods are added, more final outcomes become possible.

It is also important to note how the probabilities of final prices change as the number of periods increases. In the single-period case, there are two possible outcomes, each of which has a 50 percent chance of occurring. In the two-period case, however, there are three possible outcomes; and each outcome does *not* have a 33 percent chance of occurring. If one traces along the branches of the diagram, one can observe that only one out of four ways leads to the final price of 102. Also, only one out of four ways leads to the final stock price of 98. But two out of four ways lead to the final stock price of 100. Consequently, the probabilities in the two-period case are 25 percent of reaching 102, 50 percent of reaching 100, and 25 percent of reaching 98.

If one traces along the various paths in Figure 3–4 that illustrates a three-time-period binomial example, one sees eight possible ways of arriving at one of the four possible final prices. The probabilities are 12.5 percent of ending at 103, 37.5 percent of ending at 101, 37.5 percent of ending at 99, and 12.5 percent of ending at 97.

The Four-Period Case

We now extend the binomial process to four periods and analyze the implications for option price behavior and volatility. Figure 3–5 assumes a starting price of 100 and an up or down movement of one point per period. Consequently, the range of possible prices at the end of four periods is from up four points to 104 to down four points to 96. The probability of the various final outcomes occurring are as follows: 104—6.25 percent, 102—25 percent, 100—37.5 percent, 98—25 percent, 96—6.25 percent.

Using the expected-value calculations presented earlier, we see that the stock price has an expected value of 100 (see calculations in Figure 3–5) and the 100 call option has an expected value of .75 (calculations are also in Figure 3–5).

Moving Out One Period

The expected value calculations just presented were made from a starting price of 100, which is point A in Figure 3–5. If we assume that during the first period the stock price rises one point to 101 indicated by point B

FIGURE 3–5
Expected Value Calculations (One-Point Volatility, Four Time Periods, Starting Price 100)

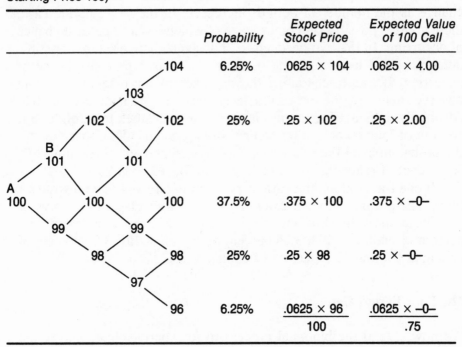

		Probability	Expected Stock Price	Expected Value of 100 Call
104		6.25%	.0625 × 104	.0625 × 4.00
102	102	25%	.25 × 102	.25 × 2.00
100	100	37.5%	.375 × 100	.375 × –0–
98	98	25%	.25 × 98	.25 × –0–
96		6.25%	.0625 × 96	.0625 × –0–
			100	.75

in Figure 3–5, new expected values for both the stock price and the call can be calculated.

Figure 3–6 shows the new situation. With the stock at 101 and only three periods remaining, the range of possible final outcomes has been reduced to 104 at the high end and 98 on the low end. The dashed lines represent the outcomes that are no longer possible. There is also a new set of probabilities for each of these possible outcomes, because now only eight possible ways exist to get to the remaining outcomes. The probabilities are: 104—12.5 percent, 102—37.5 percent, 100—37.5 percent, 98—12.5 percent.

The expected value calculations show that the new expected value of the stock price is 101 and the new expected value of the 100 call is 1.25. The calculations are shown on Figure 3–6.

These new expected value calculations are consistent with the concept of delta presented earlier and illustrated in Tables 2–1 and 2–2 in Chapter 2. When the stock price moves up by one full point, the theoret-

FIGURE 3–6
Expected Value Calculations (One-Point Volatility, Three Time Periods, Starting Price 101)

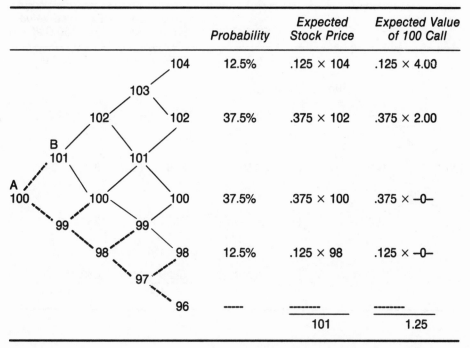

	Probability	Expected Stock Price	Expected Value of 100 Call
104	12.5%	.125 × 104	.125 × 4.00
102	37.5%	.375 × 102	.375 × 2.00
100	37.5%	.375 × 100	.375 × –0–
98	12.5%	.125 × 98	.125 × –0–
96	-----	-------- 101	-------- 1.25

ical value of the 100 call moves up by less than one point, in this case by .50.

Changing the Movement in the Binomial Example

If the size of the up or down movement is increased from one point per period to two points per period in the four-period example, the results are consistent with the concepts just presented. Figure 3–7 shows a four-period example in which the underlying stock price starts at 100 and moves up or down two points during each of four time periods. The range of possible outcomes has expanded to 108 at the high and 92 at the low, with the probabilities of each final outcome as follows: 108—6.25 percent, 104—25 percent, 100—37.5 percent, 96—25 percent, 92—6.25 percent. The expected value of the stock at the end of four periods is 100, and the expected value of the 100 call is 1.50 (the calculations are shown in Figure 3–7).

FIGURE 3–7
Expected Value Calculations (Two-Point Volatility, Four Time Periods, Starting Price 100)

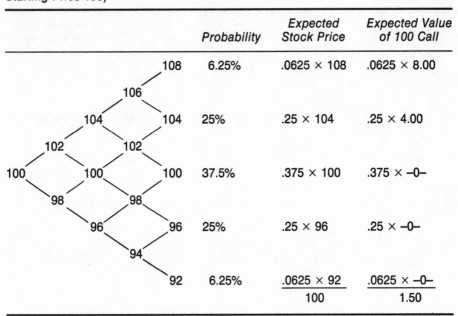

		Probability	Expected Stock Price	Expected Value of 100 Call
	108	6.25%	.0625 × 108	.0625 × 8.00
	104	25%	.25 × 104	.25 × 4.00
	100	37.5%	.375 × 100	.375 × –0–
	96	25%	.25 × 96	.25 × –0–
	92	6.25%	.0625 × 92	.0625 × –0–
			100	1.50

Figure 3–8 shows a situation in which the starting stock price is 101, there are three time periods to expiration, and the expected volatility is two points per period. It should be noted that Figure 3–8 does not follow directly from Figure 3–7. However, the numbers calculated in Figure 3–8 are required to complete the upcoming discussion on implied volatility and changes in implied volatility. Using the price of 101 as the starting point in Figure 3–8, the new expected value of the stock is 101, and the new expected value of the 100 call is 2.00.

The calculations in Figure 3–8 are consistent with the earlier example in Figure 3–5 and Figure 3–6. Although the stock price is one point higher in Figure 3–8 than Figure 3–7, the expected value of the 100 call is less than one point higher, just as the one point stock price rise between Figure 3–5 and Figure 3–6 resulted in a less-than-one-point increase in the 100 call.

The comparison of the one-point movement and two-point movement four-period examples is also consistent with the narrow movement and wide movement one-period examples presented earlier. Wider

FIGURE 3–8
Expected Value Calculations (Two-Point Volatility, Three Time Periods,
Starting Price 101)

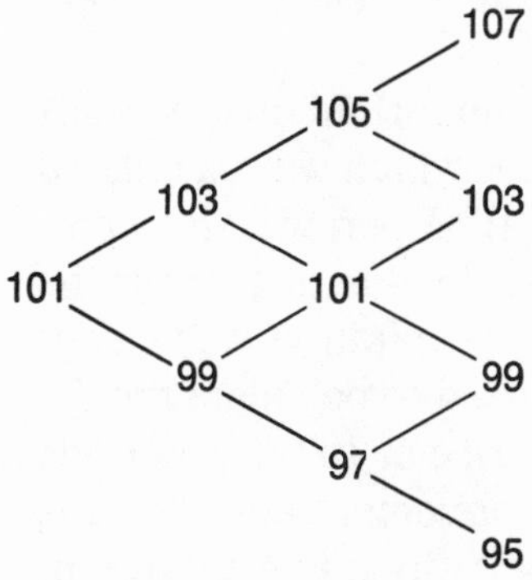

	Probability	Expected Stock Price	Expected Value of 100 Call
107	12.5%	.125 × 107	.125 × 7.00
105			
103 103	37.5%	.375 × 103	.375 × 3.00
101 101			
99 99	37.5%	.375 × 99	.375 × –0–
97			
95	12.5%	.125 × 95	.125 × –0–
		101	2.00

movements per period result in a higher expected value for the 100 call,
but not for the underlying stock price.

We now have all the information we need to explain the concepts of
expected volatility, implied volatility, and changes in implied volatility.

EXPECTED VOLATILITY

Referring back to Figure 3–5, the expected stock value of 100 is the
same as the starting price of 100, and, given the assumption that movement can only be up one point or down one point per period for four
periods, the expected value of the 100 call is .75. Another term for
expected value is theoretical value. Statistically, if the four-period event
occurred many times, then the average final outcome would be .75. Of
course, no single final outcome would equal .75 because, under the
assumptions about the stock price movement, the only possible option
price outcomes are whole numbers 0, 2, and 4.

The theoretical value (or expected value) was calculated from the
distribution that resulted from the assumption about movement. In the
real world, the future is unknown, and the daily price change is not

limited to a finite up or down amount. Furthermore, the size of possible movement is not constant. Consequently, in the examples presented above, it was not the known distribution that led to the theoretical values of the 100 call; it was the *expected* distribution. If we substitute the word *volatility* for *distribution,* which is common practice in discussions about options, it can be said that *the theoretical values were calculated using the expected volatility.*

Looking back at Figure 3–6, there are some important observations to be made about the theoretical call value of 1.25, which was calculated after the one-point price rise to 101 in the first time period. This comment may startle some readers, but the theoretical value of 1.25 for the 100 call with the stock at 101 three periods from expiration was calculated using the same expected volatility as that used to calculate the .75 theoretical value for the 100 call with the stock price at 100 four periods prior to expiration. The one point up or down movement per period is the same—there is just one fewer period; and the stock has a different starting price. But the expected movement, or volatility, is the same. This is a crucial point to understand: the price of $.75 for the 100 call in Figure 3–5 and the price of $1.25 for the 100 call in Figure 3–6 are calculated using the same expected volatility.

IMPLIED VOLATILITY

We now look at the same information from a different angle. Suppose it is four periods prior to expiration, the stock is trading at 100, and the 100 call is trading in the market at .75. It can be said that this price *implies* the distribution in Figure 3–5. Again, substituting the word *volatility* for *distribution,* we can say that the price of .75 for the 100 call (when the stock is trading at 100 four periods prior to expiration) implies the volatility in Figure 3–5.

It follows from this that the price of 1.25 for the 100 call with the stock trading at 101 three periods prior to expiration implies the same volatility.

What, then, can be said about the prices of 1.50 in Figure 3–7 and 2.00 in Figure 3–8? Obviously, these prices imply a larger per-period up or down movement. In other words, these prices imply a higher volatility.

Implied Volatility versus Expected Volatility

Expected volatility is one investor's expectation about what will happen; it is that investor's prediction for the future. For example, given a stock price of 100, if an investor expects the four-period distribution in Figure 3–5, then that investor will calculate an expected (or theoretical) value of .75. Also, given a stock price of 100, if an investor expects the four-period distribution in Figure 3–7, then that investor will calculate a theoretical value of 1.50. Similarly, given a stock price of 101, if an investor expects the three-period distribution in either Figure 3–6 or Figure 3–8, that investor will calculate a theoretical value of either 1.25 or 2.00, respectively.

An investor's expectation, or prediction, may come from experience, from historical data, or from some other source. But as was shown in the preceding discussion, one's choice of volatility will affect the resulting theoretical value.

Implied volatility is the volatility derived from looking at the current market price of an option. Using different words to express the same concept: *implied volatility* is the volatility number that justifies the current market price of an option. For example, if the stock is trading at 100 and the 100 call is trading at a price of .75, this price implies a one point per period volatility as shown in Figure 3–5. Similarly, if the stock is trading at 100 and the 100 call is trading at 1.50, that price implies a two point per period volatility as show in Figure 3–7. Also, if there are three periods to expiration, the stock is trading at 101, and the 100 call is trading at either 1.25 or 2.00, then the distributions in Figure 3–6 or Figure 3–8, respectively, in three periods would be implied.

Some traders think of implied volatility as the market's expected volatility. Given the market price of an option, the volatility implied by that price must be, it is reasoned, the expectation of the market.

Changes in Implied Volatility

Changes in implied volatility are often difficult for the options newcomer to understand. It is very important to see that an option price does not imply a direction for the underlying price movement. Calls, puts, and the underlying security always have a price relationship with each other called put–call parity, which was explained in Chapter 2. Consequently, option prices imply a distribution—or volatility—not a direction. If an option price changes without the price of the underlying security changing, then market forces are bringing about a change in the implied distribution or implied volatility.

As an example of a change in implied volatility, consider a situation in which the stock price is 100, there are four periods to expiration, and the 100 call is trading in the market at a price of .75. Now imagine that without any passage of time and without any change in the underlying stock price, the 100 call trades up in price to 1.50. How could such an occurrence be explained? Obviously, an increase in demand for the call has driven up the price. But, in terms of implied volatility, the market has changed its expectation about the distribution of prices of the underlying stock in the upcoming four periods. Specifically, when the price of the 100 call was .75, the market was expecting the distribution illustrated in Figure 3–5. With the 100 call trading at 1.50, however, the market has changed its expectation to the distribution illustrated in Figure 3–7. In other words, the implied volatility changed: the market's expectation for the upcoming four-period distribution of prices of the underlying stock changed from that pictured in Figure 3–5 to that pictured in Figure 3–7.

In the real world, of course, both time and price of the underlying change. To illustrate how implied volatility can fluctuate given changes in time and price of the underlying, consider a situation in which there are four periods to expiration, the stock is trading at 100, and the 100 call is trading in the market at .75. This option price implies the distribution—or volatility—in Figure 3–5 as discussed above. Now imagine that in the course of one period the stock price rises from 100 to 101 and the 100 call price rises in market trading from .75 to 2.00. What has happened?

If the market's expectation for volatility for the next three periods had remained constant, then one would expect the 100 call to have risen in price from .75 to 1.25. In this case, the 1.25 market price would imply the distribution in Figure 3–6. The price of 2.00, however, given three periods to expiration, implies the distribution illustrated in Figure 3–8. The change in price of the 100 call from .75 to 2.00 happened because the market's expectation for volatility in the remaining three periods increased.

To understand what happens when the market's expectation for volatility decreases, consider a situation in which there are four periods to expiration, the stock is trading at 100, and the 100 call is trading at 1.50. Given these circumstances, the market's expectation for volatility is two points per period and is illustrated in Figure 3–7. If the price of the stock trades up to 101 and the 100 call trades *down* to 1.25, then the market's expectation for volatility for the next three periods has changed. The market now expects the distribution in Figure 3–6. The market's expectation for volatility in the remaining three periods has decreased from two points per period to one point per period.

REAL WORLD EXPERIENCE

Can such things happen? This is a reasonable question for an options newcomer to ask. Although such price behavior seems counterintuitive, in fact, changes in volatility are quite common.

The conclusion is obvious: changes in implied volatility can affect the results of trading options. Therefore, traders of options should take time to learn more about this important factor.

THE MEANING OF "20 PERCENT" VOLATILITY

A natural question at this point is, What exactly does the volatility percentage number mean? Essentially, this percentage figure is a statistical measure of the width of the expected distribution of the underlying security. The higher the volatility percentage, the wider the expected distribution. In statistical parlance, the volatility percentage is the standard deviation of the bell-shaped curve that theoretically illustrates the possible price outcomes. For the layperson, this means that a security with 20 percent volatility is expected, two-thirds of the time, to be within a range 20 percent higher or lower than the current price in one year. A security with 30 percent volatility is expected, two-thirds of the time, to be within a range 30 percent higher or lower in one year. Obviously, the security with 30 percent volatility has a greater chance of experiencing a larger price change. Consequently, options on that security will have higher values, assuming other factors are equal.

Rather than learning the mathematics of volatility, option traders should be aware of this concept and incorporate it into their decision-making process. Since trading decisions are largely subjective, learning to incorporate expectations about volatility is just another subjective component.

VOLATILITY AND AVERAGE PRICE MOVEMENTS

Probability tables exist so that if a standard deviation is known (or assumed), then the likelihood or probability, of an event occurring can be determined. Although these probabilities can be calculated exactly, the following approximations are sufficient for traders of options.

- Approximately two out of three outcomes will occur within one standard deviation of the mean.
- Approximately 19 out of 20 outcomes will occur within two standard deviations of the mean.
- Approximately 369 out of 370 outcomes will occur within three standard deviations of the mean.

This concept is related to price movement of stock prices in the following manner: the volatility percentage for a given stock price represents one standard deviation of price movement for a one-year period. For example, if the stock price is $50 and the volatility is 10 percent, then a price change of one standard deviation for a one-year time period is $5 (10% X $50). This means that, over three one-year periods, it is probable that in two of three years the stock will be trading in a range between $45 ($50 − $5) and $55 ($50 + $5) and outside that range in one year, assuming a stock price of $50 at the beginning of each year. Similarly, over 20 one-year periods, it is expected the stock will be trading in a range between $40 ($50 − 2 × $5) and $60 ($50 + 2 × $5) in 19 of these years and outside that range in one year, once again assuming a $50 price at the beginning of each year. Also, over 370 one-year periods, it is expected the stock will be trading in a range between $35 ($50 − 3 × $5) and $65 ($50 + 3 × $5) in 369 of these years and outside that range in one year.

Because a one-year time frame is generally not useful for options traders, the following formula can be used to calculate a price change of one standard deviation over a period of time: *The annual volatility percentage divided by the square root of the time (expressed in years) times the stock price.*

Example 1. If a stock is trading at $50 with a volatility of 25 percent, then the *monthly* standard deviation of price change is:

$$(25\% \div \sqrt{12}) \times \$50 = \$3.62 = 3\ 5/8$$

This means that over three one-month periods, it is expected that a stock trading at 25 percent volatility and starting at $50 will trade between 46 3/8 and 53 5/8 two out of three times and outside that range on the other occasion. It also means that over 20 one-month periods, it is expected that this stock will trade in a range between 42 3/4 and 57 1/4 19 times out of 20 and outside that range once. And, it means there are 369 chances out of 370 that this stock will trade in a range between 37 1/8 and 62 7/8.

Example 2.   If a stock is trading at $50 with a volatility of 25 percent, then the *daily* standard deviation of price change is:

$$(25\% \div \sqrt{252}) \times \$50 = \$0.78 = 3/4$$

This means that over three one-day periods, it is expected that a stock trading at 25 percent volatility and starting at $50 will trade in a range between 49 1/4 and 50 3/4 two out of three times and outside that range on the other occasion. During 20 one-day periods, it is expected that this stock will trade in a range between 48 1/2 and 51 1/2 19 times out of 20 and outside that range once. And, there are 369 chances out of 370 that this stock will trade in a range between 47 3/4 and 52 1/4.

In the daily calculation, the square root of 252 is used instead of the square root of 365, because there are approximately 252 trading days in a year. Therefore, one trading day is 1/252 of a trading year.

As a final example, for a 90-day option, which has a life of one-fourth of a year, the volatility percentage is divided by the square root of 4, or 2. Consequently, for the sample $50 stock with a volatility of 25 percent, a move of one standard deviation for 90 days is:

$$(25\% \div \sqrt{4}) \times \$50 = \$6.25 = 6 \ 1/4$$

This means that over three one-quarter periods, it is expected that a stock trading at 25 percent volatility and starting at $50 will trade between $43.75 and $56.25 two of the three times and outside that range once. It also means that over 20 one-quarter periods, it is expected that this stock will trade in a range between $37.50 and $62.50 19 times out of 20 and outside that range once. Finally, it means there are 369 chances out of 370 that this stock will trade in a range between $31.25 and $68.75.

VOLATILITY AND IMPLIED PRICE RANGES

Table 3–2 summarizes the estimated standard deviation of price movement indicated by volatility percentages at 30, 60, and 90 days. As an example, consider row four, 30 percent volatility. Given 60 days to

TABLE 3–2
Statistical Price Distribution of Volatility

Implied Volatility	Price Range Expectations %		
	30 Days	60 Days	90 Days
15%	4.35%	6.13%	7.50%
20	5.75	8.17	10.00
25	7.25	10.21	12.50
30	8.65	12.26	15.00
35	10.15	14.30	17.50
40	11.55	16.34	20.00
45	13.00	18.38	22.50
50	14.45	20.43	25.00
55	15.90	22.47	27.50
60	17.35	24.51	30.00

Two-thirds of the time, the underlying will be no more than the indicated percentage up or down from the starting price.

expiration, if an option is trading at 30 percent volatility, the implication is that the standard deviation of price movement is 12.26 percent of the stock's current price. If the stock in question is trading at $70, 12.26 percent is $8.58; and the market expects that two-thirds of the time this stock will trade in a range between $78.58 and $61.42 from now until option expiration (in 60 days).

Using This Concept of Price Ranges

This concept of implied price ranges sounds much more difficult to use than it is. First, investors must remember that the option price does not imply a direction; it only implies a possible range of movement—up or down. Second, investors must have a realistic expectation about option price behavior given a price change in the underlying stock. Tables 3–3 and 3–4 show how a $50 call can be expected to behave given changes in stock price and time to expiration under two different volatility assumptions. Table 3–3 shows that if options are trading at a volatility level of 25 percent, and if the stock price rises from $46 at eight weeks prior to expiration to $50 at four weeks prior to expiration, then the expectation would be for the $50 call to rise from 1/2 to 1 1/2. If however, the $50 call were to rise to 2 1/4, as shown in Table 3–4, then the market's expectation for volatility would have increased from 25 percent to 40

TABLE 3–3
$50 Call—25 Percent Volatility

Stock Price	8 Weeks	6 Weeks	4 Weeks	2 Weeks	Expiration
$51	2 5/8	2 3/8	2	1 5/8	1
$50	2	1 3/4	1 1/2	1	0
$49	1 1/2	1 1/4	1	5/8	0
$48	1 1/8	7/8	5/8	1/4	0
$47	3/4	5/8	3/8	1/8	0
$46	1/2	3/8	3/16	1/16	0

percent. If instead, the $50 call rose to a price less than 1 1/2, then the market's expectation for volatility would have decreased. When buying options, an investor would obviously prefer to have volatility increase as the stock moved in the desired direction. Likewise, when selling options, an investor would prefer to have volatility decrease as the stock moved in the desired direction. However, the most important factor is whether or not the stock moves in the predicted direction in the predicted time frame.

Overvalued and Undervalued

Overvalued and *undervalued* are terms that are used and misunderstood as often as volatility. A common misconception is that buying under-valued options and selling over-valued options is good. In fact, *neither is necessarily good*! For example, an investor who purchases an under-valued call can still lose money if the underlying stock declines in price.

TABLE 3–4
$50 Call—40 Percent Volatility

Stock Price	8 Weeks	6 Weeks	4 Weeks	2 Weeks	Expiration
$51	3 3/4	3 3/8	2 7/8	2 1/8	1
$50	3 1/4	2 3/4	2 1/4	1 5/8	0
$49	2 3/4	2 1/4	1 3/4	1 1/8	0
$48	2 1/4	1 7/8	1 3/8	3/4	0
$47	1 7/8	1 1/2	1	1/2	0
$46	1 1/2	1 1/8	3/4	1/4	0

There are many important factors in option trading decisions, and, frequently, too much emphasis is placed on the misunderstood concepts of overvalued and undervalued.

In order to understand what the terms overvalued and undervalued mean, we must first understand what is meant by *value*. Usually, the terms *theoretical value* or *fair value* are what is said when talking about value. Recognizing how theoretical values are derived will provide some insight into the meaning of *overvalued* and *undervalued*.

THE BASIS FOR THEORETICAL VALUE

As discussed above, an option's value depends on the distribution of possible prices of the underlying security in the time remaining to expiration. In other words, the theoretical value of an option depends on future volatility, the price fluctuations of the underlying security that occur between now and expiration. But future volatility is unknown, because one cannot know for certain what the future holds. Consequently, because future volatility is unknown, calculations of theoretical values are only estimates. That's right! So-called theoretical values are only estimates of value, because future volatility is unknown. What, then, is meant when someone says, "The theoretical value of an option is . . ."?

As discussed in Chapter 2, the theoretical value of an option depends on several inputs: the price of the underlying stock, the time to expiration, the strike price, interest rates, and a volatility estimate. Of this list, all are known except the volatility estimate. And, it is important to note, it is only a volatility estimate. Consequently, since one of the most important inputs into theoretical value is only an estimate, that makes the resulting theoretical value only an estimate. This means that when someone states, "The theoretical value of an option is . . . ," only an estimate of theoretical value is being presented based on an estimate of volatility. Taken in this context, option traders might be as wary of option theoretical values as they are of market price forecasts.

Something can only be over or under relative to something else. In the case of an option being overvalued or undervalued, two prices are being compared: the current market price of an option and the price generated by someone's theoretical value calculation. What is the difference between the two? Since all inputs that go into an option's value are known except the volatility estimate, the difference must be related to the volatility estimate. In fact, this is the case. As discussed above, the market price of an option implies a volatility, the so-called *implied volatility*. If that implied volatility figure had been used to calculate the option's theoretical value, then the result of the calculation would be exactly the same as the market price of the option. Consequently, the theoretical value of the option would equal the market price of the option. But, obviously, a different number for the volatility estimate was used because a different price was calculated.

If the volatility estimate used to calculate theoretical value is higher than the volatility implied by the market price, then the calculated option value will be higher than the market price. This leads to the conclusion that the market price of the option is under theoretical value. Therefore, it is reasoned, the option is undervalued.

If the volatility estimate used to calculate theoretical value is lower than the volatility implied by the market price, then the calculated option value will be lower than the market price. This leads to the conclusion that the market price of the option is over theoretical value. Therefore, it is reasoned, the option is overvalued.

Of course, all this assumes one believes the volatility estimate used by the generator of theoretical values. If one does not believe those estimates, then one probably should not place much faith in the theoretical values.

Perhaps the biggest misconception about the strategy of buying undervalued options and selling overvalued options is that, somehow, when an option returns to fair value, a profit will result. Nothing could be further from the truth! While the volatility estimate is a component of an option's price, a much bigger component is the price of the underlying security.

Refer to Table 3–3 and consider a situation in which it is eight weeks prior to expiration, the stock is $51, and a trader buys the $50 call for 2 5/8, which is equal to a volatility level of 25 percent. If the stock declines to $48 over the next six weeks and the call is sold at a volatility level of 40 percent, has the trader made or lost money?

Table 3–4 shows $50 call values assuming 40 percent volatility. At two weeks prior to expiration, with the stock at $48, the $50 call is valued at 3/4 (40 percent volatility). Selling at this price results in a 1 7/8 loss. While this is less than a 2 3/8 loss that would have resulted if the call were sold at the 25 percent volatility level of 1/4 indicated in Table 3–3, the result is still a loss. Even though the trader bought 25 percent volatility and sold 40 percent volatility, the result was a loss; because the stock price decline had a greater effect on the call price than did the increase in volatility. This simple example makes a very important point: in the vast majority of cases, a trader's price and time forecast for the underlying is far more important than the forecast for implied volatility.

FOCUS ON IMPLIED VOLATILITY

Although a forecast for changes in implied volatility plays second fiddle to forecasting the change in price of the underlying, knowing about implied volatility may help traders improve results. Rather than focusing on overvalued or undervalued options, traders should be aware of implied volatility levels and how much they can change. Unfortunately, there are no hard and fast rules about what volatility is low and what is high. Knowledge of implied volatility changes should become part of the subjective decision-making process for option traders. There is nothing wrong, per se, with buying a high volatility or selling a low volatility, because price changes in the underlying stock are a far more important factor in option price changes. However, changes in implied volatility may be either the icing on the cake—or the vinegar in the soup: when the trade is completed, the result may be a little bigger or a little smaller because of a change in implied volatility.

SUMMARY

Volatility is a frequently used and frequently misunderstood word. The discussion in this chapter covered several important concepts about volatility. Most investors intuitively understand that volatility relates to price fluctuations in the underlying security, and this is correct. Mathematically, volatility is the annualized standard deviation of daily stock returns. Consequently, option prices imply a range of stock price movement—up or down—not a direction of movement. Higher option prices imply higher stock price volatility, which means a wider possible range of movement.

The stock price volatility implied by an option's price is referred to as the market expectation of volatility or implied volatility. Volatility is the only unknown input in the option pricing formula. Therefore theoretical value calculations use expected volatility, a trader's estimate of future volatility.

The terms *overvalued* and *undervalued* are properly seen as a comparison of expected volatility and implied volatility. Expected volatility is the percentage used to calculate theoretical values, and implied volatility is the percentage that justifies the current market price of an option. When expected volatility is higher than implied volatility, an option will appear undervalued. When expected volatility is lower than implied volatility, an option will appear overvalued. When expected volatility is equal to implied volatility, an option will appear fairly valued.

Very often investors place too much emphasis on trying to buy undervalued options and sell overvalued options. While volatility is a component of an option's value, the biggest component of an option's value is the price of the underlying stock. Consequently, most investors should concentrate on market forecasting and stock selection, and place less emphasis on forecasting volatility.

CHAPTER 4

OPTION STRATEGIES: ANALYSIS AND SELECTION

The investor who adds options to the list of investment products to achieve financial goals gains a unique advantage. They increase the number of ways this investor can manage financial assets by giving him or her the power to create positions that precisely reflect his or her expectations of the underlying security and, at the same time, balance risk-reward tolerance.

This means that options increase control over financial assets by providing alternatives that were unavailable in the past. Prior to the establishment of listed options markets, there was no effective way to hedge without disrupting the allocation of assets in the portfolio. In the past, there were only two choices—Buy 'em when you like 'em, sell 'em when you don't. Today, investors discover that they can, for example, sell calls or buy puts to establish a hedge; they reserve selling for the time they no longer desire any involvement with the underlying asset. These investors also discover that options give them more control over the speculative side of their investing; they can select from strategies that run the gamut from limited to unlimited risk and from small to large capital requirements.

Many options investors spend a lot of time acquiring technical knowledge of pricing behavior. This is a worthy goal, but above all, remember that options are derivative instruments. Options cannot exist without an underlying asset. As such, there are only two important factors that direct the investor to the proper strategy. The first and foremost is the investor's opinion of the underlying security. There are strategies to take advantage of a bullish, bearish, neutral, or uncertain opinion. Any decision made without a specific opinion of the potential movement of the underlying security is unsubstantiated and has a high probability of failure. The second factor concerns the profits the investor desires if his opinion is correct and his willingness to accept any losses that accompany his strategy if his opinion is wrong.

From speculation to hedging, options can be used to construct scenarios that maximize payoff for outcomes the investor considers most likely, while controlling exposure to losses from those outcomes he considers less likely. There are ways to express the degree of one's opinion, each with its own particular risk-reward profile. One can buy calls outright to get a leveraged bullish position, or use strategies that require a smaller cash outlay but have less profit potential. This requires understanding the trade-offs that go with every decision and the motivation one brings to strategy selection.

Options are often thought of as merely speculative instruments. This is not true. An option strategy by itself is neither speculative nor conservative. The investor using options must also understand that it is the way a strategy is selected, managed, and capitalized that determines its "personality." The goal of this and following chapters is to help the investor gain such understanding so as to use options to their fullest.

This chapter describes essential options strategies in words and illustrations. The pictures show how each strategy evolves from the day it is established until the options' expiration date. The discussion that accompanies each diagram explains how the strategy works, why an investor might select the strategy, and how to evaluate a particular risk-reward profile. The reader is encouraged to refer to this chapter periodically for review, especially if he or she has formulated an opinion on the underlying security and is ready to enter the options market but remains unclear about the risk-reward profiles of the strategies being considered.

Description of Diagrams

Each strategy diagram is constructed using the following conventions:

1. The horizontal axis represents the price of the underlying security advancing from lower prices at the left to higher prices toward the right.
2. The vertical axis represents profit/loss; profit is in the area above the horizontal axis, loss below.
3. To emphasize the importance of the effects of time decay, arrows point in the direction of decreasing time until expiration. The straight-segment line represents the profit/loss of the strategy at options' expiration, the dashed line the profit/loss when the position was initiated.

4. Strike prices of options used in the strategy are indicated by roman numerals; lower strikes by lower numbers and vice versa.
5. A break-even point is always located at any point where the position plot crosses the horizontal axis.

CALL BUYING

Without question, call buying is the most popular option strategy. It is a way to put a bullish opinion into action. If the price of the underlying security advances enough, the long-call buyer can have profits many times the initial investment of the option premium. The potential to reap such large profits is what attracts investors. It is an attraction that often results in frustrating and disappointing experiences. A better understanding of the ways call buying should be used will go a long way toward lessening the possibility of disappointment from the start.

Call buyers must know from the outset what they want from their position. If they don't, they can get results very different from what's expected. For instance, if they do not want a speculative position, yet unknowingly use the reasoning of the speculative buyer, they expose themselves to much greater risks than acceptable. If the underlying security moves in their favor, their profits are much greater than they expected, and this result usually leads to the investors' thinking they chose wisely. They are then apt to continue buying calls in a speculative manner only to be extremely dissatisfied when their forecast for the behavior of the underlying is wrong. The problem is that they did not start with an honest appraisal of their motives.

This section is divided into segments that discuss the motives, expectations, and concerns that accompany speculative and nonspeculative call-buying decisions. You will soon discover why it is important to know the difference.

Expected Behavior

A call buyer is subject to profits and losses outlined in the summary and Figure 4–1, all at expiration. Throughout this section, a $50 strike price call option on XYZ stock is used as a model. As an example, start with XYZ at $50 per share and the 90-day call at $3. Given this option price, you can calculate the break-even points and maximum profit and loss at expiration as follows:

FIGURE 4–1
Long Call

| Description: | Buy call option with strike price I. |

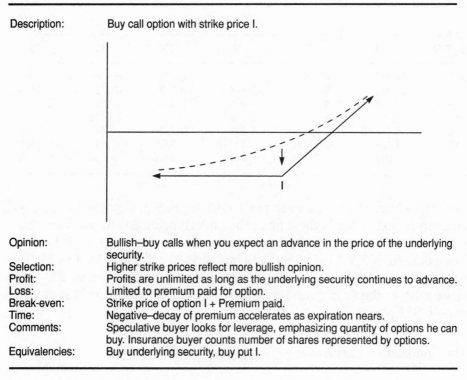

Opinion:	Bullish–buy calls when you expect an advance in the price of the underlying security.
Selection:	Higher strike prices reflect more bullish opinion.
Profit:	Profits are unlimited as long as the underlying security continues to advance.
Loss:	Limited to premium paid for option.
Break-even:	Strike price of option I + Premium paid.
Time:	Negative–decay of premium accelerates as expiration nears.
Comments:	Speculative buyer looks for leverage, emphasizing quantity of options he can buy. Insurance buyer counts number of shares represented by options.
Equivalencies:	Buy underlying security, buy put I.

Break-even: $53 = Strike price ($50) + Premium ($3).

Maximum loss: $3 ($300 per option) = The premium paid if XYZ is below $50 at expiration.

Maximum profit: Unlimited given by (Price of XYZ − $50 − $3).

At-expiration analysis, however, does not provide insight into what happens to a call option before the expiration date. Take a look at the expected effects of time and price movement on the $50 call option in Table 4–1.

The Break-Even Point

You can see that, regardless of when the option is purchased, the underlying security must be above its current price for a long call to break even. This is, after all, a bullish strategy, and one expects the price to

TABLE 4–1
Expected Price Variation of $50 Strike Call

Price	Days to Expiration					
of XYZ	90	75	60	45	30	15
$56	7 1/2	7 1/4	7	6 5/8	6 3/8	6 1/8
54	5 3/4	5 1/2	5 1/4	4 7/8	4 1/2	4 1/4
52	4 1/4	4	3 5/8	3 1/4	2 15/16	2 7/16
50	3	2 11/16	2 3/8	2	1 9/16	1 1/16
48	1 15/16	1 5/8	1 3/8	1 1/16	3/4	5/16
46	1 1/8	15/16	11/16	1/2	1/4	1/16
44	5/8	7/16	5/16	3/16	1/16	1/16

rise. However, the break-even price (strike price plus premium) at expiration is simply the highest price the underlying needs to reach for the position to break even. Before expiration, the break-even point is lower. For example, if XYZ is $48 and you buy the $50 call for $1 15/16 with 90 days left before expiration, the option can still break even at $50 per share after 45 days. In contrast, the break-even at expiration is approximately $52 per share.

The Speculative Call Buyer

The speculative call buyer uses options for their leverage. He is attracted to the percentage gains he can achieve on his investment from a rise in the price of the underlying. He also understands that if the underlying does not make the move he needs, he can lose most, if not all, of the investment. His goal is to select calls that balance his desire for profits with the possibility of the option's expiring worthless.

To achieve this balance, the speculative call buyer must address the issues of intrinsic value, i.e., out-of-the-money or in-the-money, time decay, and delta.

In-the-Money versus Out-of-the-Money

If XYZ is $48 per share, the 90-day, $50 call is out-of-the-money. The option has a premium of $1 15/16 and an expiration break-even price of about $52, 4 points above the current price. If XYZ is $52, the call is in-the-money. The option has a premium of $4 1/4 and a break-even price of $54 1/4, only 2 1/4 points above the current price.

Because the out-of-the-money call needs a larger advance in XYZ to reach the break-even point, buying it is more bullish than the purchase of in-the-money calls. A more bullish position is riskier. For accepting more risk, the speculative buyer of out-of-the-money calls should have better results if the stock behaves as expected. This is exactly what happens. First, the cost of the out-of-the-money option is lower, $1 15/16 versus $4 1/4 for the other kind. For equivalent dollar amounts, he could buy more out-of-the-money options. This is a key to understanding the thinking of the speculative call buyer. The desire for big profits leads to an emphasis on the quantity purchased. Second, an out-of-the money call performs relatively better if XYZ moves higher in price shortly after the option is purchased. After 15 days, the out-of-the money call can double in price, to $4, if XYZ rises from $48 to $52. For the in-the-money option to double, i.e., trade from $4 1/4 to $8 1/2 in 15 days, XYZ would have to trade up to $57 1/2. The emphasis on quantity validates the percentage comparisons the speculative option buyer uses.

This does not mean that the out-of-the-money call is better. As time passes, the break-even point approaches the price at expiration. The prospective out-of-the-money call buyer should be aware that a decline in XYZ makes it difficult for the call to break even, even if the stock rallies. Track the call price through the following path:

1. When XYZ is $48, buy the 90-day call for $1 15/16.
2. After 30 days, XYZ is $46; the call is trading at $11/16.
3. By the end of the next 30 days, XYZ must rally to $50 3/4, or 10 percent, for the call to break even.

Out-of-the-money calls are on their own if the underlying makes this kind of a move; they have no intrinsic value and can lose 100 percent of their premium. In-the-money calls start with the support of their intrinsic value. The next segment addresses the trade-offs between time decay and intrinsic value.

Time Decay and Intrinsic Value
For the speculative call buyer, the advantages of buying at-the-money or out-of-the-money calls are balanced by the premium decay they experience. These types of call options lose 100 percent of their premium if the price of the underlying is not above the option's strike price at expiration. On the other hand, for in-the-money options to lose all of

their premium, the underlying must have declined to the strike price at expiration. The difference is the intrinsic value carried by the in-the-money options and the impact its presence has on the decay of the total premium.

Go back to the table and concentrate on the price changes of the $50 call option if the price of XYZ were to remain at $46, 4 points out-of-the-money, for the entire 90 days until expiration. The option has no intrinsic value, and this call is trading at only $1 1/8. The premium drops to $11/16 ($68.75) after 30 days. This is a loss of about 40 percent of the initial premium. Over the next 30 days, the decay is even greater. The option decays to $1/4, a further decline of 65 percent.

In-the-money call options also experience premium decay over time, but less than 100 percent of the total option premium. This is because these options have intrinsic value. Only time premium can decay; intrinsic value cannot. Going back to the price table, with XYZ at $54, the $50 call is $5 3/4. If the stock is $54 at expiration, the call will be worth its intrinsic value of $4. This limits the loss to $1 3/4, or 30 percent of the original premium.

Given equivalent dollar amounts, a call option position becomes less speculative the farther the call is in-the-money. The $5 3/4 premium of the in-the-money one is almost twice that of the at-the-money. The dollar profit of the in-the-money option from an advance in XYZ is closer to the profit from owning the stock, but when compared to the number of at- or out-of-the-money calls that can be purchased, this gain is made on fewer options. The smaller quantity and the smaller likelihood of the option's expiring worthless makes a position in in-the-money calls less speculative.

Delta and the Speculative Call Buyer

The delta of an option is defined as a local measure of the rate of change in an option's theoretical value for a change in the price of the underlying security. Delta underlies the speculative call buyer's emphasis on quantity. Table 4–2 shows the deltas of the $50 call for various prices of XYZ.

As a call goes deeper in-the-money, it becomes more sensitive to price changes in XYZ. At $54 per share, the $50 call can be expected to change about 80 cents for every point change in XYZ. At $50, the sensitivity is 59 cents. If the speculative buyer has $600, he can buy two at-the-money calls or one in-the-money call. The at-the-money position has a delta of 1.20 (2 × .60). The in-the-money call has a delta of .80.

TABLE 4–2
Deltas

Price of XYZ	Price of 90-Day Call	Option Delta
$54	$5 3/4	.80
52	4 1/4	.70
50	3	.59
48	1 15/16	.46
46	1 1/8	.33
44	5/8	.21

Furthermore, the delta of the at-the-money calls can go from .59 to 1.00. The delta of the in-the-money can also go to 1.00, but it will do so starting from .80. This exemplifies the leverage the speculative buyer gets when buying more options for the same amount of money.

Conclusions about Speculative Call Buying

Speculative buyers have to balance many aspects of call behavior to create the right position. Most important of all is for investors to recognize that they are using calls speculatively. If they are concerned about how time decay, intrinsic value, and delta affect the performance of their investment, there is a good chance that they are speculative buyers. If they compare the number of options of different strike prices they can buy with a fixed number of dollars, they are definitely speculative buyers.

The Insurance Value of Calls

However, the investor who stands ready to buy 1,000 shares of XYZ at $50—but instead spends $3,000 for 10 at-the-money calls—is not speculating. He is making an investment decision to use the call options to protect a possible $50,000 commitment.

Why can call options be described as a kind of insurance? The upcoming section on put buying presents evidence that a long put plus long stock is equivalent to a call option. The protection provided by the put option is easy to comprehend: Puts increase in value as the underlying security falls farther below the strike price, protecting against part of the loss in the long position in the underlying. The insurance analogy, however, is sometimes more difficult to grasp when applied to calls. The following excerpt by Herbert Filer may bring the point home:

> It happened in November 1957, after the market had had a severe break. A man with a southern drawl and wearing a big ten-gallon hat, walked into our office and wanted to speak to the "boss." "You know," he said, "I bought a lot of your calls and I tore them up—lost my money." I thought maybe he was going to pull a gun on me . . . he said, "Don't worry—how lucky it was that I bought calls instead of stock. If I had bought the stocks way up there I would have gone broke!"[1]

Indeed, calls resemble insurance, too. The buyer wants to protect the cash he would have used to buy the underlying security and preserve the opportunity to profit from an advance. Nor is insurance free. A premium must be paid.

The "insurance investor" has a view of call options that is different from the speculative buyer's. To the insurance buyer, the premium of a call option is the cost of wanting insurance on his capital. He understands that the seller of a call option says, in effect, to the buyer, "If, for the next three months you don't want to lose money from a direct investment in this stock should it go down, and still participate if it goes up, you are going to have to compensate me for assuming this risk instead of you." Part of that compensation is a risk premium measured by the expected volatility of the stock in exchange for the ability to let the call expire worthless. The rest is an interest payment to the seller.

In-the-Money or Out-of-the-Money?
The investor who uses call options as insurance sees out-of-the-money and in-the-money options as different types of insurance policies. In contrast, the speculator sees out-of-the-money calls as an opportunity to gain more leverage by buying increasing quantities of less expensive options. The insurance buyer of an out-of-the-money call sees it as a cheap policy with a large deductible. The deductible is the amount the underlying must move for the option to be worth anything at expiration. It is the amount of the increase in the price of the underlying the investor is willing to give up. By contrast, the in-the-money call is like an expensive policy with no deductible. It is already worth its intrinsic

---

[1] Herbert Filer, *Understanding Put and Call Options* (New York: Crown Publishers, 1959).

value and lets the investor participate now. A wise insurance buyer always balances the deductible with the premium he pays.

The Real Difference

The biggest difference between the speculative and the insurance buyer is that the insurance buyer does not count the number of options he can buy. Because he is protecting a capital commitment to a predetermined number of shares, he counts the round lots of stock the options represent at expiration. He buys the same quantity, no matter which strike price he selects. The investor using calls this way has no need for leverage.

Which Approach?

Neither approach to call buying is more correct than the other. There is room in the option market for speculative and insurance call buyers. The most important thing is to understand which one you are at any given time. If you do that, you will make better decisions and will have better experiences with this strategy.

PUT BUYING

A long put position by itself expresses bearishness. The underlying security must go down in price for this position to be profitable. The investor who buys puts in expectation of a decline in the underlying security is attracted by the potential for a very large percentage gain on the premium he pays. This is the speculative approach to buying puts. However, a put option can be used conservatively. Puts can be very effective as term insurance policies to protect the value of an investment in the underlying security. Speculative and insurance buyers view put options differently. We'll explore different ways to use put buying, motives behind their use, and expected results in this section.

General Behavior

At expiration, the put buyer is subject to profits and losses as outlined in the summary and Figure 4–2. We'll use the $50 strike price put option on XYZ stock as an example, and start with XYZ at $50 per share and the 90-day put at $2. Given this option price, you can calculate the

FIGURE 4–2
Long Put

Description:	Buy put option with strike price I.

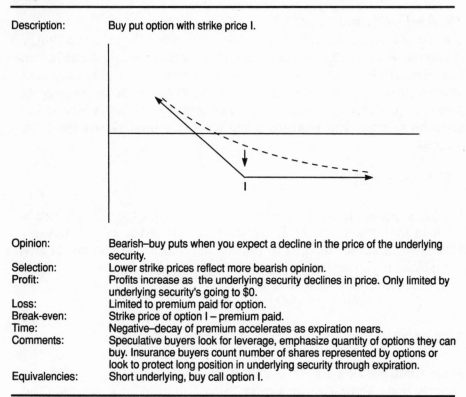

Opinion:	Bearish–buy puts when you expect a decline in the price of the underlying security.
Selection:	Lower strike prices reflect more bearish opinion.
Profit:	Profits increase as the underlying security declines in price. Only limited by underlying security's going to $0.
Loss:	Limited to premium paid for option.
Break-even:	Strike price of option I – premium paid.
Time:	Negative–decay of premium accelerates as expiration nears.
Comments:	Speculative buyers look for leverage, emphasize quantity of options they can buy. Insurance buyers count number of shares represented by options or look to protect long position in underlying security through expiration.
Equivalencies:	Short underlying, buy call option I.

break-even points, and maximum profit and loss at expiration as follows:

Break-even: $48 = Strike price ($50) − Premium ($2).

Maximum loss: $2 ($200 per option) = The premium paid for the option.

Maximum profit: $48 = Strike price ($50) − Premium ($2). Occurs if the underlying goes to $0.

To get a better feel for how put options behave over time, refer to Table 4–3, summarizing the expected effects of price and time on the premium of the $50 put.

Many investors believe that put options behave exactly like calls, but in the opposite direction. This is an incorrect assumption. There are

TABLE 4–3
Expected Price Variation of $50 Strike Price Put Option

Price of XYZ	Days to Expiration					
	90	75	60	45	30	15
$54	13/16	9/16	1/2	3/8	1/4	1/16
52	1 1/4	1 1/8	1	13/16	9/16	5/16
50	2	1 7/8	1 11/16	1 1/2	1 1/4	15/16
48	2 15/16	2 13/16	2 11/16	2 9/16	2 3/8	2 3/16
46	4 1/4	4 1/8	4	4	4	4
44	6	6	6	6	6	6

differences. Lack of awareness of these differences can lead to unrealistic expectations or mismanagement of put option positions.

The most obvious difference is that at-the-money calls and puts do not have the same price. The effect of dividends notwithstanding, at-the-money calls will be priced higher than at-the-money puts. The put-call parity equation shows why this is true. In the example given, XYZ does not pay a dividend, the risk-free rate is 8 percent, and the expected annual volatility is 25 percent. Based on these conditions, the 90-day at-the-money call is $3 and the put is $2.

Time Decay

The astute investor can draw some interesting conclusions regarding the behavior of put options from the pricing table. First of all, puts decay slower than calls do. In 45 days, if XYZ remains at $50 per share, the $50 put loses 1/2 point of time premium and is worth $1 1/2. The $50 call, which starts with a premium of $3, loses 1 point. The put declines 25 percent; the call declines 33 percent. Over the next 30 days, the call loses an additional $15/16 or 47 percent. The put only loses $9/16 or 38 percent. This should give some solace to the out-of-the-money put buyer, but don't get too comfortable. The erosion of the premium eventually attacks the put as well. There is no escape!

In another observation, as puts go farther in-the-money, they lose their time premium faster than calls do. At $44, the $50 put, with 75 days left, has a value of $6. If XYZ were $56, the $50 call, also 6 points in-the-money, has a value of $7 1/4. The call retains 1 1/4 points of time premium.

Out-of-the-Money versus In-the-Money Puts

To the speculative buyer, the bearishness of a long put position is directly related to the amount a put is out-of-the-money. The underlying has to decline farther for an out-of-the-money put to break even at expiration than for an in-the-money put to break even. The price table shows that if you buy the $50 put when XYZ is $52, the break-even is $48 3/4. If you buy the same put when XYZ is $48, the break-even is $47. XYZ must decline $3 1/4 for the out-of-the-money, but only $1 for the in-the-money to break even.

There is always balance in the options market. The advantage the speculator gets for buying out-of-the-money puts is the potential for large percentage gains. For example, XYZ is $46 per share at expiration; the $50 put is priced at $4. The investor who went long on this put 90 days prior when XYZ was $54, paid $13/16 for the option. The increase of $3 3/16 in the price of the put is 392 percent of the original premium. By contrast, the investor who waited 15 days and went long on the same put when XYZ had already dropped to $50, paid $1 7/8. The put now gains $2 1/8 from its purchase price, or 113 percent of the starting premium. A speculative buyer can make this percentage comparison because his or her tendency is to maximize the number of options purchased with a given amount of premium dollars to spend. Given the relationship of the premiums in the above example, the investor can purchase 23 out-of-the-money puts for every 10 at-the-money puts.

The speculative buyer making this comparison to maximize the leverage of his position must be aware that the chance of losing the entire premium increases with the distance the puts are out-of-the-money. In-the-money puts provide less leverage; they are more expensive, so the speculative buyer cannot buy so many. However, they have a greater chance of providing some profit and a smaller chance of expiring worthless. This is the omnipresent trade-off between in-the-money and out-of-the-money options with which the speculative buyer must contend.

A Strategic Application

We observed that put options go to parity more quickly than calls. This makes in-the-money put options an attractive strategic alternative to the short sale of stock. If XYZ were $46 with 90 days before expiration, the

$50 put would not have much time premium remaining. Buying the put at $4 1/4 is similar to being short the stock—the option is very sensitive to price changes in XYZ. This position has advantages over a short sale. First, no stock needs to be borrowed and no margin balance is created. Second, should XYZ rally, the risk of the put is limited to the premium paid. A short sale of XYZ is exposed to unlimited losses.

Term Insurance

The other major use for put options is like insurance. An investor who owns XYZ stock is concerned that there can be a drop in the stock's price over the next 90 days. This conclusion may be the result of technical or fundamental analysis on the stock or on the market. Whatever the reasoning, this investor needs to protect his investment over the time period in question, but he does not want to sell the stock and give up further profits if his forecast is wrong. This investor can purchase a term insurance policy on XYZ for the next 90 days by buying the $50 put option for $2 in the same quantity as the number of round lots he owns.

The $50 put allows the holder to sell the stock at $50 per share anytime between the day the option is bought and expiration. The out-of-the-money $45 put, which allows him to sell the stock 5 points lower, is less valuable because the investor is leaving his stock open to more of a decline. The $45 put is $1/2. The in-the-money put, which allows him to sell the stock at $55 is more valuable. The investor is not picking up any part of a decline. And the $55 put is $5.

This does not mean that the $45 put is an inferior choice. If the owner of XYZ wants very low-cost insurance and is willing to accept $5 more of the risk of XYZ himself, the out-of-the-money put might be the better choice. Here is where the real decision is made. If you want more protection, you also have to give up more of the upside. The $50 put is $2. So the investor gives up the first 2 points of any rally in the stock in exchange for being able to sell the stock at $50. The $45 put has only a 50 cent upside opportunity cost.

Difference between Speculation and Insurance
The motivation of the investor using puts like insurance is different from that of the investor using puts to profit from a forecasted decline in the underlying security. The speculative put buyer has to balance the characteristics of put option behavior, time decay, intrinsic value, and delta, to come up with the proper position. The insurance buyer only needs to

FIGURE 4–3
Buy Stock, Buy Put

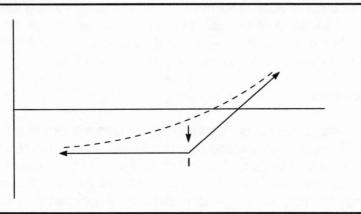

address the deductibility he is willing to accept, given the costs of the insurance. Furthermore, buying a put as insurance on a stock is certainly not bearish. The insurance buyer would much rather see his stock rally substantially than have to use the policy. If this investor were truly bearish, he would be wise to simply sell the stock.

An Interesting Equivalence

The reader with more options experience may have noticed that the purchase of a put, while holding a long position in the stock, is a strategy with a limited loss and (after subtracting the put premium) unlimited profit. Figure 4–3 is the profit/loss diagram of the result of owning XYZ at $50 and a $50 put bought for $2 at expiration. It looks exactly like the diagram of a call option at expiration. Indeed, a long put, long stock position is the same as a long call option position. When a put is bought on a stock as insurance, it turns that stock into a call for the life of the option.

CALL SELLING

Call selling achieves its maximum profit if the price of the underlying security is below the call's strike price at expiration. However, call selling is not necessarily a bearish posture. The sold call only needs to expire worthless for the investor to realize his maximum profit, and the underlying may not have to decline to satisfy this criterion. In fact, call selling can be very successful when used as a neutral strategy. Remember that, in the options market, the opposite of a bullish strategy is not a bearish strategy. Instead, it is a *not*-bullish strategy! To illustrate, call selling is a not-bullish strategy. (The method discussed here does not involve ownership of the underlying security. This strategy, named *covered call selling,* is discussed under its own heading.)

Still using the XYZ, 90-day, $50 strike price, at-the-money call option with a $3 premium, the seller is taking a position that has the following characteristics at expiration:

Break-even: $53 = Strike price ($50) + Premium ($3).

Maximum profit: $3 ($300 per option) = The premium received for the option.

Maximum loss: Unlimited.

Option selling techniques are limited profit strategies. Regardless of how far below $50 the price of XYZ goes, the $3 is as good as it's going to get. The call cannot do any better for the seller than expire worthless. This is why the payoff diagram of call selling becomes horizontal as the price of XYZ declines below the strike price of the call (Figure 4–4).

Furthermore, a short call position is exposed to large losses if the underlying advances far beyond the strike price of the option. Examine Table 4–4 of expiration values of various call options over a range of closing prices for XYZ at expiration. One can see that the call option seller cannot be bullish!

TABLE 4–4
Expiration Prices of Various Call Options

Option Strike Price	Closing Price of XYZ at Expiration				
	45	49	53	57	61
$45	0	4	8	12	16
50	0	0	3	7	11
55	0	0	0	2	6

FIGURE 4–4
Short Call

Description: Sell call option with strike price I without ownership of underlying security.

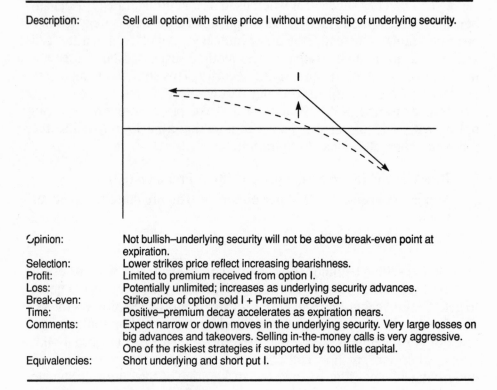

Opinion: Not bullish–underlying security will not be above break-even point at
                       expiration.
Selection: Lower strikes price reflect increasing bearishness.
Profit: Limited to premium received from option I.
Loss: Potentially unlimited; increases as underlying security advances.
Break-even: Strike price of option sold I + Premium received.
Time: Positive–premium decay accelerates as expiration nears.
Comments: Expect narrow or down moves in the underlying security. Very large losses on
                       big advances and takeovers. Selling in-the-money calls is very aggressive.
                       One of the riskiest strategies if supported by too little capital.
Equivalencies: Short underlying and short put I.

Motivation of the Call Seller

It seems that call selling is a strategy with very high risk for a small
potential return. How, then, can the call seller justify using this technique? The answer is twofold. First, he is agreeing with the option
market's estimate of the potential movement of the underlying. (The
call buyer is the one looking for a greater move.) You have seen that
expected volatility, or price movement, has a large influence on an
option's premium. The call seller believes that the potential price movement of the underlying will not be greater than that implied by the
premium. If he thought that it could be greater, he would do something
else!

Second, the seller is acutely aware of the negative effect of passing
time on option premiums. Unlike the call buyer, the call seller eagerly

TABLE 4–5
Expected Price of $50 Strike Call

Price of XYZ	Days to Expiration					
	90	75	60	45	30	15
$50	3	2 11/16	2 3/8	2	1 9/16	1 1/16

awaits the last weeks prior to expiration when premium decay acceler-ates. In Table 4–5, here's what happens to an at-the-money call.

In-the-Money, At-the-Money, and Out-of-the-Money

The call seller must consider the relationship of the price of the underly-ing to the strike price of the option sold. The at-the-money call, because the strike price is close to the current price of the underlying, makes its maximum profit if the underlying stays where it is, i.e., at about the strike price, and can make some profit even if the underlying advances slightly. This is because the break-even point is above the current price. The sale of an at-the-money call happens to be a neutral strategy that is also profitable if the underlying drops in price.

Out-of-the-money calls have the greatest probability of expiring worthless. Their premiums are lower, resulting in less potential profit, but the seller of out-of-the-money calls gets a cushion against a rise in the price of the underlying. It can be very enticing to sell cheap, out-of-the-money calls continually and watch them expire. The trouble is that they do not always expire worthless.

Consider the following. XYZ has traded at around $52 1/2 per share for the last 120 days. During this time, an investor sold the $55 calls twice, i.e., over two expirations, for a total of $275. Both times, the options expired worthless and the $275 was kept as profit.

Recently, the investor has sold another $55 call with 45 days before expiration for $1 1/4 ($125). The stock is at $53 1/2. Prior to the next morning's opening, favorable news has come out on the stock. It could be a new buy recommendation or, even worse for the naked short call, a takeover bid. The stock finally opens at $57 1/4 and the $55 calls are $4 1/8 ($412.50). Buying the short option back at $4 1/8 creates a net loss for the investor after four months!

In-the-money calls have higher premiums than at- or out-of-the-money options. The sale of such an option is more bearish than the sale of either of the other two types because the strike price of an in-the-money call is lower than the current price of the underlying. The underlying must decline in price for a short, in-the-money call to reach its maximum profit. The break-even point is usually not much higher than the current price of the underlying, and it is lower than the break-even point of the at-the-money call.

Sale of an in-the-money call is an aggressive strategy that can lose quite a bit of money very quickly if the underlying begins to move higher. In-the-money calls have less time premium than at-the-money calls. If the $50 call is trading at $3, the $45 call is about $6 3/8. This in-the-money call does have a high dollar premium, but it has only $1 3/8 of time premium and a break-even of $51 3/8. There is not much room for error.

Another difficulty with in-the-money calls is they become less sensitive to declines in the price of the underlying. This is because the delta of a call option decreases if the price of the underlying goes down; the in-the-money call starts to look more and more like an at-the-money call. The option will continue to drop in price but will lose less on each subsequent drop. Table 4–6 shows the prices and deltas of the $45 call with 75 days left before expiration. If the investor is truly bearish, there is a better strategy to express that opinion.

It should be of more than passing interest that this discussion of the differences between the three types of call options has shown that the aspects of call behavior that hurt buyers will help sellers (and vice versa).

TABLE 4–6
How Delta Changes

XYZ Price	Option Price	Option Delta
$49	$5 1/4	.83
48	4 1/2	.78
47	3 3/4	.72
46	3	.65
45	2 7/16	.58

How Much Premium Is Enough?

It would seem that it is always best for the seller of naked calls to collect as much premium as possible. This could not be farther from the truth. Do not be enticed by large premiums. Higher call option premiums (the effect of interest rates notwithstanding), as a percent of the price of the underlying security, come from an expectation of higher volatility. This, in turn, implies an expectation of greater price movement. There are many investors who consistently sell calls for high premiums. They are also the ones who consistently buy back in-the-money calls for *even greater* premiums. At no time should an investor put premium level above break-even analysis. The call seller must always ask this question, "Do I think the underlying will be below the break-even price of the call option I am going to sell at expiration?" If the answer is an unequivocal, "Yes," then, and only then should a call be sold.

Capital Commitment and Risk

It is important to note that naked call selling is a capital-intensive strategy. Without a position in the underlying, short calls are considered *naked*. Most firms require that a high minimum amount of equity be present in the account before allowing naked call selling to begin. There is also a margin requirement for each short call in the account, which could increase as the underlying increases.

The amount of capital used to support call selling determines the risk of the strategy. Investors who get into trouble with call selling usually do so because they short more options than they are willing to be short stock. If there is a big rise in the price of the underlying, the investor, who initially sold as many calls as his capital allowed, might be unable to support the now in-the-money calls.

PUT SELLING

A short put position is profitable if the underlying security closes above the break-even point (i.e., strike price minus premium) at option expiration. The maximum profit is limited to the premium received and is achieved when the price of the underlying is above the strike price at expiration (horizontal line in payoff diagram, Figure 4–5).

FIGURE 4–5
Short Put

Description: Sell put option with strike price I.

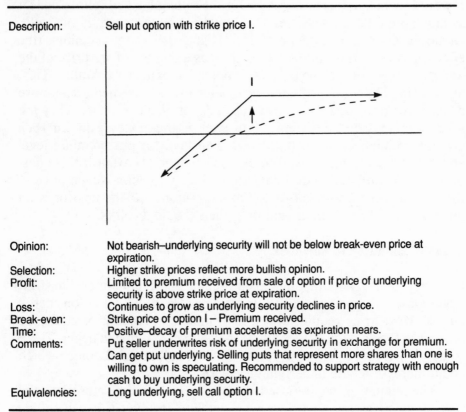

Opinion: Not bearish–underlying security will not be below break-even price at
                expiration.
Selection: Higher strike prices reflect more bullish opinion.
Profit: Limited to premium received from sale of option if price of underlying
                security is above strike price at expiration.
Loss: Continues to grow as underlying security declines in price.
Break-even: Strike price of option I – Premium received.
Time: Positive–decay of premium accelerates as expiration nears.
Comments: Put seller underwrites risk of underlying security in exchange for premium.
                Can get put underlying. Selling puts that represent more shares than one is
                willing to own is speculating. Recommended to support strategy with enough
                cash to buy underlying security.
Equivalencies: Long underlying, sell call option I.

Assuming the $50 strike price put with 90 days to expiration is $2,
the short put has these characteristics at expiration:

Break-even: $48 = Strike price ($50) − Premium ($2)

Maximum profit: $2 ($200 per option) at prices above $50

Maximum loss: $48 = Strike price ($50) − Premium ($2). Occurs if
the underlying goes to $0.

Put Selling and Insurance

Put selling can be compared to the activity of insurance underwriting.
Insurance companies receive premiums from those they insure and, in
return, accept certain risks. The insurance could be on a person's home,

car, or life. Businesses insure inventories, plants, and equipment. Should the policyholder suffer a loss, he can make a claim and collect from the insurance company. If he never makes a claim, the insurance company keeps the premium. This is the essence of put selling. In exchange for the put option premium, the seller accepts the downside risk of the underlying security.

Insurance companies spend a lot of time and money to determine how much risk is in a policy. Their goal is to charge a premium that accurately reflects the probability that the policy will be paid off. This is no different from the options market. When an investor sells a put option, he has entered into a position that requires him to pay off the buyer of the put by accepting the stock at the strike price. The premium he receives is the option market's assessment of the potential price movement of the underlying for the time remaining to expiration of the option.

Motivation to Sell Puts

One goal of an investor who chooses to sell puts might be to act as an underwriter and collect option premiums. He makes money if the underlying is above the break-even point at expiration; however, he must be ready to accept substantial losses if the underlying declines far below the strike price. If XYZ is below $50 at expiration, the short put is worth the difference between the final price of XYZ and the $50 strike price, as shown in Table 4–7. Except for the $2 premium received, the put seller has assumed the risk of the stock's price falling below the strike price.

Another goal could be to acquire stock. A short put position can result in assignment, requiring the purchase of the underlying security

TABLE 4–7
Expiration Profit/Loss of Short Put

XYZ at Expiration	Value of $50 Put	Profit/ (Loss)
$50	$ 0	$ 200
47	300	(100)
44	600	(400)
41	900	(700)
35	1,500	(1,300)

at the strike price. Let's say a short XYZ $50 strike put option results in the purchase of 100 shares of XYZ stock at $50 per share. The $2 premium received from selling the put lowers the purchase price of the XYZ stock to $48. Assignment of a short put always results in the purchase of stock at a net price that is the break-even point! Should XYZ move beyond $50 at expiration, the put will expire worthless and the $2 premium is kept as a consolation profit.

Regardless of his motives for selling puts, it is imperative that the put seller not be bearish. No investor wants to buy a stock he doesn't like.

The Lost Opportunity

There is a second break-even price on the upside for the put seller. From our example, the upside break-even point is $52. A position in XYZ or the short put has a $2 profit if XYZ is $52 per share at expiration. Above $52, a long position in XYZ stock continues to earn profits. The put profit of the short put is limited to the $2 premium.

There is no financial loss above the upside break-even price; but there is an opportunity loss. The upside break-even price is the figure beyond which a long position in the underlying does better than the short put. The investor who wants to benefit from an increase in the price of the underlying above the upside break-even price may not find put selling the proper strategy. As for any option selling strategy, the expiration price range defined by the financial and opportunity break-even prices should match or encompass the investor's expectations.

Speculative or Conservative?

The investor who stands ready to purchase the underlying security is not speculating. This investor has the capital necessary to establish a long position in the underlying security. The assignment making him long the stock may not be his goal, but it is not a cataclysm either.

Put selling becomes speculative when the investor sells puts that represent more shares than he is willing to own. He can do this because there is only an initial margin requirement for each short put. (For margin purposes, a short put is considered uncovered regardless of the amount of capital supporting the activity.) This investor has the possibility of a bigger loss than he is prepared to accept. That is speculation.

COVERED CALL SELLING

A covered call combines a short call with a long position in the underlying security. The two covered call strategies—covered writing and overwriting—are explained here. Covered call selling, whether via buy-writes or overwrites, allows an investor to profit from a correct forecast of the limit of price performance of the underlying.

In exchange for receiving the option premium, the covered call seller has limited the profit he can realize from a gain in the price of the security on which he has sold the call. The call buyer can take possession of the underlying at the strike price via exercise, so a covered call seller makes his maximum profit if the underlying security is above the call's strike price at expiration. The profit is the option premium received plus the gain from the advance, if any, of the price of the underlying up to the strike price. If the sold call is in-the-money, the loss from selling the underlying below its purchase price must be subtracted. The option premium also provides a partial hedge against a decline in the price of the underlying (Figure 4–6).

Covered Writing

When an investor buys stock and sells call options simultaneously, the strategy is called *covered writing* or *buy-writing*. Say that an investor buys 500 shares of XYZ stock at $40 per share and at the same time sells five of the 90-day $40 calls for $2 1/4 each. The total premium, excluding commissions, is $1,125. The cost of the stock, also excluding commissions, is $20,000. At expiration, his profit/loss can be seen in Table 4–8.

TABLE 4–8
Profit/Loss

Price of XYZ	Value of $40 Call	Profit/(Loss) on Calls	Profit/(Loss) on Stock	Total Profit/(Loss)
$30	$ 0	$1,125	$(5,000)	$(3,875)
35	0	1,125	(2,500)	(1,375)
39	0	1,125	(500)	625
40	0	1,125	0	1,125
41	1	625	500	1,125
45	5	(1,375)	2,500	1,125
50	10	(3,875)	5,000	1,125

FIGURE 4–6
Covered Call

Description: Buy or already own underlying security; sell call option with strike price I.

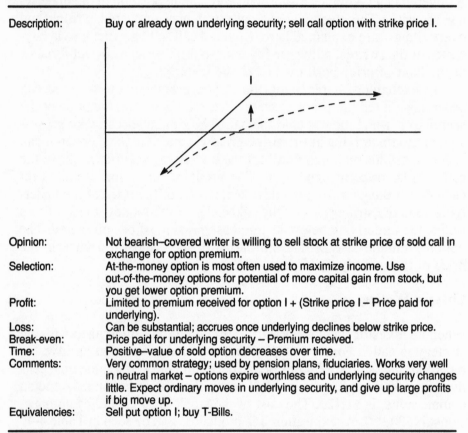

Opinion: Not bearish–covered writer is willing to sell stock at strike price of sold call in
                     exchange for option premium.
Selection: At-the-money option is most often used to maximize income. Use
                     out-of-the-money options for potential of more capital gain from stock, but
                     you get lower option premium.
Profit: Limited to premium received for option I + (Strike price I – Price paid for
                     underlying).
Loss: Can be substantial; accrues once underlying declines below strike price.
Break-even: Price paid for underlying security – Premium received.
Time: Positive–value of sold option decreases over time.
Comments: Very common strategy; used by pension plans, fiduciaries. Works very well
                     in neutral market – options expire worthless and underlying security changes
                     little. Expect ordinary moves in underlying security, and give up large profits
                     if big move up.
Equivalencies: Sell put option I; buy T-Bills.

Above $40, at expiration, the profit of the covered write is limited to the
premium received for the options. Below $40, the position loses $1,125
less than the stock investment. Whenever the call is assigned, the covered writer sells XYZ at $40 and realizes the maximum profit of $1,125.

Profits or Protection?
Like any other option strategy, the covered write can be used to express
varying degrees of one's opinion. At-the-money buy-writes are neutral.
They realize most, if not all, of their profit from the option premium.

Out-of-the-money buy-writes are bullish. Say, for example, that the
stock was purchased at $37 1/2 and the option sold for about $1 1/8. The
option premium is lower because the call is out-of-the-money. How-

ever, the position has greater potential profit than the at-the-money buy-write because there is profit to be made on the advance of XYZ to the strike price. The maximum profit on this buy-write, for 500 shares, is $1,812.50. The option premium provides $562.50; the stock, $1,250. In the first example, the stock provided no additional profit.

Another difference in the two positions is that the out-of-the-money provides less protection against a decline ($1 1/8 per share versus the at-the-money's $2 1/4 per share). This is always the trade-off in selecting a covered write in a stock. The potential for larger profits is balanced by the smaller premium.

How Much Premium?

High premiums alone do not make a good covered write. Option premium levels and risk, as defined by volatility, are directly related. If there are two $25 stocks, HVL (high volatility) and LVL (low volatility), their respective 120-day call premiums might be $2 1/8 and $1 1/2, representing 8 1/2 and 6 percent of the stock price. The covered write on HVL is not necessarily the superior one. Its possible return is higher, but it comes with the additional risk of owning a stock that could have a wider range of price movement than LVL.

Your main criterion should be your opinion of the underlying. If you do not want to own the underlying if it is not called away, you should not purchase it for the sole purpose of collecting high option premiums.

Overwriting

The other type of covered call selling is *overwriting*. In this strategy, the investor already owns the underlying security and now sells call options. He or she may have bought the security yesterday, six months ago, or six years ago.

The investor now feels that the probability of a move in the price of the underlying is small. Without options, this investor can take only one of two possible actions—sell it or hold it. Only selling allows him to extract any money from his holding.

Overwriting provides a third alternative. This investor can select among expirations to balance the premium received, the selling price *if called,* and the timeframe over which he expects the underlying to underperform. There can be 50-, 80-, and 140-day call options available with strike prices 2 points and 7 points out-of-the-money. For a stock at $53 per share, the following call options and prices might exist:

Option Strike Price	50-Day Call	80-Day Call	140-Day Call
$55	1 3/16	1 3/4	2 3/4
60	1/4	9/16	1 7/16

Whichever option he chooses, the overwriter must be aware that, in exchange for the premium received, he has *sold* the right of ownership of his stock at the strike price to *someone else*! He has capped the appreciation of the stock at the strike price. The premium is not "free money." It comes with an opportunity cost that prevents additional profits above the strike price plus premium and a financial cost of providing only as much protection as the premium. The overwriter concludes that the financial and opportunity break-even prices given by the call he sells limit the range of prices he expects.

Covered or Naked?

Addition of a long position in the underlying security makes the covered call seller very different from the naked call seller. That is, the investor who sells naked calls has a position with limited profit if the underlying is below the strike price and unlimited risk if it rallies substantially. He is neutral with a bearish bias. The covered call writer has limited profit if the underlying is above the strike price and risk if the underlying declines substantially. He is neutral with a bullish bias.

The difference is the price range over which the investor wants to take his risk. It is very important that an investor with a neutral opinion also consider on which side of the market he is willing to take risk if he is wrong.

Covered Writing and Put Selling

Compare the expiration profit/loss diagrams of covered call selling and put selling. They have the exact same shape! This can come as a surprise to many investors who feel that any option selling strategy is extremely risky.

If covered call writing is the equivalent strategy, it should have the same characteristics as put selling:

1. The covered call seller is willing to forgo any additional profits from the stock on movements beyond the strike price. So is the put seller.
2. The put seller underwrites the risk of the stock through expiration. In covered call selling, in exchange for the premium of the call option, the investor maintains the risk of the underlying.
3. The break-even point of both strategies is lower than the current price of the underlying.

BULL SPREADS

A *bull call spread* is created by purchasing one call option and simultaneously selling another call option with a higher strike price, as in the following example (XYZ at 80 3/4).

Buy 1 XYZ 90-day $80 call	$5 1/4
Sell 1 XYZ 90-day $85 call	− 2 7/8
Net cost of bull call spread	$2 3/8

A bull call spread is a combination of two options—one long, one short. The result is a position that has limited risk and profit. The limited risk is the net premium paid for the spread. If XYZ is below $80 at expiration, both call options will expire worthless and the investor will lose the $2 3/8 he paid for the spread. The profit from the spread is limited because the short $85 call has value if XYZ is above $85 at expiration. This value erases any additional profits gained from the long $80 call. In Table 4–9, you can see what the $80 to $85 bull call spread looks like at expiration. This example demonstrates that a spread can only be worth as much as the difference between the strike prices of the options! For prices of XYZ between $80 and $85, the $80 call advances without any offsetting effect from the $85 call. Above $85, this effect limits the spread's value. Table 4–9 shows the expiration points of maximum profit, and break-even. The maximum profit is $2 5/8 ($262.50) per spread—the maximum value of the spread, $500, minus the initial cost of $237.50. Maximum profit is realized at every price of XYZ above $85 at expiration. The break-even point is $82 3/8. At $82 3/8, the long $80 call is worth $2 3/8, and the short $85 is worth nothing. The break-even point of a bullish call

TABLE 4–9
Bull Spread

Price of XYZ	Value of Long $80 Call	Value of Short $85 Call	Value of Spread
$75	$ 0	0	$ 0
80	0	0	0
81	100	0	100
82	200	0	200
83	300	0	300
84	400	0	400
85	500	0	500
90	1,000	($500)	500
95	1,500	(1,000)	500

spread is the strike price of the long call plus the net premium paid for the spread. The bull call spread strategy is drawn in Figure 4–7, showing the limited loss, limited profit characteristics.

Motivation of the Bull Spreader

The bull spread can be used by the bullish investor who may not be entirely comfortable with a long call position. He may not be bullish enough to warrant the purchase of a call option straight out. He may have a target price (thus being willing to forgo additional profits from any advance beyond that target) or he may be uncertain as to the size of the advance, hesitating to "pay" to profit from every price of XYZ above the break-even point of a long call. Given these opinions, a hedged strategy is appropriate. The bull call spread is the particular hedged option position that satisfies this investor.

Many investors with bullish opinions delay buying calls when premiums seem a little too rich for them. The decision to wait can result in a lost opportunity. The bull spread lets these investors establish a bullish position now. Later on, naked long calls can be purchased. There's nothing wrong with starting with a hedged position.

The Trade-Offs of Spreading

The major trade-off of spreading is the elimination of the unlimited profit potential that goes with a long option position. In the example, the cost of the spread versus the long $80 call option is lowered because of

FIGURE 4–7
Bull Spread

Description:	Buy call with strike price I; sell call with strike price II.

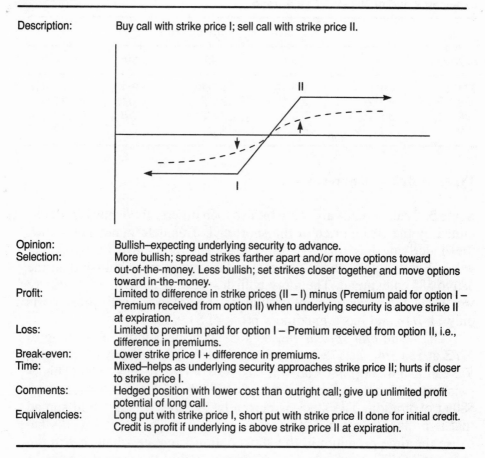

Opinion:	Bullish–expecting underlying security to advance.
Selection:	More bullish; spread strikes farther apart and/or move options toward out-of-the-money. Less bullish; set strikes closer together and move options toward in-the-money.
Profit:	Limited to difference in strike prices (II – I) minus (Premium paid for option I – Premium received from option II) when underlying security is above strike II at expiration.
Loss:	Limited to premium paid for option I – Premium received from option II, i.e., difference in premiums.
Break-even:	Lower strike price I + difference in premiums.
Time:	Mixed–helps as underlying security approaches strike price II; hurts if closer to strike price I.
Comments:	Hedged position with lower cost than outright call; give up unlimited profit potential of long call.
Equivalencies:	Long put with strike price I, short put with strike price II done for initial credit. Credit is profit if underlying is above strike price II at expiration.

the premium received from the short $85 call option. Therefore, the call spread has less risk, on a dollar-for-dollar basis, than the long call. For this lower cost, the buyer of the spread gives up additional profits from every price of XYZ above $85 per share at expiration.

There is another important trade-off besides the limitation of profits. It is the time trade-off. Here is Table 4–10, summarizing the performance of the $80 to $85 spread over different prices and time. If XYZ advanced to $90 per share in 15 days (75 days to expiration), the spread is worth about $3 7/8 and the investor has to wait 75 days for the remaining $1 1/8. The $80 call, on the other hand, is trading at 11 7/8! The spreader trades in immediate performance for a lower cost of entry.

TABLE 4–10
Expected Value of $80–$85 Call Spread

Price of XYZ	Days to Expiration				
	75	60	45	30	15
$78	1 11/16	1 9/16	1 7/16	1 3/16	13/16
82	2 1/2	2 1/2	2 1/2	2 7/16	2 3/8
86	3 5/16	3 3/8	3 1/2	3 5/8	3 15/16
90	3 15/16	4 1/16	4 1/4	4 7/16	4 3/4

Types of Bull Call Spreads

Some bull call spreads are more bullish than others. Bullishness is determined by the strike price of the short call. This determines how much the underlying has to move for the spread to achieve its maximum value. For example, the $85 to $90 call spread is more bullish than the $80 to $85 call spread. The more bullish spread is more likely to expire worthless, but it can be more profitable. The $85 to $90 call spread costs only $1 7/16 and has a maximum profit of $3 9/16.

The name *bull spread* can be somewhat inaccurate. Returning to XYZ at $80 3/4, the $75 call option is $8 1/2. The bull spread of a long $75 call and a short $80 call will cost $3 1/4 ($8 1/2 − $5 1/4). This 5-point spread has a maximum profit of $1 3/4 (5 − 3 1/4) if XYZ is at least $80 at expiration. The stock is currently $80 3/4. This is a bull spread that is profitable, even if XYZ does not move! The spread works because the time premium in the short option is greater than that in the long option. The time premium, however, makes the spread a position that does not reach its maximum profit if the underlying advances quickly. The full advantage of selling more time premium than is bought is not gained until the expiration date is very close.

But the *spread* between the options' strike prices can be larger than 5 points (for stocks with fractional strike prices, spreads less than 5 points can be possible). A $75 to $85 call spread costs $5 5/8 ($8 1/2 − $2 7/8). Break-even is $80 5/8. The distance between the strikes is 10 points and, therefore, the maximum profit is $4 3/8 if XYZ is above $85 at expiration ($10 − $5 5/8).

The break-even point of this spread is very close to the current price of the stock—$80 3/4. At expiration, the spread has the same results as the stock between $75 and $85. Below $75, the spread is

FIGURE 4–8
Comparison of Spread, Long Call, and Long Stock

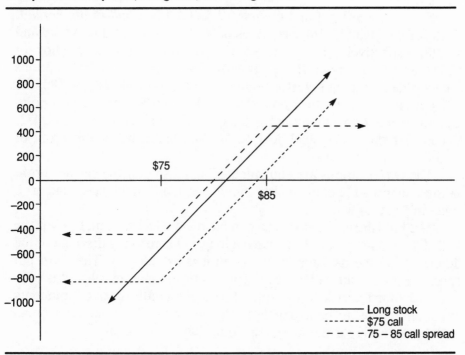

worthless and the loss is $562.50; the owner of XYZ stock continues to suffer losses. Above $85, the spread is worth $10 and the profit is limited to $437.50. The owner of XYZ stock continues to profit. This spread might be suitable for an investor who wants to profit from a rally in the stock to at least $85 over the next 90 days, but who does not want to be subject to additional losses if XYZ drops below $75. Figure 4–8 compares the spread to owning the stock or the $75 call.

The Bullish Put Spread

In the put market, the bull call spread has an equivalent—sell the higher strike put and buy the lower strike put. This would create a net credit because the premium of the sold put is higher than the one of the purchased put. The maximum profit of this position is the credit. If the price of the underlying is above the strike price of the short put at expiration, both options expire worthless. On the risk side, if the price of the underlying is below the lower strike price at expiration, the seller of this spread can lose the difference in the strike prices minus that initial credit.

Selling the $85 put and buying the $80 put is a *bullish put spread*. With XYZ still at $80 3/4, the prices of 90-day puts would be $5 3/8 and $2 7/8, respectively. The "sale" of the put spread creates an inflow of $2 1/2 ($250) per spread. If XYZ is above $85 at expiration, both options are worthless and the investor retains the $250 as profit. Below $80, the $85 put is always worth 5 points more than the $80 put. The 5 point maximum value of the spread results in the maximum loss of $2 1/2. Recall that the call spread cost $2 3/8 and had a maximum profit of $2 5/8.

The two positions are equivalent! The reason for the smaller profit in the put spread is explained in the discussion of the box spread arbitrage in Chapter 8.

The bullish *short put* spread can have a distinct advantage over the bullish *long call* spread. Because the long call spread results in an initial debit, it must be paid for in full when it is established. The short put spread results in an initial credit. Under current margin rules, it is only necessary for the risk of the spread, i.e., the credit received minus its maximum value, to be available in the account. There need not be an initial cash outlay if the margin account has excess equity.

Two Special Risks of Early Assignment

Dividends concern the call spreader. If the options of a call spread are far enough in-the-money the day before the ex-dividend date of the stock, the short call can be assigned. There is no stock risk because the long option can be exercised the next day. However, the stock that is delivered against the assignment is delivered cum-dividend, i.e., with the dividend. The stock that is purchased via exercise is purchased ex-dividend. The risk to the investor in this situation is the dividend. This is a sudden additional cost that lowers his profit in the position.

The second special situation that a spreader should be aware of involves spreads of American index options (see Chapter 2). If the short option in an index spread of this type is assigned early, the cash settlement mechanism of index options creates a debit in the account for the amount that the short option is in-the-money at the end of that business day, adjusted by the multiplier of the index. When the long option is exercised, the amount credited to the account will be determined by the settlement value of the index on the DAY it is exercised. There is a full one day's risk if the long option is not sold at some time during the next trading day!

BEAR SPREADS

The *bear spread* is commonly established with puts. It is a hedged strategy consisting of a long put and a short put with a lower strike price. The cost of the spread is the difference between the premium paid for the long option and the premium received for the short option:

Buy 1 XYZ 90-day $80 put	$2 1/2
Sell 1 XYZ 90-day $75 put	− 1
Net cost of bear put spread	$1 1/2

Like the bull call spread, the bear put spread is a position that has limited risk and limited profit (Figure 4–9). Risk is limited to the net premium paid for the spread. If XYZ is above $80 at expiration, both put options expire worthless, and the investor loses the $1 1/2 he paid for the spread. The profit from the spread is also limited because the short $75 put has value if XYZ is below $75 at expiration. This value erases any additional profits gained from the long $80 put. The $80 to $75 bear put spread in Table 4–11 looks like this at expiration.

The value of the spread at expiration, and hence, its profit, is limited at prices of XYZ below $75. The value of the $80 put is unaffected

TABLE 4–11
Bear Spread

Price of XYZ	Value of Long $80 Put	Value of Short $75 Put	Value of Spread	Profit/(Loss) in Spread
$85	$ 0	0	$ 0	($150)
80	0	0	0	($150)
79	100	0	100	(50)
78	200	0	200	50
77	300	0	300	150
76	400	0	400	250
75	500	0	500	350
70	1,000	($500)	500	350
65	1,500	($1,000)	500	350

FIGURE 4–9
Bear Spread

Description: Buy put with strike price II; sell put with strike price I.

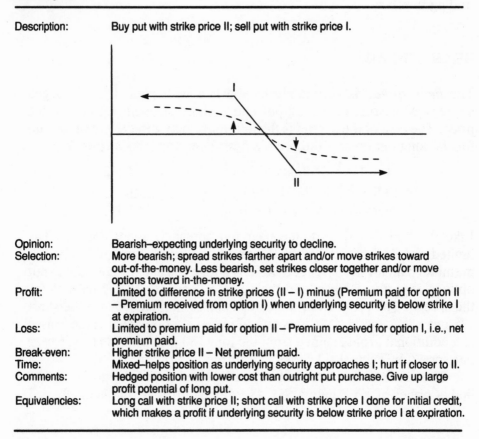

Opinion: Bearish–expecting underlying security to decline.
Selection: More bearish; spread strikes farther apart and/or move strikes toward
               out-of-the-money. Less bearish, set strikes closer together and/or move
               options toward in-the-money.
Profit: Limited to difference in strike prices (II – I) minus (Premium paid for option II
               – Premium received from option I) when underlying security is below strike I
               at expiration.
Loss: Limited to premium paid for option II – Premium received for option I, i.e., net
               premium paid.
Break-even: Higher strike price II – Net premium paid.
Time: Mixed–helps position as underlying security approaches I; hurt if closer to II.
Comments: Hedged position with lower cost than outright put purchase. Give up large
               profit potential of long put.
Equivalencies: Long call with strike price II; short call with strike price I done for initial credit,
               which makes a profit if underlying security is below strike price I at expiration.

by the $75 put until the latter is in-the-money. The spread is worthless for prices above $80. Table 4–11 also shows that the break-even point for a bear put spread is the strike price of the long put minus the net premium paid to establish the spread. In this example, the break-even price, at expiration, is $78 1/2.

Motivation of the Bear Spreader

The rationale for using the bear spread is similar to that for the bull spread. Investors feel the cost of entry into a long put position is too high, but they want to establish a position now. Investors who may have a price target on the underlying are willing to give up the substantial profits that accompany a long option position. The difference is that these investors select a bear spread when they expect the underlying to decline.

Trade-Offs of Bear Spreading

Besides limited profits, there is a performance trade-off because of time. Before expiration, the time premium remaining in the options prevents the spread from reaching its full value if the underlying declines soon after the spread is purchased. When choosing a spread over a naked long position, the spread needs to be held. Table 4–12 shows the value of the $80 to $75 put spread for various prices of XYZ in 15 day intervals.

If XYZ were to decline to $74 with 60 days remaining to expiration, the $80 put would be worth $6 1/8 and the $75 put, $2 15/16. The spread would be worth $3 3/16. It takes the entire 60 days for the spread to gain the remaining $1 13/16. The spreader trades in immediate performance for a lower cost of entry into a position!

Types of Bear Put Spreads

A bear spread is not limited to 5 points. The $85 to $75 put spread costs about $4 1/2. The break-even price for this position at expiration is $80 1/2, i.e., strike price $85 minus $4 1/2. If XYZ is below $75 at expiration, the spread is worth 10 points. It is worth comparing this spread to the $80 to $75 spread in which both options are out-of-the-money. The profit of each spread is truncated when the stock reaches $75 at expiration. The out-of-the-money spread has a maximum value of

TABLE 4–12
Bear Spread

Price of XYZ	Days to Option Expiration				
	75	60	45	30	15
$82	1 3/8	1 5/16	1 3/16	1	11/16
80	1 3/4	1 3/4	1 11/16	1 9/16	1 5/16
78	2 3/16	2 3/16	2 3/16	2 3/16	2 3/16
76	2 5/8	2 11/16	2 3/4	2 7/8	3 1/8
74	3 1/16	3 3/16	3 5/16	3 5/8	4 1/16

$5 and a maximum profit of $3 1/2. The $85 to $75 spread has a maximum value of $10 and a maximum profit of $5 1/2.

Spreads can be used speculatively. For example, if the investor places similar dollar amounts into each spread, the $80 to $75 spread in which both options are out-of-the-money is a more speculative position and should have a greater potential return. This out-of-the-money spread can have a 233 percent profit ($3 1/2 on $1 1/2). The spread is worthless if XYZ is above $80 at expiration. The 10-point spread can have a 122 percent profit ($5 1/2 on $4 1/2), breaks even at $80 1/2, and only expires worthless if XYZ is above $85 at expiration.

Taking the comparison one step farther, the $85 to $80 put spread costs $2 5/8. The break-even point of this spread is $82 3/8, and the maximum profit is 90 percent ($2 3/8 on $2 5/8). However, the stock is only $3/4 above the price at which the spread achieves its maximum value of 5. As a position that is less bearish than either the $80 to $75 or the $85 to $75, this spread should have less potential than either, and it does. The three positions are compared in Figure 4–10.

FIGURE 4–10
Comparison of Three Put Spreads

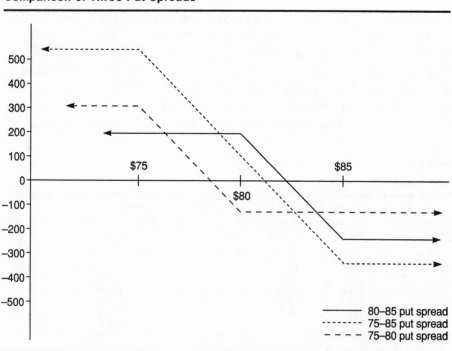

The bearishness of a put spread is determined by the strike price of the short option. The farther out-of-the-money that put is, the farther the underlying must drop to bring the spread to its maximum value. The most aggressive spreads have both options out-of-the-money and a large difference in their strike prices. The least aggressive spreads have both options in-the-money and a small difference in their strike prices.

The Bearish Call Spread

Calls can be used to establish *bear spreads* just as puts can be used to create bull spreads. Let's go back to the $75 to $80 bull call spread from the previous section. The $80 call was $5 1/4 and the $75 call was $8 1/2. The bear call spread is the result of selling the $75 call and buying the $80 call for a credit of $3 1/4. Should XYZ be below $75 at expiration, both options expire worthless. If XYZ is above $80, the spread is worth $5, resulting in a loss of $1 3/4. The put spread had a maximum profit of $3 1/2 for an investment of $1 1/2. Both positions are equivalent. As a credit spread, the risk of the position has to be available and can usually be satisfied with excess margin.

Summary of Spreading

The general rules of spreading are simple:

1. A spread can only be worth as much as the difference of the strike prices of the options that define it.
2. If a spread is purchased, the maximum profit is the maximum value of the spread minus the net amount paid. The maximum loss is the amount paid.
3. If a spread is sold, the maximum profit is the net amount received. The maximum loss is the maximum value of the spread minus that amount.
4. Spreads must be done in a margin account. If a spread is sold, the difference between the credit received and the maximum value of the spread must be available.

LONG STRADDLE

A *long straddle* consists of a long call and a long put with the same strike price and expiration date. By now you know that long calls are profitable if the underlying goes up, and long puts are profitable if the underlying goes down. A long straddle is profitable if the underlying goes up or down substantially.

Motivation

The long straddle is best suited to an environment in which the investor feels a large move is possible, but is unsure as to its direction. Consider a long straddle in a situation where an upcoming earnings report on a stock is expected, or the report of an economic statistic which can move the market is due. A technician can buy a straddle on a stock that has reached a very significant support or resistance level and is expecting the stock to either punch through that level or bounce right off it. In each case, the underlying could respond with a large move in either direction.

At Expiration

XYZ is at $80. The 90-day $80 call is $4 3/4; the 90-day put is $3 1/4. The $80 straddle costs $8 ($800 per straddle). Table 4–13 shows what the profit/loss looks like at expiration. The graph of this table gives the characteristic V shape profit/loss profile of the long straddle. It appears to straddle the strike price (see Figure 4–11).

The break-even points of a straddle at expiration are the strike price plus or minus the total premium paid for the call and the put. In this example, the break-even points are $72 ($80 strike price minus $8 cost) and $88 ($80 strike price plus $8 cost).

TABLE 4–13
Peculiar Straddle Shape Evident

Price of XYZ	Long $80 Call	Long $80 Put	Total Value of Straddle	Profit/(Loss) on Straddle
$65	$ 0	$1,500	$1,500	$700
70	0	1,000	1,000	200
75	0	500	500	(300)
80	0	0	0	(800)
85	500	0	500	(300)
90	1,000	0	1,000	200
95	1,500	0	1,500	700

FIGURE 4–11
Long Straddle

Description:	Buy call with strike price I; buy put with strike price I.

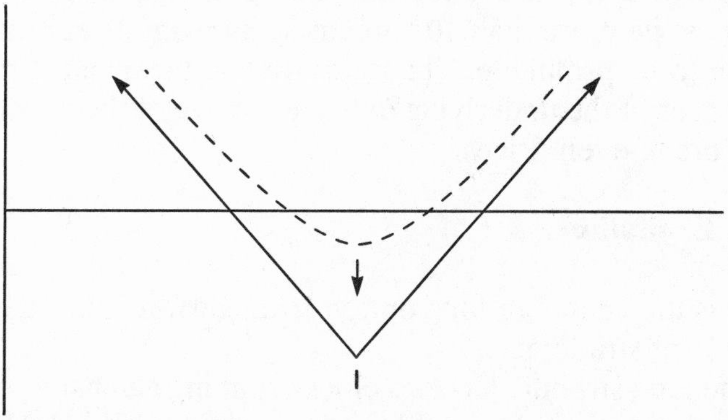

Opinion:	Uncertain–underlying security will move substantially in either direction, but you're unsure which way.
Selection:	Buy call and put with same strike price I when price of underlying security is near I.
Profit:	Increases as underlying security moves in either direction.
Loss:	Limited to sum of premiums paid for call and put.
Break-even:	On upside = Strike price I + Total premiums paid.
	On downside = Strike price I − Total premiums paid.
Time:	Very negative–position has two long options with accelerating decay as expiration nears.
Comments:	Rarely held to expiration due to time effect. Used in anticipation of news that might greatly effect underlying security in either direction.
Equivalencies:	Long 100 shares of underlying, long two puts with strike price I. Short 100 shares of underlying, long two calls with strike price I.

Risks of the Long Straddle

The risk of this strategy is quite large. Should the underlying not budge, both premiums are lost. However, the maximum loss only occurs at one price at expiration—the strike price of the options. Any move away from that single price immediately begins to lessen the loss because one of the options will have value.

Because of the opportunity to make money from a move in either direction, this strategy can seem too good to be true. In a way, it is. A long call option has a break-even point of the strike price plus the premium; a long put, the strike price minus the premium. The break-even points for the long straddle are the strike price plus and minus the sum of both premiums. A long straddle is the same as buying a call for the price of a call and a put, and buying a put for the price of a put and a call! At expiration, the underlying must have moved enough in either direction to compensate for the total premium paid. In the example, XYZ must be more than 10 percent away from its current price for the position to be profitable. The long straddle buyer must honestly assess the chances of the underlying to make a move of the magnitude required by the break-even prices.

Before Expiration

If time is the enemy of long option strategies, it is literally twice as bad for the long straddle.

The long straddle has two clocks running against it, one for the call and one for the put. It should not be a surprise that the long straddle is very sensitive to time decay. Table 4–14 shows the expected value over time of the 90-day, $80 straddle, purchased for $8 as the price of XYZ changes. Because of a long straddle's extreme sensitivity to time, the investor long a straddle can decide to take profits if the underlying makes a large move soon after the straddle is purchased. If XYZ runs up to $90 in 15 days, the straddle is worth $12 1/4. If it remains at $90, the position begins to lose time premium. The investor who waits for a continuation of the move finds that he has given back some of that initial profit.

Another reason to consider taking profits is that the position no longer reflects the investor's initial intentions. The straddle now consists of an in-the-money call and an out-of-the-money put. The investor

TABLE 4–14
Expected Value of $80 Straddle

Price of XYZ	Days to Option Expiration				
	75	60	45	30	15
$95	16 5/8	16 1/4	15 7/8	15 1/2	15 1/4
90	12 1/4	11 3/4	11 1/4	10 3/4	10 1/4
85	9	8 1/4	7 1/2	6 5/8	5 1/2
80	7 1/4	6 1/2	5 1/2	4 1/2	3 1/4
75	7 1/2	7	6 3/8	5 3/4	5 1/4
70	10 5/8	10 1/2	10 1/4	10	10
65	15 1/8	15 1/8	15	15	15

would much rather see XYZ continue to rally. Of course, another 5-point rise in XYZ increases the value of the straddle to twice its purchase price, but the position is also susceptible to a pull-back of part of the move.

Buying a straddle close to expiration does not solve the time decay problem. As expiration approaches, there is less time for the underlying to make a move. If the expected volatility of the XYZ has not changed, the $3 1/4 cost for the 15-day straddle accurately reflects this.

Before rushing to buy this straddle close to expiration ask yourself, "Do I think that XYZ will be above $83 1/4 or below $76 3/4 in 15 days?"

Which Stocks?

One might conclude that the long straddle is best for stocks that show a tendency to make larger moves. However, it may not be wise to base one's choice solely on that basis. As you have seen numerous times, the expected movement in a stock affects option premiums directly via a higher volatility number in the pricing model.

The XYZ $80 straddle in the example had an $8 total premium. If XYZ were a more volatile stock, the premiums of the call and put would be higher. This effect increases the upside break-even point and lowers the downside break-even point by the amount of the additional premium paid. At expiration, XYZ will need to have moved farther for the straddle to be profitable.

LONG STRANGLE

The *long strangle* is very similar to the long straddle. Like the straddle, it is a strategy that reflects one's forecast of a large move in the underlying in either direction. The difference between a strangle and a straddle is that the strike prices of the call and put that make up the strangle are not the same.

At Expiration

If the underlying is between strikes, there are two straddles and two strangles from which to choose. Let's say that XYZ is $57 and the 90-day options available are:

Option	Option Price	Option	Option Price
$55 call	$4 5/8	$60 call	$2 1/8
$55 put	$1 1/2	$60 put	$3 7/8

Two strangles can be created from these four options. One consists of the long $60 call and the long $55 put, called the *out-of-the-money strangle*. The other contains the long $55 call and the long $60 put, called the *in-the-money strangle*. The profit/loss diagram of a strangle shows that this strategy's maximum loss occurs over the range of prices between strike prices. In Table 4–15, you can see how the out-of-the money strangle looks at expiration. A strangle has break-even points at expiration of the strike price of the call plus the total premium paid and the strike price of the put option minus the total premium paid. For the strangle in this example, the break-even points are $51 3/8 and $63 5/8. This is a range of plus and minus 10 percent of XYZ's current price of $57 (Figure 4–12).

In-the-Money or Out-of-the-Money?

The out-of-the-money strangle of the $60 call and $55 put costs $3 5/8. By contrast, the in-the-money strangle of the $55 call and $60 put costs $8 1/2. Quite a difference in cost, but the positions are the same! For one, their break-even points are the same. The out-of-the-money strangle has break-even points of $63 5/8 and $51 3/8. The in-the-money strangle has break-even points of $63 1/2 (the $55 call strike plus the $8 1/2 total premium), and $51 1/2 (the $60 put strike minus the $8 1/2

TABLE 4–15
Strangle

Price of XYZ	Value of $55 Put	Value of $60 Call	Value of Strangle	Profit/Loss of Strangle
$45	$1,000	$ 0	$1,000	$637.50
50	500	0	500	137.50
55	0	0	0	(362.50)
60	0	0	0	(362.50)
65	0	500	500	137.50
70	0	1,000	1,000	637.50

FIGURE 4–12
Long Strangle

Description:	Long put with strike price I; long call with strike price II.

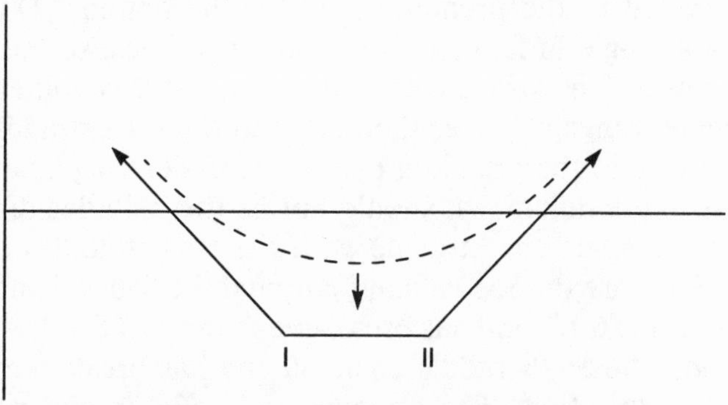

Opinion:	Uncertain–expect underlying security to move substantially, but unsure which way.
Selection:	Buy put I and call II when price of underlying security is between strike prices.
Profit:	Increases as underlying security moves in either direction.
Loss:	Limited to sum of premiums paid for call and put.
Break-even:	On upside = Strike price II + Total premiums paid.
	On downside = Strike price I – Total premiums paid.
Time:	Very negative–position has two long options with accelerating decay as expiration nears.
Comments:	Rarely held to expiration due to time effect. Used in anticipation of news that might greatly effect underlying security in either direction. Costs less than long straddle, but needs bigger move to reach break-even points.
Equivalencies:	Long 100 shares of underlying; buy put I, buy put II. Short 100 shares of underlying; buy call I; buy call II. Buy call I, buy put II.

premium). If the positions are the same, they must also have the same risk. The maximum loss of the out-of-the-money strangle is $3 5/8: the maximum loss of its counterpart is $3 1/2.

Why is the risk of the in-the-money strangle only $3 1/2 if it costs $8 1/2? If XYZ is somewhere between $55 and $60, at expiration, the sum of the values of the put and call are $5. For instance, XYZ is $58 at expiration. The $55 call would be $3, and the $60 put is $2. At $56, the call is $1, and the put is $4. Since the sum of the call and put premium will always be $5, the $8 1/2 premium paid for the strangle can only decrease by $3 1/2. This is the risk of the in-the-money strangle.

Strangle or Straddle?

A strangle of an out-of-the-money call and put costs less than the strad-dle of the at-the-money call and put. As with any long option position, loss is limited to the premium paid for the options. Do not consider buying a strangle in favor of a straddle just because the initial invest-ment is lower. The strangle can cost less, but it is vulnerable to losses over a wider range of prices than the straddle. The straddle only suffers complete loss of the premium paid if the underlying lands at the strike price. Absolute dollar risk should not be the only deciding factor.

Now compare the strangle with the two straddles available. The two straddles are the $55 call and put, and the $60 call and put. The $55 straddle costs $6 1/8 and has break-even points of $61 1/8 and $48 7/8 at expiration. The $60 straddle costs $6 and has break-even points of 66 and 54 at expiration. The strangle costs $3 5/8 and has break-even points of $63 5/8 and $51 3/8.

FIGURE 4–13
Comparison of Straddles and Strangle

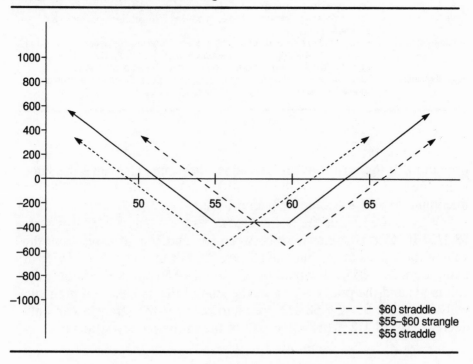

Which is the best of the three? When a stock is between strike prices, such as $57 in our example, the strangle creates a position which balances the profit potential from a movement of the underlying in either direction. The break-even points of the strangle are 6 5/8 points above and 5 5/8 points below the current price. Neither of the straddles does this. The break-even points of the $55 straddle are 4 1/8 points above and 8 1/8 points below XYZ's current price; the $60 straddle, 9 points above and 3 points below. All three positions are presented in Figure 4–13.

What if XYZ were $55? The 90-day options might be priced as follows:

Option	Price	Option	Price	Option	Price
$50 call	$6 3/4	$55 call	$3 3/8	$60 call	$1 3/8
$50 put	$ 5/8	$55 put	$2 1/4	$60 put	$5 1/8

FIGURE 4–14
Buy One Straddle or Three Strangles?

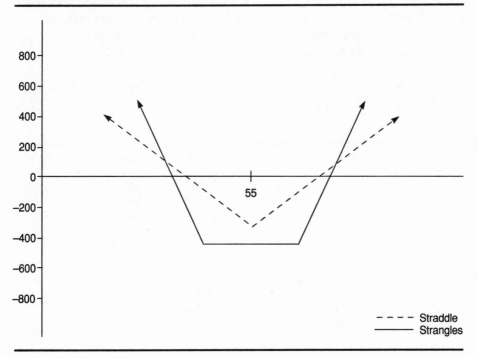

Now the $55 straddle is $5 5/8 with break-even points of $60 5/8 and $49 3/8. The $50 to $60 strangle is $2 with break-evens of $62 and $48.

Which is better? Only investors can make that decision. Do they put more emphasis on break-even analysis, absolute dollar risk, or leverage? In terms of leverage, investors can establish three $50 to $60 strangles for almost the same dollar risk as one straddle. The strangles will be a position with six long options (three calls and puts) versus the straddle's two (one call and put). If XYZ makes a big move, the three strangles are much more profitable than the one straddle. However, there is one very important trade-off: the entire premium paid for the strangles is lost if XYZ is between the strike prices of the options. The straddle only suffers total loss of the premium paid at the singular point of the strike price. This is a very aggressive and speculative way to compare strangles to straddles. Figure 4–14 shows why this type of comparison can be so dangerous.

SHORT BUTTERFLY

The *butterfly*, so named because of the "wings" in its profit/loss diagram, is a four-option position. That is, the common short butterfly is created from the purchase of two calls of the same strike price and the sale of one each of the closest in-the-money and out-of-the-money call options.

Assume XYZ is at $55. Use these 90-day option prices from the long strangle discussion.

Option	Price	Option	Price	Option	Price
$50 call	$6 3/4	$55 call	$3 3/8	$60 call	$1 3/8
$50 put	$ 5/8	$55 put	$2 1/4	$60 put	$5 1/8

The short butterfly is:

Short	1	$50 call	$6 3/4	
Long	2	$55 calls	(6 3/4)	(2 × 3 3/8)
Short	1	$60 call	1 3/8	
Net credit			$1 3/8	

At Expiration

The $1 3/8 credit, the maximum profit of this strategy, is achieved if XYZ is above $60 or below $50 at expiration. Below $50, all of the options expire worthless, and the investor keeps the entire net premium received. Above $60, the total value of the two long $55 calls are the same as the total value for the short $50 and $60 calls. For example, at $65, the long $55s are $10 each, for a total of $20. The short $50 is $15 and the short $60 is $5, for a total of $20. The break-even prices for the butterfly are the strike price of the short in-the-money call plus the credit received, and the short out-of-the-money call minus the credit received (Figure 4–15).

FIGURE 4–15
Short Butterfly

Description:	Sell 1 of each call with strike price I and III; buy 2 calls with strike price II.

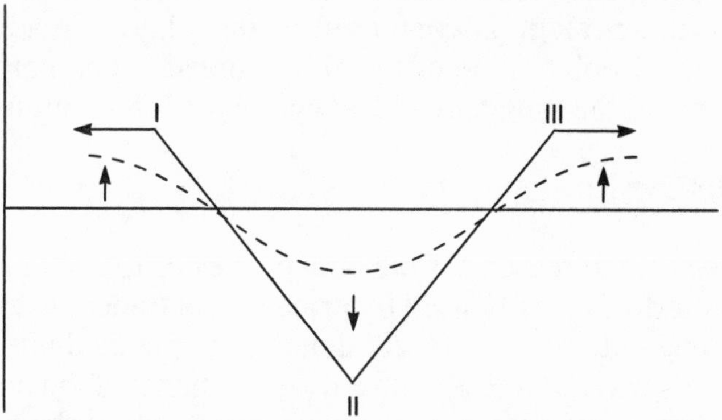

Opinion:	Uncertain–expect underlying security to be below I or above III at expiration.
Selection:	Use when price of underlying security is near strike price II.
Profit:	Net amount of premium received from sales and purchases if underlying below I or above III at expiration.
Loss:	Limited to value of short spread, strike price II – strike price I, less initial credit if underlying at strike price II at expiration.
Break-even:	On upside = Strike price III – Net premium received.
	On downside = Strike price I + Net premium received.
Time:	Mixed–most dramatic in last month.
Comments:	Cheaper than straddle or strangle because of sold options. Profits truncated at strikes I and III. Done mostly by arbitrageurs to take advantage of pricing relationship among four options. Rarely done by public.
Equivalencies:	Use all puts.

The maximum loss occurs at the strike price of the long options, the middle strike. At this price, the investor has a position that is short two options, one worth 5 points and another that is worthless. Unfortunately, the two that were purchased are also worthless. The maximum loss, then, is the value of the in-the-money short option minus the credit collected. In this example it is $3 5/8 ($5 − $1 3/8).

1 Butterfly = 2 Spreads

A short butterfly is a strategy that combines two spreads: a bullish long and a bearish short. This description confirms the limited profit, limited loss of this technique. Spreads were discussed earlier in the chapter. They were described as having both limited profit and limited loss. As a combination of spreads, the butterfly retains these characteristics.

If you break down the example into its spread components, the $1 3/8 credit also results. The $50 to $55 call spread is sold for a $3 3/8 point credit. The $55 to $60 call spread is bought for a $2 point debit. Above $60, each spread is worth its full value, in this example 5 points. Because the strategy is composed of one short spread and one long spread, the 5 point value of the short spread is counteracted by the 5 point asset in the long spread leaving the $1 3/8 credit as profit.

When to Use

There is no good reason for the public investor to use this strategy. The short butterfly is mostly used by professional traders to exploit mispricings among options. It is rarely done in the public domain.

Here's why. The short butterfly loses money if the underlying stays about where it is—assuming the long options are at-the-money. It loses less as the underlying moves away from the middle strike. The short butterfly looks like the long straddle at prices around the middle strike, and, based on this comparison, it appears that the short butterfly should be used when the investor expects the underlying to be somewhere other than the middle strike price at expiration. The $55 straddle costs $5 5/8. The short butterfly has a maximum loss of $3 5/8 at $55. The butterfly looks better at these prices.

On the other hand, the failure of the short butterfly is its inability to provide additional profit should the underlying make a substantial move. The long straddle has the potential for very large profits if the underlying moves well beyond a break-even point. The maximum profit of the butterfly, $1 3/8, is reached very close to the break-even points. The short butterfly hedges away too much of the profit that can be made from a move in the underlying away from the middle strike.

SHORT CONDOR

The *short condor* is a variation of the short butterfly. It also requires four options and is the combination of a short and a long spread. The difference is that the strike prices of the long options are separated. The name condor comes from the larger "wingspan" of the profit/loss diagram, which distinguishes it from the butterfly (Figure 4–16).

FIGURE 4–16
Short Condor

| Description: | Buy calls with strike prices II and III. Sell calls with strike prices I and IV. |

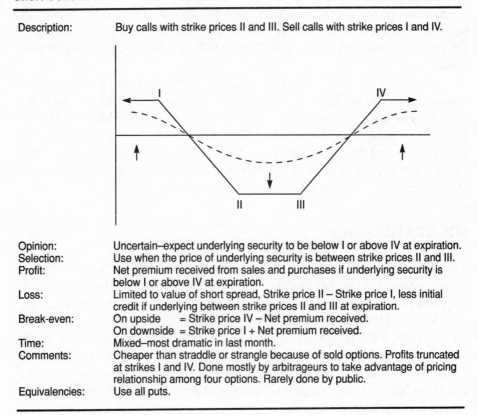

Opinion:	Uncertain—expect underlying security to be below I or above IV at expiration.
Selection:	Use when the price of underlying security is between strike prices II and III.
Profit:	Net premium received from sales and purchases if underlying security is below I or above IV at expiration.
Loss:	Limited to value of short spread, Strike price II – Strike price I, less initial credit if underlying between strike prices II and III at expiration.
Break-even:	On upside = Strike price IV – Net premium received.
	On downside = Strike price I + Net premium received.
Time:	Mixed—most dramatic in last month.
Comments:	Cheaper than straddle or strangle because of sold options. Profits truncated at strikes I and IV. Done mostly by arbitrageurs to take advantage of pricing relationship among four options. Rarely done by public.
Equivalencies:	Use all puts.

An example of a short condor position would be:

Short 1 XYZ $85 call: $9 7/8

Long 1 XYZ $90 call: 6 1/2

Long 1 XYZ $95 call: 4

Short 1 XYZ $100 call: 2 1/4

These are 90-day option prices when XYZ is $92. The net credit of these four transactions is $1 5/8. As with the short butterfly, it is also the maximum profit if XYZ is above $100 or below $85 at expiration. The short call spread in this example is $85 to $90; the long spread is $95 to $100. The break-even prices for the condor are the strike price of the short in-the-money call plus the credit received, $86 5/8, and the short out-of-the-money call minus the credit received, $98 3/8.

The short condor suffers its maximum loss over the range of prices between the two long call strike prices. For the short butterfly, it is a single price. Here the risk is $3 3/8—the 5 points the short $85–$90 call spread will be worth between $90 and $95 minus the maximum $1 5/8 potential profit. Above $95 at expiration, the $95 call gains in value. This gain is unchecked by the short $100 call until XYZ goes above $100.

The short condor, with a distance between the long strikes, can be compared to the strangle. The $90 put is $2 7/8, so the $90 put, $95 call strangle costs $6 7/8. Break-even points are $83 1/8 and $101 7/8. The $6 7/8 is lost between $90 and $95. The conclusion reached is that the premium saved by establishing a short condor may not be worth the limited profit potential of the position. Indeed, one could say that the short condor is a strangle that has had its wings clipped!

SHORT STRADDLE

The *short straddle* earns very large profits in a neutral market. No other option strategy is so profitable. Of course, using this technique means very unique and substantial risks if the market does not remain neutral.

A short straddle consists of a short call and a short put of the same strike price. XYZ is at $80. The 90-day $80 call is $4 3/4; the 90-day put is $3 1/4. The $80 straddle can be sold for $8 ($800 per straddle). In Table 4–16, there is a profit/loss picture. The only difference between the short and the long straddles is that the profits have been changed to losses and vice versa.

TABLE 4–16
Short Straddle

Price of XYZ	Short $80 Call	Short $80 Put	Total Value of Straddle	Profit/(Loss) on Straddle
$65	$ 0	$1,500	$1,500	$(700)
70	0	1,000	1,000	(200)
75	0	500	500	300
80	0	0	0	800
85	500	0	500	300
90	1,000	0	1,000	(200)
95	1,500	0	1,500	(700)

The graph of the short straddle is the inverted *V* shape profit/loss profile of the short straddle appearing to straddle the strike price (Figure 4–17).

Maximum profit is the total premium received; however, there is only one price where this maximum profit is realized—the strike price of the sold options. If the underlying is anywhere other than the strike price, but still within the break-even points, there is a profit, but it is smaller. Outside the break-even points, the potential loss in this strategy is unlimited. The straddle seller has given the potential for unlimited profits *to the buyer*.

The break-even prices at expiration are the strike price of the options sold plus and minus the total premium received.

Motivation

Before options, there was no way for an investor to profit directly from correctly forecasting a narrowly trading market. The only way to improve investment performance was to allocate assets properly. However, asset allocation provides only relative opportunity profit by maximizing investment in sectors that are outperforming and minimizing investment in those underperforming. Without options, there is no way to make money. The short straddle and the three strategies that follow are designed to be profitable when very little happens.

The seller of a straddle expects (needs) the underlying to move in a narrow range around the strike price. In this example, the break-even points are $72 ($80 strike price minus $8 credit) and $88 ($80 strike price plus $8 credit), the same as for the long straddle, some 10 percent away from the current price.

FIGURE 4–17
Short Straddle

Description: Sell call with strike price I; sell put with strike price I.

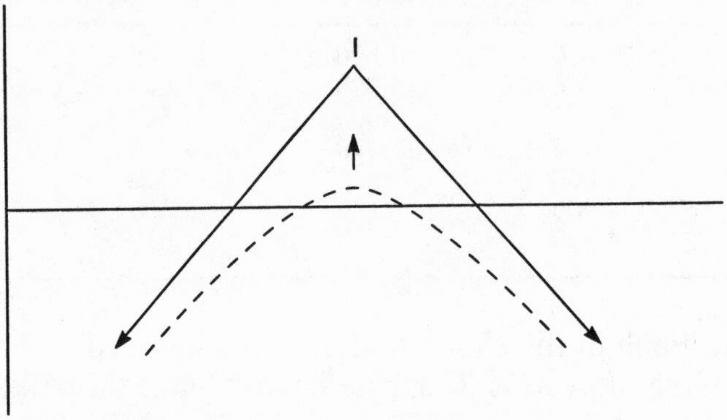

Opinion: Neutral–underlying security will not move substantially in either direction.
Selection: Sell call and put with same strike price I when price of underlying security is
                near strike price I.
Profit: Limited to sum of premiums received for call and put.
Loss: Increases as underlying security moves in either direction.
Break-even: On upside   = Strike price I + Premiums received.
                On downside = Strike price I − Premiums received.
Time: Very positive–position has two short options experiencing accelerating decay
                as expiration nears.
Comments: Expecting very ordinary moves in underlying security, within range of
                break-even points. Great when it works, very large losses when it doesn't.
Equivalencies: Long 100 shares of underlying, short two calls strike price I. Short 100
                shares of underlying, short two puts strike price I.

The investor should select this straddle position only if he expects XYZ to trade within plus-or-minus 10 percent of $80 over the next 90 days. Many investors continually forget that selection of the proper option strategy must address the expected price movement of the underlying over time and the consequences of unexpected outcomes. The short straddle is a strategy that could have serious financial results if the underlying moves substantially away from the strike price, e.g., as a result of a takeover bid or a dividend cut.

Time Decay

Say that the straddle sold at $8. If XYZ were to remain at $80, the straddle would drop to $6 1/2 in 30 days. After another 30 days, the straddle decays to $4 5/8. The overall decay is 42 percent. Time is the best friend of all short option strategies!

Risks and Capital Management

The short straddle assumes all the risk of long stock at prices below the downside break-even point at expiration and all the risk of a short position in the stock for prices above the upside break-even point. In effect, the position gets "longer" as prices go down, and "shorter" as prices go up! In more technical terms, as the underlying moves lower, the delta of the put approaches -1; as the underlying moves higher, the call delta approaches $+1$.

The possibility of extensive losses cannot be overemphasized. Short straddles and strangles are very attractive techniques. They beckon the investor with the lure of "free money." After all, these strategies require only a margin deposit, which can very often be satisfied with the loan value of securities in the investor's account. This loan value can be used over and over again producing very large returns. This reasoning often results in investors using too much of that loan value in naked option strategies.

Consequences of this type of capital management can be disastrous. It only takes the sale of one ill-timed, short position for the investor to feel the full force of his error. The lack of additional margin to support the increasing requirement can force him to close some or all of the position early. As described earlier, the loss from buying back a short option could eliminate much, if not all, of not only the profits of previous successful positions, but the investor's capital as well.

Capital Required

Since this strategy has naked options, it needs to be supported by an initial margin deposit that is based on the current requirements. This can be higher than the exchange minimums, and your brokerage firm can impose additional criteria. However, since a short straddle can only be unprofitable on one side of the trade (i.e., the underlying is either going up or going down), the requirement will only be the greater of the put or call margin plus the premium of the other side.

SHORT STRANGLE

The goal of the short strangle is to profit from movement in the underlying security over a range of prices. These price limits are defined by the strike prices of the options sold—one call and one put per strangle.

FIGURE 4–18
Short Strangle

Description:	Sell put with strike price I; sell call with strike price II.

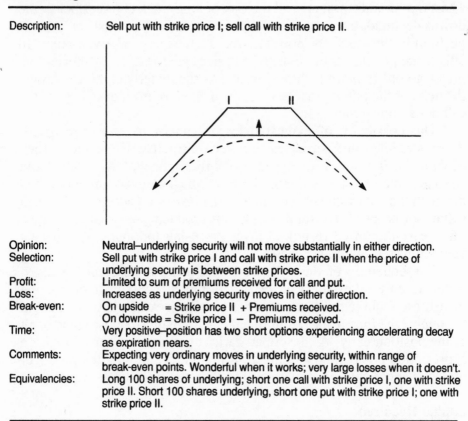

Opinion:	Neutral–underlying security will not move substantially in either direction.
Selection:	Sell put with strike price I and call with strike price II when the price of underlying security is between strike prices.
Profit:	Limited to sum of premiums received for call and put.
Loss:	Increases as underlying security moves in either direction.
Break-even:	On upside = Strike price II + Premiums received.
	On downside = Strike price I − Premiums received.
Time:	Very positive–position has two short options experiencing accelerating decay as expiration nears.
Comments:	Expecting very ordinary moves in underlying security, within range of break-even points. Wonderful when it works; very large losses when it doesn't.
Equivalencies:	Long 100 shares of underlying; short one call with strike price I, one with strike price II. Short 100 shares underlying, short one put with strike price I; one with strike price II.

Unlike the short straddle, the strike prices of the call and put are different. For example, XYZ is $57 and the 90-day options are:

Option	Option Price	Option	Option Price
$55 call	$4 5/8	$60 call	$2 1/8
$55 put	$1 1/2	$60 put	$3 7/8

The out-of-the-money strangle, made up of the $55 put and the $60 call, brings in $3 5/8 in total premium. Break-even points at expiration are $63 5/8 and $51 3/8. These prices are 10 percent above and 9.8 percent below the current price. When the underlying is between strike prices, the strangle more accurately reflects the investor's neutral opinion (Figure 4–18).

Other comparisons between the short straddle and short strangle are:

1. The short strangle usually brings in less premium because it is most often done with out-of-the-money options.
2. The maximum profit is achieved if the underlying is between the strike prices at expiration. For the straddle, it is at a singular price.
3. As with the short straddle, the short strangle is exposed to unlimited losses if the underlying makes a substantial move to the upside or the downside. The position gets longer as the underlying goes lower and gets shorter as it goes higher.

A sensible alternative is to start with some protection in place when the position is established. This is examined in the next two sections.

LONG BUTTERFLY

A *long butterfly* is the sale of two at-the-money calls and the purchase of an out- and an in-the-money call. Recall that the short butterfly was described as the combination of two spreads that limited the profit and loss of the position. The same is true for the long butterfly. The difference is that the spreads are reversed. Instead of the middle strike being the long calls, they are the short calls.

XYZ is at $85; the 60-day option prices are:

Option	Price	Option	Price	Option	Price
$80 call	$7 1/4	$85 call	$4	$90 call	$2
$80 put	$1 1/8	$85 put	$2 3/4	$90 put	$5 3/4

The long butterfly is:

Long 1 $80 call	$7 1/4	
Short 2 $85 calls	8	(2 × $4)
Long 1 $90 call	2	
Net debit	$1 1/4	

The net debit is the maximum loss of this position if XYZ is below $80 or above $90 at expiration. Below $80, all options expire worthless. Above $90, the long $80 to $85 spread is worth 5 points; so is the short $85 to $90 spread. The values cancel each other out, resulting in the 1 1/4 loss of the initial investment.

Profit, maximized at $85, is 3 3/4. At this price, the $80 call is worth 5 points, and all the other options expire worthless.

Break-even points for the long butterfly are the lowest strike price plus the initial debit and the highest strike price less the initial debit. In this example, these prices are $88 3/4 and $81 1/4 respectively (Figure 4–19).

FIGURE 4–19
Long Butterfly

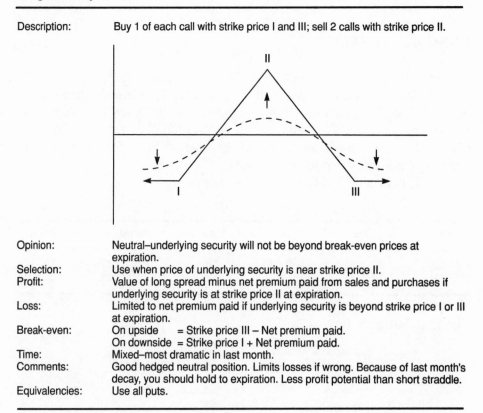

Description:	Buy 1 of each call with strike price I and III; sell 2 calls with strike price II.
Opinion:	Neutral–underlying security will not be beyond break-even prices at expiration.
Selection:	Use when price of underlying security is near strike price II.
Profit:	Value of long spread minus net premium paid from sales and purchases if underlying security is at strike price II at expiration.
Loss:	Limited to net premium paid if underlying security is beyond strike price I or III at expiration.
Break-even:	On upside = Strike price III – Net premium paid. On downside = Strike price I + Net premium paid.
Time:	Mixed–most dramatic in last month.
Comments:	Good hedged neutral position. Limits losses if wrong. Because of last month's decay, you should hold to expiration. Less profit potential than short straddle.
Equivalencies:	Use all puts.

Motivation

The long butterfly is used by the investor who wants to profit from a forecast of a narrow trading range for the underlying but is unwilling to accept the risk of unlimited losses that comes with the sale of either a straddle or strangle.

The long butterfly, then, can be an attractive alternative to the short straddle. First, though, one might ask, "How can a butterfly spread of call options be compared to a straddle composed of a call and a put?" The answer is something that the investor using options should always remember when analyzing and deciding among strategies: "Place the emphasis on the risk-reward implications of the strategies!" Options can be combined in many different ways to achieve similar results. Put-call parity shows why this is true.

The $85 straddle can be sold for $6 3/4 ($675), the sum of the call and put premiums. This is 3 points more premium than the maximum profit of the butterfly. Instead of selling one straddle for $6 3/4, the investor can buy two butterfly spreads for a total investment of $2 1/2. The $1 1/4 outlay per butterfly is the maximum loss. The maximum profit is $750 ($3 3/4 per butterfly), $75 more than the single straddle.

Break-even points for the straddle are $91 3/4 and $78 1/4. For the butterflies, they are $88 3/4 and $81 1/4. The performance difference is evident in Figure 4–20. One straddle is being compared to two butterflies. Therefore, the profit from the butterflies declines twice as fast. In the diagram, the slopes of the lines from the point of maximum profit demonstrate this effect. The long butterfly can be an effective neutral strategy especially for those who would find the excessive losses possible with short straddles hard to accept. The trade-off is the increased speed at which the butterfly achieves its maximum loss.

The Directional Butterfly

The long butterfly has a unique and interesting application for the investor with a directional bias. A long butterfly that can be placed entirely out-of-the-money can be very profitable if the underlying moves "into" the profit range of the position. XYZ is $105 and 90-day options are:

$110 call: $3 1/2
$115 call: $1 7/8
$120 call: $1

FIGURE 4–20
Comparison of Two Long Butterfly Spreads to Short Straddle

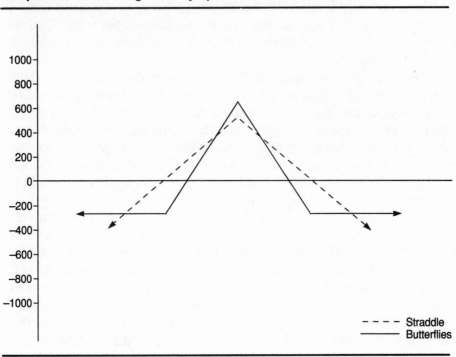

The butterfly of a long $110, long $120, and short two $115 calls costs $3/4. That is an investment of $75, excluding commissions. If XYZ closes at $115 on expiration Friday, the butterfly is worth its maximum value of 5 points, a 4-to-1 profit. The break-even points are $110 3/4 and $119 1/4.

The caveat is that the investor selecting this type of position cannot be too bullish. Profits will decline between $115 and $119 1/4, and the $3/4 is lost if XYZ is above $120 at expiration. This might be acceptable to the investor with a specific target price and the time frame in mind.

This long butterfly has a very low cost of entry—lower than any of the individual calls or spreads. It is the epitome of the power of options:

> Options allow the investor to maximize his participation in outcomes he considers most likely by creating positions that minimize or eliminate participation or create losses for outcomes he considers less likely.

LONG CONDOR

We need not elaborate on the *long condor*. It has the same risk-reward characteristics as the long butterfly except for the separation of the strike prices of the sold options (Figure 4–21).

Because of the long distance between the two long options, perhaps 15 points or more, the long condor is more effective when used with higher-priced securities. For instance, the long condor on a $52 stock could be the long $45 call, short the $50 and $55 calls, and long the $60 call. This 60-day condor would cost $3 1/4 and have only $1 3/4 points potential profit. The 60-day long condor for an $82 stock—long $75 call,

FIGURE 4–21
Long Condor

Description:	Sell calls with strike prices II and III; buy calls with strike prices I and IV.

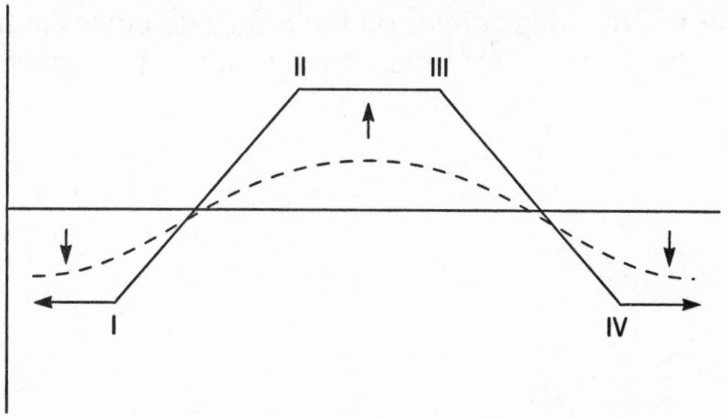

Opinion:	Neutral–underlying security will not be beyond break-even prices at expiration.
Selection:	Use when price of underlying security is between strike prices.
Profit:	Value of long spread minus net premium paid from sales and purchases if underlying security is between strike prices II and III at expiration.
Loss:	Limited to net premium paid if underlying security is above strike price IV or below strike price I at expiration.
Break-even:	On upside = Strike price IV − Net premium paid.
	On downside = Strike price I + Net premium paid.
Time:	Mixed–most dramatic in last month.
Comments:	Good hedged neutral position. Limits losses if you're wrong. Because of last month's decay, you should hold to expiration. Less profit potential than short strangle.
Equivalencies:	Use all puts.

short $80 and $85 calls, long $90 call—would cost $2 3/8 and have 2 5/8 points potential profit. Individual 60-day option prices could be:

XYZ at $52		Position	XYZ at $82	
$45 call	$7 3/4	Long	$75 call	$8 3/4
50 call	3 5/8	Short	80 call	5
55 call	1 3/16	Short	85 call	2 1/2
60 call	5/16	Long	90 call	1 1/8
Cost:	$3 1/4		Cost:	$2 3/8

The difference in profitability comes not from the absolute distance between the long options, but from the relative distance. The $45 call is 7 points or 13.5 percent below the stock price. The $75 call is also 7 points below the stock price, but is only 8.5 percent below the current price. Again, the option market has proved that prices accurately reflect options' relation to the price of the underlying. The seemingly better profit/loss of the long condor on the $82 stock comes at the expense of bringing the points of maximum loss closer to the current price.

CHAPTER 5

NEW PRODUCT STRATEGIES

Chapter 4 described and analyzed the most common option strategies: under what market conditions they best perform, potential profits, extent of risk taken, and how the passage of time affects their profitability. This fifth chapter describes how some of the risk/reward profiles of Chapter 4 can be replicated using some of the products that have been created and listed over the past few years: LEAPS®, CAPS®, End-of-Quarter, and FLEX™ options.

These new products merit attention because they are more than the results of brainstorming sessions by rocket scientists; these products can be useful to investors for implementing various strategies. For instance, CAPS® options enable investors to enter into positions that normally require two securities to be transacted with a simple buy or sell order. This presents two clear advantages:

1. The investor does not have to buy or sell one security, and following confirmation that the first trade has been executed, sell/buy the second security.
2. In real life trading, where commissions can have a substantial impact on the profitability of a trade, buying or selling an index CAPS® can substantially reduce the transaction costs vis-à-vis establishing an equivalent position in index options.

It should not be concluded that CAPS® options are nothing but a way to trade index options with lower commissions. Some features of CAPS® differentiate them from index options, and these differences will be highlighted in a later section.

LEAPS®

In the consumer goods business, LEAPS® (Long-term Equity AnticiPation Securities) would not be classified as a new product but as a line extension. This would be a fairly accurate assessment as LEAPS® do not differ in any manner from regular puts and calls, except that their expiration date may be as many as 39 months away. These longer-term options could therefore be used to enter into all of the strategies described in Chapter 4. But does this make sense? Should all the strategies that we used with one-, three-, and six-month options be implemented with one- and two-year options? There is probably no easy answer to the above questions, but the next few pages cover a few of the strategies for which LEAPS® are most appropriate.

Before discussing strategies using LEAPS®, it is important to take a closer look at how time, volatility, dividends, and interest rates affect the prices of LEAPS®. One of the important points made in the fundamentals chapter (see page 32) is the relationship between an at-the-money option's time premium and the number of days to expiration. It has already been shown that if a 30-day option has a value of $1, a 60-day option will have an approximate value of $1 \times \sqrt{2} = 1.41$. Extending the time decay line to longer-term options, we obtain the following approximate values:

If the 1-month option = $1 then the 2-month option = $1 \times \sqrt{2} =$ 1.41

If the 1-month option = $1 then the 3-month option = $1 \times \sqrt{3} =$ 1.73

If the 1-month option = $1 then the 12-month option = $1 \times \sqrt{12} =$ 3.46

If the 1-month option = $1 then the 24-month option = $1 \times \sqrt{24} =$ 4.90

If the 1-month option = $1 then the 36-month option = $1 \times \sqrt{36} =$ 6.00

From the above data, we can conduct the following analysis (which assumes that all factors remain constant except the passage of time):

	Shorter-Term Options	LEAPS®
Value and time to expiration	$1.73/3 months	$6.00/36 months
Assume position is held for	1 month	12 months
New value and time to expiration	$1.41/2 months	$4.90/24 months
Percent decrease in option value	18.5%	18.3%

The table above shows us that a three-month at-the-money option will lose 18.5 percent of its value after one month, all other things being equal. A three-year at-the-money option will lose 18.3 percent of its value after one year. It is important to understand that an at-the-money option will lose just over 18 percent of its value during the first third of its life.

The difference between LEAPS® and shorter-term options is the absolute value of "first third of its life". In the above example, the shorter-term option lost 18 percent of its value in 1 month, whereas the LEAPS® lost the same percentage over 12 months. This clearly shows how time will erode a LEAPS® premium: proportionately no differently than a shorter-term option, absolutely over a much longer time frame.

From the above, one may be tempted to conclude that LEAPS® should be bought and not sold. And although LEAPS® are a natural for some buy-side strategies, the rationale of selling them will be made in a subsequent section.

The fundamentals chapter (Chapter 2) showed how volatility, dividends, and short-term interest rates were three of the factors that changed the theoretical values of options. These factors also affect the prices of LEAPS®, but whereas with shorter-term options volatility was the most prevalent of these three variables, with LEAPS® dividends and interest rates have a more marked effect. To gauge this phenomenon, assume the following:

Stock price = $50

Volatility = 30 percent

Strike price = $50

Annual dividend = $1.24

Short-term interest rate = 3.5 percent

From the above, we can calculate the following option values, using the Black-Scholes option pricing model.

Value of 3-month call = $3.03	Value of 36-month call = $10.09
Assume volatility rises to 31%	Assume volatility rises to 31%
Value of 3-month call = $3.13	Value of 36-month call = $10.39
Percent change in call value = +3.3%	Percent change in call value = +2.97%
Assume short-term interest rates rise to 4.0%	Assume short-term interest rates rise to 4.0%
Value of 3-month call = $3.06	Value of 36-month call = $10.37
Percent change in call value = +0.99%	Percent change in call value = +2.78%
Assume dividend is increased to $1.48	Assume dividend is increased to $1.48
Value of 3-month call = $3.00	Value of 36-month call = $9.68
Percent change in call value = −0.99%	Percent change in call value = −4.06%

The effect of a change in volatility is about the same on the shorter-term option and the LEAPS®; a 1-percent increase in expected volatility results in a 3-percent increase in the price of both options. But changes in interest rates and dividends have a markedly more profound effect on the LEAPS® than on the shorter-term option. A rise of 1/2 of 1 percent in interest rates increases the value of the short term call by about 1 percent and the value of the LEAPS® by close to 3 percent; raising the yield of the underlying stock by 0.48 percent reduces the value of the short-term option by 1 percent and that of the LEAPS® by 4 percent.

So although one cannot ignore volatility in the pricing and trading of longer-term options, one must give substantially more weight to possible changes in interest rates and dividend yield.

A final note on the effects of dividends and interest rates on the pricing of LEAPS®. The dividend amount used in option pricing models is the dividend that will be paid during the lifetime of the option. For a short-term option, this amount can be known with relative accuracy: most corporations have a set dividend policy, the dividends are paid on regular quarterly dates, and market participants know when to expect dividend increases. In other words, there are few major surprises.

But when one wants to price a longer-term option, the uncertainty about the future flow of dividends increases. What will ABC Corporation's dividend be three years from now? Will the dividend continue to be increased at the same rate it has been increased in the past? Could external events force the corporation to cut or eliminate its dividend? And in the case of a company that currently does not pay any dividend, could the board of directors declare an initial and subsequent regular dividends?

The longer an option's time to expiration, the greater the uncertainty about the underlying's future dividend flow becomes, making the pricing of these options somewhat more complex.

The same uncertainty exists regarding short-term interest rates. The input required by option pricing models is the short-term risk-free rate, commonly accepted to be the Treasury-bill rate. It is easy to determine what the risk-free rate is today, and one can make the assumption that this rate will not vary greatly over the next month or two. But what about over the next three years? Where will T bill rates be 24, 30, or 36 months from now? The same uncertainty that exists as to the future flow of dividends presents itself as to the future level of short-term interest rates. These factors make it somewhat more difficult to calculate the theoretical values of longer-term options.

One last theoretical concept that merits our attention is that of delta. In Chapter 2, the concepts of delta and gamma were explained. Those who have fully grasped these two concepts will quickly understand that LEAPS® have lower gammas than the equivalent short-term options. If you have not yet mastered the Greek alphabet, the next paragraph will try to clarify these concepts.

The delta of an option is the price change in the option's value that can be expected for a $1 price change in the underlying stock. For example, based on the assumptions below, a 3-month at-the-money call will have a delta of 0.53, and a 36-month at-the-money call a delta of 0.58. This means that if the price of the underlying stock goes up $1, the theoretical value of the 3-month call should rise by $0.53 and that of the 36-month call by $0.58. But as was seen in Chapter 2, deltas are not static. As the calls go further in-the-money, the 3- and 36-month options will see both of their deltas approach 1.00. The major difference is that the delta of the 3-month option will rise to 1.00 much more rapidly than that of the 36-month option. This can best be seen in Figure 5–1, which graphs the deltas of a 3- and a 36-month option for various stock prices. The assumptions made in calculating the options' deltas are:

Strike price = $50
Annual dividend = $1.24
Volatility = 30 percent
Short-term interest rates = 3.5 percent

Figure 5–1 is important in understanding how the value of a long-term option will behave as the price of the underlying fluctuates. As a call goes in-the-money, its delta will rise more slowly than that of a comparable short-term option. Buyers and writers of long-term call options should be fully aware of this phenomenon and should anticipate the smaller price changes associated with LEAPS®.

The above discussion focused on the deltas of shorter- and longer-term call options. The same conclusions can be drawn regarding shorter- and longer-term put options. As the price of the underlying stock declines, the delta of a longer-term put option can be expected to increase less rapidly than that of the equivalent shorter-term put.

We asked earlier if all option strategies could be initiated using LEAPS®. A better question would probably have been to ask which option strategies best lend themselves to the longer-term nature of LEAPS®. In the following pages we give four examples of LEAPS®

FIGURE 5–1
Deltas of 3- and 36-Month Call Options

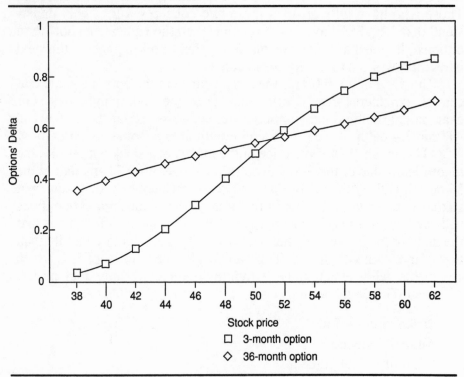

Buying Calls as an Alternative to Using Margin

applications. These in no way represent the best LEAPS® strategies or the only appropriate ones. They are intended to show how flexible longer-term options can be, and this brief inventory should by no means be considered exhaustive.

Buying Calls as an Alternative to Using Margin

In order to leverage a stock purchase, certain investors buy shares on margin, that is, they put up only a fraction of the full value of the stock purchased and borrow the balance of the required funds from their broker. Current margin regulations permit an investor to borrow up to 50 percent of the market value of the purchased securities. To understand why an investor would want to borrow part of the purchase price of an equity position, compare the returns obtained by the following two investors: investor A buys 200 shares of XYZ Corp. at $50 and pays the

TABLE 5–1

Price of XYZ Corp.	Investor A			Investor B			
	Value of 200 Shares	Profit	Return on Investment (%)	Value of 400 Shares	Financing Cost	Profit	Return on Investment (%)
$50	$10,000	$ 0	0%	$20,000	$(100)	$ (100)	−1%
52	10,400	400	4	20,800	(100)	700	7
54	10,800	800	8	21,600	(100)	1,500	15
56	11,200	1,200	12	22,400	(100)	2,300	23
58	11,600	1,600	16	23,000	(100)	3,100	31
60	12,000	2,000	20	24,000	(100)	3,900	39

full cost of $10,000. He holds the stock for a three-month period, and then resells it. Investor B buys 400 shares of XYZ Corp. at $50, puts up $10,000 and borrows an additional $10,000 from his broker. His cost of funds is 4 percent per annum, and he also resells the stock after three months.

Table 5–1 gives the profits and returns on funds invested for both investors when the price of XYZ Corp. remains unchanged or advances. As can be clearly seen, for all stock prices above $50, investor B's return as a percent of funds invested is greater than investor A's. This is the attraction of leverage.

But, as many have found out at their own expense, leverage works both ways. Table 5–2 gives the returns on investment for the investors when the price of XYZ Corp., contrary to their expectations, declines.

Does Table 5–2 mean that purchasing stocks on margin is a "bad" strategy and should not be used? No. What it means is that there is considerable risk in using margin when purchasing stocks, and only

TABLE 5–2

Price of XYZ Corp.	Investor A			Investor B			
	Value of 200 Shares	Loss	Return on Investment (%)	Value of 400 Shares	Financing Cost	Loss	Return on Investment (%)
$50	$10,000	$ 0	0%	$20,000	$(100)	$ (100)	−1%
48	9,600	(400)	−4	19,200	(100)	(900)	−9
46	9,200	(800)	−8	18,400	(100)	(1,700)	−17
44	8,800	(1,200)	−12	17,600	(100)	(2,500)	−25
42	8,400	(1,600)	−16	16,800	(100)	(3,300)	−33
40	8,000	(2,000)	−20	16,000	(100)	(4,100)	−41

those investors who are able to sustain this amount of risk should engage in leveraged purchases.

For those investors who are capable of taking on this high amount of risk, LEAPS® offer an alternative to purchasing shares on margin. Taking the example above, on a $50 stock, paying no dividends, with a volatility of 30 percent, the following LEAPS® could be available:

24-month $50 call = 10

24-month $35 call = 18 3/4

An investor could replicate the purchase of 400 shares using 50 percent margin by buying four of the 24-month $35 calls at 18 3/4. The cost of these options would be $7,500 (400 × 18 3/4). Table 5–3 compares the results of the LEAPS® purchase to those of buying the stock on margin. Because the purchase of the four LEAPS® requires only $7,500 versus the $10,000 needed to buy 400 shares on margin, it is assumed that the LEAPS® buyer maintains $2,500 in cash, making both initial investments worth $10,000. We have also assumed that no interest is earned on this $2,500 cash balance.

Compare the two far right-hand columns in Table 5–3. The returns from the LEAPS® purchase and from the stock purchased on margin are virtually the same. It is therefore possible to replicate a margin purchase through the use of longer-term options. Two questions come to mind: why bother with options since the above numbers do not appear to

TABLE 5–3

Stock Price	LEAPS Price	Value of LEAPS	Cash	Profit (Loss)	Return on Investment (%)	Return on Investment: Stock Purchased on Margin (%)
$60	$27 1/2	$11,000	$2,500	$3,500	+35%	39%
58	25 5/8	10,250	2,500	2,750	+27	31
56	23 3/4	9,500	2,500	2,000	+20	23
54	21 7/8	8,750	2,500	1,250	+12.5	15
52	20	8,000	2,500	500	+5	7
50	18 1/4	7,300	2,500	(200)	−2	−1
48	16 1/2	6,600	2,500	(900)	−9	−9
46	14 3/4	5,900	2,500	(1,600)	−16	−17
44	13 1/8	5,250	2,500	(2,250)	−22.5	−25
42	11 1/2	4,600	2,500	(2,900)	−29	−33
40	10	4,000	2,500	(3,500)	−35	−41

indicate any advantage of this strategy over the margin stock purchase, and second, why use LEAPS® in an example where the time horizon is three months?

Let's first answer the latter question. The time frame in our example was three months. But this may not have been the original time frame of the investor when the position was initiated. Often an investor will be bullish on a particular equity but may be unsure as to exactly when the stock's potential will be realized. Using LEAPS® can be the appropriate strategy when the expected timing of an anticipated move cannot be determined with certainty or is expected to occur over the longer term.

Last comes the question of why LEAPS® should be considered as a substitute to a purchase on margin. There are two differences between using LEAPS® and buying stock on margin: interest costs and the possibility of margin calls.

The buyer of LEAPS® knows exactly what his maximum outlay will be. The longer-term options must be fully paid for initially and represent the maximum cost until the LEAPS® expire. The investor who purchases stocks on margin must pay interest on the funds borrowed, usually on a monthly basis. The full extent of these financing costs cannot be known initially because interest rates may fluctuate from month to month. Second, if an investor fully margins a stock position by borrowing the maximum 50 percent permitted, he subjects himself to the possibility of margin calls. The amount of money a broker will lend is based on the current value of the stock held as collateral. If the value of the stock declines, the value of the maximum loan permitted falls, and the investor must make up the shortfall by depositing additional cash or marketable securities. This is known as a *margin call* and can be as much a psychological strain as it is a financial one. The LEAPS® buyer does not risk an eventual margin call.

One last point that can be made in favor of LEAPS®: they permit the investor to adjust the amount of leverage desired over a wider range. By purchasing stock on margin, the investor's margin requirement can range from 100 percent (purchasing stock on a full cash basis) to 50 percent (borrowing the maximum allowed from a broker). LEAPS® can further reduce the margin required; in our example the 35 LEAPS® calls were purchased for 18 3/4 or 37.5 percent of the stock price. Of course, increasing the amount of leverage used will raise both the potential returns and the risk assumed. It is for each individual investor to determine the amount of risk they are willing to take on.

Covered Writing

At first glance, using LEAPS® for covered writing may appear counterintuitive. Time decay is slowest for longer-term options. So why
would one write LEAPS®, which will, when first sold, show very little
time erosion? Consider the following example.

Stock price = $52
3-month 55 strike call = $2
Dividend = none
24-month 55 strike call = $9

Ignoring the impact of commissions, covered writes using the above
stock and options give us the following potential returns.

	3-Month Call	24-Month Call
Return if stock unchanged (annualized)	16.0%	10.5%
Return if calls assigned (annualized)	40.0%	14.0%

The three-month call shows higher annualized returns both for a static
stock price and for when the investor is assigned. Once again we ask,
what can be the justification for using LEAPS® in a covered write?

The short-term option has potential annualized returns of 16 percent (stock static) and 40 percent (calls assigned). But these potential
returns are only for a three-month period and represent actual returns of
4 percent (static) and 10 percent (assigned). What happens after this
initial three-month period? Assuming that the stock is unchanged, the
investor would have to sell another three-month call with a strike price
of 55 at $2 to generate the same return over the next three months.
There is obviously no guarantee that the investor will be able to sell a
second three-month call option for $2. Maybe option prices will be
lower because of lower anticipated volatility. Maybe the price of the
stock will have moved down a point or two depressing the call premium.

Of course other factors in the marketplace could mean that after
three months the investor would be in a position to sell a second three-
month call at a price higher than the initial one at $2. But the fact
remains that the short-term covered write has a risk. We may want to

call this reinvestment risk, roll-over risk, or premium risk; the name is of little importance. The risk is real.

The investor using LEAPS® to establish a covered write reduces this investment risk. He has written a $9 option and locked in his potential static and called returns for the next 24 months. Covered writes using LEAPS® should appeal to more conservative investors whose prime focus is consistency of returns.

Here is another example of how LEAPS® can be used to initiate a covered write. Assume a $52 stock price, no dividends, and a 30 percent volatility; the following options could then be listed:

	3-Month Calls	24-Month Calls
Strike = 55	$2	$9
Strike = 65	$ 5/16	$5 5/8
Strike = 75	$ 1/16	$3 5/8

An investor could be reluctant to sell either the 3-month or 24-month option struck at 55 because she believes the stock will rally to a higher price. On the other hand, she would not hesitate to sell a 65 or a 75 call whose strike prices are closer to her fundamental target price. In this situation, selling a three-month option makes little economic sense: the premium is so low that selling this option would not produce a significant dollar amount in absolute terms.

This example illustrates another advantage of LEAPS®: the possibility of selecting strike prices that are meaningful to the investor and still maintain the economic viability of the trade.

Although no covered write should be initiated by purchasing a stock on which the investor does not have a favorable fundamental opinion, this point needs to be emphasized when using LEAPS® as part of a covered write. In the above examples, the investors are entering into a two-year strategy. They should have a fundamental opinion that is favorable over the next two years. Finally, it should be noted that these long-term covered writes do not bind the investor for the full two-year period. Should the investors' opinions on the stock change to such an extent that they no longer wish to hold these stocks as part of their portfolios, the covered write can be completely unwound by repurchasing the written option and selling the stock.

Purchasing Long-Term Insurance

Using put options to insure equity holdings is certainly not a novel proposition. Using LEAPS® put options to insure stocks addresses two of the concerns investors have when purchasing short-term put options: the timing decision and the annualized cost.

More than one investor has forecasted a marked decline in the price of a stock and seen that same stock head south shortly after his put options expired. By purchasing LEAPS®, the element of timing, so crucial when buying and selling shorter-term options, becomes less critical. And if the anticipated correction does not materialize, there is no need to hold the put options until expiration; there is a secondary market where they can be resold once one's opinion has reverted back to bullish.

One of the most often heard arguments against purchasing puts as insurance is the relatively high cost of the options on an annualized basis. Let's look at an example with the following assumptions:

Stock price = $52
Volatility = 30 percent
Strike price = 50
Interest rates = 3.5 percent
Dividend = none

Using a standard option pricing model, we get the following values:

Time to Expiration (Months)	Option Premium	Premium as % of Stock Price	Annualized Premium as % of Stock Price
1	7/8	1.75%	21%
2	1 1/2	3.00	18
3	2	4.00	16
6	3	6.00	12
12	4 1/4	8.50	8.5
24	5 7/8	11.75	5.9
36	6 7/8	13.75	4.6

The investor who insures his holdings for a three-month period, for example, must pay an option premium equal to 4 percent of the stock price, or an annualized cost of insuring of 16 percent. For too many investors this cost appears prohibitive. But, as the table clearly demonstrates, the annualized cost of insuring holdings diminishes the longer the term to expiration.

What if an investor does not need insurance for the longer term but is only concerned about a correction over, say, the next six months. It may still make sense for an investor to purchase LEAPS® as insurance, hold them over the term desired, and resell them if the anticipated correction does not materialize.

For example, consider a portfolio manager who expects the price of a stock to move down over the next six months but is not willing or able to sell this stock. The first solution that comes to mind is that he should purchase a six-month put at $3. But he could also purchase a 12-month put at 4 1/4 and hold it for a 6-month period.

In six months, if the stock is unchanged he can resell the longer-term option, which would then still have six months to go before expiration. Assuming other factors remain the same, he could resell this option at 3, for a net cost of insuring his position of 1 1/4. Had he purchased the six-month option and the stock remained unchanged, his insurance cost would have been $3.

Of course this lower cost of insurance does have a flip side: if the price of the stock declines, the protection offered by the put option will be lower since its initial cost was higher. So the lower cost of insuring through the purchase of the 12-month put option resulted in a reduction in coverage offered by this option.

The preceeding example demonstrated how longer-term options can reduce the annualized cost of insurance. Is this true for all options? It must be pointed out that the option used was close to the money: the option had a strike price of 50 when the stock price was 52. What if the manager had only been looking for "disaster" insurance and only wanted to protect against a major downdraft in the stock price? What if a $45 strike price had been more suited to his needs? Consider the table at the top of the next page for a $45 strike price when the stock is at $52.

The annualized premium column is quite revealing. As time to expiration increases, the annualized cost of insurance at first increases and then decreases. A 2-month and a 24-month option have very similar annualized costs. The one-month option has the lowest annualized cost, although the low premium level is the one that would be most affected by the bid-ask spread.

The preceding discussion offers no panacea to the investor looking to insure certain holdings. What it reveals are the numerous possibilities

Time to Expiration (Months)	Option Premium	Premium as % of Stock Price	Annualized Premium as % of Stock Price
1	1/16	0.13%	1.50%
2	5/16	0.63	3.75
3	9/16	1.13	4.50
6	1 5/16	2.63	5.25
12	2 3/8	4.75	4.75
24	3 7/8	7.75	3.88
36	4 3/4	9.50	3.17

available based on the investor's desired level of protection and time frame. Before purchasing puts as insurance, an investor should create tables similar to ones in this section to help determine which option series best fits his current needs.

Purchasing a Collar

At times, especially in a low interest rate environment, some stock yields may compare favorably to the yields available on short-term money-market instruments such as Treasury bills.

An argument can then be made for purchasing such high-yielding stocks. But then a different problem surfaces: risk of loss of principal. Yield-oriented investors are usually risk averse and unwilling to risk their principal. A possible solution is to insure the investment through the purchase of put options. However, a new problem arises: puts cost money, although as seen in the previous section, it is possible to reduce the annualized cost of insurance through the purchase of close-to-the-money longer-term options. But what if even this cost is considered too high?

The cost of insurance can be further reduced if an investor is willing to forgo the upside potential from a given point onwards. This is accomplished by selling a call option in addition to purchasing a put option. This strategy is known as a *collar*, a *hedgewrap*, or a *fence*, and can best be illustrated by the following example.

Stock price = $52
24-month 55 call = $7
Stock yield = 3.5%
24-month 50 put = $7

A yield-oriented investor can purchase the above stock and at the same time buy the two-year 50 put and write the two-year 55 call. The two option transactions are done at the same price, so the stock price becomes the initial cost of the whole position.

Because the investor has purchased a 50 put, the risk on the stock is now limited to $2. The written call reduces the upside potential to $3, from the current $52 to the $55 strike price. What the investor has done is capture the stock's yield over the next two years with limited risk to principal and limited upside potential.

Two risks of this position must be underscored: the possibility of early exercise on the calls and the safety of the dividend.

Early assignment on calls is relatively rare but does occur more often with higher-yielding stocks. Should the stock price rise significantly above the $55 call strike price, it would be possible for the investor to get assigned early and see the position unwound before its full two-year term.

Finally, if an investor is committing to this strategy for two years, he should feel reasonably secure that the current dividend will be maintained or increased over this period. Fundamental research, not options, is required here.

INDEX LEAP®

The four previous examples illustrated some of the uses of equity LEAPS®. Also listed on the options exchanges are LEAPS® options on various indices. These index LEAPS® are similar to the shorter-term index options except for their further out expiration dates and the fact that, for the most part, they trade off and settle on a long-term index equal to one-tenth of the underlying index of the corresponding shorter-term options.

To illustrate this last point, consider the options on the Standard & Poor's 100 Index (OEX). Assume that the cash OEX index is at 400. The index underlying the longer-term S&P 100 options will therefore be at 40 (400 ÷ 10), and one would expect to have index LEAPS® with strike prices of 37 1/2, 40, and 42 1/2 listed for trading. It therefore follows that 10 OEX LEAPS® cover the same value of underlying as one short-term OEX contract.

Index LEAPS® offer opportunities to investors looking to establish a long-term position in the overall market or in one market sector, or who are looking to insure their holdings for a longer period of time. All in all, index LEAPS® add to the multifarious alternatives made available to both institutional and individual investors.

CAPS®

If one were asked to define CAPS® options in the briefest terms, the most succinct formula would probably be: "packaged index bull and bear spreads." As we shall see, this definition does not capture all of the intricacies of CAPS® but certainly conveys its essence.

CAPS® are currently listed on the Standard & Poor's 100 Index, the Standard & Poor's 500 Index, the Institutional Index, and the Major Market Index. There are CAPS® calls and CAPS® puts, with the former being akin to call spreads and the latter akin to put spreads. An illustration will best explain how CAPS® work.

Assume the Standard & Poor's 100 Index (OEX) cash index is at 405. An investor can take a moderately bullish stance in the options market by purchasing a three-month 400 call and by simultaneously writing a three-month 430 call. This, as we have seen in Chapter 4, is a bull call spread. An alternative to this bull call spread would be the 400–430 CAPS® call. This CAPS® call is similar to the 400/430 call spread in that *its risk is limited to the initial price paid for the CAPS®* and *its maximum value is 30 points*. But the CAPS® differs from the call spread as follows:

- The buyer of the CAPS® cannot exercise it prior to expiration, whereas the investor who has purchased the 400/430 call spread on the OEX can exercise the long leg of the spread or be assigned on the short leg at any time.
- At expiration, the CAPS® will be automatically exercised if the cash index closes at any level above 400. The CAPS® will settle in cash, and the settlement value will be equal to the cash index level minus 400 if the cash index closes at 430 or lower, or 30 points if the cash index closes above 430. In other words, the settlement value will be equivalent to the in-the-money amount as determined from the lower strike price of the CAPS® (i.e., 400), up to a maximum of 30 points (i.e., the capped level reached at 430).
- The CAPS® option will be automatically exercised prior to expiration if the underlying index closes at or above the option's cap price of 430.

Primarily, it is the differences in when CAPS® options are exercised that differentiate them from standard bull and bear spreads. CAPS® are European type options as long as the underlying index remains below the cap price on a closing basis. But once the cap price is reached (on a closing basis), CAPS® are automatically exercised.

Based on the exercise characteristics of CAPS®, should a 400–430 CAPS® call be worth more, less, or the same as a 400/430 bull call spread? It is possible to answer this question without taking a course in advanced mathematics. Ask yourself the following question: when will the CAPS® and the bull spread trade at or be worth their maximum value?

Prior to expiration, a 400/430 bull call spread will be worth or will trade at 30 only if the index is above 430 and there is no time value left in the short 430 calls. This will occur only if the time to expiration is quite short or the index has moved substantially above the 430 level.

A 400–430 CAPS®, on the other hand, will be worth its maximum value on the first day the underlying index closes at or above 430.

A second point to keep in mind is that the index has to close above the capped price only once for the CAPS® to reach its maximum value. With a call spread, the index could trade above the upper strike price on a number of occasions, but if it has moved back below that level at expiration, the spread may be worth less than its potential maximum.

The above two arguments lead us to conclude that the odds of a CAPS® call reaching its maximum value are greater than those of the equivalent bull spread reaching its maximum value. This would appear to make the CAPS® more valuable, and this is what has been observed in the marketplace so far.

It should be noted that CAPS® are not available for all strike price intervals listed in the equivalent index options. For example, capped OEX options are currently listed with 30 point intervals (such as the 400–430 interval in our example) and with specific expiration months.

Strategy Equivalencies

CAPS® will let investors replicate some of the strategies explained in the previous chapter with more ease and sometimes lower transaction costs. The purchase or sale of a CAPS® is equivalent to two call or put transactions; but the CAPS® is bought or sold at one price, making the transaction somewhat more straightforward.

The equivalencies given below are subject to the different exercise characteristics of CAPS® and index options. Investors should be aware of the different risks of early exercise (for index options) and of automatic exercise (for CAPS®) before entering into any of these strategies.

Index Option Strategy	Equivalent CAPS® Strategy	
Bull call spread	Long	CAPS® Call
Bear call spread	Short	CAPS® Call
Bear put spread	Long	CAPS® Put
Bull put spread	Short	CAPS® Put

In addition to these basic spreading strategies, CAPS® can be used to replicate more complex ones such as butterflies and condors. We shall illustrate one such possibility, the long butterfly, but the interested reader should, as an exercise, replicate a short butterfly and both long and short condors using CAPS®.

A long butterfly, as was seen in the last chapter, consists of the purchase of a call with a lower strike price, the sale of two calls with a middle strike price, and the purchase of one call with a higher strike price. It was also pointed out that an equivalent position used all puts. The importance of this equivalency will become apparent shortly.

Assume an investor is looking to replicate a 370–400–430 butterfly. The first equivalent strategy that comes to mind using call CAPS® is to purchase the 370–400 CAPS® call, and to sell the 400–430 CAPS® call. The problem with this position is that if the index closes above 400, the 370–400 CAPS® call will be automatically exercised, leaving the investor short the 400–430 CAPS® call. To circumvent this problem, one must use one CAPS® call and one CAPS® put in constructing the CAPS® butterfly. This is done by selling the 400–430 CAPS® call as described above and also selling the 370–400 CAPS® put. Note that the purchase of a butterfly using CAPS® is arrived at by the sale of two CAPS®.

This CAPS® butterfly will have a pay-off diagram with the same shape as the pay-off diagram that uses index options, although one would expect the CAPS® butterfly to have a slightly higher profit potential. This reflects the fact that, as noted above, one expects CAPS® to trade at a higher price level than the equivalent option spread.

This slightly higher profit potential is offset by the risk of automatic exercise, and of the additional risk of double exercise. If an investor constructs a 370–400–430 CAPS® butterfly, the CAPS® call would be automatically exercised if the index moved above 430, and the CAPS® put would be automatically exercised on a closing index value of 370 or lower. There is therefore a risk that half the butterfly could collapse before expiration on a move to one of the outer strike prices.

There is a small risk that the investor will be assigned on both the CAPS® put and call. Assume, in the case of a 370–400–430 butterfly, that the market at first rises strongly and closes above 430. The 400–430 CAPS® call is then automatically exercised, the investor with the short position assigned and his account debited 30 points ($3,000). If at that point the market reverses direction, and moves to or below the 370 level, the 370-400 CAPS® put would then also be automatically exercised, and the investor with the short position would have his account debited another 30 points ($3,000).

This means that the actual risk of a 370–400–430 CAPS® butterfly is 60 points less the initial premium received, not 30 points less the initial premium. Although the risk of a double assignment is relatively low, it must be kept in mind. The best way to prevent such an event happening is to close out the remaining CAPS® should the first be assigned. For example, with a 370–400–430 CAPS® butterfly, if the market rallies to or above 430, the short 370–400 CAPS® put should be repurchased. Since the CAPS® put to be repurchased will then be at least 30 points out-of-the-money, one can expect it to be trading at a relatively low premium.

Finally, the following table gives CAPS® positions that are equivalent (except for the different exercise characteristics) to some of the more complex option strategies of the previous chapter. Strike prices are used to clarify the illustrations.

	Option Strategy		Equivalent CAPS® Strategy
Long	370–400–430 butterfly	Short Short	400–430 CAPS® call and 370–400 CAPS® put
Short	370–400–430 butterfly	Long Long	400–430 CAPS® call and 370–400 CAPS® put
Long	360–390–420–450 condor	Short Short	420–450 CAPS® call and 360–390 CAPS® put
Short	360–390–420–450 condor	Long Long	420–450 CAPS® call and 360–390 CAPS® put

OTHER NEW PRODUCTS

LEAPS® were first listed in October 1990 and CAPS® in November 1991. Since then, a number of new products have either been listed or should be listed shortly. This section gives a brief description of the latest newcomers to the world of derivatives.

FLEX™ Options

Listed in February 1993, FLEX™ Options (FLexible EXchange options) offer larger market participants the ultimate in option flexibility: the ability to set the expiration date up to five years from creation (with the exception of few black-out dates), the exercise style (American, European, or Capped), the strike price, and the settlement value determination of options on the Standard & Poor's 100, Standard & Poor's 500, and Russell 2000 indices. Because of the minimum size requirement ($10,000,000 of notional principal), these options are not for the smaller investors.

For years, a growing number of participants have turned to the over-the-counter options market when listed options did not meet their specific needs. An OTC option dealer would customize an option contract to the user's exact specifications, and an agreement would be struck. The options' terms would seldom be identical to those of listed options, meaning greater flexibility, but the end-user would have to assume counterparty risk.

Listed options are guaranteed by The Options Clearing Corporation (which has been granted a triple A rating by Standard & Poor's), which will make good on an option if its writer becomes insolvent. An over-the-counter option is guaranteed by its issuer, whether a bank, investment dealer, or other financial institution. Should this party be unable to meet its obligations, the holder of the option has no immediate recourse.

FLEX™ options were designed to address this counterparty risk: they offer the same flexibility as OTC options, with the added security of the OCC's top-notch credit rating. FLEX™ options also play an essential role in the price discovery process. When an OTC option is transacted between two parties, the price of this option is not made public.

Any FLEX™ option traded results in the term and the premium of the option being publicly disseminated, informing all interested market participants of the exact level where business is presently being transacted.

End-of-Quarter Options

For a number of institutional users, index options that expire on the Saturday following the third Friday of an expiration month pose a problem: these institutions' accounting periods close at the end of the month, leaving a gap between an option's expiration and the close of the accounting period, or forcing the institution to trade options that extend beyond the end of the calendar's quarters. End-of-quarter options were listed in February 1993 to address this problem. They are currently available on the following indices: Standard & Poor's 500 (SPX), Major Market (XMI), Institutional (XII), and Mid-Cap (MID) indices. The terms of these options are similar to those of regular options except that they will trade until the close of business on the last business day of each quarter and that they will settle on the closing value of the index (SPX options, for example, currently settle on a value based on the opening price of all the component stocks).

End-of-quarter options therefore permit a perfect match of the hedge offered by the options and an institution's quarterly accounting periods.

The Volatility Index

The importance of volatility in option pricing has already been underscored and will be repeated in subsequent chapters. Implied volatility reflects the market's consensus as to expected volatility. But an accurate and readily available measure of implied volatility was at times difficult to obtain before the CBOE started disseminating the value of its volatility index (VIX) in January of 1993.

VIX measures the average weighted implied volatility of eight series of options on the Standard & Poor's 100 Index. The implied volatility of the two calls and two puts that are closest to the money in the near-term month and the two calls and two puts closest to the money in the second-nearest expiration month are averaged to determine the value of VIX.[1] As Figure 5–2 shows, implied volatility has ranged from a

---

[1] Options are removed from the index's calculation during their last week of trading to prevent distorting the index.

FIGURE 5–2
VIX: Historical Levels (1986–1993)

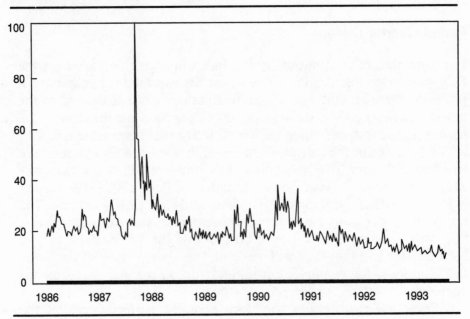

low of 8 percent to over 100 percent over the last 8 years. Chapter 9 discusses VIX in somewhat more detail.

As of this chapter's writing, options on VIX were not yet listed for trading, although this remains a possibility. VIX options would offer market participants the purest play on the market's volatility.

PART 2

TRADING
STRATEGIES

CHAPTER 6

OPTIONS FOR THE SMALL INVESTOR

An old riddle asks: What does everybody give and nobody take? The answer, of course, is advice!

The small investor is bombarded with advice about options. It ranges from dire dissuasions to paeans to the power of leverage. Unfortunately, the advice so proffered is seldom directed to small investors. Perhaps we should define their investment needs. Certainly advice is not needed on hedging portfolios of $500,000. Nor do they need to be told how to buy 50 calls on any one stock. Instead, this chapter speaks to intelligent people in the marketplace who lack more than the basics in option trading knowledge. For them, we can say: "Yes, you can improve your investing and trading techniques by the sensible utilization of options."

Let's start with someone who has been smart . . . a long position has been taken in a stock at $20 which has subsequently risen to $40. A *double* is nice, but perhaps the stock will move up even farther. For the cautious, a simple option technique such as the following can be very advantageous.

GETTING IN

The Protective Put

This strategy consists of simply buying one put for each hundred shares owned. In this example, you could buy a 40 strike put with an expiration of two to three months. This might cost about 1 1/2 to 2 points per put ($150 to $200). If the stock returned to $20, it could still be sold at $40 by exercising the put. If the stock continued to rise, the put could expire worthless or be sold for a small amount. There are, of course, some potential negatives here. If the stock stayed in a narrow band—very close to $40—the purchase would seem wasteful, but predicting the future successfully is very difficult, and the put acquisition *did* allow you to sleep at night without worrying about the subsequent move-ment—whether up or down—in the stock.

Opening this chapter with the protective put strategy emphasizes that options have more than one characteristic. While leverage is well known, the protective capacity of options is not. Options can be used to protect, to hedge, and even, as in this example, to insure.

The Married Put

This refers to the simultaneous purchase of both stock and equivalent number of puts on that stock. If these are identified with each other (often by a trailer on the brokerage confirmation), they are said to be *married*. At times, there has been a tax benefit to this technique, but this is not its sole advantage. *Warning*: No one should enter into any tax-related transaction without advice from a tax professional.

The married put is simply the protective put before the profit has accrued. If the stock, during the life of the put, rises by more than the put's cost, the investor will have a profit. If the stock should fall rather than rise, the loss will be limited to the stock's cost less the put's strike and the put's cost.

Example

Buy 500 shares of XYZ @ 31.

Buy 5 XYZ 3-month 30 puts @ 1.

Maximum loss would be (31 − 30) + 1, per hundred shares.

Phrased another way, you have bought two securities at a cost per hundred of $32 (31 + 1). By exercising the put, you can always recover $30. Therefore the maximum loss is 2 points or 6.25 percent of the initial investment. See Table 6–1.

Couldn't the same goal be accomplished by entering a *stop order* 6 percent below a purchase price? No. Stop orders, while beautiful in theory, do not always work so well in practice. A random sale of 100 shares can touch off a stop; a stop order can be filled at a price disturb-ingly below its expected level. When you own a put, *you* control the time and price at which your stock will be sold. The protective put can be especially attractive in four cases: (1) you are afraid of entering the market, (2) you want to buy the particular stock, but are nervous about

TABLE 6–1
Married Put

<table>
<tr><td colspan="5" align="center">XYZ   31   XYZ   3-month 30 put 1</td></tr>
<tr><td></td><td></td><td colspan="2" align="center">Profit/Loss</td></tr>
<tr><td>Percent Up/Down</td><td>Price at Expiration</td><td>Stock</td><td>Stock and Put</td></tr>
<tr><td>+20%</td><td>$37 1/4</td><td>+6 1/4</td><td>+5 1/4</td></tr>
<tr><td>+10</td><td>34 1/8</td><td>+3 1/8</td><td>+2 1/8</td></tr>
<tr><td>+5</td><td>32 1/2</td><td>+1 1/2</td><td>+ 1/2</td></tr>
<tr><td>–0–</td><td>31</td><td>–0–</td><td>–1</td></tr>
<tr><td>–5</td><td>29 1/2</td><td>–1 1/2</td><td>–2</td></tr>
<tr><td>–10</td><td>27 7/8</td><td>–3 1/8</td><td>–2</td></tr>
<tr><td>–20</td><td>24 3/4</td><td>–6 1/4</td><td>–2</td></tr>
</table>

both its current price and the possibility of its "getting away from you," (3) the stock involved is highly volatile, (4) the stock has a high dividend yield. In this example, if the stock were to go ex-dividend by 50 cents during the life of the put, the risk would be lowered to 1 1/2 points or 4.7 percent.

There are two common criticisms to counter for protective and married puts. When the stock rises, the Monday morning option quarterback says, "You didn't really need the puts and the money was wasted." This is akin, in our view, to the man who calls his insurance broker to complain that, after he bought home insurance, his house didn't burn down!

The second critic is more sophisticated. He says that the 2 to 5 percent cost for three-month protective puts is deceptive; the percentages should be annualized, producing adjusted figures of 8 to 20 percent. This is too expensive and so, he concludes, protective puts cost too much to be practical. Here the basic premise is wrong. You *always* want your house insured, but you need not always insure a stock or an accumulated profit. Protective puts are like every other option strategy: they should be used, not constantly, but when desirable.

Put Purchase versus Short Sale

The obvious way to hedge a short sale is with a long call in a position analogous to the married put. For the following reasons we deem a put purchase as greatly superior to a short sale:

FIGURE 6–1
Short XYZ @ 50 versus Long XYZ 50 Put @ 3

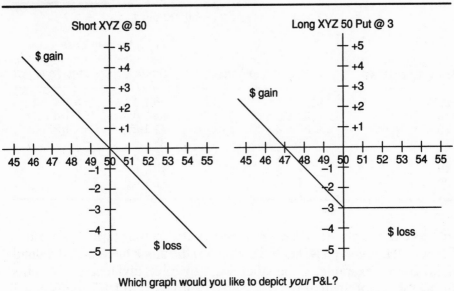

Which graph would you like to depict *your* P&L?

- Your loss is limited—you can lose at most the cost of the put; in the short sale your risk is unlimited.
- You do not need an uptick.
- You do not owe out dividends.
- You never receive a margin call.
- You cannot be panicked into covering.
- You do not have a stop order touched off or filled badly.
- You cannot be involuntarily "bought in" (forced to repurchase the stock).

See Figure 6–1.

BUYING CALLS

With the reams of literature on call buying, is there really anything new to say on the subject? Yes.

First, make sure the call you have selected really fits your expectations for the stock's movement. If you are trying to "scalp" a few points from the stock, you probably shouldn't buy a call at all. If you are looking for a modest rise, you should buy a slightly-in-the-money call. If you anticipate a very large move in the stock, you can buy a slightly-out-of-the-money call. Finally, if you are predicting an absolutely fabulous move in a very brief time (for example, from a takeover), you can contemplate a far-out-of-the-money call. The last strategy should be used sparingly; too often it results in that dreaded actualization of the oft-voiced theoretical warning: loss of 100 percent of investment.

Assume you are considering buying calls on each of three different stocks. They are all trading at the same price—42—but are otherwise quite dissimilar. They are very different in expected *volatility* (how violently or placidly the stock will fluctuate), and you have various expectations for them.

Modest Company	Average volatility	Expected rise—"moderate"
Largemove Inc.	Above average volatility	Expected rise—"healthy"
Fabulous Possibility Co.	Very high volatility	Expected rise—"super"

	2-month calls		
	40	45	50
Modest Company	4	1 3/8	1/8
Largemove Inc.	5	1 3/4	1/4
Fabulous Possibility Co.	6	2 1/4	1/2

Note: Underscore indicates suggested call.

If you are correct in your expectations, you might see moves like this:

Modest Company	+10%	to	46
Largemove Inc.	+15%	to	48 1/4
Fabulous Possibility Co.	+30%	to	55 1/4

		Calls at Expiration			Increase		
		40	45	50	40	45	50
Modest	46	6	1	0	50%	−27%	−100%
Largemove	48 1/4	8 1/4	3 1/4	0	65	86	−100
Fabulous	55 1/4	15 1/4	10 1/4	5 1/4	154	356	950

Note: Underscore indicates suggested call.

Note that, with the expected moves fulfilled, money might be made on many calls (but not usually on far-out-of-the-money). The percentage gain worked out best when the type of call was matched with the expected move.

Of course, you must also note that life sometimes has its little disappointments. If, for example, any of the stocks ended unchanged at 42 you would lose respectively 50, 100, and 100 percent on the three choices.

This is an excellent place to take cognizance of an important point. Buying equal *numerical* amounts of calls is being discussed here. If you had bought equal *dollar* amounts of calls, that would have greatly improved the performance of the farther-out-of-the-money calls. Do not equivocate: that is an extraordinarily **dangerous** way to trade options. When your losses can run to 50 percent or even 100 percent of your investment, you should take care that the loss will be a relatively small dollar amount.

EXPIRATION CYCLES

When *listed options* first began trading, they had quarterly expirations. These were the nearest three months of January, April, July, and October. Later, two other cycles were added: February, May, August, and November, and March, June, September, and December. When *index options* started trading, they expired on a monthly rather than quarterly basis. The popularity of sequential expirations led to the current system. A hybrid type is now used. Equity options all have four expirations (even though some newspapers print only three). These are the nearest two plus two additional taken from one of the original quarterly cycles.

Thus IBM, for instance, would have in January the nearest two months—January and February plus April and July. After the January expiration, the months would be February and March plus April and July. After the February expiration, there would be March and April plus July and October. See Table 6–2.

One result of this system is that you never have to buy the nearest month; there is always a second *spot month*. This is especially important when the near month is halfway or more through its evolution. You do not have to run the risk of the story on the stock materializing, but only after the call has expired. Instead, you can buy the next month out. And it will be only one month away, not three. Thus it won't cost much more, but will significantly increase the probability of making a profit.

TABLE 6–2
Cycles

When Spot Month is	Expiration Months Will Be		
	(newly added month in boldface)		
January	Jan **Feb** Apr Jul	Jan Feb May **Aug**	Jan **Feb** Mar Jun
February	Feb **Mar** Apr Jul	Feb **Mar** May Aug	Feb Mar Jun **Sep**
March	Mar Apr Jul **Oct**	May **Apr** May Aug	Mar **Apr** Jun Sep
April	Apr **May** Jul Oct	Apr May Aug **Nov**	Apr **May** Jun Sep
May	May **Jun** Jul Oct	May **Jun** Aug Nov	May Jun Sep **Dec**
June	Jun Jul Oct **Jan**	Jun **Jul** Aug Nov	Jun **Jul** Sep Dec
July	Jul **Aug** Oct Jan	Jul Aug Nov **Feb**	Jul **Aug** Sep Dec
August	Aug **Sep** Oct Jan	Aug **Sep** Nov Feb	Aug Sep Dec **Mar**
September	Sep Oct Jan **Apr**	Sep **Oct** Nov Feb	Sep **Oct** Dec Mar
October	Oct **Nov** Jan Apr	Oct Nov Feb **May**	Oct **Nov** Dec Mar
November	Nov **Dec** Jan Apr	Nov **Dec** Feb May	Nov Dec Mar **Jun**
December	Dec Jan Apr **Jul**	Dec **Jan** Feb May	Dec **Jan** Mar Jun

Another new thing one can say about buying calls is to take advantage of their low price. No, we do not mean leverage. For example, the fact that a call sells for 10 percent of the price of its underlying stock does not mean you have to buy 10 calls for every 100 shares of stock you were planning to purchase. Instead, you could buy two calls on each of four or five stocks in the same industry. This strategy takes advantage of the lower prices, but for safety through diversification rather than for leverage. It allows you to participate in projected profits but removes the risk of "right church, wrong pew."

It is worth noting that the *package approach* will often do much better with options than with stocks. This is because with stocks, rises and falls could tend to cancel each other out. With options, the leverage

Stock	Price	Call (Market Strike)
Mammoth Mainframes	$150	$7 1/2
Colossal Computers Co.	90	4 1/2
Growing Graphics Group	50	3 1/2
Average Abacus Assoc.	40	3
Inflated Interactions, Inc.	30	2 1/2
Sprouting Systems	20	2

Note: Prices for calls and stocks do not have linear relationships because there are many different determinants involved.

effect operates on the upside while there is a limit to losses on the downside. Now look at the package approach for both computer stocks and their options.

Before continuing, it is necessary to note that the sum of these call premiums is $2,300. Buying four or five calls of each means investing on the order of magnitude of $10,000. The only people who should consider such an investment are those who are very familiar with the risks involved and who could afford the potential loss. This hypothetical example illustrates the advantage of the package approach. Still, you would have to be bullish on the market overall, very bullish on the computer group, and willing and able to monitor the positions closely. Here is a possible outcome:

	Stock at Expiration	Call Value	Call +/−	Stock +/−
Mammoth Mainframes	$170	$20	+12 1/2	+20
Colossal Computers Co.	80	0	− 4 1/2	−10
Growing Graphics Group	62	12	+ 8 1/2	+12
Average Abacus Assoc.	40	0	− 3	0
Inflated Interactions, Inc.	15	0	− 2 1/2	−15
Sprouting Systems	25	5	+ 3	+ 5
Total			+14	+12

The result: the option package is up more than the stock package. Even more important, the stock gain is 12/380 (3.2 percent), while the option gain is a whopping 14/23 (60.9 percent)!

COVERED CALL WRITING

Covered call writing refers to stock purchased (or owned) and an equivalent number of calls written against that position.

Example

Buy 500 XYZ @ 40.
Write 5 XYZ 6-month 40-strike Calls @ 4.

In order to see what the motivation for such a position is, we look at reward and risk. If the stock is above 40 at expiration, the call will be assigned (you will sell the stock at the agreed-upon price of 40). That is what was paid, so your profit (per hundred shares/1 call) would be $400. As a percentage, this is $400 earned on $3,600 deposited. (Only $3,600 is needed to pay for the stock; the other $400 is in the account from the call sale). This is a percentage return of 11.1 percent, which becomes 22.2 percent on an annualized basis. Returns are annualized in order to make uniform comparisons possible.

Now let's go back to our specific strategy. What's the risk you would take in exchange for this nice reward? There are two separate and indeed very different risks that a covered call writer takes. First and foremost, there is the risk that the stock will go down. In our example, if the stock were held to expiration and was then selling at, say 30, there would be a *loss*. Stock bought at forty and selling at thirty results in a one thousand dollar loss for each hundred shares. In this case, however, the loss would be somewhat attenuated by the call premium of $400. That would reduce the loss to only $600. But it would still be a *loss*. Thus we see the first risk as very similar to the risk of a far better-known strategy: owning stock.

The second risk can be seen if we again posit holding the stock until expiration, but this time assume that it is then trading at 70. How much money would be lost in that case? None. You would have to fulfill the terms of the contract—that is, deliver stock out at the agreed strike of 40. You would profit by the amount of the call premium—$400, but that would be all of the profit. Someone who had bought the stock and had not sold a call would have a greater profit: $3,000. This second risk, then, is one of opportunity, not of dollars.

In each of the two risks, the option premium can be regarded as a payment for assuming that risk. In the down case, it would cushion the loss. On the upside it would give you some profit to make up for missing a larger one. Now we see the conceptual answer: this strategy should be used by someone who believes the stock will go up, not down, over the life of the call. S/he also believes the rise will not be a substantial one. In brief, someone who could be labeled "mildly bullish." It also has to be someone who has an attitude toward risk that is very different from the one implicit in the profile of the call buyer. There is no question here of either tripling one's money or of losing anywhere near 100 percent of invested capital. The risk can be likened to a banker's risk. You—the covered call writer—are lending money. And the underlying stock is your collateral for the loan.

There are two final points to consider. First, do not let yourself be

FIGURE 6–2
Covered Write Comparisons

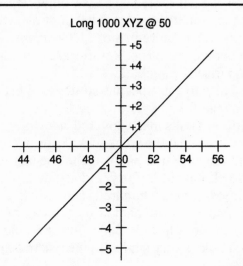

Long 1000 XYZ @ 50

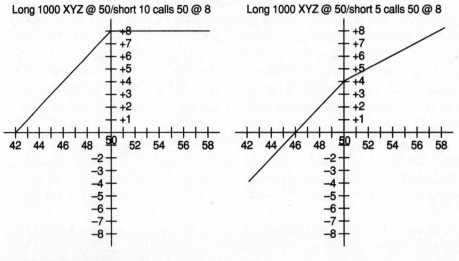

Long 1000 XYZ @ 50/short 10 calls 50 @ 8

Long 1000 XYZ @ 50/short 5 calls 50 @ 8

Note: Profit and loss in one point units.

seduced by the alleged return on a covered call write. Additional reward is always accompanied by additional risk. These high returns are not actually returns; they are projections of returns. These projections tacitly assume that the stock will not decline. This leads to an explicit rule: never write a call on a stock that you are not willing to own, even if it declines.

The other point goes back to opportunity risk. There have been a lot of takeovers where covered call writers did not participate in very, very large moves. While in theory call writers should not mind that—their stance is to let the buyer try for the long shot—in practice many have become disillusioned and discouraged in these situations. While the number of takeovers has been high, the number of rumored takeovers has been much, much higher. This suggests a strategic solution. Buy as much stock as you are comfortable with; simultaneously write calls on only half the position. With premiums on rumored stocks so high, you still achieve a good return; if the wonderful takeover does come to fruition, half the position achieves the good return, and you are participating fully in the great takeover rise on the other half of the position. Earlier comments about being comfortable with the stock and price apply here with added emphasis. See Figure 6–2.

UNCOVERED PUT WRITING

This strategy fell into disrepute in October 1987, when very large losses hit traders who had written large quantities of uncovered index puts. Nevertheless it is a viable technique and can be used with some restrictions in mind. First, you are dealing here with equity options. That distinction is extremely important. If you have erred in writing an index put, you end up with a debit in your account after it is assigned. This debit does not change if the index subsequently recovers. If you write an equity put that is subsequently assigned, you end up with stock in your account. While its cost could be above its price at the time of writing the put, the same would be true of stock purchased at that time and retained. Afterward, you are subject to the familiar risks of stock ownership.

Remarks about being comfortable with the underlying stock apply with equal force to writing uncovered equity puts and writing covered calls.

The great advantage in put writing over covered call writing is the lower initial investment. Policies vary at brokerage firms, but the *minimum* initial margin requirement for an uncovered equity put is 20 percent of the stock price, less any out-of-the-money amount with a minimum of 10 percent of the stock price. The premium must also be left in the account. For a covered call, you are dealing with stock purchase, and so 50 percent must be posted (and reduced by the call premium left in the account). A moment's thought reveals that even with lower put premiums, a higher return can be generated with a similar risk-reward profile. See Table 6–3.

It must be noted that leverage cuts two ways. While the return for the put write is greater than the corresponding call write, the risk (in percentage terms) can be greater as well. The same rule we derived before is applicable here: never write a put on a stock you are not willing to own.

Although we have indicated that the percentage loss might be greater in the put write, there is one class of investors who are less bothered by that. These people are more concerned with stock price level than return. If, for example, you thought that XYZ stock, currently at 39, would be a superb buy at 33, you could write a 35- strike put for 2. Your viewpoint would be that you would either make the $200 per

TABLE 6–3
Put Write versus Covered Call

XYZ = 50		6-month 50 call = 4	6-month 50 put = 3		
Covered Call Write					*Uncovered Put Write*
Successful return (margin)					
Collateral	=	50% of $5,000		=	20% of $5,000
	=	$2,500		=	$1,000
Minus call premium	=	400	Leave put premium		
Out-of-pocket	=	$2,100	Out-of-pocket	=	$1,000
Return = 400/2100	=	19%	Return = 300/1000	=	30%
Annualized return					
(assumes can be repeated)	=	38%		=	60%
Opportunity loss point	=	54		=	53
Break-even point	=	46		=	47
Unsuccessful return (margin)					
Assume stock falls to $45					
Loss on stock	=	$500		=	$500
Minus call premium	=	400	Minus put premium	=	300
Net loss		(100)			(200)
Return = (100)/2100	=	−4.8%	Return = (200)/1000	=	−20%

Note: Commissions not included.

put (whatever that might be in percentage terms), or own the stock at the very attractive level.

Two other observations are pertinent here. First, the balance of the money that would have been used for stock purchase (cash or margin) can be invested in Treasury bills, thereby enhancing the return without increasing the risk. Second, as with buying calls, the diversification method can be used here. That is, puts might be written on more than one stock to take advantage of the reduced requirements. What should not be done is to write these puts in an amount inappropriate to the possible risk. Contracting to purchase a large quantity of stock because you think that "it can't go down *there*" is not a good approach.

While this has been oversimplified—there is no consideration given to commissions, dividends, or margin interest (although this would apply to the call, not to the put)—the bottom line is that the two strategies have a quite similar risk-reward profile.

If you combine the last two strategies you get covered straddle writing.

COVERED STRADDLE WRITING

Straddle means many different things to different people. To the IRS, a covered call write is a straddle. To the commodities crowds, a position of long pork bellies and short soybeans is a straddle. So we had better start with a definition. A *straddle* means equal numbers of puts and calls on the same underlying security, with the same expiration and striking price. This means that you can be long or short straddles. Later there is a look at long straddles (or their close cousins—*combinations*), but now it's time to examine short straddles.

But what's a *covered straddle*? Are you covered against the separate risk of a short call and a short put? Yes and no. Being discussed here is the strategic position of long stock/short call/short put. This combines the covered call and the uncovered put (with the same strike). Why would anybody want to do that? Indeed, this could be an appropriate posture if your stock expectations were extremely bullish and/or you wanted to commit less money at this time. Now for a look at "the last word in stocks"—XYZ Corp.

XYZ 50   XYZ 50 call 4   XYZ 50 put 3

TABLE 6–4
Profit and Loss

Stock Price at Expiration	XYZ 50	50 call $4		50 put $3
		Covered Call Write		Covered Straddle Write
$51		+4		+7
50		+4		+7
49		+3		+5
48		+2		+3
47		+1		+1
46 1/2		+1/2	Break-even	0
46	Break-even	0		−1

By now, you are familiar with posting $2,100 for the covered call write (50 percent of $5,000 less the call premium) and posting $1,000 for the short put (20 percent of $5,000 and leaving the put premium). Thus the initial requirement would be $3,100. The results for this collateral would be: stock up a lot or a little, stock called away and profit from both premiums; stock down, buy a second lot of stock and have its cost reduced by both premiums.

Another way of looking at the procedure is to contrast it with buying twice as much stock. You would spend more money, post more margin, and pay more in commissions, but your profit percentage might not be higher. See Table 6–4.

SYSTEMATIC WRITING

This term usually refers to the investor whose business, so to speak, is covered call writing. It is contrasted to the trader who occasionally makes use of that strategy to produce incremental income, obtain a downside cushion, or scale out.

Here, *systematic writing* refers to an almost mechanical approach. Start off by writing puts on the stock you have selected. If the stock rises, you are ahead by the premium. If the stock falls, you are assigned on the puts and now own the stock. Then write covered straddles. If the stock rises, you are assigned on the calls and have collected three premiums. If the stock falls, you will be assigned again and have a double position in the stock. Now write as many calls as you are long

TABLE 6–5
Systematic Writing

Jan 3	XYZ 51		No position
Jan 3	XYZ 51	Sell XYZ Mar 50 put 2	
Mar 20	XYZ 48 1/2	Mar 50 put assigned	Long 100 XYZ @ 48 (50 − 2)
Mar 21	XYZ 48 3/4	Sell XYZ Jun 50 call 3	
		Sell XYZ Jun 50 put 4	Straddle 7
Jun 19	XYZ 47	Jun 50 calls expire	
		Jun 50 puts assigned	Long 200 XYZ
			100 @ 48
			100 @ 43 (50 − 7)
			Avg 200 @ 45 1/2
Jun 20	XYZ 48 1/2	Sell 2 Sep 50 call 3	

Alternate Possibilities

Sep 18	XYZ 52	2 Sep 50 calls assigned	Sep 18 XYZ 48 2 Sep 50
			calls expire
		Sell 200 XYZ 53	Cost basis reduced to 42 1/2
		(50 + 3)	(45 1/2 − 3)
	Net profit (53 − 45 1/2) = 7 1/2 × 2		
		= $1,500	
	No position		Long 200 XYZ adjusted cost
			42 1/2
	Ready to sell more options		
	Same or another stock		Ready to sell more calls

Note: In either possibility shown, although the stock ended not far from its starting price, you were able to make a good profit.

stock. If the stock rises, you are assigned and have collected four premiums. If the stock falls, you will be long and wrong. But the resulting unrealized loss will have come not from options, but because you chose a stock that went down three times when you had predicted an upward move each time. Even then, you would own the stock at a cost basis that was reduced by four option premiums. See Table 6–5 and Figure 6–3.

SPREADS

Although these examples and illustrations have not referred to commissions, commissions certainly affect the profitability of any option strategy. This is not an effort to hide transaction costs but merely to simplify concepts and calculations. However, when it comes to spreads, com-

FIGURE 6-3 Systematic Writing Flow Chart

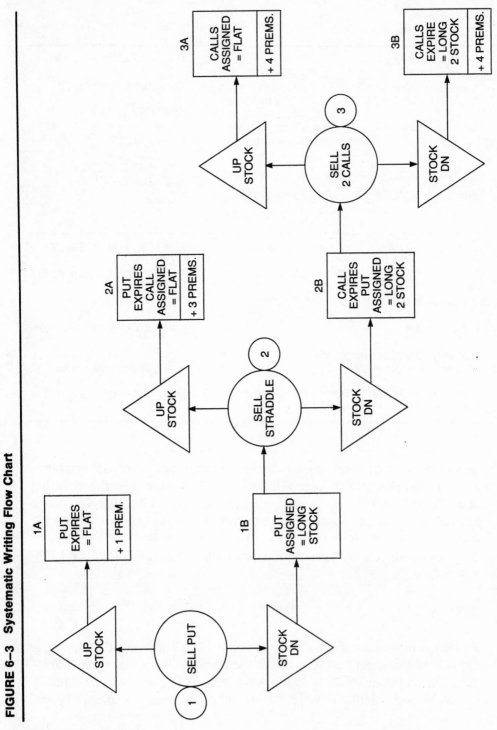

missions *do* multiply. A spread of any sort has at least one long option position and at least one short one. This means two commissions going into the trade and perhaps two more to get out. Further, spreads have limited profit potential. The combination of these two factors argues against most spreading tactics for the small investor. An exception may be made for the far out calendar spread.

Far Out Calendar Spread

A calendar spread usually involves the purchase of a farther month option and the simultaneous sale of a nearer month. These will usually be calls if bullish or puts if bearish. It is also usual to opt for a strike just out-of-the-money. Remembering what you learned about expiration cycles, you can buy, for example, the farthest-out-call both in month and strike. Then you can sell the nearest month with a strike below the long leg but still out-of-the-money. If you have selected wisely and well, the short side expires unassigned (or could be repurchased for a nominal amount), and you still own the long. Then another month can be written, and so on.

TABLE 6-6
Far Out Calendar Spread (Marvelous Multiple Company)

Fourth Week of	Stock Price	Event	Action
November	$44	July options created	Buy Jul 50 c 5
			Sell Dec 45 c 1
December	44	Dec options have expired	Sell Jan 45 c 1
January	44	Jan options have expired	No action
February	47		Sell Mar 50 c 1
March	49	Mar options have expired	Sell Apr 50 c 2*
April	49	Apr options have expired	No action
May	52	May options have expired	Sell Jun 55 c 4
June	52	June options have expired	No action
July	54	(before July options expired)	Close Jul 50 c 4
Conclusion:	Loss long call	1	
	Gain short calls	9	
	Net profit	8	

* At this point the long cost has been recovered.
Note: This particular scenario has been selected, not as "most likely," but to illustrate the mechanism involved.

It would take some luck as well as sagacity, but it is possible to sell as many as seven different short calls against the same long option. Although there would be many commissions, there could be many premiums. These would successfully shrivel the cost of the original long. Not only might this strategy lead to a very low-cost call, incredibly it could lead to a zero—or even negative—cost!

Of course there are, as always, accompanying potential negatives to view. By the time all these trades were finished, the low-cost call might be so far out-of-the-money that it wouldn't be worth very much. Also, the stock could move away quickly, resulting in an assignment on one of the shorts. Obviously, such a technique requires much more monitoring than usual. Still any strategy that holds out the possibility of ending up with a call not far out-of-the-money, with time to run and zero (or less) cost deserves serious consideration. For the bears, a similar strategy does exist utilizing puts, but be aware of the lower premiums and lower liquidity in put options. See Table 6–6.

GETTING OUT

Most literature on options concentrates on what could be dubbed "getting in." Options can be a very effective tool for getting out of positions as well. One way of achieving this is using the protective put as a means of insuring an accumulated profit. There are two other methods, as follows, for getting out of a position.

Scaling Out

Scaling out means making stock sales at successively higher prices. The justification for covered call writing is the return versus the risk, but that is in the context of a zero starting position. If you are long a stock and have reached the stage of ambivalence about its retention, you can write out-of-the-money nearer-term calls against it. This provides a downside cushion and can get you out at a price higher than the current market. If your position is a larger one and your ambivalence has an upward bias, you can write successively higher strikes on portions of the position. This strategy is akin to scaling out (making stock sales at successively higher prices) but could result in higher net returns. See Table 6–7.

TABLE 6–7
How Covered Call Writing Can Beat Scaling Out

Long 2,000	Supreme Scaling Co. @ 40	
	Stock has risen slowly to 48, then spurts to 53	
	Sell 5 55 c @ 3	

Stock Price at Expiration	*Action*	*Effective Price*
56	500 called	58 (55 + 3)
	Sell 5 60 c @ 2	
61	500 called	62 (60 + 2)
64	Sell 5 65 c @ 4	
66	500 called	69 (65 + 4)
	Sell 5 70 c @ 1	
66	70 calls expire	
	Sell 500 @ 66	67 (66 + 1)

Note: Although the stock never rose above 66, this method achieved an average sale price of 64 (not far from the stock's high). Indeed, half of the stock was sold at effective prices above the high for the year!

Replacement Therapy

This cutely titled technique involves selling out the stock and replacing it with calls. Depending on your outlook, these can be in-, at-, or out-of-the-money calls. In any case, you will have gotten both your profit and most of your capital out of the market. Yet you will retain the possibility of participation in farther upside moves in the stock. See Table 6–8.

Enhancement

This is surely a welcome topic! What to do when things are going well is a pleasant problem to encounter. Still, because an option position is going the right way doesn't mean you should just forget about it. Look at a few possibilities. An option (put or call) that you have bought has doubled in value since its purchase. It still has a fair amount of time to run. You could use OPM.

OPM

OPM can be used in three ways. Here are three examples:

1. Simply sell out half the position. The other half has no upside limit on profits, but you have gotten your *own* capital out of the market.

TABLE 6–8
Replacement Therapy

Long 1,000 Recombinant Replacement cost 40—stock @ 50
Sell 1,000 @ 50, Buy 10 2 mos. 50 calls @ 3
$10,000 profit reduced by call purchase to $7,000
$50,000 investment reduced to $3,000

Stock Price at Expiration	Additional Profit/Loss
$60	$7,000
58	5,000
56	3,000
54	1,000
52	−1,000
50	−3,000
40	−3,000

Note: The remaining $47,000 is free to be deployed elsewhere. It could be invested in another stock or stocks, in calls or puts, or in Treasury securities.

Example

You are long 10 XYZ calls, original cost 3, now at 6.

Sell 5 calls @ 6 = $3,000 = 10 × $300 = Original cost.

If stock continues up, you still profit, albeit less than maximally.

If stock reverses, you can still eke out some profits. You might make not a penny more, but you don't lose a cent of your original principal. You are still speculating, but with Other People's Money!

2. Sell an equal quantity of a higher/lower (for calls/puts) strike in the same month if that premium is at least equal to your original cost. This creates a spread that limits upside gains, but you can profit by up to the difference between the strikes. And again, this is OPM.

Example

Long 10 XYZ 50 calls cost 3, now at 6.

Sell 10 XYZ 55 calls @ 3.

If XYZ ends at 55 or higher, you earn an additional profit of 5 points, 10 times. If the stock ends between 50 and 55, you make some additional profit. And, if the stock ends below 50, you make no more, but your principal is intact.

3. Sell all the options and invest only the *profits* in a different strike and/or month. Once more, you have the potential to pyramid profits with OPM.

Example

Long 10 XYZ Jan 50 calls 3, now at 6.
Close 10 Jan 50 calls @ 6 = $6,000.
Buy 10 Feb 55 calls @ 3 = $3,000.

You could profit more—you have gained a month's time—if the stock moved still higher. Once again, if the stock fails, your principal is preserved.

Added Profits
Enhancement is not limited to long options. One very common situation is the rapid upward movement of a stock soon after you have done a covered call write. With the earlier comments on expiration cycles in mind, you can do a *diagonal roll*. This consists of buying back the short call and simultaneously writing the next strike one month farther out. Often, this can be accomplished for a nominal cost, equal dollars, or even a small credit. The point here is that, at no extra risk, you have placed yourself in a position to be assigned one strike higher for added profits.

Diagonal Rolling

Example

Jan 2	Buy 500 DDD 38.
	Sell 5 Feb 40 calls 2 1/2.
Feb 1	DDD at 43.
	Buy 5 Feb 40 calls 3 1/2 close.
	Sell 5 Mar 45 calls 3 1/4 open.

Note that the premium received on the original covered write on Diagonal Data Distributors (DDD) has become irrelevant. So long as you can make the diagonal switch for a low debit or credit, you have little to no additional risk should the stock reverse. You could gain an additional 5 points if the stock continued its uptrend past 45. In fact, you might repeat the maneuver.

Once you have alerted yourself to enhancement possibilities, many option positions can be thus improved. Like any other market stake, you don't have to do it just because it's there. In all the examples here, the unstated assumption is that the underlying stock will continue to move in the same direction.

REDUCED-RISK TRADING

For the scalpers and market pinpoint-timers, there is a wonderful option strategy available. Start by buying a *combination*—equal quantities of puts and calls on the same underlying stock, with the same expiration month, but with different strikes. These will usually consist of a call strike above the market price of the stock and a put with a strike price below it. This technique is well known: traders use it to profit from a large stock move in *either* direction. The strategy can also be employed in a slightly different fashion.

Assume that after your double purchase, the stock moves down to below the put strike and then hesitates. If you believe it is about to turn up, you could buy stock at that point. If your assumption is correct, you could sell the stock at a point when you thought it would again reverse its trend. If you were wrong, the risk was limited because you could always exercise the put. Similarly, if the stock first rose, you could short it, then buy it back while being protected by the long call. If you are able to get off a couple of good trades, you will probably recover the original cost of the combination. Once that has happened you will be in the stance of having no money invested, and being able to trade back and forth while always being protected. While this trading technique sounds wonderful, it should be attempted by only the most nimble. See Table 6–9.

There is even an enhancement to this tricky technique. When the stock is at your predicted action point, take an offsetting position in options instead of stock! Substitute the sale of an out-of-the-money call for short stock and the sale of an out-of-the-money put for long stock. In addition to leverage (approximately 20 to 25 percent for the short options instead of 50 percent for the long or short stock), you will also have premium decay working for you. See Table 6–10.

TABLE 6–9
Example of Reduced-Risk Trading

Date	XYZ Stock Price	Action
Jan 3	$50	Buy XYZ Feb 55 call @ 1 3/8
4	49 1/2	Buy XYZ Feb 45 put @ 1
5	49 3/4	
6	48 3/4	
9	47 5/8	
10	47	
11	46 1/2	Buy XYZ 46 1/2
12	47	
13	47 1/2	
16	48 1/4	
17	49	Sell XYZ 49 close out, profit 2 1/2
18	49 7/8	
19	50 1/2	
20	51 1/4	
23	51	
24	52 3/8	
25	53 5/8	Sell short XYZ 53 5/8
26	54	
27	54 1/8	
30	53 1/2	
31	53	
Feb 1	52 5/8	
2	52 1/8	
3	51 1/2	
6	51 1/4	Buy XYZ 51 1/4 cover short, profit 2 3/8
7	51	
8	52 1/2	
9	52 7/8	
10	53 3/4	
13	54 7/8	
14	55 5/8	Sell short XYZ 55 5/8
15	56	
16	56 1/2	
17	56 1/8	Exercise Feb 55 call to cover short, profit 5/8. Feb 45 put expires 0.

Conclusion:	Total *scalp* profit	5 1/2
	Combination spread cost	2 3/8
	Net profit	3 1/8

Note: The timing here was far from perfect. Nevertheless profits resulted—more than 100 percent of investment (excluding commissions) was gained. It is well to recall the answer of Baron Rothschild when asked how he made all his money: "I always got out too soon."

TABLE 6–10
Reduced-Risk Trading—Using Options!

Date	Action
Jan 11	Sell Feb 40 put 1 1/2
Jan 17	Buy Feb 40 put 1/2 close, profit 1
Jan 25	Sell Feb 60 call 2 7/8
Feb 6	Buy Feb 60 call 3/4 close, profit 2 1/8
Feb 14	Sell Feb 60 call 1 3/4
Feb 17	Feb 60 call expires, profit 1 3/4
	Sell Feb 55 call 1 1/8
	Feb 45 put expires
Conclusion: Option "scalps" profit	6
Combination spread cost	2 3/8
Net profit	3 5/8

Note: Refer to Table 6–9; here, option trades are substituted for stock and similar profit was made while less money was tied up.

REPAIR

Option Repair

Repair techniques should be a part of every trader's arsenal. They help fix an option and/or stock position that is not going according to plan. Very often, that position might be *repaired*—that is, the profit probability can be increased or the losses can be reduced. While there is an abundance of advice to option traders and investors, that advice usually deals with initiation and occasionally with closure. There has been almost no counseling on what to do when positions go awry. Profits are wonderful, but in real life we have to know what to do about losses.

Let's start with the most frequent position: long calls.

Time - early Jan
XYZ 82 1/2
Mar 100 calls 2 1/4
Mar 95 calls 3 1/8
Mar 90 calls 4 3/8
Mar 85 calls 6 1/4
Mar 80 calls 8 1/4

Assume that you own 12 XYZ Mar 100 calls (purchased in the heat of bullish passion) and have become disturbed about the stock's performance. You still expect a rally, but are dubious about it taking XYZ above 100 (more than 20 percent higher than its current price). Let's (pun intended) look at our options.

1. Hold and Hope
Not so good. Here you frequently find yourself saying:

"*It will come back, I _know_ it will*" followed by,

"*It will come back, I _think_ it will.*" and then,

"*It will come back, I _hope_ it will.*" and maybe even,

"*It will come back, I _pray_ it will.*"

By the time the hope stage has been reached, it is usually much too late. So you'd better survey some more realistic possibilities.

2. Bite the Bullet
Take (what's left of) the money and run! All too often that's the best way to proceed, although it might be the most underutilized strategy. It's not used so much as it should be because it implies taking a double hit—one to the wallet and one to the ego. The latter is preferable to the former for: "He who fights and runs away/lives to fight another day." And don't forget the improved judgment that results from a difficult experience like this.

If you have elected to eschew both the stubborn hold and the immediate sale, there are other possibilities to evaluate. The most important consideration is to forget about your original cost; it is now irrelevant. Your goal is no longer to produce profits; it is to salvage something from a position that no longer has its previous potential.

3. Trade In
Trade in your *nearly impossibles* for fewer *might-do-it* options or an even smaller number of *more probables*.

Replace the 12 100s @ 2 1/4 with	6	90s @ 4 3/8.
or with	4	85s @ 6 1/4.
or even with	3	80s @ 8 3/4.

None of these shifts requires capital infusion. The old 12 generate $2,700 and the new calls cost $2,625, $2,500, and $2,625, respectively.

You can't make the great killing you originally lusted after, but keeping half a loaf is better than buying the whole bread and watching it all rot away.

What will happen, if at expiration, XYZ has made a good recovery? A rise of 15 percent would bring XYZ to 94 7/8.

Calls struck at	90	would be worth	4 7/8 × 6 = $2,925.
Calls struck at	85	would be worth	9 7/8 × 4 = $3,950.
Calls struck at	80	would be worth	14 7/8 × 3 = $4,462.50.

Of course, you must also remember:

Calls struck at	100	would be worth	0 × 12 = 0.

On the downside, no more money is lost compared to retention of the original 12 calls. Now, a cynic could comment: "If the market does rebound to the upside, you have lost all your profit potential." To demonstrate that this is wrong, calculate break-even points (B/E). Not the usual call purchase B/E point (strike plus premium), but the strategic B/E point. This will allow you to evaluate the comparative efficacy of the strategies. We will ascertain the XYZ price, at option expiration, above which Hold would have outperformed the Trade-In tactic.

Trade in to 90	S/B/E 110	Stock needs to rise 33.3%.
Trade in to 85	S/B/E 107 1/2	Stock needs to rise 30.3%.
Trade in to 80	S/B/E 106 5/8	Stock needs to rise 29.2%.

We can verify one of these S/B/Es as an example. An XYZ close at 110 at expiration would produce an intrinsic value of 10 points for each of the 12 calls struck at 100. This total of $12,000 is exactly equal to the worth—20 points each—of the six calls struck at 90.

4. Better Switch

The switch advocated here is not of calls, but of strategies: Change the long call position to a bull spread. This can be done by selling out the calls to close the position, writing an equal number of the same calls to open a new, short position, and buying an equal number of calls with a lower strike. Here is an example.

Position:	Long	12 XYZ	Mar 100 calls.
Action:	Sell	12 XYZ	Mar 100 calls @ 2 1/4 closing.
	Sell	12 XYZ	Mar 100 calls @ 2 1/4 opening.
	Buy	12 XYZ	Mar 90 calls @ 4 3/8 opening.

New position: Long   12 XYZ   Mar 90 calls.

                     Short   12 XYZ   Mar 100 calls.

Once again, this switch did not require additional capital; a total of 24 calls sold at 2 1/4 produced $5,400 and the 12 calls purchased at 4 3/8 cost only $5,250. We can again calculate the S/B/E. And again it is 110. That is due to XYZ, at expiration, closing above 100, making the 12 spreads worth 10 points apiece. To get more than 10 points each from the original long 12 calls would require a close above 110. In summary: below 90, each position described does just as poorly; between 90 and 110, this Switch works out better; only above 110 does Hold emerge as the superior strategy.

Note: these repair suggestions might not always be executable at zero cost. They still might be worthwhile doing at small debits.

All spreads must be done in a margin account that has been approved for this type of options trading. In addition to whatever costs were necessary to produce the spread positions, many firms might ask for additional collateral.

Stock Repair

There is another position worth going through the repair review. Although it is seldom talked about from that perspective, it is a strategy that does involve substantial risk: buying naked stock!

The repair strategy examined here is similar to the Better Switch one. Suppose that you are long not 12 XYZ calls, but 1,200 shares of XYZ stock purchased at a price of $100 per share and now selling for 82 1/2. If your outlook is for the stock to recover well, but not all the way, there is an option strategy that can implement that view quite well. Buy 12 XYZ Mar 85 calls @ 6 1/4 and sell 24 Mar 95 calls @ 3 1/8 to produce this position:

Long 1,200 XYZ.
Long 12 calls Mar 85.
Short 24 calls Mar 95.

As before, no additional money is needed (but see the note at the end of the call repair section), and there are no uncovered calls. You now have a combined position of a covered call and a bull spread. There is no additional risk on the downside. On the upside, thanks to your marvelous maneuver, the break-even point for the stock has been lowered. Instead of 100, it has become 92 1/2. To see this, observe the position in a rearranged form:

Long 1,200 XYZ.   Short 12 XYZ Mar 95 calls.

Long 12 XYZ Mar 85 calls.   Short 12 XYZ Mar 95 calls.

If the stock, at option expiration is 92 1/2 (and you sell it out), you would lose 7 1/2 points per 100 shares. The long calls struck at 85 would each be worth the same 7 1/2 points, while the 95 strike calls would expire worthless. The net result would be a break-even. In other words, using those so-called dangerous and speculative options, you have improved a deteriorated long stock position. Even better, the B/E that was achieved (92 1/2) is very close to 91 1/4. That number is the B/E that would have resulted from a straight averaging down (buy an equal second lot at 82 1/2 and sell both out at 91 1/4). Using options, you obtained a B/E only about a point away from the more traditional technique. We will note impassively that those who do not deign to touch an option would have had the pleasure of spending $1,200 \times 82\ 1/2 = \$99,000$ to get to their B/E! Further, for their almost six-figure expenditure, they would have incurred a doubled downside risk. The final comment here is that the S/B/E is 105. That is, a rise of 22 1/2 points (27.3 percent) would be necessary for Hold to be a superior strategy to Repair.

SUMMARY AND CONCLUSION

Risk Transfer

All too often, option critics erroneously attribute losses to options themselves. These securities are described as speculative, dangerous, and immoral. In fact, options are special securities for the transfer of risk. The risk can be increased as with leverage in long calls; reduced as in married puts or covered calls; or all but eliminated as in protective puts and OPM trading. Option trading is very different from the more familiar stock trading in several ways. These differences are absolutely vital to comprehend and must be constantly kept in mind. We will label the major aspects (although these categories are neither exclusive nor exhaustive) as price, time, KISSes, and discipline.

Price and Time

We are all used to thinking that options are cheap (i.e., low priced) compared to stocks, but we may not have fully appreciated the implications. A *point*—$1 per share, $100 per 100 shares, or 1 option—isn't much. Well, it may not be much for stocks, but it's enormous for options. One point on a $50 stock is 2 percent, but the same point on that stock's $4 option is a whopping 25 percent! The moral is that you have to trade options in a much more controlled fashion than you trade stocks.

What is true for price is even more so for time. With stocks you can often afford the luxury of waiting out an adverse move. With options, that waiting period is anathema; it could kill your chances as expiration approaches. In fact, the option buyer will, "always hear/Time's wingéd chariot hurrying near." We observe that time is the friend, not the enemy, of the option *writer*.

As for discipline, it is essential in all aspects of investing, but perhaps nowhere more so than with options. With long options, you run the risk of premium decay up to and including 100 percent loss of investment. With short covered options, you risk loss of opportunity. And with short uncovered options, you face the specter of almost unlimited losses. These negatives are offset by the positive aspects of options: limited risk, good returns, and the lovely lure of leverage.

With these considerations in mind, what should be the approach of the rational investor or trader in options? First, some elementary but effective rules.

A Lot of KISSes

We'll commence with the well-known *KISS* strategy—Keep it Simple, Sweetheart—and extend it to simple, sensible, safe, suitable, and small.

- Keep it simple—don't attempt a diagonal weighted calendar straddle spread if you really just need to buy a call.
- Keep it sensible—don't buy options too far out-of-the-money because they appear cheap. Even more, don't sell uncovered options because they're "free money—the stock just can't go that far." The first often produces a 100 percent loss. The second can lead to losses that are fearsome in their magnitude.
- Keep it safe—don't ever risk more than you would be extremely sorry to lose.
- Keep it suitable—just because you read about some alleged mastermind doing something weird and wonderful with options doesn't mean you should try to emulate the operation. Don't try trades or techniques that will take you beyond the *sleeping point*.

* Keep it small—remember the advantages discussed in the buying calls section. It's often better to achieve greater safety through diversification than to try for maximum leverage.

A Little Discipline

Despite all the KISSes, we should note that option losses sometime occur because of the wrong stock, the wrong strategy, and the wrong timing. But beyond these, be aware that decision making for options is radically different from the superficially similar process with stocks. What is needed here is a clarity of viewpoint. Whenever you contemplate an option trade, start out with EYE—Establish Your Expectations. Maybe even write your expectations down on a piece of paper. This can inhibit the rationalizing rituals that so often blind people to the misperformance of their option positions. When a critical point is reached, find that piece of paper and burn it! (Clear your desk first.) This can free you from the now-erroneous expectations.

With these broken, it is time to CYE—Change Your Expectations. How do you know when a critical point is reached? The strange but significant answer to this question is: any way at all! This means that when you EYE, you should not only have at least an approximate idea of when you want to close profitably, you should also have a clear view of an exit point to stem losses. It does not matter whether that exit point is arrived at by fundamental research of the stock involved, by technical readings of the position, by managerial evaluation of the company, by listening to an investment guru, by checking cycles, by gazing at astrological analyses, or by reading chicken entrails! What does matter is that you make the choice that is comfortable for *you* in order to select the exit point. And even more important, when that point is reached, use discipline to stay with your resolve. CYE or lose your money or your opportunity. Phrased succinctly:

If you don't EYE and CYE, you will soon say BYE to your dollars.

Afterword

We have come to the end of this chapter and tried to be instructive without preaching. The chapter started by suggesting that much advice was offered and little accepted. Perhaps our advice will be treated differently. We cannot pretend that options are a panacea. We do believe that there is a plenum, if not a plethora, of option opportunities for both traders and investors. To refrain or refuse to trade with options is sadly to neglect one of the most valuable vehicles in the entire universe of investments. We have tried to explicate some of the myriad possibilities in the large world of options. Naturally, these pages have been able to cover only a small part thereof. For those further interested, there are other chapters in this book and other books to peruse. We hope you will become an option user, even if not an advocate.

CHAPTER 7

INSTITUTIONAL USES
OF OPTIONS

A portfolio manager has many responsibilities beyond those related to specific equity selection. Some involve the broader issues of market timing, portfolio asset allocation, and trade execution. The need to deal with these responsibilities and the ever present pressures to reduce cost were among the driving forces that led to the creation of index options.

Index options have been the fastest growing segment of the industry in recent years, and certain index options markets have become extremely liquid. Because markets are liquid and able to handle sizeable orders, index options are in fact, as well as in theory, a beneficial tool for the knowledgeable portfolio manager.

This chapter explains how a wide variety of options strategies can be used to manage risk and to increase returns. The importance of having a market view is stressed, as we analyze different strategies that can be used in different market environments. We first look at portfolio insurance, comparing equity put options and index puts, and the advantages of each. We then look at five strategies that *decrease* market exposure and compare the results of each. The next area to consider is how to *increase* market exposure using index call buying strategies. Finally, other portfolio strategies, such as covered call writing, are discussed, as well as suggestions for portfolio repair and recommendations for handling special situations.

INTRODUCTION TO PORTFOLIO INSURANCE

A Look at Index and Equity Options

Perhaps the most basic use of index options is to insure or to hedge a portfolio against a broad market decline while, at the same time, allowing that portfolio to participate in any market advance. The table below shows the similarities between buying index put options and a standard insurance policy on a car or home.

Insurance Policy	Purchase of Index Put Options
Risk premium	Option time premium
Value of asset	Index level
Face value of policy	Option strike price
Amount of deductible	Index level minus strike price (out-of-the-money amount)
Duration	Time until expiration

It is easy to demonstrate how the purchase of index put options can protect the value of a well-diversified portfolio, the makeup of which generally matches the index on which the option is purchased. This concept is illustrated first in a simplified six-stock, $162,600 portfolio that is assumed to track the performance of the S&P 100 Index. The potential problem with this assumption for larger portfolios is discussed later.

Consider the six-stock group shown below. Closing prices were taken from *The Wall Street Journal* for November 4, 1993, 78 days from January expiration.

Issue	Number of Shares	Price	Value
AT&T	500	56 3/4	28,375
Bristol-Myers Squibb	400	59 7/8	23,950
General Motors	600	48 7/8	29,325
Exxon	400	64 7/8	25,950
DuPont	600	48 1/2	29,100
Merck	800	32 3/8	25,900
			$162,600

The question here is simply, other than liquidating the portfolio, what can a manager do to protect a portfolio from an expected short-term market decline? Buying puts, of course, is appropriate; but there are two types of put options from which to choose: individual equity options and index options. So the next step is to analyze potential performance of both types, then compare the results. A portfolio of equity puts that matches the equity holdings in the sample portfolio would look like this (again, closing prices for November 4, 1993):

Issue	Price	Put Options	Price	Quantity	Cost
AT&T	56 3/4	Jan 55	1 9/16	5	781.25
Bristol-Myers Squibb	59 7/8	Jan 55	13/16	4	325.00
General Motors	48 7/8	Jan 45	1 1/16	6	637.50
Exxon	64 7/8	Jan 60	9/16	4	225.00
DuPont	48 1/2	Jan 45	7/8	6	525.00
Merck	32 3/8	Jan 30	5/8	8	500.00
					$2,993.75

How this group of put options would profit with a stock market decline is shown in the next table. Assume that each stock has declined 15 percent (to match the decline in the overall market) at the time of option expiration; thus, there is no time premium left in the option prices.

Issue	Price (down 15%)	New Option Price	Quantity	Value
AT&T	48 1/4	6.75	5	3,375
Bristol-Myers Squibb	50 7/8	4.125	4	1,650
General Motors	41 1/2	3.5	6	2,100
Exxon	55 1/8	4.875	4	1,950
DuPont	41 1/4	3.75	6	2,250
Merck	27 1/2	2.5	8	2,000

Total put option value after 15% market decline	$13,325
Total put option cost	2,994
Total put option profit	10,331

Original portfolio value	$162,600.00
15% decline in value	24,390.00
Profit on put options	−10,331.00
Portfolio declined by:	$ 14,059.00

The $10,331 put option profit is the payoff from the insurance policy. This profit directly reduces the total decline of $24,390 in the value of the equities in the portfolio. As a result, the total portfolio declined in value by $14,059 ($24,390 − $10,331). This is only an 8.6 percent decline compared to the overall market and uninsured portfolio decline of 15 percent.

A second insurance strategy is to purchase index put options. On November 3, 1993, the S&P 100 closed at a level of 425.63, and the January 420 put option closed at $9.

First, it's necessary to calculate the number of options required to insure the equity portfolio. S&P 100 (OEX) options represent a cash settlement value equal to 100 times the index. This means that each option with a strike price of 425 represents a market value of $42,500 (425 × $100). In the example, the equity portfolio has a total beginning value of $162,600. Using the January 420 put options to insure this portfolio requires purchasing 4 puts ($162,600 divided by $42,000 = 3.87). Obviously, some rounding is always involved in this calculation. At the closing price of 9, the purchase of 4 put options would cost a total of $3,600 (4 × $900.00). (For the sake of simplicity, commissions and taxes are not included in this example. However, these are real world factors that must be considered when implementing any actual investment strategy.)

The next task is to calculate how this insurance strategy benefits the portfolio. First, calculate the index level after a 15 percent decline. Then determine the option price assuming no time premium (a conservative assumption). Finally, calculate the put option profit and resulting benefit to the portfolio.

1. A 15-percent decline in the index from 425.63 results in a level of 361.79 (425.63 × .85).
2. At an index level of 361.79, the 420 put option, at expiration, has a value of $58.21 (420 − 361.79).
3. At $58.21, each index option has a profit of $4,921 ($5,821 − $900) for a total put option profit of $19,684 ($4,921 × 4).

The following table summarizes the effect of these two portfolio strategies.

	S&P 100 Index	Equity Portfolio	Equity Put Options	Four Index Put Options
Beginning value	425.63	162,600	2,994.00	3,600
Ending value	361.79	138,210	13,325.00	23,284
Change in value	−15%	−24,390	+10,331.00	+19,684

In this example, the payoff favors the index option purchase. The difference is $9,353, which is about 6 percent of the $162,600 portfolio. While the index puts here would have been the wiser choice, that will not always be the case. There are other important items to consider as well. A closer look at the two alternatives reveals several differences that become important as the portfolio in question gets bigger.

Consider first the issue of manageability. In the simple example given, the purchase of four options is required. All stock issues were chosen with the January option series available 78 days out. In the real world, however, stocks in a diversified portfolio might not have options with 78 days remaining. Due to the way option series are structured and are opened, there are times when only options with 30, 60, 120, and 210 days are available. This means that matching a portfolio of equity puts with an equity portfolio will inevitably result in the purchase of puts with different expirations. When different quantities of puts are added to the variety of expiration months, the management problem becomes obvious.

By contrast, when using equity options, the risk of error is more than losing money. There is also the risk of portfolio disruption. When puts are in-the-money at expiration, there is a great likelihood of automatic exercise. This means that stocks will be automatically sold. For taxable portfolios, the result can be significant. Extra commission charges from selling stocks and buying them back are other negatives.

There is also the possibility that listed put options are not available on some equities. And even though over-the-counter put options can be available, these options markets are generally not as liquid as the listed options markets. The manager is left to contend with the problems of liquid markets, such as wide bid/ask spreads and the possible difficulty of entering into or offsetting an options position.

Advantages of Index Options

Fortunately, index options can remedy some of the disadvantages of equity options. First, consider the issue of *manageability*. When insuring a portfolio with index options, one quantity of one option series is used. The problem of portfolio disruption is also absent. With the cash settlement feature of index options, there is no risk that individual equities will be sold by automatic exercise.

A *lower option commission* is another advantage. As previously discussed, at a strike price of 420, one index option covers a market equivalent of $42,000. Compared with a put option on a $50 stock that only covers $5,000 in value (for 100 shares), only one index option is required for every eight equity options. This ratio, of course, would be different for every portfolio, depending on the average stock price in the portfolio. The good news is that commission discounts would probably result from buying one larger quantity of index options, compared to buying several smaller quantities of equity puts.

The relative advantages of index options apply to many situations and have fueled the growth of index option markets; however, these advantages do not apply in certain situations. For example, in times of market uncertainty, the index options strategy may not be cheaper than an equity option strategy. That index options could be more expensive than equity options seems counterintuitive. Index options represent a diversified portfolio, and diversification generally implies less risk of a broad decline. Consequently, put options with less risk should be cheaper. Yet, in times of market uncertainty, the implied volatility for index options can be higher than for a group of equity options, resulting in a higher price for index options.

In the simple example given, the index put strategy requires a cash outlay of $3,600, and the equity put strategy requires $2,994. Consider also commissions and payoffs. Commissions for four index puts are obviously less than commissions for 33 equity puts on five stocks.

Overall, the payoff issue is much more uncertain and depends entirely on how well the portfolio in question moves with the index on which the puts are purchased. As long as the two move in tandem, the index put payoff will equal the equity option payoff. However, portfolios weighted unlike the index being used have a significant risk of behaving differently. If the manager of a specialized portfolio sees an imminent decline in its equities, there may not be a useful index option available.

STRATEGIC CONSIDERATIONS OF PORTFOLIO INSURANCE

To implement a portfolio insurance strategy, you must evaluate alternatives. Using a general example, the following section illustrates how each strategy can perform and discusses considerations used in selection.

The Alternatives

We look at five alternatives in terms of performance, then as a function of the portfolio manager's outlook, followed by the cost and risk of each alternative. We then compare the strategies using seven criteria.

Consider the investment alternatives of a portfolio manager with a bearish outlook. One choice is *selling the portfolio*. While this has many wide-ranging implications, it is the ultimate insurance policy. When the portfolio is in cash, it has no risk if a market decline occurs. The second alternative, a variation on this strategy, is *selling stock index futures contracts*. Although it is not within the realm of this book, this strategy has attracted a considerable following.

INDEX PUT BUYING STRATEGIES

Decreasing Market Exposure

Strategy alternatives 3, 4, and 5 are index put option strategies. The third alternative is an index option strategy similar to the example of the five-stock $162,600 portfolio. This method is generally known as *buying a portfolio equivalent of at-the-money puts*. The fourth alternative involves buying the same number of index puts as in the third method, but with a lower strike price. This strategy is called *buying a portfolio equivalent of out-of-the-money puts*. The final technique is not one that appears obvious to most investors because it involves buying a quantity of puts that is greater than the portfolio equivalent number in strategies 3 and 4. Generally this strategy involves the purchase of a greater number of out-of-the-money puts, so it could be called *buying a portfolio multiple of out-of-the-money puts*.

How the Strategies Perform

Figure 7–1 illustrates how the portfolio can change in value (vertical axis), given a change in the overall market (horizontal axis) for each of the five alternatives. Lines represent the outcome at expiration. Of course, the strategies would have been implemented at some point prior to expiration.

FIGURE 7–1
Portfolio Insurance Strategies

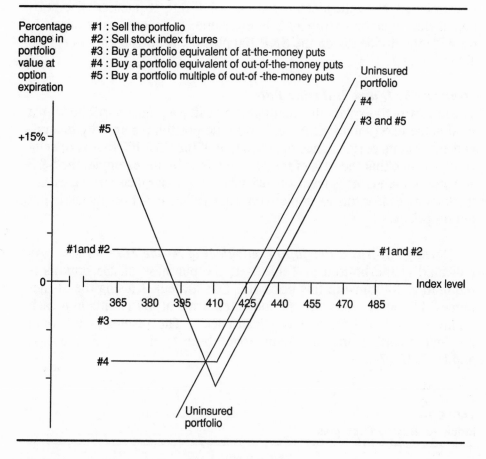

Percentage change in portfolio value at option expiration

#1 : Sell the portfolio
#2 : Sell stock index futures
#3 : Buy a portfolio equivalent of at-the-money puts
#4 : Buy a portfolio equivalent of out-of-the-money puts
#5 : Buy a portfolio multiple of out-of -the-money puts

Strategy 1: Selling the Portfolio

Converting the portfolio to cash, of course, eliminates risk from market fluctuation. Consequently, the return, regardless of market movement, will be a straight line above zero market movement equal to the interest earned during this time period.

Strategy 2: Selling Stock Index Futures

It is not within the scope of this discussion to cover all the practical difficulties in the execution of this strategy. Suffice it to say that the object of selling stock index futures against an equity portfolio is to eliminate the risk of downside market movement while still owning the portfolio. As a result, at the end of the time period when this strategy is implemented, the return can equal the T-bill rate of interest. The horizontal line depicting strategy 2 is the same, in theory, as strategy 1, because the dividends on the S&P 100 plus the futures premium equals T-bill interest.

Strategies 3, 4, and 5: Buying Puts

The best way to explain this method is by using a model portfolio with a total value of $10 million. Assume that the portfolio is broadly diversified and that its performance matches that of the S&P 100 Index. Specifically, assume that the beta of the portfolio is 1. In this example, the S&P 100 Index stands at a level of 425 when the insurance strategies are implemented. For this example, you can use Table 7–1 on available put option prices.

Strategy 3: Buy a Portfolio Equivalent of At-the-Money Puts.   As indicated at the bottom of Table 7–1, the purchase of 235 options is required to fully insure this portfolio. For strategy 3, using the at-the-money 425 put options and the indicated price of $11 results in a cash outlay of $258,500 for 90-day "insurance." The results of the total portfolio's performance are summarized both by line #3, Figure 7–1, and by Table 7–2.

TABLE 7–1
Index Put Buying Strategies

	S&P 100 at 425
90-Day Put Strike Price	*Option Price*
425	11
420	9
415	7
410	5 3/4
405	4 7/8
400	3 3/4

Calculating portfolio equivalent quantity of options. Number of Puts = Portfolio dollar value ÷ (Index level × Multiplier).
For a $10 million portfolio: $10,000,000 ÷ (425 × 100) = 235

TABLE 7–2
Strategy 3: Buying a Portfolio Equivalent of At-The-Money Puts to Insure a $10 Million Portfolio

Index Level at Option Expiration	Index Percent Change	Equity Portfolio Value ($)*	Put Option Value ($)	Total Portfolio Value ($)	Portfolio Percent Change
365	−14.1%	$ 8,367,949	$1,411,765	$ 9,779,714	−2.2%
380	−10.6	8,708,901	1,058,824	9,767,725	−2.3
395	−7.1	9,049,854	705,882	9,755,736	−2.4
410	−3.5	9,400,548	352,941	9,753,489	−2.5
425	0	9,741,500	0	9,741,500	−2.6
440	+3.5	10,082,453	0	10,082,453	+0.8
455	+7.1	10,433,147	0	10,433,147	+4.3
470	+10.6	10,774,099	0	10,774,099	+7.7
485	+14.1	11,115,052	0	11,115,052	+11.2

235 put options (90-day expiration) with a strike price of 425 are purchased for $258,500 (235 × $1100). The balance of $9,741,500 remains invested in a diversified portfolio of equities that matches the performance of the S&P 100.
* Dividends are not included.

Table 7–2 and line #3 in Figure 7–1 demonstrate the two important concepts about portfolio insurance. First, on the downside, the loss in portfolio value is limited to a maximum percentage, even though the market average could fall farther. On the upside, the portfolio remains intact and participates in a market rally; however, on the upside, the portfolio underperforms during the market rally because part of the portfolio is spent (and lost) on the put insurance.

A comparison of Figure 7–1 and Table 7–2 reveals an apparent inconsistency. Line #3 in Figure 7–1 is horizontal and represents a constant maximum loss. The Portfolio Percent Change column in Table 7–2, however, indicates that a market decline of increasing proportion actually results in a smaller portfolio loss. How can this inconsistency be explained?

In theory, as represented by line #3 in Figure 7–1, the maximum loss in the event of a stable or declining market is the cost of the put options, which act like insurance on the portfolio. In the event of a market rise, the portfolio underperforms the market by the cost of the insurance. In practice, however, paying for the put options reduces the amount invested in equities. The result is that 235 puts represent $10 million in market value while only $9,741,500 is invested in equities. On the downside, the puts will rise slightly faster than the decrease in the equities; and on the upside, the equities will rise slightly less than the theoretical $10 million portfolio. It is possible to purchase a number of puts such that a maximum loss will result in the event of a stable or declining market. That number is determined by the use of a linear programming optimizing technique that finds the number of puts equal to the portfolio value being insured. The issue here is that the cost of the put options is part of the total capital whose performance is being measured. Some writers have tried to avoid this issue by assuming that the cost of the put options equals the dividend income or that the puts are purchased with funds outside of the portfolio being insured. A complete discussion of portfolio performance evaluation is beyond the scope of this book, but portfolio managers must face this issue when using option-buying strategies.

Strategy 4: Buying a Portfolio Equivalent of Out-of-the-Money Puts. Out-of-the-money puts cost less than at-the-money ones, but if out of-the-money puts are used, the equity portfolio is uninsured against a market decline between the current market level and the strike price of the puts. Consequently, this portfolio insurance strategy is similar to purchasing a policy with a large deductible. In comparison, purchasing at-the-money puts is similar to buying a policy with no deductible.

As Table 7–3 indicates, the purchase of 235 puts with a strike price of 410 (15 points below the current market level) requires a cash outlay of $135,125.

With the out-of-the-money puts, the maximum loss in the portfolio is 4.8 percent. This occurs if the market declines to an index level of 410. At this point, the equity portfolio has declined 3.5 percent and the options—at a cost of 1.4 percent—expire worthless. On the upside, the insured portfolio underperforms the market by 1.4 percent—the cost of the put options.

Strategy 5: Buying a Portfolio Multiple of Out-of-the-Money Puts. This put-buying strategy has two significant differences from strategies 3 and 4. You can observe the first difference in line #5 in Figure 7–1. With this strategy, the portfolio can actually show an increase in value with a market decline. This occurs because the quantity of puts purchased represents a larger market value than the equity portfolio.

TABLE 7–3
Strategy 4: Buying a Portfolio Equivalent of Out-of-The-Money Puts

Index Level at Option Expiration	Index Percent Change	Equity Portfolio Value ($)*	Put Option Value ($)	Total Portfolio Value ($)	Portfolio Percent Change
365	−14.1%	$ 8,473,928	$1,058,824	$ 9,532,752	−4.7%
380	−10.6	8,819,198	705,882	9,525,080	−4.8
395	−7.1	9,164,469	352,941	9,517,410	−4.8
410	−3.5	9,519,604	0	9,519,604	−4.8
425	0	9,864,875	0	9,864,875	−1.4
440	+3.5	10,210,146	0	10,210,146	+2.1
455	+7.1	10,565,281	0	10,565,281	+5.7
470	+10.6	10,910,552	0	10,910,552	+9.1
485	+14.1	11,255,822	0	11,255,822	+12.6

To insure a $10 million portfolio, 235 put options (90-day expiration) with a strike price of 410 are purchased for $135,125 (235 × $575). The balance of $9,864,875 remains invested in a diversified portfolio of equities that matches the performance of the S&P 100.
* Dividends not included.

The second significant difference is that there are no strict guidelines as to how many puts to buy. Table 7–4 shows how this strategy performs at different market levels. The reasoning behind the choice of 449 options is as follows: $258,500 was the cost of the at-the-money puts in strategy 3. That dollar amount was chosen as an acceptable amount to risk in terms of underperforming the market in the event of a market rally. Out-of-the-money puts were purchased instead of at-the-money puts due to the desire to take advantage of the leverage feature of options. Obviously, a portfolio manager would have a different market forecast for strategy 5 than for strategy 3.

The cash outlay cost of this strategy is the same as for strategy 3—$258,500. As a result, this portfolio will underperform the market by 2.6 percent if the market remains at the current level of 425 or rallies.

If the market declines slightly, you risk losing a maximum of 6.1 percent. That happens if the market declines to an index level of 410, at which point the equity portfolio has declined 3.5 percent and the puts expiring worthless represent a 2.6 percent loss. Below the index level of 410, however, the leverage effect of the put options comes into play. At an index level of 395 and a market decline of 7.1 percent, the puts have

TABLE 7–4
Strategy 5: Buying a Portfolio Multiple of Out-of-The-Money Puts

Index Level at Option Expiration	Index Percent Change	Equity Portfolio Value ($)*	Put Option Value ($)	Total Portfolio Value ($)	Portfolio Percent Change
365	−14.1%	$ 8,367,949	$2,020,500	$10,388,449	+3.9%
380	−10.6	8,708,901	1,347,000	10,055,901	+0.6
395	−7.1	9,049,854	673,500	9,723,354	−2.8
410	−3.5	9,400,548	0	9,400,548	−6.0
425	0	9,741,500	0	9,741,500	−2.6
440	+3.5	10,082,453	0	10,082,453	+0.8
455	+7.1	10,433,147	0	10,433,147	+4.3
470	+10.6	10,774,099	0	10,774,099	+7.7
485	+14.1	11,115,052	0	11,115,052	+11.2

Use $258,500 to purchase 449 put options (90-day expiration) with a strike price of 410 ($258,500 divided by $575). The balance of $9,741,500 remains invested in a diversified portfolio of equities that matches the performance of the S&P 100.
* Dividends are not included.

increased in value from the cost of $258,500 to $673,500 value, and the result is only a 2.8 percent overall portfolio decline. As the market continues to decline, the leverage effect of the puts boosts portfolio performance to a profit position. At an index level of 380, a 10.6 percent market decline, the portfolio shows a .6 percent profit. And at an index level of 365, a 14.1 percent market decline, the portfolio shows a 3.9 percent profit.

All three put option strategies are summarized in Table 7–5.

Choosing a Portfolio Insurance Strategy

In analyzing or choosing an option strategy, there are a number of important considerations. The first is the cost of the strategy; the second, the risk. Another important consideration is the portfolio manager's opinion of the market. Unfortunately, a vague opinion will not suffice. Because the most popularly traded options typically have a life of less than six months, market opinion must be specific in terms of direction, percentage of movement, and duration. The portfolio manager must also be able to articulate the advantage that options can bring to this particular investment situation.

TABLE 7–5
Comparison of Results for Strategies 3, 4, and 5

Index Level at Option Expiration	Percent Change	Percent Change Strategy 3	Percent Change Strategy 4	Percent Change Strategy 5
365	−14.1%	−2.2%	−4.7%	+3.9%
380	−10.6	−2.3	−4.8	+0.6
395	−7.1	−2.4	−4.8	−2.8
410	−3.5	−2.5	−4.8	−6.0
425	0	−2.6	−1.4	−2.6
440	+3.5	+.8	+2.1	+0.8
455	+7.1	+4.3	+5.7	+4.3
470	+10.6	+7.7	+9.1	+7.7
485	+14.1	+11.2	+12.6	+11.2

Initial portfolio value = $10,000,000.
S&P 100 at 425.
Strategy 3: Buying 235 at-the-money puts (a portfolio equivalent quantity).
Strategy 4: Buying 235 out-of-the-money puts (a portfolio equivalent quantity).
Strategy 5: Buying 449 out-of-the-money puts (a portfolio multiple quantity).

When the specific market opinion is formulated and the desired benefit is identified, the time frame should then be chosen. As you can see, some strategies are implemented for the life of the option, perhaps as long as six months, and others are implemented for less than one month, at which point the option position is liquidated.

The portfolio manager should also take into account the implied volatility level of options. While it is always better to buy something at the best possible price, the exact level of implied volatility is more important in some situations than in others.

Finally, the expected frequency of use for each strategy deserves discussion.

For a summary of the analytical process in choosing one of these strategies, see the grid in Table 7–6, followed by a detailed explanation of each column.

Column 1: Selling the Portfolio

Selling the portfolio is, in effect, the ultimate insurance policy. Once in cash, there is no risk if the market declines. It is obvious, however, that selling an entire portfolio is not done lightly or frequently. In fact, this

TABLE 7–6
Portfolio Insurance Strategy Grid

	Strategy 1: Selling the Portfolio	Strategy 2: Selling Stock Index Futures	Strategy 3: Buying a Portfolio Equivalent of At-the-Money Puts	Strategy 4: Buying a Portfolio Equivalent of Out-of-the-Money Puts	Strategy 5: Buying a Portfolio Multiple of Out-of-the-Money Puts
Cost	Commissions and impact on market	Discount or premium of futures to real market level	2.6%	1.4%	2.6%
Risk	Miss market rally	Miss market rally	Perform 2.6% worse than market	Maximum loss 4.8%	Maximum loss 6%
Specific market opinion	Long-term bearish	Bearish 4–12 months	Bearish 3 months	Bullish, but worried	Short-term very bearish
Benefit of options	n.a.	n.a.	Market timing portfolio hedge	Disaster insurance	Leverage profit from market decline
Time frame of strategy	1 1/2–3 years	4–12 months	1–3 months	3–6 months	2–4 weeks; will liquidate if market does not begin to move
Implied volatility	n.a.	n.a.	Should buy options at low end of implied volatility range	Relatively unimportant; do not want to buy extremely high implied volatility	Very important; must buy options at low end of implied volatility range
Expected frequency of use	Once in 5–10 years	Once every 2–3 years	Once per year	Once every 18–24 months	10 times in 20 years

n.a.: Not applicable.

would be a major policy decision that would probably occur only at the end of a market cycle. There would undoubtedly be strong fundamental economic considerations, perhaps the forecast of a prolonged recession. Consequently, the portfolio manager would not simply be bearish, he would be predicting a 25 to 40 percent market decline over one to three years. This strategy simply would not be practical for a three-month or even a six-month period.

In the cost/risk area, however, this strategy has many ramifications. For a portfolio of any size, converting all equities to cash is not easy or inexpensive, and commissions are only part of the cost. The true full cost includes the spread between the current market price and the sale price of the equities. An increase in the supply of a given stock can drive down its price and, for large blocks of stock, this can be a significant discount. For taxable portfolios, this strategy has considerable cost consequences. For individuals with long-term holdings at a very low cost basis, this strategy is virtually impractical.

The ultimate test of cash conversion is the price at which the portfolio is repurchased. The risk, therefore, is being wrong in the market forecast and missing a bull market move. If the repurchase occurs at a market level higher than at the time of sale, this strategy results in an opportunity loss, rather than a recognizable trading loss.

Column 2: Selling Stock Index Futures

As stated earlier it is not within the purview of this book to discuss all the technicalities of using stock index futures. However, a stock index futures contract is equivalent to some dollar value portfolio that matches the underlying index, and a portfolio manager seeking protection against a market decline can sell stock index futures contracts against a broadly based equity portfolio with the goal of becoming "neutral the market." Although this is never perfectly achievable, the concept is that the loss experienced by an equity portfolio during a market decline is offset by the profit from the short stock index futures contracts.

This strategy has the advantage of not disrupting the existing equity holdings, which is especially important to taxable portfolios. Other advantages are lower commissions and ease of execution. The ease of execution, however, has been called into question by the October 1987 crash. Nevertheless, the subsequent recovery has shown that this strategy can be implemented satisfactorily for portfolios with values that extend to hundreds of millions of dollars.

Because of the relative ease of entry and exit, the portfolio manager has more flexibility in acting upon bearish market forecasts. If, for example, the institutional investor predicts a 10 percent market correction over three to six months, it would not be practical to sell the portfolio with the goal of buying it all back at a price 10 percent lower. Use of stock index futures contracts, however, could protect a portfolio during this time period.

The risk of this strategy, as with selling all holdings, is missing a market rally. The cost, in addition to commissions, includes any discount or premium to the index at which the futures contracts trades are executed.

Column 3: Buying a Portfolio Equivalent of At-the-Money Index Puts

Although index put options are available with maturities in excess of one year, the most liquid series are in the first six months. Consequently, at the current time, it seems best to limit option insurance strategies to that time frame.

The market opinion required to make a portfolio insurance strategy appropriate must take into account the expected move relative to the price of the option. In the example discussed earlier, the 90-day at-the-money 425 puts were priced at $11 or 2.6 percent of the index value. This means that the market must decline 2.6 percent for the put position to break even at option expiration. As such, the portfolio manager must have a strong expectation that a market decline in excess of 2.6 percent is likely to occur. To understand why such an expectation is essential, look at the cost/risk of this strategy. The risk is underperforming the market by 2.6 percent—the cost of the put options. If the market remains at the same level or rallies, the put options expire worthless, and this insured portfolio underperforms the market by 2.6 percent.

Why would a manager be willing to risk underperforming the market by 2.6 percent during a 90-day period (a 10.4 percent annual rate)? The manager is willing to take this risk because he or she has an extremely bearish view and hopes to beat the market performance by profiting from owning the puts. Clearly, the objective of the option purchase is to have profit and thereby to limit or insure against portfolio losses.

Because the puts in this case are at-the-money, they have the highest price change response to the level of implied volatility. In fact, during the period of 1986 to 1987, at-the-money put options traded as low as 3 percent of the index (11 percent implied volatility) to 15 percent of the index (45 percent implied volatility). The higher number, of course, occurred in the aftermath of the October 1987 crash. This means that knowledge of implied volatility levels and an opinion about future levels are vital.

Column 4: Buying a Portfolio Equivalent of Out-of-the-Money Puts

What are the implications of buying puts with a strike price below the current market level? At first glance it may seem that there are only two differences between this strategy and buying at-the-money puts: a lower cash outlay (1.4 versus 2.6 percent) and a greater maximum portfolio decline (4.8 versus 2.6 percent). In fact, the other considerations for this strategy—market opinion, time frame, option objective, and implied volatility—are significantly different as well.

Market opinion, as with any equity investment decision, is the place to start. A manager who had a high expectation of a market decline would be willing to pay more for portfolio insurance and would buy at-the-money puts. One who is less certain, but has that "nagging feeling" that a market correction is within the realm of possibility, would be willing to pay a smaller amount.

To make this distinction clearer, consider the following two scenarios. In the first, after a two-and-a-half-year bull market, a portfolio manager sees that gradually rising interest rates have not yet been digested by the market. Further, the latest research reports indicate that three major industries are facing labor negotiations and that walkouts in one or two are likely. This institutional investor feels that another major negative development is all it would take to send the market down, and his market experience and knowledge of the political and economic situation make him believe that such an event is likely. In this scenario, the 2.6 percent cost of at-the-money puts is warranted.

In the second scenario, the market has been moving sideways for four months after a 60-day 8 percent rally. The research reports are favorable, and the portfolio manager's fundamental outlook is positive. Experience, however, suggests that all may not be as it seems. Bullish sentiment is high, the advance-decline line is sloping downward, and institutional cash holdings are at a low level. The portfolio manager is bullish, but is facing this quandary: Will the overbought condition be resolved by more sideways movement, or by a market correction? The manager is clearly willing to ride out a minor market correction, but he believes in the possibility of a short sharp correction. In this scenario, cheaper insurance is desired. The out-of-the-money puts are the best choice, because the portfolio manager is bullish in the longer term and does not want the expensive cost of at-the-money puts to significantly reduce performance relative to market averages.

What time frame is relevant for purchasing out-of-the-money puts? Because the certainty of the market decline is less than in the first scenario, and because the cash cost is lower per unit of time for longer options, this strategy seems more appropriate for five-, six-, or seven-month options. The overall cost of the strategy is low and, with the timing in doubt, it is best to allow as much time as possible for the insurance to remain in effect.

The level of implied volatility and the objective in using options also need to be addressed. A low level of implied volatility is always favorable when buying options but is less important when buying out-of-the-money puts than when buying at-the-money puts. Although the change in option price has a nearly linear relationship to the change in volatility (because the overall cost of the out-of-the-money puts is relatively low), a higher level of implied volatility does not significantly change the cost of this strategy as a percentage of the total portfolio. Of course, in extreme conditions such as the aftermath of October 19, 1987, this may not be true, but in normal times, the level of implied volatility does not greatly affect the decision to implement this tactic.

In this portfolio insurance strategy, the objective in purchasing the options is to have them expire—worthless! Strange as it may sound, the portfolio manager actually hopes that these out-of-the-money put options expire worthless. After all, a homeowner does not hope that the house burns down so that the insurance policy will provide some compensation. Similarly, a portfolio manager who buys out-of-the-money puts does not hope that the market declines so that the portfolio will decrease in value by a lesser percentage than the overall market. This is a hard concept for many investors to digest. But there are times when the experienced money manager recognizes that a sharp market correction, even though not expected, has a probability of occurring that is high enough to justify the expenditure of 1 1/2 to 2 percent of the portfolio on out-of-the-money puts for three to six months of insurance.

Column 5: Buying a Portfolio Multiple of Out-of-the-Money Puts

Strategy 5 has the possibility of actually profiting from a market decline. The cost of the options is 2.6 percent of the portfolio—the same as strategy 3. However, the risk is the greatest of any of the put buying strategies. If the overall market drops to an index level of 410 (equivalent to the strike price of the puts), the portfolio loses 6 percent, which would compare to an overall market decline of 3.5 percent.

How often is this strategy useful? To quantify the answer, Table 7–4 shows that with a nearly 15 percent market decline, the strategy of buying a portfolio multiple of out-of-the-money puts will actually show a positive return for the entire portfolio. Since 90-day puts are used in the example, it seems reasonable to ask how often the Dow Jones Industrial Average (DJIA) declined by 15 percent or more in 90 days. If this has never happened, the discussion of this method would be no more than an academic exercise. This is a severe yardstick—a 15 percent or greater decline in 90 days. The number of such occurrences is shown in Table 7–7. This has happened 11 times between 1969 and 1993, less than once every two years. With a less strict test, say 12 percent in 100 days, the number of such occurrences is close to once per year. This knowledge should open the eyes of many portfolio managers to the possible benefits of this option strategy.

TABLE 7–7
11 Times in 24 Years

	Start Date	DJIA	Finish Date	DJIA	Number of Days	Percent Decline
1.	5/14/69	974	7/30/69	788	77	19.0%
2.	11/10/69	871	2/3/70	738	85	15.2
3.	4/9/70	798	5/27/70	631	48	20.9
4.	10/29/73	999	12/5/73	783	37	21.4
5.	6/11/74	865	8/29/74	651	79	24.7
6.	11/6/74	692	12/9/74	570	33	17.6
7.	7/22/77	972	10/19/77	809	89	16.7
8.	2/13/80	918	3/27/80	729	42	20.5
9.	6/30/81	988	9/28/81	807	90	18.3
10.	8/25/87	2,722	10/19/87	1,738	55	36.0
11.	7/16/90	2,999	10/11/90	2,365	87	21.4

Between 1969 and 1993 the Dow Jones Industrial Average fell more than 15 percent in less than 90 days—11 times.

The objective of this strategy is to take advantage of the leverage aspect of the options and to profit from the anticipated market decline. In order for a portfolio manager to take the risk of performing 10 percent worse than the market, he must be extremely confident of his market opinion. In fact, this strategy has no direct insurance analogy. It is more of a speculation on a market decline.

What, then, are the key elements to making this strategy successful? The answer to this question has two parts: the knowledge of implied volatility levels and the choice of the appropriate time frame.

Although the implied volatility level was not significant in strategy 4 (buying a portfolio equivalent of out-of-the-money puts), implied volatility levels are critical in buying a portfolio multiple of out-of-the-money puts. The implied volatility level is important for three reasons. First, because the quantity of options purchased is determined by the dollar amount (or portfolio percentage) allocated, more options can be purchased if the price (implied volatility level) is low. For this example, 2.6 percent of the portfolio was chosen because this is the same amount invested in at-the-money puts in strategy 3. Using this amount clearly demonstrates the effect of leverage when using out-of-the-money options. However, there is no specific rule for the amount allocated when using this strategy.

A second reason the level of implied volatility is important when implementing this strategy is if the puts are purchased at a high implied volatility level, then they will decrease in price rapidly should implied volatility levels decline. This could happen with or without the market declining as expected. Third, an increase in implied volatility, in addition to appreciation from market movement, greatly adds to the options' increase in price. Consequently, the ideal time to implement this strategy is when implied volatility is low and expected to increase.

The best time frame is similar to the one chosen for any speculation—usually very short. Since success depends on a sharp market move (which, by definition, must be unexpected by the general market), it is likely that in two to four weeks this speculative strategy will prove to work or not. That is the point to sell the options with a profit or no more than a small loss. This is a major difference from the other put buying strategies, in which the plan is to hold them until expiration. With this strategy, however, the plan is to sell the options within two to four weeks of their purchase if the anticipated market decline has not begun.

The fact that this method calls for holding the options for no more than a month does not imply that options with four weeks left until expiration are the best buy. Actually, options with a strike price 15 index points below the current market level that have 90 days or longer until expiration are the preferred choice here. Time decay in option prices is significant in the last 30 days, and option-buying strategies using these very short-term options must be planned carefully. If 90-day put options are purchased, they will increase in price either from a sharp down move or an increase in volatility. Perhaps both will happen. When using the 90-day or longer-term options, portfolio managers must have the discipline to liquidate the position at the point when either the strategy has worked successfully, or it has been judged to be unsuccessful.

Where the Insurance Analogy Breaks Down

The term *portfolio insurance* is not used in a strict sense to mean the insurance used by property owners. In fact, many attributes of those policies do not apply to portfolio insurance. First, the home or car owner hopes that he or she never has to make a claim on the policy. Second, mortgage lenders and many state laws require certain types of insurance. Third, home insurance, at least, generally costs less than 1 percent annually of the market value of the insured property. Finally, payoffs from home and car insurance can be several hundred times the premium.

There is certainly no requirement that portfolio managers purchase portfolio insurance. The motivation behind buying put options is a negative market forecast and can entail a desire to profit from the put-option purchase. In the previous example of buying at-the-money puts (strategy 3), the total cost of insuring the portfolio for 90 days comes to 2.6 percent of the portfolio; that implies an annual rate of 10.4 percent, which is unquestionably too expensive to be used continuously. Although there are stories of options going up 1,000 percent, most success stories deal with options doubling or tripling rather than multiplying several hundred times.

The conclusion to be drawn from these differences is that portfolio insurance strategies are more properly called *market timing strategies*. They give the portfolio manager several alternatives to use for the purpose of increasing returns and managing market risk. Before the birth of these option products, the range of alternatives available was limited to owning stocks, investing in cash, or having a combination of the two.

MARKET TIMING

Although market timing has its critics, many professional investors recognize that a manager who changes the portfolio mix between equities and cash is essentially making market timing decisions. Almost by definition, unless a portfolio manager has 100 percent invested in equities all the time, he is a market timer. Consider a portfolio manager who, over the course of time, is "fully invested" at one point, "maintaining cash reserves for buying opportunities" at another point, and "largely in cash waiting for the market to bottom" at a third point in time. Many portfolio managers who make these statements also say, "I am not a market timer." But the motivation behind each of these statements is a market opinion and therefore a market timing opinion. "I am fully invested" means "I am bullish." In this case, the portfolio manager would not be using any of the portfolio insurance strategies discussed above.

"I am maintaining cash reserves for buying opportunities" means "I am long-term bullish but short-term bearish." This situation might dictate being fully invested and employing one of the put-buying strategies.

"I am largely in cash" means "I am bearish" and might indicate use of the put-buying strategy that profits from a sharp down move. Indeed, looking at portfolio insurance strategies in the light of market timing decisions can give the portfolio manager additional insight into the nature of these tools and their appropriate use.

DYNAMIC HEDGING CAN REDUCE MARKET EXPOSURE USING PUTS

Index put options can be used on a very short-term basis (one to three weeks) to decrease a portfolio's exposure to the equity market during a temporary market decline or during the time it takes to sell individual equities. An example of when this strategy is appropriate is a situation in which a portfolio manager has decided to reduce the equity allocation and is concerned about the effect of a market decline during the two-week period that it will take to select and sell individual equities. To begin with, assume that the S&P 500 Index is at 455. Anticipating a moderate decline in the market, a portfolio manager decides to reduce equity exposure by $7.5 million through the purchase of index puts. A two-month, at-the-money S&P 500 put with a 455 strike is selling at $6 3/4 and has an estimated delta of −.55. The manager reduces equity exposure by purchasing 300 index puts [7.5 million/($100 multiplier × 455 index × .55 delta)]. The cost of this position is $202,500 ($675 option premium × 300 options).

Two weeks later, the manager selects the equities to sell. If the index now stands at 450 and the S&P 500 put is $9 7/8, the put position has a value of $296,250, representing a profit of $93,750. Assuming that the equities declined by the same proportion as the index, this profit offsets the $82,418 loss incurred on the sale of the equities.

This strategy is called *dynamic hedging* because the number of index options purchased depends on the delta of the option being used. Because an option's delta changes with market movement, the use of this strategy can involve the buying and selling of options during the hedging period.

In the previous example, if the market had moved to an index level of 450 before the individual equities had been chosen, the delta of the 455 put options would have risen to −.68. This would have changed the portfolio market value represented by the put options to $9,180,000 (450 × $100 × .68 × 300). Meanwhile, the equity portfolio would be $7,417,582 ($7,500,000 − $82,418). At the index level of 450, only 242 options would be required to hedge the equity portfolio [$7,417,582/(450 × $100 multiplier × .68 delta)]. Consequently, 58 of the options would be sold, and the portfolio manager would have a new position of *delta equality*—long $7,417,582 of equities and short $7,417,582 represented by index put options. Adjusting the option position could then be repeated until the time when the individual equities were sold, at which point the put options would also be sold.

This dynamic feature could also work if only part of the equities were sold at one time. For example, if the equities were sold in three blocks, each on a different day, the put options could also be sold in three blocks. The goal would be to maintain a short market position in options equal to the long market position in equities until both positions were sold. In this way, the equity market exposure of the portfolio would have been reduced during the period it took to implement the selling program.

Dynamic hedging is perhaps the most frequently misunderstood strategy. It is confused with insurance strategies, and its essentially short-term use is often overlooked. Successful use depends on knowledge of implied volatility levels and the option time decay curve. The portfolio manager must decide on the time period of the dynamic hedge and then carefully examine the possible returns from the options, given a change in market level and implied volatility. If these elements are carefully integrated, a manager can see how effective this tool can be.

INDEX CALL BUYING STRATEGIES

Increasing Market Exposure with Limited Risk

Because index call options replicate a dollar portfolio of the underlying index, it is possible to match a portfolio's total dollar investment by purchasing index call options. The advantages of doing this are similar to the advantages of buying call options on individual equities. For the limited risk of the premium paid, the call buyer can participate in a broad market advance.

There are four general ways to employ index call buying. Three are variations on the same concept of buying calls with the goal of participating in a broad market rally while having limited risk on the downside. These three strategies are: (1) buying a portfolio equivalent quantity of at-the-money index calls, (2) buying a portfolio equivalent quantity of out-of-the-money calls, and (3) buying a portfolio multiple of out-of-the-money calls.

The fourth method of employing index call options is a short-term market timing tool used when increasing a portfolio's equity exposure. Proper use requires knowledge of implied volatility levels and the option's time decay curve, as will be discussed.

In the following examples, assume that the portfolio in question has $10 million in cash and the S&P 100 Index and related options closed at the prices indicated in Table 7–8.

The 90/10 Strategy

A tactic traditionally known as the *90/10 strategy* enables portfolio managers to achieve two goals simultaneously: capital preservation and potential appreciation from a market rally. This method involves the purchase of index call options with a small portion of a portfolio's capital—say 10 percent—and the purchase of low risk cash equivalents with the remaining 90 percent. Hence the name 90/10. The maximum risk is the premium paid for the calls, and, above the break-even index

TABLE 7–8
Index Call Buying Strategies

90-Day Call Strike Price	Call Option Price
425	8 3/4
430	6
435	4
440	2
445	1 1/2
450	3/4
455	1/4

90-day Treasury bills pay 3.0 percent annual rate.
  Calculating portfolio equivalent quantity of options:
Number of calls = Portfolio dollar value ÷ (Index level × Multiplier).
For a $10 million portfolio: 10,000,000 ÷ (425 × 100) = 235.

level implied by the call price, the index call options allow the portfolio to participate dollar for dollar in a market rally.

From Table 7–8, one can calculate that 235 calls is the proper quantity required to replicate a $10 million portfolio. With the S&P 100 Index at 425, each option represents a market value of $42,500 ($100 × Index level of 425), and thus 235 options are required ($10,000,000 divided by $42,500).

The at-the-money calls with a strike price of 425 are purchased at 8 3/4 each for a total cost of $205,625. The remaining balance of $9,794,375 is used to purchase 90-day Treasury bills that pay 3 percent annually, resulting in a maturity value of $9,867,833. Table 7–9 demonstrates how the portfolio of T-bills plus 235 at-the-money calls perform at various index levels.

The Percent Change column shows that the maximum loss on this portfolio is 1.3 percent (the premium paid for the index calls minus the interest earned on the cash investments). This occurs if the index level declines or remains constant and the calls expire worthless. With any market rally, however, this portfolio of at-the-money calls plus cash will participate in the market advance. If the market rallies to an index level of 485, a 14.1 percent advance, this *cash-plus-calls* portfolio increases in value by 12.8 percent. It is important to note that the maximum loss of the portfolio is also the amount by which the portfolio will underperform the market if the index level rises.

TABLE 7–9
Strategy 1: Buying a Portfolio Equivalent of At-The-Money Calls

Index Level at Option Expiration	Index Percent Change	Cash Plus Interest Earned ($)	Call Option Value ($)	Total Portfolio Value ($)	Portfolio Percent Change
365	−14.1%	$9,867,833	$ 0	$ 9,867,833	−1.3%
380	−10.6	9,867,833	0	9,867,833	−1.3
395	−7.1	9,867,833	0	9,867,833	−1.3
410	−3.5	9,867,833	0	9,867,833	−1.3
425	0	9,867,833	0	9,867,833	−1.3
440	+3.5	9,867,833	352,500	10,193,333	+1.9
455	+7.1	9,867,833	705,000	10,572,833	+5.7
470	+10.6	9,867,833	1,057,500	10,925,833	+9.3
485	+14.1	9,867,833	1,410,000	11,277,833	+12.8

To replicate a $10 million portfolio, 235 call options (90-day expiration) with a strike price of 425 are purchased for $205,625 (235 × $875). The balance of $9,794,375 is invested in Treasury bills and earns $73,457.81 ($9,794,375 × .03 × .25).

Buying a Portfolio Equivalent of At-the-Money Calls

To replicate a $10 million portfolio, 235 call options (90-day expiration) with a strike price of 425 are purchased for $205,625 (235 × $875). The balance of $9,794,375 is invested in Treasury bills and earns $73,458.

Low-Cost Participation with Out-of-the-Money Calls

Participation in a market rally can be achieved by buying out-of-the-money options. This method requires less cash outlay than buying at-the-money index call options, although participation in the rally begins at a later point in the market rise. Purchasing 235 options with a strike price of 440 at a total cost of $47,000 ($200 each × 235) is only 63 percent of the interest earned of $74,648 on the remaining cash balance of $9,953,000. Table 7–10 illustrates how this cash plus index call buying strategy performs at different index levels.

This strategy, as illustrated, has no potential for loss because the interest earned is greater than the cost of the call options. However, in many cases there would be a loss if lower strike price calls were used. The loss would be calculated by determining the difference between the cost of the calls and the interest earned. In this example, the gain is 0.28

TABLE 7–10
Strategy 2: Buying a Portfolio Equivalent of Out-of-the-Money Calls

Index Level at Option Expiration	Index Percent Change	Cash Plus Interest Earned ($)	Call Option Value ($)	Total Portfolio Value ($)	Portfolio Percent Change
365	−14.1%	$10,027,648	$ 0	$10,027,648	+0.28%
380	−10.6	10,027,648	0	10,027,648	+0.28
395	−7.1	10,027,648	0	10,027,648	+0.28
410	−3.5	10,027,648	0	10,027,648	+0.28
425	0	10,027,648	0	10,027,648	+0.28
440	+3.5	10,027,648	0	10,027,648	+0.28
455	+7.1	10,027,648	352,500	10,380,148	+3.8
470	+10.6	10,027,648	705,000	10,732,648	+7.3
485	+14.1	10,027,648	1,057,500	11,085,148	+10.8

To replicate a $10 million portfolio, 235 call options (90-day expiration) with a strike price of 440 are purchased for $47,000 (235 × 200). The balance of $9,953,000 is invested in Treasury bills and earns $74,648 (9,953,000 × .03 × .25).

percent until the index reaches a level of 440—the strike price of the options. If, for example, the market rallies to an index level of 470, a 10.6 percent advance, this cash-plus-calls portfolio will achieve a 7.3 percent increase. This portfolio has underperformed the index by approximately 3.3 percent. You can calculate this by adding the cost of the calls minus the interest earned to the difference between the strike price of the calls and the index level at the time of the call purchase. In this example, the cost of the calls minus the interest is ($27,648), or 0.3 percent of the $10 million portfolio. The difference between the strike price of the calls (440) and the index level at the time of the call purchase (425) is 15 points, or 3.5 percent of the index level. Adding these figures together gives you 3.2 percent, the amount by which the portfolio using this call buying strategy will underperform the market in a broad rally.

Leverage with Out-of-the-Money Calls

In this strategy, a quantity of out-of-the-money calls greater than the portfolio-equivalent number is purchased so that the portfolio's performance will be increased by the leverage aspect of options. Determining the quantity to be purchased is a subjective decision. One commonly employed practice is to calculate the dollar amount required to purchase at-the-money calls as in strategy 1 and then use that dollar amount to purchase as many out-of-the-money calls as possible from strategy 2. In this case, $205,625, the amount used to purchase index call options in strategy 1, will purchase 1,028 out-of-the-money 440 calls ($205,625 divided by $200 equals 1,028). The upside leverage payoff of this strategy is demonstrated in Table 7–11.

If the market rallies to an index level of 470, a 10.6 percent advance, this cash-plus-calls portfolio increases by 29.5 percent, outperforming the market by 18.9 percent. At an index level of 485, this portfolio outperforms the market by 30.8 percent.

This portfolio will continue to outperform the index at an increasing rate, because 1,028 calls with a strike price of 440 represent the portfolio equivalent of $45,232,000 ($44,000 × 1,028). By comparison, a $10 million portfolio at an index level of 425 would have grown only to $10,352,500 at an index level of 440.

Upside leverage does not come without a cost, however. For any decline in the index level, the maximum potential loss is 1.3 percent, the premium paid for the calls minus the interest earned on the cash investments. This is not the worst case for the portfolio manager who is evaluated on his performance in comparison to the performance of the

TABLE 7–11
Strategy 3: Buying a Portfolio Multiple of Out-of-the-Money Calls

Index Level at Option Expiration	Index Percent Change	Cash Plus Interest Earned ($)	Call Option Value ($)	Total Portfolio Value ($)	Portfolio Percent Change
365	−14.1%	$9,867,833	$ 0	$ 9,867,833	−1.3%
380	−10.6	9,867,833	0	9,867,833	−1.3
395	−7.1	9,867,833	0	9,867,833	−1.3
410	−3.5	9,867,833	0	9,867,833	−1.3
425	0	9,867,833	0	9,867,833	−1.3
440	+3.5	9,867,833	0	9,867,833	−1.3
455	+7.1	9,867,833	1,542,000	11,409,833	+14.1
470	+10.6	9,867,833	3,084,000	12,951,833	+29.5
485	+14.1	9,867,833	4,626,000	14,493,833	+44.9

Use $205,625 to purchase 1,028 call options (90-day expiration) with a strike price of 440 (205,625 ÷ 200). The balance of $9,794,375 is invested in Treasury bills and earns 73,458 (9,794,375 × .03 × .25).

market and his peers. The worst case for the portfolio manager occurs when the market rallies only slightly to an index level of 440. At this point, the index has risen 3.5 percent and, with the 440 calls expiring worthless, this cash-plus-calls portfolio falls by 1.3 percent. This means that the portfolio has underperformed the market by 4.8 percent.

Choosing the Appropriate Call Buying Strategy

Table 7–12 summarizes and compares the percentage changes in the portfolio for call buying strategies 1, 2, and 3 at various index levels. Different payoff opportunities for each imply that various market environments and outlooks lead to the selection of each strategy.

Again, there are important considerations in selecting the appropriate strategy. The first is the cost of the strategy; the second is the risk. Risk is defined in terms of comparing the performance of the cash-plus-calls portfolio and the overall market performance. Market opinion, in all the required specificity described earlier, must be taken into account; and the benefit to be derived from buying calls must be clearly identified. Other considerations are the time frame for implementation and the implied volatility level. Finally, no strategy can be used continuously, so the next section reviews how often a particular one might reasonably be implemented.

TABLE 7–12
Comparison of Results in Index Call Buying Strategies 1, 2, and 3

Index Level at Option Expiration	Index Percent Change	Percent Change Strategy 1	Percent Change Strategy 2	Percent Change Strategy 3
365	−14.1%	−1.3%	+0.28%	−1.3%
380	−10.6	−1.3	+0.28	−1.3
395	−7.1	−1.3	+0.28	−1.3
410	−3.5	−1.3	+0.28	−1.3
425	0	−1.3	+0.28	−1.3
440	+3.5	+1.9	+0.28	−1.3
455	+7.1	+5.7	+3.8	+14.1
470	+10.6	+9.3	+7.3	+29.5
485	+14.1	+12.8	+10.8	+44.9

Analysis for Choosing Index Call Buying Strategy 3

Gaining Leverage

The payoff table for this strategy shows the model $10 million portfolio significantly outperforming the general market in a major rally. Consequently, market opinion must be extremely bullish for the very near term. Specifically, the portfolio manager must be looking for an increase in the index level from 425 to at least 455, a 7.1 percent market advance. Above that level, the cash-plus-calls portfolio increasingly outperforms the market. This move must be expected to begin in the very near future, probably within two to four weeks.

It may be of interest to understand a statistic of market rallies. Say in the above example the market move required to outperform the market was just under 20 percent. Although it may come as a surprise to many investors, this kind of rally occurs, on average, nearly once per year. Such a rally occurred in August 1982 when the Dow Jones Industrial Average rallied from 790 to 950 (a 20 percent advance) in two weeks. Table 7–13 lists similar moves from 1969 to November 1993.

This strategy would be employed to take advantage of the leverage aspect of options. A portfolio manager who employs this strategy must be sufficiently confident of a short-term bullish market opinion that allows for a possible reward, despite the risk of underperforming the market.

The time frame for this strategy is necessarily short. The portfolio manager's unusually bullish forecast must be prompted by something—a news event, a technical condition in the market, or some other pending development. Generally speaking, in such a situation the manager will know within two weeks to a month if his or her forecast is being realized. Consequently, the time to liquidate the option position is when the strategy is successful or when it becomes apparent that it is not working.

Deciding which options to buy is another matter. Expecting a major rally to begin in the next two to four weeks does not mean that the front-month options are the right choice. This strategy is a short-term bullish volatility play, and two events can make it profitable: a market rally or an increase in implied volatility. With the front-month options so close to expiration, it is unlikely that they will benefit much from an increase in implied volatility. Also, if the market rally starts later than expected, these options can expire just before the market rallies through the strike price. Farther out options have a higher absolute cost, but have the

TABLE 7–13
22 Times in 24 Years

	Start Date	DJIA	Finish Date	DJIA	Number of Days	Percent Increase
1.	5/26/70	628	6/19/70	728	24	15.9%
2.	7/7/70	669	9/8/70	773	63	15.5
3.	11/19/70	775	2/16/71	890	89	17.9
4.	11/23/71	790	1/18/72	917	56	16.0
5.	10/16/72	921	1/11/73	1,067	87	15.8
6.	8/22/73	851	10/29/73	985	67	15.7
7.	9/30/74	598	11/6/74	692	37	15.7
8.	12/9/74	579	2/21/75	749	74	29.3
9.	4/7/75	742	6/30/75	878	84	18.3
10.	12/8/75	821	2/25/75	994	79	21.0
11.	3/1/78	743	5/17/78	858	77	15.4
12.	3/27/80	730	6/17/80	887	82	21.5
13.	8/9/82	770	10/22/82	1,051	74	36.4
14.	2/2/83	1,046	4/29/83	1,226	86	17.2
15.	10/7/85	1,324	12/30/85	1,550	84	17.0
16.	1/22/86	1,502	4/21/86	1,856	88	23.5
17.	1/5/87	1,971	4/3/87	2,390	87	21.2
18.	5/29/87	2,291	8/25/87	2,722	88	18.8
19.	12/4/87	1,766	2/29/88	2,071	86	17.2
20.	11/16/88	2,038	2/7/89	2,347	83	15.1
21.	1/09/91	2,470	3/13/91	2,955	72	19.6
22.	12/10/91	2,862	3/03/92	3,291	83	15.0

Between 1969 and November 1993 the DJIA rose more than 15 percent 22 times in less than 90 days.

advantages of benefiting from an increase in implied volatility and a longer life to enable a bullish market forecast to materialize. A portfolio manager must weigh these trade-offs when choosing which option expiration to buy.

Implied volatility is an important consideration when buying a large quantity of out-of-the-money options. If the strategy is to buy 90-day options and sell them in two to four weeks if the rally has not started, the buy decision is best implemented with a thorough knowledge of implied volatility levels. Implied volatility changes can have a greater impact on the price of 90-day out-of-the-money options than time decay. If, instead, the strategy is to buy front-month options with three to four weeks until expiration and let them expire if the rally does not occur, implied volatility is not as important. In this situation, the ap-

TABLE 7–14
Index Call Buying Strategy Selection Grid

	Strategy 1: Buying a Portfolio Equivalent of At-the-Money Calls	Strategy 2: Buying a Portfolio Equivalent of Out-of-the Money Calls	Strategy 3: Buying a Portfolio Multiple of Out-of-the Money Calls
Cost	2%	.5%	2%
Risk	Underperform general market by 1.3%	Perform with the general market	Underperform general market by 1.3%
Specific market opinion	Bullish on pending developments, worried about sharp down move	Short-term bearish but worried about missing big market advance	Very bullish short term
Benefit of options	Expensive insurance (no deductible)	Low-cost insurance	Leverage
Time frame of implementation	1 month maximum	Buy 3–6 month options, willing to let them expire	2–6 weeks, then close out if not successful
Implied volatility	Should be on low end of range	Not an important consideration	Important consideration: Need low implied volatility
Expected frequency of use	As needed, depending on cash position of portfolio	As needed, depending on cash position of portfolio	Once every year, on average

proach is to take a low-cost, short-term option risk; the total price, not implied volatility, can be the most important factor.

The considerations for index call buying strategies are summarized in Table 7–14.

Analysis for Choosing Index Call Buying Strategy 2

Strategy 2 (buying a portfolio equivalent of out-of-the-money calls) is employed for completely different reasons and has completely different criteria than does strategy 3, yet both use out-of-the-money calls.

Examining payoff Table 7–10, one can ask: Why would a portfolio manager be willing to risk underperforming the market by 3.5 percent? The answer is that he or she has a bearish outlook and purchases calls for insurance. This strategy could be employed near the end of a bear market when a portfolio manager is in cash and still bearish, but is looking for an acceptable price level at which to buy stocks. This manager is looking for the market to bottom in the next two to four months and is planning to be fully invested at that point. In the meantime, upside protection is needed in case the market rallies sharply and unexpectedly, as it so often does at the end of bear markets. By owning call options, the portfolio manager insures participation in an upside rally.

Had this strategy been employed during the 20 percent market rise in August 1982, a cash-plus-calls portfolio could have increased by 14 percent. It underperformed the market by 6 percent, but the portfolio manager was bearish and out of stocks. The cost of options was approximately equal to interest income, and the options were an insurance policy against missing a big market rally.

The optimal time frame for any conventional insurance policy is for as long as possible. With this strategy, the manager must determine over what time period the portfolio will become fully invested, and plan the option purchase for that period. Generally, with this strategy, options would be purchased with a view to carrying them until expiration. If the market did not rally while this portfolio was becoming fully invested, the options would expire worthless—similar to any insurance policy expiring when no claim is made. The benefit to the portfolio in this case is the ability to buy individual equities at a lower market level.

Implied volatility is not a major consideration here either. A few out-of-the-money options are being purchased, and changes in implied volatility is not a meaningful percentage of the total portfolio. This strategy is designed as insurance against a major market move, so it is not likely that these options would be sold in the event of a quick market run-up or an increase in implied volatility. Doing so would eliminate the insurance before the portfolio was invested in equities.

This strategy can be employed whenever one has cash to invest, and when one is short-to-medium-term bearish and waiting to buy individual equities. That might be as infrequently as at the end of each bear market cycle or as frequently as when new funds are received for investing in equities.

Analysis for Choosing Index Call Buying Strategy 1

Strategy 1 (buying a portfolio equivalent of at-the-money calls) is similar to strategy 2 in that the portfolio participates in a market rally but underperforms the market—in this case by 1.3 percent. Also, at-the-money calls are more than twice as expensive as out-of-the-money calls.

What then must the market forecast be, and why purchase these expensive calls? The market forecast must be bullish, but the reason, again, is insurance.

There are two classic situations when this strategy is appropriate. The first is a major news event such as a presidential election. The portfolio manager predicts that the market will rally sharply after the election, but he or she realizes that the election results may cause the market to decline. In this situation, underperforming the market by 1.3 percent on the upside is a favorable trade-off relative to outperforming the market on the downside—a maximum loss of 1.3 percent versus a potentially significant market decline.

The second situation is one in which the money manager cannot afford to lose due to contractual obligations and, without the limited risk nature of call options, would otherwise be forced to buy only fixed-income investments. For example, assume a corporate treasurer must make a fixed pension contribution at some point in the future. If the money is available now and the treasurer is bullish, equities would not be appropriate due to the risk of a market decline. Any available funds, however, in excess of the fixed obligation (interest or excess accumulated funds) could be used to purchase call options, thereby insuring participation in a market rally.

In this strategy, the market forecast is more important than the implied volatility level of the options. Obviously, buying options when implied volatility levels are low is always advantageous. But with this strategy, matching the market forecast to the break-even index level of the call option strategy is the determining consideration. For example, in a bull market, when new investment funds are coming to a portfolio manager, index calls may be the quickest and easiest way to commit the funds to the market.

DYNAMIC HEDGING INCREASES MARKET EXPOSURE USING CALLS

Using call options to provide additional market exposure is a strategy with different implications than the insurance and leverage strategies just discussed. The goal here is to replicate market performance during the time it takes to shift a portfolio from cash investments into individual equity issues.

For example, assume that the S&P 500 Index is currently at 462. Anticipating a rapid advance in the market, the professional manager decides to commit an added $5 million to equities. Market exposure is initially increased by purchasing S&P 500 index calls. The plan is that stocks will be purchased as specific issues are selected and the amounts to be invested in each are determined. This professional investor decides to use one-month S&P 500 calls with a 460 strike. These sell for $8 1/4 and have an estimated delta of .55. To create an immediate $5 million exposure to the market on a point-for-point basis, 196 calls are bought [$5 million exposure/($100 multiplier × 463 index value × .55 delta)]. This represents an initial outlay of $161,700 ($825 premium × 196 calls).

One week later, the manager purchases a group of stocks to make up a $5 million equity investment. Assuming that the S&P 500 advances to 470 and the calls are trading at $12 1/2, then the call position is valued at $245,000 ($1,250 × 196 calls). The calls can then be sold for a net profit of $83,300 ($245,000 − $161,700) as the stocks are purchased. Assuming that the selected stocks increased in proportion to the index, the outlay for the stocks will be $5,086,580. The $86,580 increase in stock price is mostly offset by the $83,300 profit in the option position, which provided immediate participation in the market advance.

A logical question is, what would have happened if the market declined? Quite simply, the loss on the index calls would have been largely offset by the decrease in the purchase price of the stocks. Remember that the calls were purchased so that market exposure was increased immediately, with results very nearly the same as purchasing a portfolio of equities.

This strategy is sometimes called *dynamic hedging,* because the delta of an option changes as the index level changes. We saw the reverse of this strategy in an earlier section, using put options to *reduce* market exposure. Consequently, maintaining approximate equality between the initially desired portfolio and the index options requires buying and selling options as the market fluctuates. This process is known as *adjusting* and explains why the strategy is dynamic.

In the example just given, assume that on the day the 196 calls are purchased the market rallies to an index level of 465, the options increase to 9 1/2, and the delta of each one rises to .65. At this point, a $5,000,000 equity portfolio would have risen to $5,032,468 [5,000,000 × (465/462)]; 196 calls with a delta of .65, however, replicate a $5,924,100 portfolio (196 × 465 index level × $100 multiplier × .65 delta). The proper number of calls for a $5,032,468 portfolio is 166 [$5,032,468/

(465 index level × $100 multiplier × .65 delta)]. Consequently, at the end of day one, with the index up 3 points, 30 calls would be sold so that the call option position remained in balance with the desired equity portfolio.

To make this successful, the time period must be chosen carefully, and the portfolio manager must have considerable knowledge of implied volatility levels. This is a very short-term strategy. Time decay is a significant element here. If options are held too long, it is possible that time decay can take away all, or at least most of, the profit from owning them during a market rally. Depending on which options are purchased, this strategy is most effective in the two-to-four-week time frame.

Changes in implied volatility can also affect this strategy. The call option purchaser must have a basis for believing that implied volatility is not going to decline significantly during the period that dynamic hedging is implemented. Forecasting implied volatility requires knowledge and experience, but is not an impossibly difficult task.

OTHER PORTFOLIO STRATEGIES

Reducing Volatility by Writing Covered Calls

Covered call writing is a popular strategy among institutional investors. Selling call options against individual stocks reduces the variability of returns associated with stock ownership and enhances returns in stable or declining markets. Writing S&P 500 Index calls against a well diversified portfolio can provide the same benefits on a portfoliowide basis.

For example, assume that the S&P 500 Index is at 460 and that a diversified $10 million portfolio approximately matches the index and yields 2.4 percent. Expecting the market to remain within a 10 percent range over the next three months, the manager decides to sell 90-day, at-the-money index calls with a premium of 13 3/8. Dividing the value of the portfolio by the contract size times the index level, you can determine that 217 index calls can be sold against this portfolio [$10,000,000/ (460 index level × $100 multiplier)].

Figure 7–2 illustrates the return profile for this position at expiration under different market conditions.

In Table 7–15, column 4 lists changes in the call position under different market scenarios. Assuming that the stocks increase in proportion to the index, if the market advances 10 percent by expiration, the

FIGURE 7–2
Writing Index Calls against an Equity Portfolio (reduces volatility while
increasing cash flow)

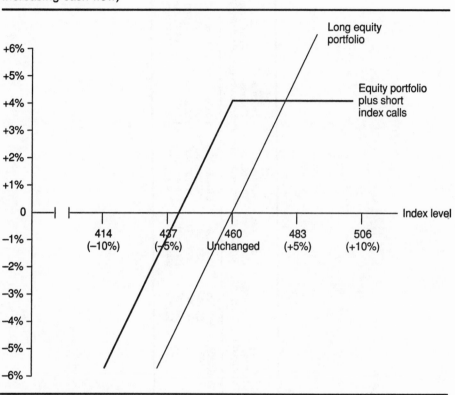

value of the portfolio will increase by $1 million. The value of the call
option at expiration is 46, which is the in-the-money amount (506 −
460). Loss on the short call position is $32 5/8, which is the in-the-
money amount minus the premium received ($46 − 13 3/8). Therefore,
the total call position shows a $707,962 loss ($3,262.50 per contract ×
217 contracts). If the call option expires unexercised, the seller will
keep the total $290,238 premium.

Column 6 in Table 7–15 shows a three-month portfolio dividend of
$60,000 (2.4 percent annual yield for three months on $10 million). The
dividend is constant and is not dependent on market movements. The
net change in the combined option/stock position is indicated in column
7, which is the sum of the value in columns 3, 4, and 6. The maximum
profit from the combined position is indicated by the horizontal line in

TABLE 7–15

Writing Index Calls on a Diversified Portfolio

(1) Range of Market Outcome (%)	(2) S&P 500 Expiration Level	(3) Change in Equity Position ($)	(4) Change in Options' Position ($)	(5) Value of Options' Position ($)	(6) Dividends ($)	(7) Profit/Loss Combined Portfolio ($)	(8) Value of Combined Portfolio ($)	(9) Percent Change (Unannualized)	(10) Profit/Loss Portfolio ($)	(11) Value of Unprotected Portfolio ($)
10%	506	$1,000,000	$(707,962)	$998,200	$60,000	$352,038	$10,352,038	3.52%	$1,060,000	$11,060,000
5	483	500,000	(208,862)	499,100	60,000	351,138	10,351,138	3.51	560,000	10,560,000
0	460	0	290,237	0	60,000	350,237	10,350,237	3.50	60,000	10,060,000
−5	437	(500,000)	290,237	0	60,000	(149,763)	9,850,237	−1.49	(440,000)	9,560,000
−10	414	(1,000,000)	290,237	0	60,000	(649,763)	9,350,237	−6.49	(940,000)	9,060,000

Figure 7–2. No matter how far the index advances, there is no potential for appreciation beyond the premium received. The numbers in column 7 of Table 7–15 do not indicate a perfectly horizontal maximum profit line due to an arithmetic technicality. The equity portfolio is assumed to be exactly $10 million at an index level of 460 and will behave proportionately with market rises and declines. The option position, however, will behave like a slightly larger portfolio if the index level rises. This happens because a 460 call priced at 13 3/8 is similar to a starting index level of 473.38. The number of contracts, 217, equates to a $10,272,237 portfolio for index price rises above 473.38.

In the case of a market decline, the combined position will outperform a position consisting of only stocks. If the market declines slightly, the value for a stock portfolio will decline proportionately to the decline in the index, less dividends of $60,000, while the value of the portfolio covered with call options may actually increase.

The premiums earned by writing covered calls provide a cushion against loss in a declining market, and extra income in a flat market. This is an effective strategy for institutional investors who (1) want to supplement the dividend income of a portfolio, (2) want to reduce the downside risk of a portfolio, (3) are willing to exchange upside potential for downside protection, or (4) believe that call premiums are overvalued.

The risk/reward characteristics of a covered writing strategy change, depending on whether in-the-money or out-of-the-money options are used. Some differences are graphically presented in Figure 7–3. A portfolio manager who writes in-the-money options exchanges upside potential for premium income that provides downside protection. The more a call is in-the-money, the more protection it provides. A manager who writes at-the-money or out-of-the-money options participates more fully in a market advance, but limits downside protection on the portfolio. Whether the option is in-the-money or out-of-the-money, however, covered call writing does not totally insulate a portfolio from a severe market decline.

The Fence Strategy

To build a *fence* around possible returns, combine two strategies previously discussed: buying an index put option for insurance and, at the same time, selling an index call to reduce volatility and enhance portfolio income. This is demonstrated graphically in Figure 7–4 and numerically in Table 7–16. With an overall market decline, the long index puts

FIGURE 7–3

Writing Index Calls against an Equity Portfolio (a comparison of strike price selection)

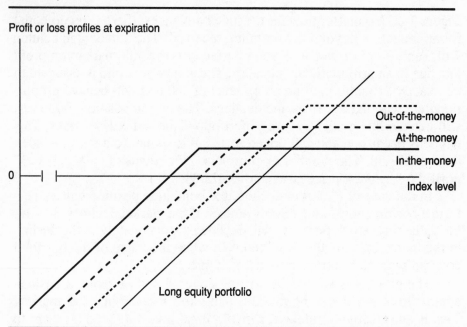

Profit or loss profiles at expiration

Out-of-the-money

At-the-money

In-the-money

Index level

0

Long equity portfolio

FIGURE 7–4
Fence Strategy

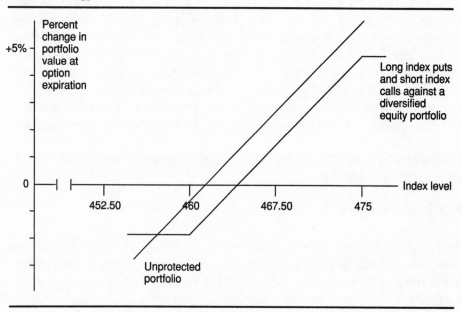

Percent change in portfolio value at option expiration

+5%

0

Index level

452.50   460   467.50   475

Long index puts and short index calls against a diversified equity portfolio

Unprotected portfolio

TABLE 7–16
The Fence Strategy with a Diversified Portfolio

(1) Range of Market Outcome (%)	(2) S&P 500 Expiration Level	(3) Change in Equity Position ($)	(4) Change in Options' Position ($)	(5) Value of Options' Position ($)	(6) Dividends ($)	(7) Profit/Loss Combined Portfolio ($)	(8) Value of Combined Portfolio ($)	(9) Percent Change (Unannualized)	(10) Profit/Loss Portfolio ($)	(11) Value of Unprotected Portfolio ($)
10.0%	509	$1,000,000	$(788,400)	$(734,400)	$60,000	$271,600	$10,271,600	2.71%	$1,000,000	$11,000,000
2.6	475	260,000	(54,000)	0	60,000	266,000	10,266,000	2.66	260,000	10,260,000
1.5	470	150,000	(54,000)	0	60,000	156,000	10,156,000	1.56	150,000	10,150,000
0	463	0	(54,000)	432,000	60,000	6,000	10,006,000	0.06	0	10,000,000
−5	440	(500,000)	378,000	432,000	60,000	(62,000)	9,938,000	−0.62	(500,000)	9,500,000
−10	417	(1,000,000)	874,800	928,800	60,000	(65,200)	9,934,800	−0.65	(1,000,000)	9,000,000

limit the possible loss, while the returns from a market advance are limited by the sale of the index calls.

There is no real insurance analogy for the combination of these two strategies. This strategy is based on the portfolio manager's desire to lower the net cost of insurance (the put purchase) by giving up some upside profit potential (the covered call sale). A portfolio manager who expects the market to decline sharply, but feels that implied volatility levels are too high, might consider simultaneously selling a call option and buying a put option.

For example, with the S&P 500 Index at 463, a $10 million portfolio can be insured for 60 days by buying 216 index put options with a strike price of 460 [$10,000,000/(463.00 × $100)]. At a price of 5 5/8 each, the total cost is $121,500 (216 × 562.50). The index level at which the put option purchase breaks even is 454.38 (460 − 5 5/8). This represents a market decline of 1.8 percent (463.00 − 454.38)/463.00). The cost of the puts could be reduced by selling the index calls with a 475 strike price for $3 1/8 each. The total premium received from the sale of 216 calls would be $67,500 ($312.50 × 216). This would lower the net cost of the strategy to $54,000.

Sale of the calls would also raise the downside break-even index level to 457.50 (460.00 − 2.50) which represents a market decline of 1.2 percent. While this level of downside protection is attractive compared to the break-even level of the put purchase alone, this benefit is not achieved without a cost. That cost is the opportunity cost limiting the upside potential of the portfolio to an index level of 475. Above that level, the short calls will lose as the market (and the portfolio) rises.

The risk/reward profile for the combined strategy of buying a put and selling a call is presented in Table 7–16. This table describes the returns the investment manager could expect from a $10 million portfolio protected by the fence strategy (purchase of puts strike 460 and sale of calls strike 475). Figure 7–4 presents a picture of the return profile at option expiration.

In the fence strategy, the long put limits the downside risk, and the short call limits the upside potential. The fence is often seen as a low cost method of buying insurance, and it is frequently thought to be excellent if the insurance can be bought for "nothing." In some cases, calls that are closer to the money can be sold for a premium equal to or greater than the cost of puts, which are slightly farther from the money. Note, however, that focusing exclusively on the cost of the strategy ignores other important factors central to portfolio management. General issues of managing risk and reward are, by their very nature, subjective. Any investment decision is a decision that the prevailing market price is wrong in some sense. The decision to buy a stock presumes that the market is valuing a stock too low. Option trading decisions are no different in this basic sense. Portfolio managers buy puts as insurance because they believe the put premiums relative to current market levels and their market forecast represent a fair risk/reward ratio relative to owning a portfolio without insurance.

At a given decision point, a portfolio manager should consider the fence strategy as a viable alternative, but not because of its low cost alone. The first consideration should be the *market forecast*. The second should be the *portfolio's objective,* and third should be the *knowledge of current implied volatility levels*.

The Portfolio Repair Strategy

A variation of the repair strategy for individual equity issues discussed in Chapter 6 can also benefit broadly based portfolios that have experienced a 10 to 15 percent decline. Assume that $10 million was invested in a diversified group of equities, the performance of which closely follows the S&P 500 Index when it was at 450. If the index had subsequently declined 12 percent to 396, the portfolio would have a value of approximately $8.8 million. By using options on the S&P 500 index, the break-even point on this portfolio can be lowered to an index level of approximately 425, instead of 450. Here's how it works.

The strategy is to buy one near-the-money call option and sell two out-of-the-money call options at a total net cost that is very low. With the S&P 500 Index at 396, the 400 calls are near-the-money calls. An $8.8 million portfolio equivalent of these calls comes to 220 [$8,800,000 ÷ (400 × 100)]. At a price of $14 each, the cost of 220 calls is $308,000. The second part of the strategy is to sell twice as many index calls with a strike price of 425. At a price of $6 1/2 each, 440 of these calls can be sold for $286,000. This reduces the total cost of the strategy to $22,000 (not including transaction costs).

What has this accomplished? The long near-the-money index calls essentially double the market exposure of the equity portfolio. This means that the portfolio can recoup its losses in half the market rise required by the equity portfolio alone.

Portfolio appreciation, however, is limited to the level of the short index call options—in this case an S&P 500 Index level of 425. Above that point, at expiration, the short calls begin to appreciate in value and, therefore, offset additional gains in the long calls and the equity portfolio. How this strategy works is demonstrated in tabular form in Table 7–17.

In the example just given, note the use of S&P 500 Index options, instead of the more popular S&P 100 Index options. The reason this was done relates to the early exercise feature of American options. Because index options are cash settled, there is an additional risk in applying the repair strategy to a portfolio, a risk that does not exist when using equity options to repair a loss on an individual stock.

In the case of the equity options repair strategy, early exercise does not create additional risk, because the exercised short call can be met by delivering stock or by assuming a short stock position, which can then be met by the exercise of the lower strike price call option. For instance, assume the owner of a $44 stock decided to repair his unrealized loss by purchasing one $45 call and selling two $50 calls with the same expiration date. Assume the stock then rose to $55 and, one week prior to expiration, both short $50 calls were exercised. Against one of these $50 calls he delivered his long 100 shares of stock; against the other $50 call he exercised his $45 call, which enabled him to deliver stock against the

TABLE 7–17
Portfolio Values at Option Expiration

Equity Portfolio ($)*	Index Level	Percent Gain	Long 220 400 Calls P/(L) ($)	Short 440 425 Calls P/(L) ($)	Total Portfolio Value ($)*
$ 8,800,000	396	—	$ (308,000)	+$286,000	$ 8,778,000
8,900,000	400	1.00%	(308,000)	+286,000	8,878,000
9,000,000	405	2.27	(198,000)	+286,000	9,088,000
9,100,000	410	3.53	(88,000)	+286,000	9,298,000
9,200,000	415	4.80	+22,000	+286,000	9,508,000
9,300,000	420	6.06	+132,000	+286,000	9,718,000
9,400,000	425	7.57	+242,000	+286,000	10,000,000
9,500,000	430	8.58	+352,000	+66,000	10,000,000
9,600,000	435	9.85	+462,000	(154,000)	10,000,000
9,700,000	440	11.11	+572,000	(374,000)	10,000,000
9,800,000	445	12.37	+682,000	(594,000)	10,000,000
9,900,000	450	13.64	+792,000	(814,000)	10,000,000
10,000,000	455	14.90	+ 902,000	(1,034,000)	10,000,000
10,100,000	460	16.16	+1,012,000	(1,254,000)	10,000,000

* Numbers are rounded.

second short call as well. Between the time the notice was received of the exercise and the time he was able to exercise his $45 call, there was no market exposure because the short $50 call (when exercised) turned into short stock. As the short stock fluctuated, the long $45 call also fluctuated because it was deep-in-the-money.

Yet in the case of index options, the portfolio manager must deliver cash against a call that is exercised—an obligation that never changes. He is still left with the long portfolio and the long call options that have the lower strike. Consequently, he is long twice what is desired until he can sell the long call options. If the market opens substantially lower, the long calls would be sold at an index level below the level where he had to settle the short calls exercised against him.

The way to avoid this *overnight risk* or *early exercise risk* is to use European style options, such as the S&P 500 Index options, on which early exercise is not permitted. No early exercise privilege means these options are generally cheaper. Sometimes this will affect the pricing relationship of at-the-money and out-of-the-money options. As a result, it can be necessary to use different strike prices than optimally desired or to use an expiration farther out than with American style options.

Selling Equity Puts: A Portfolio Management View

Selling equity puts is, without question, the most controversial of all option strategies. It is viewed as highly risky and very speculative. Some critics have gone so far as to blame the October 19, 1987, crash in part on a large number of *naked* (or uncovered) put sellers. But is all this true?

Chapter 4 demonstrated that selling puts has exactly the same pay-off diagram as covered writing does. In Chapter 2, the discussion of put-call parity also demonstrated that the two strategies are identical.

Nevertheless, selling puts continues to be vilified while covered writing is accepted as a safe, conservative strategy. During an Options Institute class in July 1993, an opinion poll was taken of 32 participants. Twenty-two said that selling puts was "risky," and 28 said that selling puts was "inappropriate for institutions." Twenty-five said selling puts was "inappropriate for individuals." In contrast, 29 people said that covered writing is "conservative." Only five thought that covered writing was "inappropriate for individuals."

Why the difference? There seem to be three reasons. First, do not overlook that options are complicated. People may believe that the two strategies are different, because they have not been introduced to the concept of put-call parity. They may have also heard or read about the risk of *naked put selling*.

Second, for some inexplicable reason, there is a tendency to analyze a covered write from the point of view of, "How much can I make?" whereas the tendency is to analyze selling puts from the point of view of, "How much can I lose?"

Third, the use of margin changes the profit or loss potential of an option as a percentage of capital. And, typically, the put seller uses margin while the covered writer does not. Consequently, stories about losses from selling puts on margin—so-called *naked puts*—tend to be more dramatic than stories from covered writers who can brag that "The $2 call I sold expired worthless," even though the stock declined $10.

This discussion is a good introduction for considering equity put selling from a portfolio management perspective, because a comparison of the institutional investor and the individual speculator is most instructive. Their goals are different, the capital they manage is different, and the way they can benefit from options is often different.

It is important to make a clear distinction between a portfolio manager and a speculator. A speculator, for the purposes of this discussion, has limited capital, uses margin, and concentrates on one or two stock or option positions at a time.

The portfolio manager, by comparison, does not use margin and is constantly preoccupied with a portfolio of securities, probably at least 25 individual issues. Absolute quantity of capital is not the distinguishing feature, because there are many very large speculators. However, a portfolio manager has diversified his investments so that he does not consider himself to have limited capital.

With these clear distinctions in mind, the first obvious difference is in the willingness to buy the stock on which the puts are sold. The speculator has no intention of buying and owning the stocks. If the stocks are put to the speculator, this means that he was wrong. The stocks would be sold immediately. The portfolio manager, however, has sold puts on stocks that he is willing to own and that he would like to buy at a price below the current market price. In fact, when a money manager sells puts on a group of stocks, he fully expects to get some delivered to him. Thus, delivery of stock is not viewed as being wrong; it is viewed as buying a good stock at a good price.

There is a sharp difference in goals between the speculator and the portfolio manager. The speculator simply wants to collect the premium from the sale of the put option. The institutional investor, however, is content with either of these two outcomes: collecting the premium or taking delivery of the stock. The result over time is income enhancement to the portfolio by collecting option premiums.

The very different risk profiles of the two investors is not so obvious. The speculator, as a result of selling puts on margin, stands the risk of losing a high percentage of capital. This is especially true if a speculator is *fully margined*. A portfolio manager views the risk profile quite differently. First, selling puts for the portfolio manager is actually less risky than owning stock! Because selling a put is similar to buying stock at a lower price, the cash-collateralized put seller loses less than the owner of a stock when the market declines. Second, because the portfolio manager sells puts on stock considered desirable for the portfolio, he or she would be very disappointed if the market rallies and these stocks were not in the portfolio. Consequently, the risk for this professional manager is missing the big market rally—quite a difference from the speculator who does not care what happens to a stock when it is above the strike price of the sold put.

This difference in perceived risk implies a significantly different market opinion when initiating the put selling strategy. The speculator is neutral to bullish and does not want the stock to decline. Anything else is OK. The speculator is not wildly bullish, or he would buy calls. The portfolio manager, however, has the goal of buying stocks cheaper. If a manager thought prices would rally, he would buy stocks now. To sell puts, therefore, the manager must be forecasting a neutral to bearish market. In the absence of options, a manager would be placing bids for stock under the market, expecting prices to dip so that the bids could be filled. Selling puts can accomplish the same result without a stock dipping to the desired price, as long as the stock stays below the strike price of the put.

For example, assume that a stock is trading at $50 and the appropriate $50 put option can be sold for $2. A portfolio manager, who is short-term bearish but willing to buy this stock, could place an order to buy the stock at $48. If the stock price drops to $48 1/2 and rallies back to $50, the manager still owns no stock. If the stock dropped to $45, the stock would have been purchased at $48 and would have experienced a $3 loss. If the stock rose to $55, the portfolio manager would have been wrong and made nothing.

Selling the $50 put option, however, makes two of these situations better and has the same outcome as the third. If the put is exercised, the portfolio manager has effectively bought the stock at $48. If the stock price declines to $45, there is a $3 loss exactly as just described. At $50 the portfolio manager is a buyer of stock at $48, gaining a $2 profit. In the case of the rally to $55, he or she still collects the $2 option premium. This is a nice consolation prize when the short-term market forecast was wrong!

Viewed in its proper context, cash-collateralized put selling is a valuable income enhancement strategy for portfolio managers.

COVERED WRITING VERSUS PUT SELLING: FINDING A DIFFERENCE WHERE THERE IS NONE

Starting from a cash investment and going to either a covered write or a short put results in exactly the same payoff diagram. But if these strategies are used over time to enhance portfolio performance, there is a difference in timing as to when each should be implemented.

A portfolio manager who is fully invested, but is willing to sell some of the equities at higher prices, finds the strategy of selling covered calls attractive. This means that the manager is neutral to bullish and looking for a place to raise cash.

The portfolio manager most likely to sell puts, however, has cash and is looking for lower prices at which he hopes to buy stocks. Selling puts is the appropriate strategy with this neutral to short-term bearish market opinion.

When considering the market cycle over the course of several months, the distinction is very obvious. A portfolio manager should be a covered call seller when willing to sell stocks and a cash-collateralized put seller when willing to buy stocks.

CHAPTER 8

THE BUSINESS OF MARKET MAKING

For any option order that enters the pit, market makers must bid to buy or offer to sell. They are required to make a two-sided market on demand. In fulfilling these responsibilities, the market maker's goal is to accept only the amount of risk he is able to bear and to control his overall risk by trading away the particular risks he is unwilling or unable to retain for himself.

THE ROLE OF OPTIONS MARKET MAKERS

Beyond that, the market-making function is a critical component in the investment and capital formation process for four reasons. First, market makers add liquidity to the financial markets. Whether backed by large or small amounts of capital, each one has a willingness to assume risk and therefore contributes to the overall market's ability to facilitate the purchase and sale of securities with reduced price fluctuations.

Second, price efficiency is increased by the market-making function. As will be discussed later, many market makers conduct their trading through *hedging*—a process by which one security is bought and another with equal or similar risk characteristics is sold. By acting in this way, market makers keep the prices of similar securities in line with each other, no matter where the security is traded. This condition is called *price efficiency* and the presence of options market makers increases price efficiency.

Third, because hedging keeps prices efficient, options market makers also increase the ability of financial markets to transfer risk. Financial markets are composed of many participants who are willing to accept particular risks in the expectation of adequate compensation because they are better situated to accept those risks, or perhaps more expert in controlling them. The hedging process conducted by options market makers transfers risk between different market participants who would not, for a number of reasons, trade among themselves.

Fourth, by bidding, offering, and trading, options market makers provide valuable price information that is transmitted across all markets and is used in the decision-making process of other participants.

The Business of Market Making

Market making in the option pits is a business—one with its own special set of risks and rewards. Actually, the job is notorious for both big rewards and high risks; however, this reputation is only partly deserved. In some crucial respects, the "high rollers" label that often comes to mind when you think of floor traders can be misleading. In fact, the real job centers in controlling and minimizing risks. Despite the job's reputation, it's not the high-rolling gamblers who are successful over the long run.

The skill of market making is looking at trades, not in isolation, but in combinations to be bundled together as packages. A market maker attempts to trade those combinations that allow him to realize a profit and, at the same time, allow him to hedge away unwanted exposure by means of offsetting trades. The market maker's ideal trade is an *arbitrage*—a trade where there is a profit to be taken without retaining any accompanying risk.

Arbitrage trades are typically found in shades and colorations, not in pure, perfect form. A pure arbitrage—a truly rare find—is one where exactly the same fungible product can be bought and sold simultaneously at two different prices, bringing a genuinely riskless profit. Any variation from this incurs risk. Once, perhaps, there were such trades, when stock traders bought a stock in New York and jumped on their horses to ride hell-bent for Philadelphia to sell it at a price a point higher. But even then there was risk. Either the horse or the stock could take a tumble during the ride!

What options market makers typically look for, however, is not the perfect arbitrage, but a *synthetic arbitrage*. They try to synthesize one instrument out of a combination of others, and then to buy and sell the same package of risks for a profit. Their goal is to establish this low-risk combination of offsetting trades for a net profit on the whole package.

Measuring and evaluating risks can be a highly mathematical task, so that eliminating them is a highly quantitative enterprise. Ultimately, a synthetic arbitrage is a *mathematical arbitrage,* one where the mathematical characteristics of one set of instruments are combined to offset the mathematical characteristics of another. It should be clear that the market maker's job demands the fast thinking and discipline for which it is renowned, as well as complex analysis and careful judgment. A large part of being successful lies in the ability to spot synthetic arbitrage trades.

Large and Small Operations

A fair portion of market makers are "independents," trading for their own accounts. They trade as individuals relying on their experience and on the information they can gather standing in the pits. They can rely on PCs to help tally their trades and look over their positions after the close of the markets, and they may well have computer printouts or "sheets " of theoretical option prices over a range of underlying prices and volatilities. Most independent market makers usually trade without computer backup during the day. However some exchanges have set up pilot programs whereby market makers can compute option prices and keep track of their positions using hand-held computers.

As financial markets in stocks, currencies, and interest rate and other instruments have evolved and become increasingly sophisticated and interdependent, so have the options markets matured. Over the years, a range of firms have developed; they vary in their theoretical sophistication, in the complexity of their organizations, and in the power and complexity of their computer systems. Some are well capitalized, with perhaps $100 to $200 million or more behind them. They have developed sophisticated proprietary computer systems that employ their own quantitative approach to help evaluate and control their positions. They are not brokers; they do not serve customers. Instead, they are organizations trading for their own accounts.

These large firms can have dozens of traders both upstairs (off the trading floor) and down (actually in the pits on various trading floors). These firms maintain a presence on the floors of the exchanges that trade underlying instruments as well as on the floors of various options exchanges. They are organized to gather and make use of a wide range of information, both from the floors and from outside the pits. For example, their upstairs operations monitor news from many sources and relay it internally. They relay not only the news, but its anticipated impact, in the form of output from their computer models.

In between the independent market maker and the very large organization are firms with various structures, sizes, and styles. Some are simply organized teams of individual traders. Others try to differentiate roles so that some members concentrate on gathering information and providing analysis from outside the pits, while others function on the floors.

Styles of Options Trading

Besides differences in size and organization, there are differences in style among traders and trading organizations. The techniques market makers use to limit risk are multifaceted. While this section describes various styles, it is necessary to recognize that market makers can use any or all of these techniques during a day, depending on the ebb and flow of orders into the pits and the types of trades possible.

Day traders tend to hold small positions for very short times to reduce their risk and they often do not make any real attempt to hedge risks during the day. *Theoretical traders* buy what their quantitative models say, in theory, is cheap and sell what is overpriced. *Spread traders* make markets primarily in spread positions, which they then incorporate into their own overall positions. *Premium sellers* tend to sell more options than they buy because this strategy pays off as long as nothing out of the ordinary happens, but they must hurry to hedge their risks when an unusually large move does occur. And then there are those risk takers who "get a hunch, and bet a bunch."

These differences in style reflect not only how market makers take on risk and try to control it, but also how their attitudes differ. Some, such as the small independent day traders, or *scalpers,* are willing to accept the risks of briefly holding a long or short position. Others (often, but not exclusively, the larger organizations) make every attempt to hedge away as much of their risk as they can. This makes it possible for them to trade more theoretically and to hold their positions for longer periods—perhaps weeks—while they wait for prices to behave in a way that makes the theoretical edge pay off.

Together, these various styles for managing risk determine the role of the options market within the broader financial markets. The different styles of market making (arbitrageurs, day traders, theoretical traders, spreaders, and scalpers) determine how risk is distributed throughout the options markets and how much risk is transferred from the pits to outside markets.

HOW MARKET MAKERS PRICE OPTIONS

In a sense, the key to successful market making is very simple. The prescription for success is: Buy options that are cheap, sell those that are expensive, and yet eliminate the risks.

Market makers use a variety of approaches to the business, but few, if any, simply buy calls or sell puts when they are bullish and buy puts or sell calls when they're bearish. While most will *scalp* trades or *leg* into spreads on a short-term basis, they will generally not try to employ the long-term strategy of taking advantage of moves in underlying prices. The risk of simply taking direction bets, or taking on any one kind of exposure for that matter, is just too great. Those who do so don't survive over the long run.

All market makers attempt to control the risks of their positions, most of them by spreading options against other options or the underlying stocks or index futures. Easy as the prescription for synthetic arbitrage sounds, there is great skill in knowing how to follow it. First, the market maker must know what is mispriced. Second, he needs to know how to hedge away the unwanted risks. The two problems can be treated as different sides of the same coin. If the market maker can enter two or more offsetting trades that cancel out the risk, and if he can do this for a net profit, he has solved both problems.

Relative Pricing and Arbitrage Spreads

Market makers in the pit often don't need to worry about whether an option is actually overpriced or underpriced in some absolute sense. What matters is whether an option is mispriced *relative* to the underlying security or to other options at any given point in time so that the market maker can create a spread and reduce the risk of buying or selling the option.

There are a few such basic arbitrage spreads that will be examined in detail later. These spreads determine the price relationships that the underlying instrument and their various options should have to each other. When the basic price relationships don't hold, there is an opportunity for profit. The first thing that market makers learn to do when they enter the pit is to watch for the basic arbitrages. If the arbitrages are there to be done at current prices, traders spread options against options, or options against the underlying security, until their own buying and selling pressure forces the prices back into line and the possibility of further arbitrage disappears.

Synthetic Equivalents

To expand on this point, a market maker quickly learns to think in terms of synthetic equivalents. He compares prices of different combinations of puts, calls, and stock that have the very same risk exposure. Then, by buying the underpriced and selling the overpriced, he takes advantage of any mispricings and, at the same time, cancels out his net exposure by establishing an arbitrage spread. In fact, this basic technique is a fundamental part of the way that a market maker thinks when he considers what he can do at current prices.

Looking at option positions in terms of synthetic equivalents reveals alternatives. Pricing synthetic equivalents is part of the apparent "magic" in market making. It is key to understanding the professional's ability to begin making bids and offers within seconds after walking into a pit.

Let's first consider some forms of risk and examine some simple ways that the risk of one position can offset the risk in another. Owning a stock (being long the stock) is the most obvious way to take on exposure to the direction the stock price moves. Assume you are simply bullish. If the stock rises, you make money; if it falls, you lose. In either direction, the value of your position varies dollar for dollar with any change in stock price. So if you are long a stock, you clearly have direction risk.

There is an equivalent way of being long or bullish about direction—an equivalent way to acquire the same exposure with the same risk. By holding a combination of a long call and a short put (with the same strike and expiration), your exposure to movements in the stock price is identical to owning the stock itself. So a position combining a long call with a short put is called *synthetic long stock*. Why is this so? Suppose XYZ stock is trading at $100.

1. If you own the stock, you gain a dollar for every point it rises above $100 and lose a dollar for each point it falls. Now consider two at-the-money options.
2. If you own a $100 call, at expiration your position is worth a dollar for each point the stock has risen over $100. On the other hand, your call is worth nothing if the stock falls below $100.

3. If you are short a put, your position has lost a dollar for each point the stock has fallen below $100 by expiration. The short put has no value at expiration if the stock is above $100.

So the combination of (2) and (3), a long call and a short put, is synthetically equivalent to (1), holding long stock. If the stock price rises, the call is worth a dollar for each point the stock is above $100 and the short put is worthless. But should the stock fall, the long call has no value and the short put loses a dollar for each point below $100. Think for a minute about how you might take advantage of synthetically equivalent positions. At expiration, synthetic long stock and real long stock show the same net gain or loss with any change in stock price. The two equivalent positions have the same potential for gain and the same risk of loss when the stock price moves. Thus, by buying one and selling the other, you can eliminate the most significant form of position risk, namely, exposure to the direction of price movement. Buying stock and selling synthetic stock, or the reverse, results in no net direction exposure. The positions cancel one another because what you make on one, you lose on the other.

Not only is there a synthetic equivalent for long stock, there is a synthetic equivalent for any option or stock position. (See Table 8–1.) Market makers quickly learn to price options in terms of the basic stock and option positions, together with their synthetic equivalents. If prices of any options (or stocks for that matter) get out of line with other prices, market makers quickly spot the discrepancy and consider how to use the mispricing to position themselves in the option and its synthetic counterpart.

TABLE 8–1
Synthetic Equivalents for Stocks and Options

Position	Synthetic Equivalent
Long stock	Long call, short put
Long call	Long stock, long put
Long put	Short stock, long call
Short stock	Short call, long put
Short call	Short stock, short put
Short put	Long stock, short call

Conversions and Reversals

You've had a brief look at the basic idea of buying one instrument and selling its synthetic equivalent. Ready for more?

The two most basic forms of option arbitrage are the *conversion* and reverse conversion or *reversal*. If a market maker can buy long stock and sell synthetic long stock (or the reverse) for a net price difference that more than covers his costs, the combination of trades ought to net a profit with no direction risk. What matters is not the price of the call, put, or stock itself in isolation, but the relative price of the offsetting pieces.

For example, suppose a market maker finds 100 calls, expiring in 30 days, trading at $4 1/4 and the puts at $3 1/4 with the underlying stock trading at $100. He simply puts together the three pieces: selling the call, buying the put, and buying the stock. He takes in $1 and, at the same time, hedges away his exposure to any changes in the price of the stock prior to expiration.

Assume that carrying the stock until expiration (tying up his funds at $100 per share) costs him $100 × 10% interest rate × 1/12 of a year = 83 cents. His net profit, assuming no other costs and risks, is about 17 cents, which he can earn with no stock price exposure. All calculations should be multiplied by 100 because options cover 100 shares of stock. Furthermore, of course, appropriate interest rates need to be used in the calculation to reflect actual costs.

There is no reason to think of a conversion exclusively in terms of long stock and short synthetic stock. From Table 8–1, it is clear that a conversion can be viewed in terms of the other pieces. A conversion can be either a long call and a short synthetic call, or a short put and a long synthetic put, as well as long stock and short synthetic stock.

Of course, the opposite strategy, a *reverse conversion* or reversal, can be established if the call and put prices are out of line in the opposite direction. If, for example, the $100 call were offered at $4 and the put were $3 1/2 bid, a market maker could buy the underpriced call and sell the expensive put for a net debit to his account of 50 cents. He could then earn interest on the $100 he received from the short sale of the stock to generate a net positive return with no direction exposure.

Exclusive Deal on Interest
Readers may not be familiar with the concept of earning interest when stock is sold short because brokerage firms generally do not pay interest

to individual customers. Market makers, however, who short large quantities of stock are allowed to keep the cash received when borrowed stock is sold. The cash is then invested in T-bills, and the interest income is a significant part of the profit from a reverse conversion position.

It should be apparent that the current level of interest rates determines whether a conversion or reversal is profitable. For that reason, these spreads are known as *interest rate plays*. Using his own appropriate current interest rate, a market maker calculates his "cost of carry" for the position, including the receipt of a dividend (long stock) or the payment of one (short stock). He then knows the size of the credit or debit that would make a conversion or reversal profitable, and he can examine current option prices with those values in mind.

Market makers who enter into conversions and reversals have largely eliminated their stock price risk, but they are still subject to the risk that interest rates will move against them prior to expiration. (For that reason, market makers may try to balance the number of conversions they put on against the number of reversals in order to hedge their interest rate exposure.)

There is no need to restrict this strategy to at-the-money options. As long as the put and call have the same strike price, a combination of a long call and a short put has the same direction exposure as holding the stock. However, parity, the intrinsic value of the in-the-money option, must be considered in computing the cost of carrying the spread until expiration.

For example, consider using a put and a call with a strike price of $90 and the stock trading at $100. The $90 call will be $10 in-the-money and will be trading at a price somewhere in excess of $10. Perhaps the call is trading at $12 3/4 and the put at $2. This means that the conversion, which requires buying the stock and selling the call, requires about $10 less to be invested for the holding period until expiration.

The strategy here is to put on the conversion whenever the difference between the option prices, after netting out parity, allows you to take in more than 75 cents, and to do the reversal if it costs less than 75 cents to put on the spread. This is because the cost of carry for the conversion is approximately ($100 for the stock − $10 parity received for the call) × 10% interest rate × 1/12 of a year = 75 cents.

An additional technicality to consider is that one cannot invest the full $100 price of the stock at the current rate of interest. A fee must be paid for borrowing the stock to sell short, and there are transaction costs to entering and exiting the spread. So the conversion might be profitable if the option prices differed by more than 85 cents, and the reversal might be profitable if the price difference were 55 cents or less.

To take some specific option prices, suppose a market maker finds the $90 call offered at $12 1/2 while there is $2 bid for the $90 put. He buys the call and sells the put for a total debit of $10 1/2. At the same time, he sells the stock for $100 and invests the money (minus approximately $10 he had to pay for the option spread) for a month to earn about 75 cents. After it's all over, he can buy back the stock and take off the spread. He will have taken in 75 cents in interest income and paid out 50 cents for the options, after netting out $10 parity.

Whether the options are at-the-money (or not) alters, but does not invalidate, the pricing relationship between puts and calls with the same strike. Because of these basic arbitrage spreads, at-the-money calls should be more expensive than the puts by the cost of carrying the stock until expiration. Out-of-the-money options should be priced so that the difference between the call and the put, after parity has been netted out, reflects carry costs (or interest) for the total amount invested.

If prices of any options get out of line with other prices, market makers quickly spot the mispricing, then buy whatever is cheap and sell whatever is relatively expensive—its synthetic equivalent—until their own buying and selling pressure forces prices back into line. In doing so, they are performing an important role in the stock and option markets. By forcing options and the underlying stocks to be priced appropriately relative to each other, market makers enforce pricing efficiency among the options and across the option and stock markets.

Dividends

Dividends also alter price relationships, but they do not abrogate basic pricing principles. In general, the value of a stock must be discounted by the amount of the dividend on the *ex-dividend date* (that date is the day before which an investor must have purchased the stock in order to receive the dividend). Absent of other relevant happenings, the price of a $100 stock paying a $1 dividend should be expected to fall by $1 on the ex-dividend date, and holders of record on that date should receive $1. Since the stock is worth less, an approaching ex-dividend date means that calls should be less valuable and puts more valuable. To be precise, the value of a long call and a short put together ought to be worth less by approximately the amount of the dividend than they would be without it.

The implications for conversions and reversals are fairly straightforward. If you put on the conversion—buy the stock, buy the put, and sell the call—then (since you own the stock), you can expect to receive the dividend. That means your cost of carrying the conversion is reduced by the amount of the dividend. The difference between the price you receive for selling the call and the price you must pay to buy the put—after you net out parity—needs only to exceed the new cost of carry to be profitable. That is, the call price, minus the put price after netting out parity, must be at least enough to compensate for the interest expense of holding the stock (minus the dividend that you receive). Algebraically this is expressed as:

Call price − Put price (− Call parity or + Put parity) >
Interest expense − Dividend received.

For the reversal to be profitable, the amount you must pay for the call, minus the price you receive for the put, must be less than you can expect to receive for investing the price of the stock until expiration, minus the value of the dividend that you have to pay out because you are short the stock. Algebraically this is:

Call price − Put price (− Call parity or + Put parity) <
Interest income − Dividend payout.

The basic arbitrage price relations remain intact, after some arithmetic adjustments, among all the options and their underlying stock, and market makers can establish conversions or reversals without extreme risk at all strike prices, whether or not dividends are anticipated.

Hidden Risks

From the calculations just covered, it should be apparent that arbitrage trades typically net a market maker only very small profits. The key to using these trades is to minimize any and all risks. One substantial loss can eat up all the profits from many such transactions.

This is a point well worth noting in trying to understand what a market maker does for a living. One who fails to spot a risk can lose all the profits he's made over a week, a month, or even a whole year. Two particular risks market makers must be aware of when they consider putting on reversals are especially instructive because they typify the kinds of hidden risks that many market makers learn to guard against only after harsh, expensive experience.

First, the possibility that the stock might close precisely at $100 on the day of January expiration, so that neither option is worth exercising, poses a danger to anyone carrying a synthetic long or short stock position as part of a spread. If the stock price is "pinned" precisely at the strike price at expiration so that no exercise occurs, the position can be left with direction exposure at expiration. This is sometimes referred to as *pin risk*.

Second, a reversal generates a profit because the funds received for selling the stock short can be invested until the spread is taken off—presumably until the options expire. Any reversal that involves in-the-money puts—especially if they are deep-in-the-money—involves the danger that the (short) puts will be assigned early. Early assignment would force the spread to be closed out prior to expiration. The market maker would be forced to buy back the stock when it is put to him or her. As a consequence, the interest income generated from the spread would be less, perhaps significantly less, than he or she anticipated based on the calculation for the full holding period.

Many a rookie market maker who bought out-of-the-money calls that looked cheap—intending to sell the puts and sell the stock short, then earn interest on the funds until expiration—has found himself getting "bagged" on the reversal. He thought he was hedged against any move in the price of the stock. But then he saw the price of the stock fall and found that his short puts had been exercised well in advance of expiration. Early exercise of the puts cut off the interest income he expected over the life of the options.

To see just how dangerous it can be to trade in these supposedly "riskless" arbitrage spreads, consider this extreme, but not unheard of, case. Suppose a $32 stock goes ex-dividend tomorrow and is paying a special $5 dividend. Assume further that the options expire after the ex-dividend date, but before this week is out. Entering a conversion or reversal in this stock could be a disaster for the unwary market maker. Let's see how this might work.

Ordinarily, you might expect the 30 puts, which are $2 out-of-the-money with a few days of life remaining, to be almost worthless; and you would expect the 30 calls to be worth only their inherent value of $2 because you would expect to exercise them today, prior to the ex-dividend date tomorrow. So you might consider buying the call and selling the put (and hedging with short stock) if you could pay anything less than $2.

In fact, if you pay $2 for the reversal, you will lose money. The put is worth $3, even though it is out-of-the-money! Tomorrow when the stock goes ex-dividend, the stock price can be expected to drop by $5. Thus, assuming nothing else extraordinary happens, the stock drops to $27 so that the put is $3 in-the-money. That means that later this week the put is exercised for its $3 inherent value before it expires, so the reversal should be a credit spread. That is, you should demand to be paid at least $1 to put on the reversal (because you will want to exercise your long call immediately for $2, and the short put will be worth $3 after the ex-date). Settling for anything less than a $1 credit in "buying" the synthetic stock would prove very expensive. It is the not-so-apparent risks that can prove costly to novice market makers who aren't careful in examining "riskless" trades.

Box Spreads

So far this chapter has explained why puts and calls with the same strike price must bear certain price relationships and how market makers can establish an arbitrage position if a put-call pair gets out of line. There are also other price relations that hold among options with different strike prices, and there are still other relations that hold among options with different expiration dates. Each of these relationships deserves a look.

Suppose a market maker finds two put-call pairs with different strikes that have their prices out of line in opposite respects—in one case the calls are cheap compared to the puts and in the other, the calls are expensive. For example, the $90 strike call is cheap relative to the $90 put, while the $100 strike call is expensive relative to the put.

The market maker's strategy here is to do a conversion using the $100 strike options and a reversal using the $90 strike options. Specifically, he should sell synthetic stock with the $100 strike options (sell the call and buy the put), and he should buy synthetic stock using the $90 strike. Against his short and long synthetic stock positions, he should buy and sell stock. Of course, the last step is superfluous. The two stock transactions simply net out. He can sell synthetic stock at one strike price and buy synthetic stock at another, and the option positions alone offset each other.

This strategy—long synthetic stock at one strike and short synthetic stock at another (long call, short put and short call, long put, all

TABLE 8–2
Ways of Thinking of a 90–100 Box Spread

1. Long 90 call, short 90 put, short 100 call, long 100 put
2. Long synthetic stock using 90 strike and short synthetic stock using 100 strike
3. Long 90–100 call, bull spread and long 90–100 put, bear spread
4. Short 90–100 call, bear spread and short 90–100 put, bull spread
5. Long 90–100 mambo-combo (in-the-money call and in-the-money put, also called *guts*) and short 90–100 strangle for surf and turf (out-of-the-money call and out-of-the-money put, also called *wings*)

with the same expiration)—is a basic arbitrage spread called a *box spread*. Box pricing relationships hold among options of all strike prices with the same expiration. For example, there is a 90–100 box, a 100–110 box, a 90–110 box, a 100–120 box, and so forth. If any option gets out of line, it can be bought or sold and hedged using any appropriate combination of three other options to create long and short synthetic stock at two different strikes.

As with conversion or reversal, there are various ways of thinking about a box. They are listed in Table 8–2. It is important for market makers to recognize boxes under any and all of these descriptions because it allows them to compare prices for various spreads, seen as components of other spreads, as well as for individual options and their synthetic counterparts. A mispriced call bull spread or *mambo-combo* (an in-the-money call and an in-the-money put) can be turned into a box just as readily as a mispriced put-call pair can be turned into a conversion or a box.

Box Pricing

Like conversions and reversals, box spreads should generally be regarded as interest rate plays. They are arbitrage trades in the sense that they can be expected to produce a profit whenever (1) you pay a net debit for the options that will be more than offset by the interest income returned while you hold the position, or (2) you receive a net credit that exceeds your cost of carrying the position.

To state it differently, if you buy a box, (i.e., buy synthetic stock—buy call, sell put—at the lower strike price and sell synthetic stock—buy the put and sell the call at the higher strike price), you must buy an in-the-money call and/or an in-the-money put. You are selling less expensive, out-of-the-money options. You should then expect to pay approximately the total inherent value of the in-the-money options. Normally, the four options net out to make the cost of buying a box approximately equal to the difference between the strikes. A box with strikes 5 points apart costs about $5 because of parity in the in-the-money options, and a 10-point box costs about $10 in inherent values.

More precisely (assuming no early exercise), a 10-point box should trade for the present value of $10 at expiration ($10 minus the cost of carrying the $10 investment for the life of the options). This means that boxes, like conversions and reversals, are interest rate sensitive. The price of a box spread reflects both the cost of carry for the spread for the period until the options expire and the market maker's risk from interest rate fluctuations for that period (as well as any additional costs from entering or exiting the spread).

There are some important additional factors for a market maker to keep in mind. For instance, a box comprised of American options often involves buying or selling deep-in-the-money puts, and these puts are likely to be exercised prior to expiration. If this happens, it changes the cost of carry calculations for holding the spread.

Suppose you sell a 110–120 box with the stock trading at $100 and 30 days left until expiration. That is, you sell the $110 call and the $120 put and buy the $120 call and the $110 put. You receive something in the neighborhood of $10, which is the parity value in the box (the difference between $20 for the $120 puts that you sell and $10 for the $110 puts you buy).

The Bottom Line

The question in pricing the box is: How much less than $10 should you be willing to take, given that you earn interest on the proceeds? To answer, calculate that you can invest $10 for one month at 10 percent interest to earn about 8 cents. This implies that you might be willing to sell the box for anything in excess of $9.92—8 cents less than the $10 parity value.

But there is another risk here. The deep-in-the-money $120 put will almost certainly be exercised very soon, perhaps immediately. The box does not generate 8 cents in income, since you soon have the stock put to you and, instead of the 110–120 box, you are forced to carry the $110 conversion. (You have long stock, short the $110 synthetic stock, unless you decide to exercise your own $110 put.) Clearly, you need to demand more than $10, not less, if you want to sell the box.

As a general rule, if you are short a put and the corresponding call falls below the cost of carrying the conversion, you can expect to have the stock put to you. If you have established a short box position with this in mind (so that you have covered the expense of carrying the conversion in the event of early exercise), then, when the put is exercised, selling out the "left-over" long call can produce a bonus.

Extra Premium
As can be seen, if you are selling puts that are deep-in-the-money, you need to demand extra premium. Similarly, in-the-money puts on expensive stocks command extra premium because the carrying cost for holding the stock is higher. If you sell an in-the-money put on a high-priced stock—as part of a reversal, for instance—this means that you must demand more because the put may well be exercised early, ending the income from the reversal. A market maker who is not alert to these extra complications quickly learns the painful consequences.

Advantages
Trading in conversions, reversals, and boxes gives a market maker advantages in addition to the small arbitrage profits available from the spreads themselves. Holding positions with no net exposure, but involving many options, provides a market maker with a great deal of flexibility. He has a ready inventory of long and short options, making it much easier to trade in and out of positions as the market moves. It becomes easier for him to accept some small amount of direction exposure for a short time to take advantage of movement that he sees in the market.

Consider the following example of using a box spread in a bear market. A market maker is long a box spread. He bought synthetic stock at the lower strike and sold an out-of-the-money call and bought an in-the-money put at the higher strike. Meanwhile, the stock price has dropped to a point where the short out-of-the-money call is priced below the short stock interest rebate for the stock.

The market maker can now position himself to take advantage of *bounces* in the falling market (bounces are when the market begins to go back up). He can buy in his short call with the expectation of exercising his deep-in-the-money put very soon to establish a reversal. Now, if the market bounces after he has *covered* his short call, the market maker has two alternatives available. First, he can choose to go ahead with his initial strategy by early exercising his put to establish a reversal. On the other hand, he can decide to sell out the call once again. This re-establishes the short synthetic stock position for his original box. As such, this tactic allows him to re-establish his original box to capture a *scalp profit* from the amount the call price rose during the bounce.

Jelly Rolls and More

It is November. Suppose that a market maker finds two mispriced put–call pairs. This time they have the same strike price, but differ in expiration cycle. That is, he finds an expensive call and a relatively cheap put (with a January expiration) and a cheap call and expensive put (with an April expiration), all with a $100 strike price. He then does a conversion with one pair and a reversal with the other, just as he would to establish a box. In this case, he should sell synthetic stock using the January options and buy synthetic stock using the April options. To hedge, he could buy stock to offset his January options and sell stock to offset his April position. The stock positions net out, at least until January expiration, leaving him with short January synthetic stock and long April synthetic stock.

This position is called a *jelly roll,* commonly shortened to *roll.* It is the basic arbitrage that interrelates options across various expirations, and, together with conversions and box spreads, it serves as the basis for valuing all options in relation to other options.

Jelly rolls may sound like complicated spreads—long a call with one expiration, short a call with a second expiration, and the reverse with the corresponding puts. But they are fairly easy to spot because they can be seen as two *time spreads*. And time spreads trade frequently in the pits. (See the discussion of trading time spreads later in this chapter.)

Pricing jelly rolls is fairly straightforward, once you understand conversions and reversals. A long jelly roll like the one just described (long the April 100 call, short the put and short the January 100 call, long the put) simply turns into a reversal at January expiration. To see this, consider what happens at January expiration. Either the stock price is above $100, in which case the short January call is exercised, leaving the market maker short stock and long April synthetic stock; or the stock price is below $100, in which case the long put should be exercised to produce the same position. In either case, the market maker has a reversal with three months' life left in the options. Long or short jelly rolls are priced as if they were reversals or conversions with three-month carry periods.

Of course, there are more of these basic arbitrage spreads. A spread involving put-call pairs with different strikes as well as different expirations is called a *time box*. Such a combination is a box that lasts until near-term expiration and then turns into a conversion or reversal for the time remaining until the farther-term options expire.

In each case, there are risks and complications to consider. Arbitrage spreads can seem risk free at first glance, but experienced market makers know the hidden risks involved in each kind and can quickly price the spreads to compensate. They have learned from experience which spreads require a premium and which spreads shouldn't be entered into at all.

THEORETICAL VALUES AND VOLATILITY

Options have a host of uses for end users in controlling and modifying various forms of risk. Indeed, options are capable of repackaging risks in infinitely many ways and can be used to eliminate, accept, or transfer combinations of exposure and risk. A glance at Table 8–3 should make it clear that different spreads carry different degrees of exposure. Option position risks can be classified into four fundamental types:

1. Exposure to the direction of the underlying security's price moves.
2. Exposure to the volatility of stock prices—the amount of price movement without regard to its direction.
3. Exposure to the options' time decay—the tendency of options to lose time premium as they near expiration.
4. Exposure to changes in the cost of carry (changes that derive primarily from variations in short-term interest rates or changes that can result from inaccurately forecasted dividends).

In buying or selling options, market makers take on exposure to each of these forms of risk. They can then choose either to accept them or to hedge them away, totally or partially. The arbitrage spreads discussed earlier are examples of strategies for eliminating direction exposure and, in most cases, time decay and volatility exposure.

Market makers would be fulfilling their role in its simplest form if they simply bought whatever options were undervalued, sold options that were overvalued, and then proceeded to eliminate all the risks

TABLE 8–3
Risks (and Rewards) of Arbitrage Spreads

	Direction Risk/Reward	Volatility Risk	Time Decay Risk	Interest Rate Risk
Long/short stock*	High	—	—	Low
Long naked options*	Moderate to high	—	High	Moderate
Short naked options*	Moderate to high	High	—	Moderate
Bull/bear spreads*	Moderate	Moderate	Moderate	Low
Conversion/reversal*	Low to none	Low to none	Low to none	High
Long box*	Low to none	Low to none	Low to none	High
Short box*	Moderate	Low to none	Low to none	High
Jelly roll*	Low to none	Low to none	Low to none	High
Long time spread*	Low to moderate	Low	Low	Low
Short time spread*	Moderate	Moderate	Moderate	Moderate
Backspread (long options delta neutral)	—	—	High	Low
Vertical spread (short options delta neutral)	—	High	—	Low
Long butterflys*	Low	Low	Low to moderate	Low
Short butterflys*	Low to moderate	Low to moderate	Moderate to high	Low

* Denotes spreads that are one-to-one in nature and are regularly quoted as spreads in most option pits.

entirely. Of course, this is much too simple to be practicable. In fact, market makers accept uncertainty when they buy or sell options; and, in practice, they must leave some risks unhedged. Competition often forces them to accept some risks just to be included in trades. Sometimes there are no immediate and efficient means available to eliminate all the risks. If, for example, all options are underpriced for a period, there are no expensive options to sell that will enable the market maker both to establish a hedge and to lock in his edge.

More often, market makers accept and retain particular risks with studied intent. When they find options significantly underpriced, they may well be willing to accept certain risks in buying the options as long as they can eliminate the most dramatic and potentially devastating ones.

Most simply will not accept direction risk for more than a very short time. There are many, usually individuals, whose style is to *scalp* or *day trade*, trying to take advantage of intraday price trends by buying calls and selling puts when stock prices are on the way up, or reversing the tactic when prices fall. Even these traders trade out of their positions as quickly as possible as a means of minimizing danger, and none retain any heavy exposure to the direction of stock prices overnight. It's just too easy to sustain a devastating loss when taking on this kind of exposure.

On the other hand, most market makers are willing to accept some volatility exposure that comes with being net long or net short options. For the same reasons they are unwilling to accept direction exposure—largely because a sudden big price move in the wrong direction could put them out of business—they are willing to take on volatility exposure. In other words, if they can hedge away their immediate exposure to the direction of prices, a sudden move in underlying price is unlikely to result in a major loss. Although the volatility component in option premiums can increase or decrease dramatically, even a fairly large change in volatility would be unlikely to be devastating.

Now let's look at how market makers decide when to take on volatility exposure, taking a chance in expectation of a profit. To put it another way, we'll look at how traders decide when options are over- or underpriced, when the mispricing doesn't reflect some interest rate versus cost-of-carry considerations.

A Tool for Accepting Volatility Exposure

Earlier, you saw how interest rate and dividend considerations affect price relationships among different options, and between options and their underlying stocks. You saw how market makers determine theoretically correct option values, given current prices for other options, and how they act upon relative mispricings when they discover them to create spreads sensitive only to interest rate fluctuations (and perhaps changes in dividends).

Consider for a moment the factors that affect the price of an option—the variables in the option pricing models. These include:

- The current underlying stock price.
- The strike price.
- The time remaining in the option.

- The current interest rates.
- The expected dividend.
- The projected volatility of the underlying instrument.

One can make fairly reliable projections about short-term interest rates or dividends over the next few months, and it is simple to determine a value for the current stock price, strike price, and time remaining until expiration. The one determinant of option values difficult to ascertain—and even more difficult to project—is the volatility of the underlying instrument.

If you could correctly assess how volatility will contribute to the total value of options, you would have a handle on all the components of option value. You've already seen how market makers assess the value of the interest rate and dividend contributions. Knowing the volatility component would allow them to determine a single theoretically correct price for each option.

Indeed, this is just what many try to do. They purchase volatility research or, in the case of large firms, do their own research to project the volatility of the underlying instruments over the life of the options. Then they plug those volatility numbers into one of the option pricing formulas to generate a computer printout of theoretical values, or *sheets*, for the options they are trading. Armed with such a table, a professional can price options individually. He or she can decide that an option is mispriced, even though it is in line with the current prices of its counterparts.

This greatly increases flexibility. In addition to trading in the basic arbitrage spreads that take advantage of interest rate and other carrying costs, these market makers can compare market prices and theoretical values. Then they can buy and sell options one by one, intending to repackage them into appropriate bundles to eliminate risks. With a sound idea of a theoretically correct price, a market maker can buy underpriced options or sell overpriced ones. He or she can then decide independently to hedge away those unwanted risks and retain those he or she is willing to carry.

One way for market makers to think of a table of theoretical values is as a tool for deciding when to accept volatility exposure. If the volatility component in the option value is currently mispriced, market makers can position themselves to take advantage of this by buying or selling options and hedging away other forms of risk, especially direction exposure.

Volatility Premium

Assessing the value of options is fairly straightforward, except for the portion of the premium accounted for by volatility. It is easy to calculate the advantage of holding a deep-in-the-money $90 strike call option that costs a bit more than $10 in place of the $100 stock itself, and it is easy to compute the effect on the value of an in-the-money call when the stock pays a dividend.

It is much more difficult, both in theory and in practice, to determine the value of a call option that offers the opportunity to buy a stock currently trading at $100, if and only if the stock price is above $100 on a certain date in the future. This kind of calculation involves some fairly complex statistics and analysis of probabilities.

Briefly, the value of an option is a function of how likely it is to finish in-the-money and how far in-the-money. Historical research shows that, over time, stock prices approximate what statistics calls a "log normal distribution" or "bell curve." This tells a great deal about how likely a stock's price is to be at any given level two, three, or six months from now.

First, researchers know that the chance of a stock going up by $10 in a given time period is about the same as its dropping $10. We know then that a call that is $10 out-of-the-money ought to have about the same volatility premium as a put $10 out-of-the-money. Researchers also know the put-call parity thesis: Put price minus call price should equal parity, or, a put and a call with the same strike price should have the same volatility premium.

Furthermore, knowing that stock prices are normally distributed over time, it is possible to compute about how likely a stock is to be up or down by 5, 10, or 20 percent during the life of an option. The volatility (technically the standard deviation of the distribution) of an underlying stock of, for example, 25 percent simply means that the stock has a certain likelihood (about a one-third chance) of being up or down by 25 percent in any one-year period. From this it is easy to determine the probability of any size price move for any time period—in this case, the time left in the life of an option.

A volatility number indicates how much the underlying stock is expected to fluctuate. This in turn indicates the likelihood that an option has value prior to expiration, either because it is now out-of-the-money (but may finish in-the-money), or because it is now in-the-money and offers some protection. If, over a very long period, you bought options priced exactly at their (correct) theoretical values, i.e., with the correct volatility estimate, you could expect that on the average the rate of return on a typical option would be at least as great as the rate of return for the stock. This explains the justification for the option market: Expected returns from options should equal or exceed expected returns from stocks.

An Edge and a Hedge

Another way of looking at this is that, over the long run, you would do well if you bought underpriced options and sold overpriced ones. In fact, we can say just how well you should do. Over the long run, just enough options should finish in-the-money enough of the time that you should come out ahead by the total difference between actual market prices and theoretical values. Thus, buying options that are priced below theoretical value, or selling options that are priced above value, gives an investor a theoretical edge. The difficulty is to survive for the long run, so that trading options in relation to their theoretical values has the chance to pay off.

In the short run, any trade can go against you. Buying an underpriced call, for instance, may or may not pay off, depending primarily on whether the underlying price rises by expiration. The likelihood that it pays off enough to provide a return that corresponds exactly to its theoretical value is minuscule. Trading on the basis of theoretical values pays off only as a long-term strategy.

The market maker, who accepts volatility exposure and trades on the basis of a sheet of theoretical values, must find a way to reduce the risk that buying or selling options will produce disastrous short-term results. For this purpose, market makers use a trading strategy called *delta neutral spreading*. As the name implies, it is a technique to take the worst risks out of option trading by minimizing *delta* (short for direction exposure).

Delta

Many people acquainted with options know that the price of an option generally changes more slowly than the price of the underlying stock. If the stock rises $2, an at-the-money call option can rise by only $1 and an out-of-the-money call can increase by only a few cents. An in-the-money put might lose $1.50 and an out-of-the-money put might lose 25 or 50 cents.

The delta of an option is the measure of how its price changes in relation to a move in the price of the underlying stock. Technically, delta is the rate at which the option value increases or decreases for a given change in the underlying stock price. Delta tells you how much the option price should change, given a $1 move in the stock.

Thus, a 50 delta call can be expected to change in value by 50 percent of any change in the price of the stock; and a −25 delta put should rise by 25 percent of the amount of any fall in the stock price. This also means, of course, that two 50 delta options change price at the same rate (by 100 percent) as 100 shares of stock.

Many traders are familiar with delta in terms of the *hedge ratio*—the number of options it takes, given the current price of the stock and time left in the option, to hedge 100 shares of stock. It should be clear why delta provides the hedge ratio. It takes four −25 delta puts, each moving at −25 percent the rate of change in the stock price, to protect 100 shares of stock; it takes 80 shares of short stock to offset an 80 delta call. Similarly, two short 50 delta calls hedge 100 shares of long stock, and three long 33 delta calls offset the effect of a price move on 100 shares of short stock.

In other words, delta is the number of stock shares necessary to produce a change in dollar value equivalent to any dollar change in the option. You can be *long delta*—equivalent to holding a long stock position—or *short delta,* in which case your net delta is negative and is equivalent to a short stock position. Furthermore, it is often convenient to think of the underlying stock itself in terms of deltas. One hundred shares of stock will change value at the same rate as a 100 delta option. Stock can be thought of as having 100 deltas—its value changes at 100 percent the rate of its own price, and option deltas can be thought of in terms of equivalent shares of stock.

Knowing this, it is a simple matter to neutralize the price exposure of any stock or option position, however complex. You simply calculate the *net delta* by adding and subtracting the deltas of all the component options and the underlying stock.

For example, a position consisting of four long 75 delta calls, two long −50 delta puts, and 100 shares of long stock has a net delta of +300 deltas $(4 \times 75) + (2x - 50) + 100$, so the position gains or loses value at a rate three times any change in the stock price.

To take a second example, a position including three short 50 delta calls, two short −25 delta puts, and 100 shares of short stock has a net delta of −200, that is, (−3 × 50 − [2 × −25] − 100). The overall position loses 2 points for every 1 point gain in stock price, and it gains $1 for every 50 cents the stock declines.

Curve

Things aren't quite as simple as this, however. Hedging a position against price exposure can't be done once and for all. It is important to note that delta gives the correct hedge ratio (and relative rate of price change) *only for the current price of the underlying stock,* and only for the current volatility and time until expiration. Because option prices respond to changes in underlying price in a way that is nonlinear, or curved, there is a further risk that a hedged or delta neutral position will acquire direction risk by becoming unhedged.

The term *curve* refers to this characteristic of option positions to change their direction exposure with any large move in stock price. Any sizable move in stock price produces an accompanying change in the hedge ratio. A stock price move can cause a fully hedged or "riskless" position to take on direction exposure and to become unhedged at a different underlying price. The amount of curve, or change in price exposure, is indicated by the *gamma* of an option or option position.

A market maker who finds some expensive 50 delta, at-the-money calls can't just sell 20 calls and buy 1,000 shares of stock and be done with it. This will do as a start. But he must constantly adjust the hedge as the stock price changes, or as time decay or other factors change, for they produce concomitant changes in delta.

If the stock price suddenly runs up and the calls move into the money, their deltas rise. For example, if call deltas rise to 60, the trader would be long 1,000 shares of stock or 1,000 deltas, but would now be short 20 60-delta calls or −1,200 deltas (−20 calls × 60 deltas each). His position would have acquired a net delta of −200. He would be short the equivalent of 200 shares of stock while the stock price is rising.

The solution, of course, is to rehedge the position by buying 200 more shares of stock or by buying back about three short calls. Either of these adjustments probably means that he has lost money on the spread. Either he must buy more stock at a higher price to stay hedged, or he must buy back calls that have gone up in value.

A market maker can be *long curve* (long gamma) or *short curve* (short gamma). If a market maker's position is net long options or long curve, his position responds to an upward move in the stock price by increasing its delta (and responds to a price decline by decreasing the delta). A position that is long curve multiplies the bet in the direction of any price move. Conversely, a position that is short curve responds to a major price move by increasing the bet against a continuation of the trend. Either way, the position requires constant adjustment in the face of trending prices to remain hedged and avoid taking on price exposure.

Volatility Plays

The kind of "dynamic" option trading that requires constantly adjusting a long or short option position to retain minimal price exposure—to maintain a zero net delta—allows market makers to buy and sell options to act upon their projections about volatility, yet still avoid betting on the direction prices will move. Market makers typically use a *delta neutral* strategy to implement their views when they think the volatility premium in options is mispriced. That is, when current prices do not accurately reflect the volatility they expect over the life of the options.

Market makers are often willing to take a position based on volatility projections. Sometimes this is done tacitly by relying on theoretical values that incorporate a volatility estimate. Often they establish positions quite consciously because they believe implied volatility is too high or too low and that actual volatility will differ from implied.

In fact, those market makers who concentrate on using theoretical values in making markets come to think of option prices explicitly in terms of volatility. They think and speak of options in terms of their *implied volatilities* and compare the "implied" to their own projections for volatility over the near term. Implied volatility is simply another way of thinking about current prices; it is the volatility that the current option price "implies" that the underlying stock must have over the life of the option for the price to be correct. More technically, implied volatility is the number you get if you plug the current option price into a mathematical option pricing model and run the formula backward to solve for the volatility, instead of the option price.

High option prices reflect high implied volatility. An expensive option reflects the fact that the marketplace has built a high volatility estimate into the current price of the option. It shows that the market is expecting a lot of movement in the underlying stock before expiration to justify the increase.

What market makers are doing when they buy cheap options and decide to hedge them with the underlying stock—often called *back-spreading*—is anticipating that over time the options will pay off by finishing enough in-the-money (or by offering enough protection to a stock position) to more than compensate for their current price. Conversely, by selling expensive options against a stock position, they are anticipating against high volatility, prior to expiration.

Positioning to Accept Other Types of Exposure

By buying what they think are underpriced options, traders are positioned to profit if volatility rises. They often refer to such positions by saying they are *long volatility*, and they describe positions where they have sold overpriced options to take advantage of a decline in volatility premiums as being *short volatility*. Among other risks, then, a position that is long volatility is exposed if volatility declines. What's more, a trade in favor of volatility is a trade against time passing with no action. So a trader who is long volatility is exposed to time decay, even when implied volatility remains constant.

There are other ways to make volatility plays. Just as delta measures the rate at which option price changes with a change in stock price, another measure, usually called *vega* (or sometimes *kappa* or *tau*), indicates an option's sensitivity to changes in volatility itself.

Vega tells you the rate at which you can expect an option's price to change with a 1 percent change in underlying volatility. The higher the vega, the faster an option responds if volatility kicks up, and the quicker the option loses premium if volatility dies.

It follows that at-the-money contracts can be expected to have higher vegas than out-of-the-money or deep-in-the-money options. The volatility component of their premiums is much larger and is thus more sensitive to any change in volatility. It also follows that a farther-term option has a higher vega than a near-term option. The greater time remaining for volatility to act makes their premiums more responsive to changes in volatility.

This offers market makers a variety of ways to spread options against options, and vegas against vegas, to take advantage of the different rates at which options can be expected to respond to changes in volatility.

For example, time spreads can be used to make volatility plays. By buying a time spread, a market maker can act on an expectation that volatility premium will rise. In general, by spreading options with different expirations and, at the same time, keeping the overall position delta neutral, traders can construct low-risk positions that profit when the volatility premium in one option expands or contracts faster than another.

A market maker can also trade *vega neutral* and thus hedge away his exposure to volatility changes. When he finds a disparity between two implied volatilities, by spreading one option against the other in a ratio that produces a zero net vega, he can wait for the high and low implied volatilities to come back into line, without exposing himself to the risk that volatility will change drastically in either direction.

Akin to the delta and vega thermometers, there are measures of other kinds of sensitivity and risk. They can be used to indicate risks to be avoided or eliminated, or they can be used to search out ways to take on just the exposure a market maker wants to accept.

As pointed out earlier, the mathematical measure of the curve or direction instability of an option position is the *gamma*. This measure tells you the rate at which you can expect delta to change with stock price. It indicates how fast an option position can be expected to become unhedged, if there is a move in the underlying.

Gamma can be used to recognize unstable hedges and to anticipate the size of price moves that require quick readjustment of the hedge. By buying and selling options with offsetting gammas (to reduce curve), a market maker can greatly increase the stability of his hedge across a range of underlying prices.

Just as delta is dependent on the current price of the underlying stock, it is also dependent on the time left in the life of an option and on the volatility premium built into the current price of the option. Any delta neutral spread must be adjusted to maintain its neutrality as time decay occurs. Moreover, it must be rehedged as market conditions change to produce different implied volatilities.

Similarly, a market maker can hedge away his exposure to volatility or to time decay by trying to neutralize vega and *theta*, the measure of time decay, just as he can hedge away gamma. Of course, when he does, he no longer has a position that benefits from an increase in volatility. Once all the risks are hedged away, the position becomes a pure arbitrage. All this can, in turn, demand further adjustment by buying or selling stock to compensate for the effect on the net delta of the position in neutralizing the other forms of exposure. Table 8–4 summarizes the types of risks inherent in basic spread positions.

TABLE 8–4
Types of Exposure for Basic Spreads

	No Delta	*Long Delta*	*Short Delta*
No curve	Basic arbitrage spreads (conversion, box, jelly roll)	Long or synthetic stock	Short or synthetic stock
Long curve	Long option delta-neutral spreads; long options versus stock; long straddle or strangle; option-to-option ratio spreads; net long options	Long call	Long put
Short curve	Opposite to entry directly above	Short put	Short call
No volatility	Basic arbs	Long or synthetic stock	Short or synthetic stock
Long volatility	Long at-the-money time spread; delta-neutral spreads, net long options; long straddle or strangle; (*not* option-option ratio spreads)	Long call; long time spread with stock below strike	Long put; long time spread with stock above strike
Short volatility	Opposite to entry directly above	Short put; short time spread with stock above strike	Short call; short time spread with stock below strike

	No Curve	*Long Curve*	*Short Curve*
No volatility	Basic arbs	No such spreads	No such spreads
Long volatility	Long ratio time spread (e.g., +1 May, −2 Jan. options)	Net long options	Long a-t-m time spread
Short volatility	Opposite to entry directly above	Short a-t-m time spread	Net short options

TABLE 8–4 (*concluded*)

Accompanying Risks			
No delta	No current price risk	No curve	No risk from price instability
Long delta	Downside price risk	Long curve	Risk after large price move; risk from time decay
Short delta	Upside price risk	Short curve	Risk from any large price move
No volatility	No exposure to changes in expectations		
Long volatility	Risk from decrease in volatility expectations; risk from time decay		
Short volatility	Risk from increase in volatility expectations		

Removing the Risks of Index Options

You've seen how market makers can use various combinations of equity options, together with underlying stocks, to selectively remove any or all of the risks inherent in buying and selling mispriced options. By eliminating risks selectively, they can construct positions that contain precisely the amount of exposure desired. Most frequently, they trade against the market's assessment of the volatility of a single underlying stock by buying or selling options. Then they use the stock itself to remove exposure to the direction of price movement.

In the index pits, market makers use the same approach to take positions on the volatility of the market as a whole—at least as measured by a particular index such as the S&P 100. They position themselves as net buyers or sellers of index options and then neutralize the index delta. This leaves them with no net exposure to market direction, but with a position that profits from an increase or decrease in volatility premium that reflects their own view of index volatility.

A dilemma arises when making markets in index options that traders don't encounter when they trade options against a single underlying stock. When market makers trade equity options, they have a good, "clean" underlying in the stock itself. They can be secure in the knowledge that their stock and option positions function as a bona fide hedge to offset each other because the options settle into the stock itself. Ultimately, options even turn into a stock position, either because short options are assigned or because long options are exercised directly into the stock.

On the other hand, for the S&P 100 (OEX) and other cash settled index options, there is no such underlying instrument available to provide a reliable hedge. The OEX underlying is a capitalization weighted index, containing different numbers of shares of 100 different stocks. OEX options do not settle into shares of the stocks themselves. Instead, a cash settlement at expiration compensates for the difference in value between the expiration-day index value and the strike price of the options. There is no perfect way to adopt a position in the underlying index itself, short of holding the appropriate number of shares of 100 different stocks—an alternative that is simply too cumbersome and too costly to be feasible.

Surrogates

As a result, market makers typically choose some surrogate for the underlying index. Most turn to the S&P 500 Index and use the S&P 500 Index Futures (an index futures traded at the Chicago Mercantile Exchange). Others use "baskets" of 70, 80, or more stocks as a representative sample of the 100, which they expect to move in tandem with the actual S&P 100 Index. Still others opt for some combination of stocks and futures to serve as an accurate representation to track the underlying index.

All these alternatives share the same drawback, to a greater or lesser extent. Every surrogate shows some tracking error in any given period and, consequently, all involve some *basis risk*. That is, the *basis* (or duplication in the price movement between the surrogate being used to replicate the 100 and the index itself) varies from period to period. For any given period, the surrogate can gain or lose value, relative to the S&P 100 Index itself. Therefore a market maker's hedge can gain or lose value, relative to the option position it is being used to offset. A market maker must take the risk that his hedge is ineffective to this extent every time he uses a substitute.

In addition to basis risk, market makers face problems maintaining their hedge when exercise occurs. When OEX options are exercised, it's a *cash settlement*. This means that the market makers' option positions are eliminated in favor of cash, yet the position adopted in the surrogate for the underlying S&P 100, whether a position in index futures or a basket of stocks, is unaffected by the exercise. The market maker, left with an unhedged position in his surrogate for the underlying index, must accept considerable exposure.

This represents a problem not only at expiration, but at any time the market maker (short options) finds options getting deep in-the-money. If the market maker is short deep-in-the-money, American options like the OEX, against a position in the actual stocks, the options can be exercised on any given day. This leaves the rest of the position in the stocks and equity options entirely unhedged because the index options settle for cash while the stock position remains unaffected by the early exercise. The unfortunate market maker starts the next day with a huge *leg*, totally exposed to any sudden move in the market.

Trading a Portfolio Delta-Neutral

You have seen that the basic strategy market makers use, whether they are trading equity or index options, is to buy or sell mispriced options and then to repackage options in bundles that eliminate unwanted risks. Such bundles can be small or large, combining an option or two with a position in the underlying instrument, or packaging together a number of options with different strike prices and expirations.

Furthermore, just as you can control the exposure of any position combining a single underlying stock or index and its options, you can also control various forms of exposure for a whole portfolio of stocks and options by treating the whole portfolio as one huge bundle of options and underlying instruments.

The same alternatives available for managing the exposure of a portfolio of stocks can be used to manage a portfolio of options. Fortunately, all the different types of exposure are simply additive. If volatility exposure on one contract is X and volatility exposure on another is Y, the total exposure to changes in volatility is just $X + Y$. This is also true for direction exposure and all other forms of risk. This means the overall delta or total exposure to market direction can be controlled with index products. Similarly, you can control the exposure of your portfolio as a whole to changes in market volatility and time decay with index options.

How to Do It

Starting with the most basic position, suppose you owned a portfolio of 50 or 60 stocks with no option position. Obviously such a portfolio's price exposure could be neutralized with S&P 100 (OEX) options. After all, controlling portfolio price exposure is precisely one of the purposes for which the OEX was designed.

To eliminate price exposure, first compute the *beta* of your stock portfolio relative to the S&P 100 Index, and calculate the number of options required to match the dollar value of your stock holdings. Then, by selling index calls which neutralizes the upside exposure and buying puts to protect the downside, you can design a hedge that neutralizes the portfolio against any price move.

The same general approach also works for a portfolio that includes equity options, along with the underlying stocks. However, the portfolio cannot be neutralized with this simple technique across a sizable range of market values. Remember that options change their own exposure with moves in the underlying stocks, as well as with changes in time and volatility.

At any given time and market level, the net delta for each stock, taken together with its options, indicates current exposure to price movement in that stock. Simply think of *option deltas* as shares of stock currently held. By totaling the current option deltas and the shares of actual stock held, you end up with a *net delta* which tells you your position in equivalent shares held. (Note again that this number changes over time and changes in stock price.)

If you know your current net delta stock by stock, you have a measure of your current exposure in each stock. This, in turn, enables you to neutralize your current market price exposure with index options, just as if you held a portfolio of the stocks alone. By selling index calls and buying puts, assuming your overall position is long (your portfolio's net delta is positive), you can maintain a zero net delta for the whole portfolio.

Of course, you are not restricted to using index options to control price exposure. Clearly, you can always buy and sell the stocks themselves. Furthermore, with some additional minor adjustments for beta, you can also use S&P 500 Index Futures to control your market direction exposure in much the same way you could adjust the net delta of a position in a single stock's options by buying and selling the underlying stock. You can use any index options that fit the makeup of your holdings, not only as one more tool for controlling direction exposure, but also for helping control other forms of exposure.

A good way to close this topic is with one final, provocative point. Market makers can control more risks than just their exposure to market direction at a portfolio level. A portfolio of stocks and options has a net gamma, a net vega, and a net exposure to time decay, just as it has a net delta. All these forms of risk can be addressed at both the micro-level of individual securities and at the macro-level with index products in the portfolio.

This is certainly not to say that the intricacies of how to go about controlling these risks at a portfolio level are easy, either in theory or in practice. It is to suggest, however, that market making in its purest form, where the market maker buys and sells options and eliminates all the risks it is possible to hedge, can be done in a wide variety of ways with a host of instruments.

Obviously, a market maker or market-making organization must have a fairly large position to even consider controlling exposure at a portfolio level, instead of stock by stock. Nearly all floor traders approach the task of managing their risk in discrete chunks, largely because they are standing in the pit where it's easier to control exposure a bit at a time. By bundling together combinations of options and stocks into groups (each of which is relatively free of those risks), a market maker can move on to other trades without undue concern over how each new purchase or sale will affect the exposure already inherent in the overall position.

TIME SPREADS, BUTTERFLIES, AND OTHER TRADING TOOLS

In theory at least, the basic arbitrage spreads have no exposure to underlying price movement—not to direction, size, or volatility. Often it's not easy to establish an arbitrage to lock in the edge from mispriced options. There are two other spreads that are not truly arbitrages, but that do deserve special discussion because they are staple items in a market maker's toolbox. They play a basic role in his or her strategies for bundling options into low-risk spreads to take advantage of mispricings and for trading in and out of other spread positions.

Butterflies and *time spreads* are themselves low-risk combinations of options. What's more, they can be recombined in various ways to produce arbitrage positions with even lower risks. For this reason, market makers learn to price and trade butterflies along with the basic arbitrage spreads even before they begin trading. Veteran traders keep their eyes on time spreads to give them a feel for price relations across different expirations.

While these two types of spreads retain some risks besides interest rate exposure, they are low-risk positions because all forms of exposure are at least partially hedged. However, establishing a time spread or a butterfly is to accept some risk. It is to take a position on both the price at expiration and the upcoming volatility of the underlying stock.

From Figure 8–1, it may be apparent that both kinds of spreads result in a profit or loss depending on whether the stock price lies within a particular range when expiration arrives. It might also be clear that there is indeed a volatility component to the pricing of these spreads, though it is dampened by the fact that the spreads include both long and short options.

FIGURE 8–1
Profit and Loss Profiles for Butterflies and Time Spreads

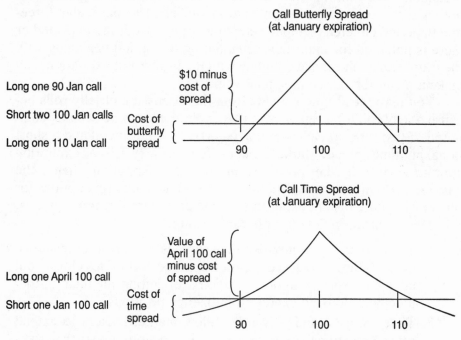

Time Spreads

A one-to-one time spread (also called a *calendar* or a *horizontal spread*) simply involves buying a call (or a put) with one expiration and selling the same strike call (put) with a different expiration. For example, buying a call time spread in November, which would result in a debit to the market maker's account, might involve buying a more expensive April call and selling a near-term January call with the same strike.

The value of a time spread at any given point during the life of the two options (including the moment of expiration for the near-term option) is just the difference between the values of the long and the short options. The spread value of a one-to-one call or put spread is the value of the more expensive farther-term option, minus the value of the nearer-term option. At near-term expiration, the expiring option is worth its intrinsic value. (If in-the-money, it is worth parity; if out-of-the-money, it is worth nothing.) At expiration, the spread is worth the value of the far-term option with parity netted out.

Assuming three months between the option expirations, the value of a time spread is three months' worth of time value or volatility premium. Note that this may not be the same as the time value of an option that expires three months from today. The particular three-month period covered is important. Whether dividends are expected or there is potential for important news during the period beginning with the near-term expiration and ending with the farther-out expiration, can make a major difference in spread value.

You may recall time spreads from the discussion of jelly rolls because a jelly roll arbitrage across two expirations can be seen as composed of two time spreads—a long (short) call time spread and a short (long) put time spread. Market makers often use jelly rolls as expiration approaches to *roll* other positions into the next expiration—hence the name *roll*. Doing so is simply a matter of trading in expiring options for others with more distant expirations—a matter of trading time spreads.

The important points to note for now are:

1. The availability of low-risk time spreads gives market makers a host of alternatives as expiration approaches besides closing out all their expiring option positions, or letting all their in-the-money options be exercised into stock positions.
2. Time spreads (and jelly rolls) allow market makers to extend pricing relationships across different expirations so that risks can be controlled, or even totally neutralized.

3. Time spreads allow market makers to manage their positions over different time periods. They can adjust their exposure in light of not only *what* they expect to happen, but also *when* they expect it to happen.

4. Time spreads, either one-to-one or in other ratios, can be used to manage other risks inherent in options besides just direction exposure. Hedging option positions with other options having different expirations provides a technique that is crucial for controlling exposure to volatility and time decay.

Primarily because they are so critical for controlling position risks, time spreads are frequently traded on the floor and priced as spreads. They are not nearly as important for their role as speculative vehicles as they are for their role as risk management tools.

Trading Time Spreads: A Conflict in Intuition

Time spreads are unusual among the strategies traders have at their disposal. They are rarely put on as freestanding spreads; more often they are used as a hedge in conjunction with other spreads. This stems from an odd combination of characteristics that make time spreads too inactive in price to make much money, but still capable of serving as an effective hedge.

It's curious that a spread that does not move enough to justify putting it on for its own sake is used to hedge something else. Although a time spread does not show the dramatic range in value that characterizes its counterparts, it responds predictably to changes in the market and can be relied on to offset the effects of another spread.

Nonetheless, time spreads are worth using as trading vehicles in their own right, and it is important to understand how they behave. These spreads have a peculiar kind of exposure to each of the various determinants of option price—underlying price, interest rates, dividends, volatility, and time. What's more, the nature of this exposure changes as time passes or as the spread moves farther in- or out-of-the-money.

Assume you're long a time spread with two months until near-term expiration (you're long a 120-day option and short a 60-day option with the same strike). Now take a look at the risks and the profit potential.

The spread, with 60 days left in the short options, does very little for a while unless something dramatic happens. An at-the-money time spread remains passive, earning little money as time decay slowly erodes the short options, until rapid time decay begins to affect the near-term options about five or six weeks prior to expiration. (In-the-money or out-of-the-money time spreads gain very little from time decay, since there is little time value to erode in the short options.) In this sense, the time spread is like a *vertical*—selling options against the underlying or against deeper in-the-money options; it profits from price stability as time goes by.

If a time spread is established at-the-money and the underlying price moves away from the strike, however, it can be expected to lose value since the spread is long time premium and the time premium in options that are away-from-the-money is much less than the time premium of those at-the-money. In this way, too, time spreads are like verticals: a move of the underlying away from the strike price produces a loss.

There are some important respects, however, in which time spreads are unlike verticals. In many ways, time spreads behave more like *backspreads*—the mirror images of verticals. This makes the behavior of time spreads seem counterintuitive to traders used to trading volatility by dealing in backspreads and verticals.

You expect a vertical, like a time spread, to gain from time decay and lose from a large price move, but in a vertical spread you are net short volatility premium. A time spread is long volatility premium. The value of the spread, after all, is just the difference in volatility premium between a long option with a lot of time (or volatility premium), and a short option with relatively little volatility premium. Consequently, a time spread is like a backspread and unlike a vertical in the way it responds to implied volatility: An increase in implied volatility benefits the spread and a decrease produces a loss or reduces the profit potential.

Yet, unlike a backspread, an at-the-money time spread is hurt by a large price move usually associated with high volatility. If prices move away from the strike, there is little of the volatility component left in the price of either option, so there is little difference between the two option prices and little value left in the spread. Not only do you lose more volatility premium in the far-term option, but there is less time value left in the near-term option left to decay. So room for profit from time decay has dried up.

For similar reasons, anything that might alter the effective expiration date—a large dividend, a takeover, a major restructuring—dramatically reduces the value of the time spread because the far-term options are worth no more than the near-terms. If this happens, the holder of the spread loses whatever he paid for it.

All this should help make clear why time spreads can seem so counterintuitive and even unpredictable. If you are long an at-the-money time spread, you want stability and you profit from time decay, despite the fact that you are long time premium. You are long volatility premium, but you don't want volatility—or at least not a big price move. You want higher implied volatility, but you don't want underlying prices to exhibit volatility by moving away from the strike price.

What makes a time spread attractive as a trading vehicle is that it allows you to bet in favor of stability and time decay, but with limited risk. You can lose only what you paid for the spread.

Furthermore, time spreads are quite predictable in various ways. Dividends and interest rate changes affect them in very predictable ways. For example, suppose you suspect interest rates are going up. Remember that a far-term call has a greater interest rate component than a near-term. An increase in interest rates benefits your far-term options more than the near-terms. You can play it the opposite way with puts where the effect of interest rates is negative.

The strategy can be inverted for dividend plays to anticipate a higher or lower dividend than generally expected. The value of calls, for example, involves subtracting the expected dividend. A dividend increase, assuming it affects two dividends prior to far-term expiration versus one before near-term expiration, reduces the price of the far-term option more than the near.

However, the most common scenario is one where nothing much changes very dramatically—not dividends, not interest rates, not implied volatility, and not any dramatic movement in underlying price. This is the kind of scenario where an at-the-money time spread can be established to produce a profit without much risk. The risk is simply that the spread value collapses if something dramatic does happen. When a time spread moves away from-the-money, it becomes very cheap.

This risk has a flip side: Time spreads that are already away from the money are very cheap, and they have the potential to expand dramatically under certain conditions. They can function as valuable hedges in combination with other spreads. They can provide cheap disaster insurance. If, for instance, your overall position has exposure at a particular price level above or below current prices, buying out-of-the-money time spreads at that level can be an effective hedge for that exposure. Out-of-the-money time spreads are a cheap hedge if the underlying price moves toward the strike.

Although they are a complex and sometimes counterintuitive trading tool, time spreads can also be extremely valuable to experienced traders who take the trouble to learn their intricacies.

Butterflies

A *butterfly spread* is a combination of four options (all calls or all puts) involving three strike prices, though just one expiration. A long butterfly—one that involves buying the "wings"—is composed of a long option, two short options at the next higher strike, and a long option at the strike above that. For example, a 50–55–60 call butterfly consists of a long $50 call, two short $55 calls, and a long $60 call. The corresponding put butterfly simply substitutes puts for calls, so it includes a long $50 put, two short $55 puts, and a long $60 put.

An alternative way to think of a butterfly is to pair the options as bull and bear spreads, also called *vertical spreads*. A long 50–55–60 butterfly is a $50–$55 call (put) bull spread combined with a $55–$60 call (put) bear spread.

Profit/Loss Profiles

Butterflies are limited risk, limited profit spreads. Taken by itself and carried to expiration, a butterfly spread succeeds or fails to make a profit depending on whether the underlying stock price closes at expiration within a particular range. The optimal result for a long butterfly is for the stock to close exactly at the middle strike price. In the example just given, having the stock close precisely at $55 would leave the two short $55 options and the long out-of-the-money option worthless with the in-the-money option worth a full $5. The spread would be worth $5 at expiration.

Any move away from the middle strike price makes the spread less valuable. The call butterfly, for instance, loses value from $55 down because the long in-the-money $50 call loses; it loses value from $55 up because the two short $55 calls produce twice as much loss as any gain from the single long $50 call.

Butterflies have limited stock price exposure, however. They cannot produce a loss greater than the premium initially paid for the spread. To return to the call butterfly at expiration, below $50 all the options, long or short, are worthless, so the spread cannot lose more than you have invested in it. At $60 the values of the long $50 call (worth $10) and the two short $55 calls (each worth −$5) cancel one another (while the $60 call is worthless). As the price escalates above $60, the two long options gain value at the same rate the two short options lose. In no case, then, should the spread result in a loss greater than the initial investment. Thus, a long butterfly is exposed to losses on either side of the middle strike price across the "body" of the butterfly, but the exposure is limited by the butterfly's "wings." Partly because of their limited loss features, butterflies are especially valuable as *inventory*—tools for trading in and out of other positions.

The way butterflies respond to price swings is unique. With options that have a great deal of time left, a butterfly does not react dramatically to moderate price moves. Only large moves produce a significant response in the spread price. So sensitivity to price movement is reduced to a minimum if expiration exceeds 60 days.

Volatility affects butterflies, but, again, their sensitivity is minimal as long as there is a lot of time remaining. Time decay does affect a butterfly, primarily because the out-of-the-money options become completely worthless, but most decay comes in the last few weeks before expiration.

This means that for the farther-out options a butterfly is a very effective tool for packaging trades into low-risk bundles to be thrown into *the spread hopper* and set aside until needed. Price movement won't hurt butterflies day by day, and they can always be taken back out of the hopper when there is an opportunity to use the inventory.

Typically, the same profit/loss profile as a butterfly can be achieved by selling the mid-strike straddle and buying the surrounding strangle— a spread nicknamed the *iron butterfly*. For example, the profit profile from a 50–55–60 call or put butterfly could be duplicated by selling the $55 straddle and buying the $50 put and $60 call or the 50–60 strangle.

You've seen how jelly rolls can be seen as combinations of time spreads, which in turn can be separated and recombined into other spreads. Similarly, butterflies can be seen as combinations of bull and bear spreads, which in turn can be recombined to form *boxes*. By buying a call butterfly, for instance, and hedging the risks by simultaneously selling a put butterfly, you can establish a *double box* or *double butterfly* spread (for example, a long 50–55 box and a short 55–60 box) that is free of direction and volatility exposure. (See Table 8–5 for a look at some of the various combinations.)

A look back at Figure 8–1 should make it clear that butterflies and time spreads have similar value (or profit/loss) profiles. For times well

TABLE 8–5
Some Ways to Think about Butterflies and Boxes

Long 50–55–60 call butterfly	Long 50 call	Short two 55 calls Long 60 call
	or	
	50–55 call bull spread	55–60 call bear spread
Long 50–55–60 put butterfly	Long 50 put	Short two 55 puts Long 60 put
	or	
	50–55 put bull spread	55–60 put bear spread
Long 50–55–60 iron butterfly	Long 50 put and 60 call	Short 55 call and short 55 put
	or	
	Long 50–60 strangle	Short 55 straddle
Double box or double butterfly	Long 50–55 box	Short 55–60 box
	or	
	Long 50–55–60 call butterfly	Long 50–55–60 put butterfly

prior to near-term expiration, the way time spread values change with underlying price is virtually identical to the way butterflies respond to price changes.

This suggests that the two spreads might be used to offset each other's risks. Not only can call butterflies be hedged against put butterflies (to form double boxes or double butterflies), and call time spreads hedged with put time spreads (to form jelly rolls), but market makers can also trade time spreads and butterflies against each other to form an indefinite number of reduced-risk positions.

What's more, each of the spreads can be extended in various ways to produce an array of spreads with an array of risk profiles. Butterflies, for instance, need not be restricted to consecutive strikes. You might, for example, want to construct a 50–55–65–70 butterfly by getting long the 50–55 call spread and short the 65–70 call spread.

The combinations for constructing different versions of the basic butterfly are limited only by the number of strikes available. A common name for any of these elongated butterflies is the *condor*. Other nicknames for this sort of spread are the *top hat, flat-top,* or *pan-head butterfly*. Condors have elongated profit patterns, hence the name. (The body is longer than a mere butterfly.) Unlike the basic, consecutive-

FIGURE 8–2
Profit Profile for a Top Hat, Flat-Top, or Pan-Head Butterfly

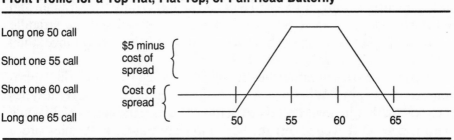

strike butterfly, there is no single point at which the profit is maximum. Instead there is a fairly large range (determined by the strikes selected and their prices) over which the spread earns its maximum profit. The profit profile at expiration is illustrated in Figure 8–2. Typically, condors are much more expensive than basic, three-strike butterflies because they have an extended profit zone. This squares with intuition: Anyone willing to take a view about the stock that requires the price to fall within a narrow range should have to pay less than someone who wants to profit across a broader range.

Trading Butterflies
Butterflies offer the trader a multitude of alternatives and almost unlimited flexibility. To see this, take another look at the equivalence between a basic call and an iron butterfly.

If you start with a call butterfly (e.g., long the 50 call, short two 55s and long a 60), then sell a 50–55 box (a totally neutral addition), notice that you end up with an iron butterfly. You end up short the $55 straddle and long the $50 put and the $60 call. It follows from this that selling the straddle and buying the strangle should put a credit in your account because, in effect, you are short a box for a large credit and long a butterfly for a small debit.

The beauty of the butterfly is that it gives the market maker the ability to make a mistake—yet various ways to correct it. He has three other sides of a trade to make up for the errant initial trade. If, for example, he buys one option, and that trade seems to be going against him, he can sell two options and wait for the third side to come his way. On the other hand, if he sells a call option and it starts to go against him, he can buy a deeper call and wait to sell the higher bear spread at a better price.

The only way a trader really gets hurt moving in and out of butter-flies is in very *whippy markets*. Then he can either buy the strangle and sell the straddle when it gets to his price; or he can sell the straddle when the market is whipping back and forth within a narrow range, then buy the strangle when it comes to his price.

Characteristics of butterflies change dramatically as time till expiration becomes short. What was a low-risk spread takes on several types of exposure that just weren't there before. But as a trading vehicle while there are several weeks left in the option contracts, butterflies are a nearly perfect trader's tool.

WHAT IT TAKES TO BECOME A MARKET MAKER

Becoming a market maker may seem a simple matter of joining an exchange and starting to trade, but there is a great deal more to it. Becoming a market maker amounts to starting a business—one that could range in size from one person trading his or her own small account independently, to a large and complex operation. Setting up such an operation requires both a heavy capital investment and a heavy investment in time, energy, and hard work.

More importantly, market-making demands some very special expertise. Developing that expertise requires native ability and a lot of homework, practice, and experience. The next part takes a careful look at the knowledge and skills market makers have to acquire. First, though, here's a brief look at some of the requirements for setting up a market-making business.

Costs and Commitments of Market Making

First, of course, are capital considerations. Trying to run any undercapitalized business is very risky. Market making is no exception; a market maker needs adequate trading capital to survive, even for the short term. Currently, "adequate" means an amount in excess of $100,000, even if the market maker plans to trade independently only in his own "small" account.

The second major capital consideration is arranging for a seat. Memberships on the major futures and options exchanges are now priced in the neighborhood of $300,000 to $500,000. In addition to full memberships, some exchanges offer less costly partial memberships or trading permits with trading rights for a limited number of products. Alternatively, seats can be leased for about $3,000 to $6,000 a month to leave capital free for trading.

Additional costs include initial fees in the neighborhood of $2,200, plus the on-going costs of doing business, such as securing office space, hiring a clerk, and obtaining computer facilities. Other daily costs to anticipate are paying the basic contract rate, arranging a volume discount, forking over fees for stock executions or index futures trades, and so on.

But it's more than a thousand dollars here, a thousand there. Ever think about where you train for trading pits? Well, nearly every business or profession has a structured and often institutionalized way to learn the ropes and get started. Doctors and lawyers go through professional schools and internships; engineers train on the job after mastering the technical material in undergraduate and graduate programs; and other businesses have lengthy formal training programs. Our industry, however, lacks a formal or standardized structure for initiating new traders into the business.

To make things worse, this is probably one of the most expensive businesses in which to get started because it involves such high financial risk. Part of the cost of entry into this business is the cost of inexperience. Not every market maker loses money in his first month, but a great many do; not every market maker blows out in his first month, but some do that too. Any tally of the cost of entry for the business of market making as a whole needs to reflect the enormous total cost of the collective experiences of all new traders.

When asked to add the total start-up costs involved for all neophytes— both the survivors and the bankrupt—to arrive at an average, the consensus among veterans is in the $50,000 to $100,000 range. That, most agree, is the *average cost* before a market maker turns the corner.

There are some ways to cut the cost of inexperience. The Options Institute at the CBOE conducts simulated trading for new market makers on its floor. Other learning tools include books, games, videotapes, seminars, classes, and paper trading. Computer-based trading simulators employ state-of-the-art technology to replicate the environment in which trading occurs. While these tools are no substitute for time on the trading floor, they offer knowledge and preparation that can contribute to the bottom line of a market maker's actual trading.

Clearly, the financial investment required for market making is substantial, and there are additional forms of investment required. Before you can trade, you need to be approved for exchange membership, a process that can take several weeks, and you need a letter of guarantee from a clearing firm. Selecting an exchange and a clearing firm are important and difficult decisions, decisions that require diligent homework.

Choosing an Exchange
The exchange the trader chooses determines the environment in which he or she will work. Every floor, indeed every pit, has a culture of its own. Although it may be hard to judge how a particular floor will feel as a place to spend long days standing in a crowd of traders, there are some key factors that determine the culture of a floor.

The first is whether an exchange is regulated by the Securities and Exchange Commission (SEC) or by the Commodity Futures Trading Commission (CFTC). This is important, not only because some of the rules are different, but also because the history and evolution of trading practices in the securities markets differ significantly from those in the futures markets. The New York Stock Exchange, as you know, is the dominant stock trading institution in the securities markets. Its long-established decorum and trading style, and its system that separates specialists providing liquidity from brokers filling customers' orders, have had an important impact on the development of SEC-regulated option markets, such as the CBOE. For example, a market maker on the CBOE, the dominant options trading institution, cannot act as both a broker (filling a customer order) and a market maker in options on the same underlying stock during the same day. This proscription has not been part of the tradition on futures exchanges, although some futures exchanges now have some restrictions on "dual trading." Capital requirements also differ between SEC and CFTC regulated exchanges.

Futures pits have a tradition where *locals* (individuals who trade for their own accounts) provide liquidity in an open outcry system that gives all those making markets equal access to trades and equal responsibility for providing liquidity and accepting risk. *Scalping*—accepting risk by simply holding unhedged long or short positions for brief periods during the day—has been the style in the futures markets for over a century. Traders can enter into spread positions to reduce their risk, but often they don't.

For that reason, trading options fits into a different environment on a futures' floor. That is not to say that there is anything about the theory of trading options on futures that makes it inherently more risky, or even very different from trading equity or cash-settled options. Options on futures do differ in some theoretical respects from equity options and from options on cash, but these are differences that a market maker can adjust to fairly quickly. Over the long term, it is the floor environment and culture that are more important considerations in choosing an exchange.

Other considerations include the volume and the volatility in the options you intend to trade. Not only does greater volume mean getting a chance at more trades, it also means that it is easier to transfer risk. Liquidity is crucial to reducing risk. On the other side of the coin is the fact that bid-ask spreads are typically wider when option volumes are lower (to compensate for the greater risk).

The volatility of the underlying instrument is important because it determines the premium and the fluctuations in premium for the options. Higher volatility produces higher premiums and more opportunities; low, steady, and unchanging volatility means that the value of options and the number of opportunities for profit are reduced. For example, CBOE's OEX is the most active option product in the world. Its volatility ranges typically between 10 and 20 percent, making it a relatively volatile product. Thus, OEX options offer both opportunities for profit and liquidity for controlling risk.

Choosing a Clearing Firm

A market maker's clearing firm plays a major role in his business. New market makers usually operate out of the clearing firm's office space, so the clearing firm influences all of his work time outside the pit. The cost structure that the market maker negotiates with the clearing firm has an impact on his cost of doing business and on his potential for success.

Many clearing firms offer a wide array of services. The basic services every one offers include clearing trades, accounting services (partial), and guaranteeing the market maker's trades. In addition, the firm might provide office space, secretarial services, educational facilities, and formal education programs. Different clearing firms offer different services and cost structures. And, of course, the costs rise with the amount of service. New traders ordinarily opt for an arrangement that offers the lowest clearing costs. Seasoned traders often demand more services, but generally they are also in a better position to negotiate rates.

An important consideration for new market makers is what a clearing firm offers to help them learn the business. Some have well developed education programs, including videotaped lectures, written materials, and perhaps even formal classes.

Partnerships and Backing

Adequate capital is crucial to success as a market maker. The arrangements between individual market makers and their backers vary greatly. In the past, backers typically negotiated a 50:50 split with a cutoff after a $50,000 loss. But in the past, a higher percentage of newcomers turned a profit. Today, typically only one out of five will be successful. A typical contract calls for a 30 percent cut for the market maker and a 70 percent cut for the backer to compensate the backer for his greater risk.

Frequently, sponsorship arrangements evolve out of an initial role as a clerk. A newcomer who learns the business by working for an experienced trader as a clerk often develops the relationship so that he takes more and more responsibility until he eventually becomes a market maker himself, backed by his mentor. Such arrangements vary from the new trader receiving a guaranteed salary and some minimal percent of profits to receiving a percentage of the profits based on a sliding scale. A typical scale might offer no participation for the first $50,000 in profits, 5 percent participation in the next $50,000, 10 percent for profits from $100,000 to $150,000, 15 percent from $150,000 to $250,000, and 20 percent above $250,000.

There are also partnerships among traders and arrangements where the backers play no role whatever in trading. An experienced team of market makers and clerks might arrange for backing up to several million dollars by negotiating participation in profits ranging anywhere from 30 percent to 70 percent.

Success

Successful traders are often asked, "What does it take to be a market maker?" Composure and the ability to respond intelligently to the unexpected, for starters. There's just no such thing as a "typical day" in the marketplace. There's rarely a day when everything goes as expected so that the market maker is prepared for everything that happens. Perhaps one of the key ingredients for being a market maker is enjoying that kind of daily variety. It's potentially very frustrating, but market makers are often people who enjoy the uncertainty, instability, and lack of structure.

What does it take to succeed instead of survive in the pits? It takes a combination of discipline and expertise, and discipline that outweighs expertise more than in most jobs. What marks the superior trader is the discipline to execute properly and the discipline to maintain the strategies he or she intended to employ. Success requires the ability to respond in a structured way in an unstructured environment.

Expertise is crucial too, especially today. Expertise among traders has risen dramatically, so competition has become very stiff, yet profit margins are small. A market maker who is going to stand out over the long run has to develop expertise out of experience. In particular, the experience the market maker gains from facing that first "crisis" is unsurpassed. How he handles it isn't as important for the long run as what he learns from it. That first crisis, and others that follow, mold a trader, and his talent for acquiring skill from experience is a major ingredient of success.

REFLECTIONS ON WHAT THE FUTURE HOLDS

The listed options business has evolved since its start in April 1973. Market makers who relied on "market feel" and "guts" have largely been replaced by arbitrage traders and mathematicians who trade for slight price discrepancies, rather than for "the big kill." This trend toward sophistication will continue, not only because of new technology, but also as a result of the increased awareness of price risk, which is inherent in any aspect of the securities business. Because the market maker's function is to transfer risk between longer-term investors, there will always be room for new and improved methods of managing this risk transfer role.

The collapse of the equity markets in October 1987 and 1989 and the shock waves sent through the currency markets with the ERM realignment in October 1992 are dramatic examples of price risk that is ever present in the securities business. In recent years, every major market has experienced similar volatility. From crude oil to Treasury bonds, and from agricultural commodities to currencies, every market in the world has attracted headlines at one time or another when price movements spell panic. The lesson for any participant is that risk management is crucial, and all investors and traders must be flexible enough to change with the evolving environment.

In addition to improved risk management, some challenges markets will face are the development of new trading techniques, applications of technology, trading structures, and extended trading hours.

New trading techniques can arise from new theoretical insights or from the listing of new products. Past milestones in the options business were the development of the Black-Scholes options pricing model, the introduction of put options, and the creation of cash-settled index options. Each created a new ball game at the time of its introduction. New products, such as exchange-traded "OTC" FLEX options, options on foreign indices, and long-dated equity options (LEAPS) have found their place with investors.

Current applications of technology continue to further the efficiency of analyzing and acting upon market information. Although computers may never replace the human decision-making process, there undoubtedly will be continuing discoveries of new ways to use the computer's ability to track prices and to identify price discrepancies. Undoubtedly, new developments will translate this information into trade execution.

Indeed, new trading structures will arise. Although the specialist system has historically dominated equity trading, and the open-outcry auction market system has been prominent in option trading, no one can say with certainty that these market structures will persist indefinitely. The CBOE has found success with the Designated Primary Market-Maker (DPM) system. More important, off-floor computer-based trading has challenged floor-based trading. Globex, in the United States, has brought electronic trading to the edge of the open outcry day and will serve to facilitate seamless trading. Trading procedures and rules for access that are suitable to computer usage will need to be adopted by the U.S. markets to hang on to the market share they currently hold.

Extended trading hours via longer hours of floor trading or via computer-based trading are the result of international financial markets. Trading around the world has grown in importance, and U.S. exchanges must face up to the challenge to maintain market share. Of course, extended hours are only part of meeting the global challenge. U.S. exchanges must continue to have markets with the most liquidity and with the highest integrity—or the business will go elsewhere.

PART 3

REAL TIME APPLICATIONS

CHAPTER 9

USING OPTION MARKET INFORMATION TO MAKE STOCK MARKET DECISIONS

Listed options are stock market derivatives. As such, it would seem that looking at option price data to make stock market decisions is putting the cart before the horse. Actually there are several logical reasons for analyzing option price data. One relates to a basic objective of the option markets, which is to determine a "fair" value for the derivative security. The *fair value* is a price for an option that favors neither the buyer nor the seller. Indeed, the listed option market is unusual in its quest for price efficiency. While the efficient market theory says that all information that is publicly known about a company is included in its price, this market is the only one that uses a mathematical model to arrive at an efficient or fair value.

As you have seen in previous chapters, the variables used in pricing models contain very useful information. First of all, option premiums contain an opinion about the future volatility of the stock price, that is, the range of prices in which the market expects the stock to trade. Second, option premiums must also take into account an expectation for short-term interest rates, since market makers finance their positions based on the spread between puts and calls. Third, option prices take into account an expectation for a stock's future dividends. For example, when a company is expected to make a change in its dividend policy, options premiums can reflect the anticipated change.

Another reason for studying this market is the nature of the use of options.

Listed options are ideal vehicles for speculation. This means they offer the potential to analyze the psychology of speculators. Options are also excellent tools for managing risk. Therefore, contained within an option price is an opinion regarding the risk of the underlying security, which is very valuable information for those who have invested, or are contemplating an investment, in a particular security.

Finally, listed options incorporate a time assumption. The time-frame is short by traditional investment analysis standards. Most options have expirations of 90 days or fewer. Few fundamental approaches to analysis cover a time period this short. Normal technical analysis does not state a time period. Indeed, with quarterly performance analysis increasing in importance, information that is directly aimed at the short term is increasingly in demand.

This chapter examines three methods of analyzing the option market. The first method seeks to determine the investment sentiment of option-oriented investors; the second examines premiums. Then the third explores the inner workings of an option pricing model in an attempt to determine the market movement expectations contained within the option price.

THE PUT–CALL RATIO

Sentiment indicators have long been a favorite technical analysis tool. Contrary indicators are those that mean the exact opposite of what they say. If such an indicator is registering a large percentage of bullish investors, the reading is considered bearish, given the assumption that most speculators are wrong most of the time. Prior to the introduction of listed options, *odd-lot volume* was a favorite contrary indicator. An odd lot is fewer than 100 shares of stock. Odd-lot buyers or sellers were generally considered to be at the bottom of the investment sophistication barrel, and thus were assumed likely to be making the wrong decision at key times in the market. The epitome of the odd-lot indicators was the number of odd-lot short sales. The arrival of listed options, along with an inflation rate that turned many odd lots into round lots, diminished the value of this indicator.

In recent years, the percentage of bullish investment advisors has become a popular sentiment indicator. Just as with individual investors, a relatively large number of bullish advisors is deemed to be bearish on Wall Street. Each week, investment advisors are polled in an effort to measure their bullishness, and the analyses are published frequently in various financial publications.

Buyers of options are generally considered speculators. Speculators are thought to be on the wrong side of the market most of the time, especially at market extremes. Logic would then suggest that an examination of the number of puts traded versus the number of calls might provide an ideal *contrary sentiment indicator.*

The CBOE publishes two put-call ratios. The S&P 100 Put-Call Ratio is calculated by dividing the number of puts traded on the popular OEX options during the analysis period by the number of calls traded. The CBOE Equity Put-Call Ratio makes the same calculation for puts and calls on individual stocks traded on the exchange. Some brokerage firms maintain their own put-call ratio calculations. The CBOE ratios can be found each week in the "Market Laboratory" section of *Barron's.*

A put-call ratio of 125 : 100 for the S&P 100 (125 puts for every 100 calls), considered as a contrarian sentiment indicator, could be viewed as a bullish reading. It takes only a 60 : 100 ratio to reach a similar conclusion for the CBOE Equity Put-Call Ratio.

The difference reflects an opinion that index traders are somehow less vulnerable to "contrary indicator disease" than individual equity players. To reach contrarian bearish readings, the ratios must record a reading of 30 : 100 (30 puts for every 100 calls) for equity options and 75 : 100 for OEX options.

Figure 9–1 shows the S&P 100 (OEX) Index graphed; it can be compared with both CBOE put-call ratios also in the figure. Some users prefer to plot a moving average to more clearly define the trend, thus helping filter out short-term "noise" that can be present in the numbers.

When using put-call ratios, it is important to remember that not all option activity reflects the trading of speculators. In fact, more than half the volume of trades comes from investment professionals and market makers. The percentage of public trades is a changing number, reflecting the overall condition of the market. It would seem logical that the value of examining put-call ratios would be greater during periods of high market interest by the public.

Remember also when viewing a put-call ratio that there is a direct, definable relative value between puts and calls. Traders on the floor of an exchange can "create" a put option by buying a call and selling the underlying stock short. They can create a call by buying a put and buying the stock. This process is known as *conversion.* They would choose to do this trade, or the reverse, if the prices for either option got out of line. This means that high call volume can generate high put volume and vice versa.

While on the subject of volume, note that option volume is a moving target. A volume of 1,000 contracts does not necessarily mean there

FIGURE 9–1
S&P 100 Index and CBOE Put/Call Ratios

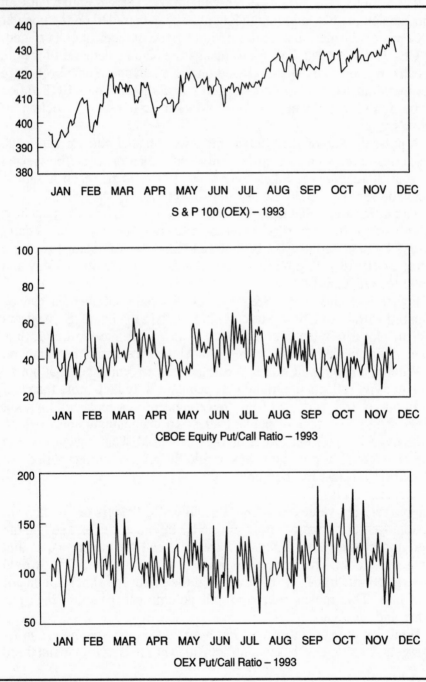

is a buyer or seller of that many options, although there might be. When an order reaches the floor of an exchange, the market maker can simply purchase the contracts for his or her own account. If the option is not desired, the trader can offset the new position by making a trade in the underlying security or another option. Offsetting a position with other option contracts pyramids the volume of such trading.

With all these caveats in mind, the put-call ratio can provide valuable market insight. As with most technical indicators, though, successful use of the number is probably more of an art than a science.

OPTION PREMIUMS

The amount by which an option price exceeds its intrinsic value is called the *premium*. An option's *intrinsic value* is the difference between the current value of the stock and the strike price of the option. Premiums are the "product" of the options market. All of the fundamental, psychological, and mathematical factors in the market are incorporated in their value. Monitoring the level of premiums and their relationship is one of the simplest—and probably one of the most important—ways option market information can be used to make stock decisions.

If the strike price of the option is at or above the price of the stock (in the case of a call), or at or below the price of the stock (in the case of a put), the entire price of the option is premium. The level of premiums is an important consideration for option traders—and for stock traders.

Traders in general want to be sellers when premiums are high, buyers when they are low. The problem is that what is relatively high or low is known for certain only *after* the fact. In other words, by looking at a chart of historical option premiums, the viewer can say what would have been the best approach for a trader to have taken. For example, if premiums had been declining, the trader should have been a seller, since the level obviously had been too high in the past.

Option Premium Indices

The CBOE calculates a dual index of option premiums. The index estimates the value of a theoretical call and put option on a stock of average market volatility selling at $100. The options have a strike price of $100 and expire in 180 days. Figure 9–2 shows the put and call premium levels, according to the CBOE Put and Call Option Premium Indices,

FIGURE 9–2
CBOE Put and Call Option Premium Indices

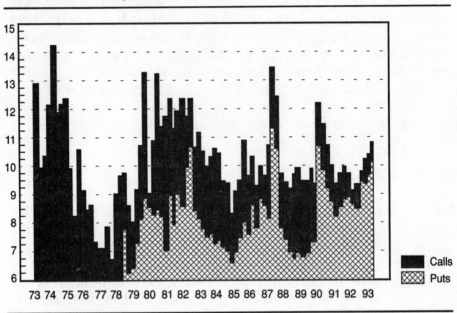

since the inception of listed option trading. As the chart shows, both put and call premium levels rise and fall together. This is due to the direct relationship between the two, and it reflects the fact that the most important factor in option pricing is the volatility assumption, which is the same for both contracts.

Of the two indices, put premium levels might be the most revealing and the easiest for investors to understand. A purchased *put option* represents the right, but not the obligation, to sell a stock at the strike price for a stated period of time. Puts are often used as insurance to protect a profit in the underlying stock. The seller of a put can be viewed as taking a position on risk equivalent to that of an insurance company. Just as in the more traditional forms of insurance, premium level is a key consideration. If insurance premiums turn out to have been too high, the insurance company will make a higher than expected profit. Higher profits attract other companies to the business and eventually lead to lower premiums. The same thing happens in the case of put options. Figure 9–3 shows the level of option premiums in 1993.

FIGURE 9–3
The CBOE Put and Call Option Premium Indices—1993

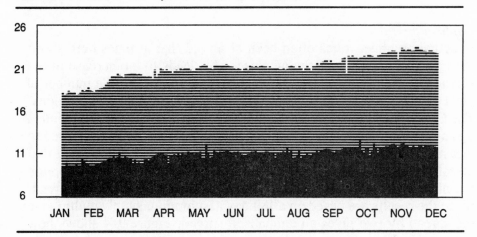

As is the case with the put-call ratio, a chart on the level of option premiums provides valuable perspective. Traditionally, one can be found each week in "The Striking Price" column of *Barron's*. This chart shows the trend of premium levels over the last six months.

The long-term picture of premium levels suggests a cycle. In the insurance business, the premium cycle is an important consideration. The same might be true for the listed option business, although the history of the business is still too short to make such a statement with certainty. If so, the volatility cycle can provide additional insight into the underlying market.

In addition, the long-term chart shows that the difference between put and call premium levels is not constant. The reason for this variance is the conversion process discussed previously. A put option can be converted into a call by simply buying the stock while holding the put. Actually, the process of conversion is one of the keys to efficient option pricing. The conversion process means that the long put, long stock position is equal in risk and return to a long call, long T-bill position. In order for this relationship to be true, the call option usually has a higher value than the put. This is true because under most conditions the dividend yield on the stock is lower than the T-bill yield. As short-term interest rates rise and fall, the spread between the value of the call and the put premium index changes. When the yield on T bills rises, the value of the equity should decline, all other factors being the same. This tends to hold the put-call relationship steady.

Confidence Index

In actual practice, it has often been observed that at times both short-term yields and stock prices increase. This leads to an increase in the spread between bond and stock yields. *Barron's* publishes a number of yield spread indicators, the best known being the Confidence Index. The Confidence Index is calculated by dividing a high-grade bond index by an intermediate-grade index. Changes in the relationship are used to measure the confidence of investors. At some point it is assumed that investors will become overconfident. The CBOE Put and Call Option Premium Indices provide a simple way of calculating a yield spread. Since the results are based on a 180-day assumption, simply multiplying the spread by two gives an annualized spread. Figure 9–4 shows how the relationship has changed in the past.

FIGURE 9–4
Option Premium Derived Yield Spread

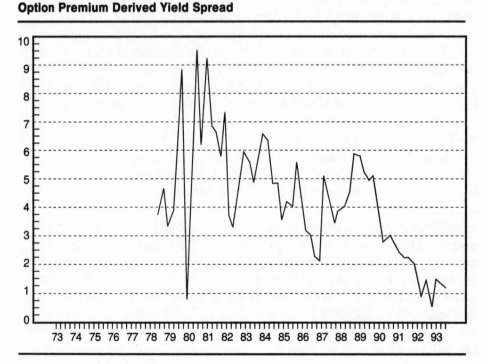

IMPLIED VOLATILITY

An option pricing model requires the following input variables: stock price, exercise price, time, interest rate, stock dividend, and expected volatility. Of these, volatility is the only unknown variable, yet it is the most important. *Volatility* is defined for pricing model purposes as the standard deviation of the daily percentage price change for the stock, annualized. To estimate the volatility of a stock, the stock price changes for a recent time period can be analyzed. The volatility for the stock determined in this manner is called *historical volatility*.

Calculating the value of an option using historic price volatility often results in a theoretical price that is different from that in the actual market. This means either that the option is out of line with its value, or that the volatility being used by others in the market varies from the historic. Because the option market has become relatively efficient since its birth in 1973, it is more often the latter reason—that expected volatility is different from historical volatility. To determine what this assumed volatility factor is, the pricing model can be employed. If the price of the option is used as an input, and the model is solved for the volatility assumption, the resulting factor is called *implied volatility*.

Implied volatility can help an investor analyze the market in several ways. A chart of implied volatility provides the same perspective as the chart of option premiums discussed in the previous section. If a stock's implied volatility has been declining, it can be assumed that option writers have been earning a higher rate than expected. If implied volatility is in an uptrend, option buyers have probably been net winners. A sudden change in the trend of implied volatility might indicate a substantial fundamental event in the company or the market.

CBOE Market Volatility Index

In 1993, the Chicago Board Options Exchange introduced the CBOE Market Volatility Index. The CBOE Market Volatility Index, known by its ticker symbol VIX, measures the volatility of the U.S. equity market. It provides investors with up-to-the-minute market estimates of expected volatility by using real-time OEX index option bid/ask quotes.

The VIX is calculated by averaging S&P 100 Stock Index at-the-money put and call implied volatilities. The availability of the index enables investors to make more informed investment decisions.

FIGURE 9–5
CBOE Market Volatility Index, 1988–1992

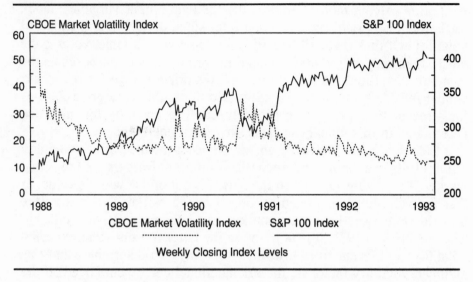

CBOE Market Volatility Index   S&P 100 Index

CBOE Market Volatility Index   S&P 100 Index

Weekly Closing Index Levels

Figure 9–5 presents the VIX history, consisting of daily minute-by-minute index values for the five-year period from January 4, 1988, through December 31, 1992. The chart also includes the S&P 100 OEX index for the same time period. Note that for the time period shown, all of the spikes in volatility accompanied market downturns and significant events that affected the market.

A study of Figure 9–5 reveals a great deal about the relationship between the market and volatility. Note the tendency of the VIX to spike upward during periods of market decline. The high level of volatility at the beginning (left side) of the chart is a direct result of the October 1987 market decline, which is not shown. Volatility then declined steadily until late 1989. The spike in volatility at that time was the result of the sharp one-day market correction in October. Another sharp increase in volatility occurred in August and September 1990, the period during which Iraq invaded Kuwait. In January 1991, volatility rose sharply again, just before the initiative led by the United States known as Operation Desert Storm. The last peak in volatility displayed in the chart reflected the downturn in the market, occurring one month before the United States presidential election in November 1992.

The tendency of market volatility to expand during market downturns is clear from the illustration above. This tendency is the subject of numerous academic studies of the options market. Perhaps the best way to understand the relationship between volatility and market declines is to look at the options market from a "put" perspective.

A put is the option market equivalent of an insurance policy. An investor may purchase a put to insure a sale price for the underlying asset. The seller (writer) of a put may be viewed as the equivalent of an insurance underwriter. The put writer accepts a premium in return for accepting a risk, which in this case is ownership of the underlying asset. In the insurance business, premiums rise following significant negative events (such as a hurricane). In the options business, market volatility, the critical factor in determining put premium levels, increases in periods of market distress.

The same factor that leads to an increase in put premium levels, increased volatility, causes call option premiums to increase at the same time. Thus, put premium levels and call premium levels move together because they are both related to volatility. This relationship is critical to the option strategist. High call premiums during periods of market distress are the opposite of what most investors would expect.

A similar pattern would be observed if we looked at a chart of the implied volatility of an individual stock. The average investor has to search a little to find volatility numbers. Many online computer services compute an implied volatility for each underlying stock every day. The *Daily Graphs Option Guide* includes the historic volatility each week in its statistical section. Sooner or later the media will discover that implied volatility is an important statistic, and it will be included along with stock dividend and price earnings multiples in the daily stock quotations page.

When looking at an implied volatility for a stock, remember that the number can vary from option to option within a family of options. It can also change for in-the-money or out-of-the-money types. For this reason, most services use a filtering process, or weight more heavily the more liquid at-the-money contracts. The most important consideration is that the service remain consistent in applying its rules. Remember also that as a stock's options become less liquid, the implied volatility becomes a volatile number. This would suggest that decisions based on implied volatility would be better for liquid issues than those less often traded.

The implied volatility of the stock is a vital consideration for a trader. The higher the implied volatility, the greater the percentage move in the underlying stock needed to double the value of the option.

TABLE 9–1
Ten-Day Price Movement of Stock Necessary to Double the Value of an At-the-Money Option with 45 Days Until Expiration

Implied Volatility	Beginning Stock Price				
	$20	$40	$60	$80	$100
15%	3/4	1 5/8	2 3/8	3 3/8	4 1/8
20	1 1/8	2	3 1/8	4 1/8	5 3/8
25	1 3/8	2 1/2	3 3/4	5	6 3/8
30	1 5/8	2 7/8	4 1/2	6	7 3/4
35	1 3/4	3 3/8	5 1/4	7	8 3/4
40	1 7/8	3 7/8	6	8	10
45	2 1/8	4 3/8	6 3/4	9	11
50	2 3/8	4 7/8	7 3/8	10	12 1/4

Table 9–1 shows the dollar price movement for the underlying stock needed to double the value of an at-the-money option. It states that a stock selling at $60, whose options assume a volatility of 30 percent, has to increase in price by 4 1/2 points for the $60 option to double in value, all other factors remaining the same. This table only considers an option with 45 days until expiration. Contracts with more days to expiration would need greater price movement. Another use for implied volatility could be to estimate the expected price range for a stock for a particular time period. This is based on the idea that an upper and lower price for the stock can be determined, above or below which the volatility would be wrong. Table 9–2 presents the implied price range for stocks of varying implied volatilities and prices over the next 45 days. This table states that a stock selling at $60 with an implied volatility of 30 percent has an implied price range of 18 points.

Price range is determined using an option pricing model. To find the upper limit, the price of the stock is increased until the dollar price movement in the option equals that of the stock. This is referred to as a *delta* of 1. The same process is used to determine the lower limit. The difference between the upper and lower limit is the expected price range. Again, the greater the time frame, the larger the expected price range.

For those who like rules of thumb (recognizing the dubious origin of the term) the approximate expected price range for a stock for the time period under consideration can be determined by multiplying the at-the-money call option price by 8.

TABLE 9–2
Implied 45-Day Price Range

Implied Volatility	Beginning Stock Price				
	$20	$40	$60	$80	$100
15%	3	6 1/2	9 1/2	13 1/2	16 1/2
20	4 1/2	8	12 1/2	16 1/2	21 1/2
25	5 1/2	10	15	20	25 1/2
30	6 1/2	11 1/2	18	24	31
35	7	13 1/2	21	28	35
40	7 1/2	15 1/2	24	32	40
45	8 1/2	17 1/2	27	36	44
50	9 1/2	19 1/2	29 1/2	40	49

At this point it is important to remember that the options market considers stocks to be efficiently priced and price movement to be random. In other words, a stock is always considered to be at the center of its expected volatility price range. Applying the implied price ranges to the table of the stock might lead to a different conclusion.

A research service in Vienna, Virginia, publishes an options market newsletter that is almost entirely devoted to an analysis of implied volatility. The firm's owner holds a belief that a stock has a longer-term price trend that is directly related to the investment fundamentals of the company. In the short term, the price of the stock bounces randomly around this trend as buy and sell orders are received and as the overall market oscillates. The more volatile the stock, the wider the range of possible price fluctuations. The research service estimates the location of each optionable entity within its expected price distribution. The information is then used to determine the most appropriate risk management strategy and stock to employ in the strategy.

The firm's approach contains three steps. Step one calls for determining the location of the overall market in its expected price range. This step determines the most appropriate risk management strategy and is considered to be 50 percent of the decision process. If the market is in the upper part of its expected price range, a defensive or bearish position is assumed. The listed options market offers a number of strategies for such a situation. In the defensive list are *overwriting* (the sale of call options against exiting stock positions) and the purchase of *protective puts* (puts purchased as insurance against a stock price decline). Possible bearish positions include the speculative *purchase of puts* or *bear spreads* (the purchase of a put combined with the sale of a lower-priced put, for example).

If the market is judged to be in the lower part of its implied range, bullish positions are considered. Possible bullish strategies include *buy-write* (the purchase of stock and sale of a call option); *underwrite* (the sale of cash-secured put options); and *buy call* and *bull spreads*. All of these positions offer the possibility of profit if the underlying stock increases in value.

The midrange for the market is possibly the most important consideration in the strategy decision process. This is because it is expected that the market will be in this area most of the time. This assumption is based on the normal distribution assumption for market values in the expected price range. Option pricing models assume that two-thirds of stock price observations will be in an area that represents one-third of the price range. If the market is in the mid-range, a strategy that would result in a profit if the price of the underlying stock is little changed would be preferred. These option positions are called *neutral strategies*. Possible neutral strategies include bull and bear spreads, *writing straddles* (the sale of a put and a call with the same strike price and expiration date), and buy-write or underwrite (discussed as bullish positions, but also applicable in the neutral area because they can produce a profit if the underlying stock price remains unchanged).

The strategy selection process just discussed can be visualized using The Option Strategy Spectrum (see Figure 9–6).

The Option Strategy Spectrum

Bullish	Neutral	Bearish
Market in lower part of expected price range	Market in middle part of expected price range	Market in upper part of expected price range

Once a market strategy has been established, the process of stock selection is started. This selection process has two parts, stock risk analysis and industry group analysis. Each stock is assigned to one of 20 industry groups. The average position of all stocks in the group is determined so that an analysis can be made about an individual issue. If the individual issue differs dramatically from that of its industry group, it can indicate that an abnormal fundamental condition exists. This is important because the implied volatility analysis assumes a "normal" market.

FIGURE 9–6
The Option Strategy Spectrum

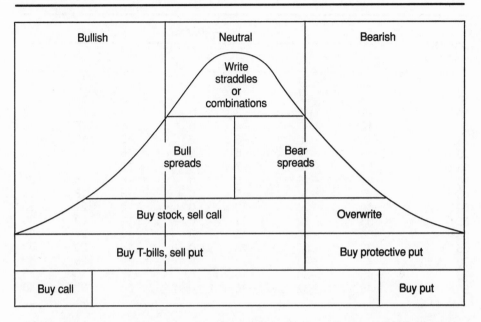

Source: The Option Strategy Spectrum was developed by Jim Yates, President of DYR Associates, Vienna, Virginia.

The analysis of the market and industry group can be viewed as market risk analysis; this evaluation constitutes 75 percent of the decision process. The final step is to identify the location of the individual stock. This step is called nonmarket risk analysis.

Table 9–3 can be used to estimate the location of a stock within its normal expected price distribution in a 90-day time frame. The needed ingredients are the stock's price, its 50-day average price, and its implied volatility. The first step in using the table is to determine the stock's percentage variation from the 50-day average. Then using the implied volatility, you can determine if this variation is sufficient to place the stock one, two, or three standard deviations above or below this trend.

The importance of volatility in the listed options market cannot be overstated. The entire market rests on the efficient market concept of randomness and lognormal price distribution. As the single most important factor in determining the value of an option, implied volatility is a critical factor in market risk analysis.

TABLE 9–3
Percentage Deviation from Trend Necessary to Attain Options Strategy Spectrum Zones for Various Levels of Implied Volatility

| Implied Volatility | Zones | | | | | |
	1	2	3	4	5	6
5	−3	−2	−1	0	1	2	3
10	−6	−4	−2	2	2	4	6
15	−9	−6	−3	3	3	6	9
20	−12	−8	−4	0	4	8	12
25	−15	−10	−5	0	5	10	15
30	−18	−12	−6	0	6	12	18
35	−21	−14	−7	0	7	14	21
40	−24	−16	−8	0	8	16	24
45	−27	−18	−9	0	9	18	27
50	−30	−20	−10	0	10	20	30
55	−33	−22	−11	0	11	22	33
60	−36	−24	−12	0	12	24	36
65	−39	−26	−13	0	13	26	39
70	−42	−28	−14	0	14	28	42
75	−45	−30	−15	0	15	30	45
80	−48	−32	−16	0	16	32	48

SUMMARY

The listed options market can be the most efficient equity market. As such, data derived from the market can provide valuable perspective regarding expectations. The perspective gained from an analysis of the listed options market, when combined with longer-term fundamental or technical analysis, should allow the investor to make significant use of a valuable risk management tool.

CHAPTER 10

INSTITUTIONAL CASE STUDIES

Development of the listed options market has dramatically enriched the set of portfolio management strategies available to institutional investors. It should be evident from the information presented in previous chapters that numerous option strategies can be designed to implement market views held by institutional and individual investors. For the institutional investor, options are best viewed as *tools* for portfolio risk management. They can be used to modify a portfolio's risk in ways not achievable with any other portfolio management technique. Understanding the proper role of options and other derivatives in portfolio risk management is a necessary component for successful institutional investment management in the 1990s.

Based on concepts presented in earlier chapters, the two cases are designed to test your knowledge of options as tools for portfolio risk management. Before institutional investors implement option-based investment strategies, they typically go through a two-step process. First is a learning process, the investment managers learn how options can be used as strategic and tactical investment tools—What strategies are appropriate? When should they be used? What is different about options compared with other portfolio management techniques? Second is an approval process, the institutional trustees or directors must change the investment plan documents to allow for trading of options and other derivative assets. The approval process usually requires an extensive educational effort for the plan trustees and investment committee members about the costs, benefits, and risks of using options. The trust plan managers making the presentation must be familiar with the characteristics of options and option strategies to earn the approval of their governing board.

The two cases presented in this chapter were developed from discussions with institutional investors and companies who provide consulting services to institutional clients. No particular institution is represented in either case, but the situations described are a collage of events that actually have taken place across several different companies.

In Case One, Lincoln Pension Trust is beginning the option implementation process. John Strong, the director of a large pension trust is trying to educate his investment strategy group and himself about the proper use of options in portfolio risk management. With a long record of achievement as a pension fund manager, John is considered a true *forward thinker* by his peers and subordinates. His experiences during the decade of the 1980s and early 1990s have convinced him that the new generation of professional fund managers must know how to use options and other derivatives in investment strategies. Lincoln Pension Trust is not a stranger to the use of derivatives, having previously used covered writing strategies in the early 1980s and dynamic portfolio insurance techniques during the period of the 1987 market crash. However, John is convinced that the options market has matured to a great extent over this period and that a much richer set of portfolio management techniques based on listed options now are available.

The analysis of this case should focus on development of the proper risk management strategies for the pension trust equity portfolio. John Strong is accumulating a growing cash pool and is uncertain about the market's future direction. What derivative strategies would you recommend in this situation? In addition, because the Trust is invested primarily in large capitalization, domestic securities, some members of the investment committee are encouraging the Trust to consider small-cap stocks and even foreign securities to gain greater benefits from diversification. Can you develop option strategies that will control risk and facilitate investment in these securities? In developing your recommendations, you may choose to analyze the market data provided in the case for the Russell 2000 Index. Premiums for three-month puts and calls are provided over a 12-year period, enabling you to construct different option-based strategies and evaluate their risk-return characteristics.

In the second case, the internal fund management of Hampton Investment Fund is trying to gain approval from their trustees to change their plan documents and allow investment in derivative securities. Using the trustee meeting as a setting, the case involves members of the trustees and the fund management team discussing the pros and cons of investment in derivative securities. The purpose of this case is to make you aware of questions about options typically raised by board members and to encourage your formulation of answers to these questions. Study of this case should enable you to avoid some of the problems and pitfalls faced by other institutional investors as they cleared the internal management hurdles to gain approval for the use of derivative securities.

You are encouraged to read each case and formulate your own answers using the suggested outline of questions provided at the end of the case. As you develop an answer for each question, reference to other chapters in the book may be of use. Afterward, you can compare your analysis to the suggested case solution. Keep in mind that the suggested solution is only one of many feasible answers that could have been developed; it is provided merely as a guide to the major points developed in the case. Each investment manager has his or her own particular trade-off for risk and return that will influence the answers. The great benefit of options is that they enable each manager to tailor a payoff pattern for the portfolio that provides the best fit for the manager's unique preferences.

CASE ONE

Lincoln Pension Trust

John Strong is the director of investment strategy for the $20 billion Lincoln Pension Trust, the pension fund for employees of Lincoln Agriculture Products. Lincoln Agriculture is a large, integrated food production and processing company headquartered in Chicago. The pension trust employs more than 30 external fixed income and equity money managers who specialize in a variety of investment strategies. In addition, the Trust has 15 internal managers whose responsibilities are divided among fixed income, equities, private investments and venture capital, and real estate.

John has been in the fund management business more than 30 years and is highly regarded by his peers as a true "forward thinker." If someone was trying a new and successful investment strategy, you could bet that John was one of the leaders of the group. He increasingly had become convinced that the pension fund manager's job should be viewed in the context of portfolio *risk management* rather than merely identifying stocks to buy and sell, or making overall asset allocation decisions that would be changed gradually over market cycles. Because of John's leadership, some of his internal managers wanted to explore the use of various derivatives—options, futures, and swaps—in their portfolio management strategies.

Last Monday, John directed two of his top managers, Rick Bowlin and Susan Jordan, to study the topic of portfolio risk management and to design various strategies using derivatives that could be considered by the investment committee later in the month. Their analysis, which would be reviewed by the other 12 members of the internal management team, was scheduled on Thursday morning. Specifically, John asked them to (1) devise for the group a workable definition of the term *risk management*, (2) illustrate how options can be used to implement portfolio risk management strategies, and (3) suggest what risk management strategies might be appropriate in today's market environment.

Lincoln Trust's Previous Experience with Options and Portfolio Risk Management

As John considered risk management strategies that would be appropriate for the Pension Trust, he remembered their two experiments with derivatives during the past 15 years—covered call writing in the 1970s and early 1980s, and portfolio insurance in the mid 1980s. Covered call writing was popular in the early years of the exchange-traded options market. Its attraction may be traced to the fact that many pension fund trustee boards and state regulators would only allow institutional investors to engage in covered call writing—the selling of individual call options against stock currently owned. This strategy was deemed prudent and conservative and was considered the only proper use of options by institutional investors. Only listed calls were available beginning in April 1973. Listed puts on individual stocks began trading in 1977 under a market test program sanctioned by the Securities and Exchange Commission, and were available only on a limited number of stocks until 1982.

For funds in the 1970s and early 1980s that followed the covered call strategy religiously by rolling over new calls when previous ones expired, it appeared to work exactly as planned. The market during this period trended sideways for extended periods, with few strong moves either up or down. The only exception was the boom in energy stocks during the late 1970s. However, the bull market that began in August 1982 demonstrated that no investment technique works forever. As the bull market roared, returns from covered call-writing portfolios badly underperformed the S&P 500 Index, as stocks were called away at strike prices far below then-current market values. Thinking about to-day's market environment, John wondered how covered call writing related to the concept of risk management and if the strategy should again be considered for use in specific market situations.

Portfolio insurance was the other experience with portfolio risk management by Lincoln Pension Trust. As the Trust's equity invest-ments appreciated from 1982 to 1985, John began searching for ways to protect the fund's value in the event of a market decline. In 1985 a strategy that was growing in popularity with institutional investors was called *dynamic portfolio insurance,* marketed by LOR (Leland, O'Brien, and Rubenstein) of California. John did not understand the technical details of the trading strategy, but he knew that it involved buying and selling S&P 500 Index futures contracts every few days as a function of the price change that occurred in the S&P 500 Index. The underlying equity portfolio held by Lincoln Trust did not have to be disturbed. As it was described to him, the portfolio insurance manager used information from an option pricing model to calculate the amount of futures contracts to buy or sell, so that the payoff at the end of the following week from the futures and equity portfolio would replicate the payoff of an equity portfolio insured by index put options.

Lincoln Trust implemented dynamic portfolio insurance in 1986, and the strategy worked as advertised until the market crash in 1987. From October 19 to 22, 1987, the dynamic insurers were unable to execute the strategy. They could not trade S&P 500 futures contracts because the tremendous volume in stocks and their exploding volatility "delinked" the stock and futures markets. The manager explained that during this period, appropriate prices for the futures could not be deter-mined because current stock prices were unavailable. High stock vol-ume caused the price quotations for stocks to run significantly behind the market, and futures traders were unwilling to quote the futures contracts because they did not know the prices of the underlying stocks. The dynamic insurers could not maintain the proper hedge with futures causing the portfolio to become uninsured. Lincoln Trust's equity port-folios suffered severe losses during the 1987 crash period, even though they were "insured." In a meeting during the week after the crash, John and the investment committee made the decision to discontinue the dynamic insurance strategy.

In spite of this bad experience, the concept of portfolio insurance appealed to John Strong. He wondered if the marketplace had evolved today to a point where the strategy could be applied using a different technique than daily or weekly hedging with futures contracts. It seemed that portfolio insurance strategies could be designed using listed index options that would not require any changes in the option positions until their expiration. It did not appear that listed options and underlying stock prices could become delinked, and the problem experienced with S&P 500 futures should be avoided. John wanted to be sure that Rick and Susan examined this strategy in their presentation. Primarily, he wanted to know the advantages and disadvantages of the different listed option contracts that would be acceptable candidates for this strategy.

The Fund's Current Investment Position

After reviewing the overall investment position of the fund, John believed that the fund and its external managers had sufficient exposure to the large capitalization stocks favored by institutional investors. In fact, two of the external managers were basically running index funds designed to track the S&P 500.

The large size of the Lincoln Pension Trust fund motivated John to explore a variety of alternative investments beyond stocks with large institutional followings. For example, during a recent investment strategy session, two of his internal equity managers argued strongly that the fund should allocate a greater portion of the portfolio to domestic, small capitalization stocks, and one manager wanted to increase the Trust funds' exposure in the foreign stock arena. The main concern about small-cap stocks expressed by some of his managers was the increased volatility that they typically exhibit compared to large-cap stocks and the thin markets in many of the issues. The problems of foreign stock investing related to a dearth of knowledge about foreign markets and the inability to obtain comparable financial statements, which would enable comparison to domestic investments.

Preparation for the Strategy Meeting

Rick and Susan began an outline of the topics they wanted to pursue for the meeting. They believed that their first task was to develop a definition of *portfolio risk management,* after which they could explore how options could be used to modify the risk inherent in equity portfolios. Rick began working on this project, while Susan volunteered to examine the different types of listed option contracts available that could be used for strategies they might recommend. To begin, Rick and Susan knew they had to define what is meant by risk; then they had to evaluate how risk can be changed or managed using different derivative securities. Pertinent segments of their report are presented below.

Definition of Risk and Portfolio Risk Management

Risk in a financial security may be defined as the degree of uncertainty about the stock's value at any future date. A speculative stock will exhibit more variability in its price over time than a conservative stock and for that reason is considered more risky. By quantifying that variability, we can estimate an investment's risk. It also should be realized that the total risk or price variability in a stock can be decomposed into two components: firm-specific risk and market risk.

Firm-specific risk is the price uncertainty caused by events unique to the company itself. These include the demand for its product, labor costs, and executive management changes. *Market risk* entails factors that affect the prices of all securities. Events such as interest rate changes, a change in the economic outlook, the federal budget, and the federal deficit are market-risk factors. When securities are combined into large portfolios, the firm-specific risk can be diversified away because random events cause some firms to prosper more than expected while others decline more than expected. However, the market risk cannot be altered. A portfolio containing more than 40 or 50 stocks will vary in price much like a broad market index such as the S&P 500 or the Russell 3000. The limit of risk reduction through diversification is the risk level of the market portfolio.

We can quantify investment return and risk by creating a distribution of the expected returns for the investment. For example, Exhibit 1 shows a familiar bell-shaped histogram representing a normal distribution of returns, with a mean, or expected return, E(r), of .10. [$E(r) = \Sigma p_i r_i$, where p_i is the probability of return r_i. The mean divides the distribution exactly in half.] A measure of risk in the distribution is the standard deviation of the returns, which is the average deviation from the expected return of each individual return weighted by its probability of occurring. The standard deviation of this distribution is .0537. (Standard deviation, σ, is calculated as $(\Sigma p_i [r_i - E(r)]^2)^{1/2}$. An investment that has a higher standard deviation has more risk, and one with lower standard deviation would be considered less risky. A virtually riskless investment such as a Treasury bill will have a standard deviation near zero.

Using past data for large stock portfolios, one usually finds that the distributions of historical returns are basically normal, meaning that the right side of the bell-shaped curve is a mirror image of the left side of the distribution. The same is true for bond portfolios, which have much

EXHIBIT 1
Symmetric Probability Distribution of Returns

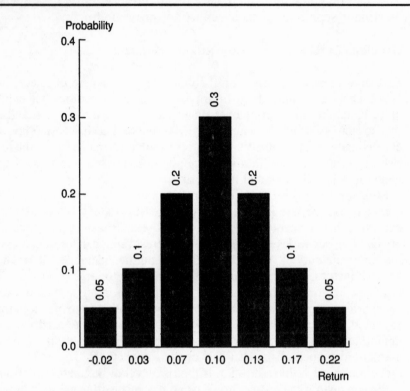

lower standard deviations than stock portfolios but still have distributions that are normal. To understand how return distributions incorporate portfolio risk, consider what happens when you transfer money from a 100 percent equity position, to 80 percent equity, 20 percent bonds as shown in Exhibit 2. Note that the expected return of the distribution falls and the standard deviation is reduced. The distribution becomes more peaked, indicating that you are more certain of getting the distribution's expected return. At the limit, conversion of the portfolio to 100 percent Treasury bills would produce a certain return of the Treasury-bill yield and would be shown as a vertical line on the expected return distribution.

Susan and Rick now felt comfortable in developing a definition for the concept of risk management. "*Portfolio risk management* means molding the expected return distribution of a portfolio to achieve the

EXHIBIT 2
Return Distributions for a Stock Portfolio Compared to an 80 Percent Stock, 20 Percent Bond Portfolio

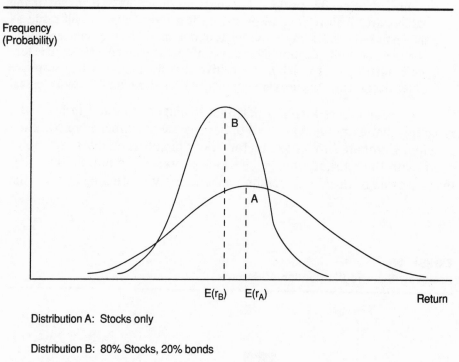

Distribution A: Stocks only

Distribution B: 80% Stocks, 20% bonds

objectives desired by the portfolio manager." Rick and Susan go on to note that

> using traditional investment strategies, portfolio managers have limited tools at hand to control the shape of the distribution. If investment alternatives are restricted to stocks, bonds, and cash, any expected return distribution will have an approximately normal shape, and only the expected return and standard deviation can be adjusted.

As a final step in describing risk management, Rick wondered if it was possible to create expected return distributions that were not normal and that might have greater appeal to equity managers in certain market environments. He recalled the term *skewness* and thought that the investment committee should be aware of its meaning because the concept may be important later as they developed risk management strategies using options.

Skewness is a risk measure for a distribution that evaluates outliers or unusually large or small returns. When a return distribution has some large returns relative to the mean and many returns near but slightly below the mean, it will exhibit positive skewness as shown in Exhibit 3A. If the outliers are small relative to the mean, negative skewness will result as shown in Exhibit 3B. For these types of distributions, the standard deviation does not fully capture all the risk of the investment. Most investors prefer distributions which have positive skewness because any surprises which occur will be returns greater than expected, rather than large losses.

Rick remembered from a portfolio management class in his MBA program, that a unique feature of options is the asymmetric payoff they provide. Compared to stocks or futures, which essentially move up or down with the market, changes in option returns are limited on either the downside or upside, depending on whether you are long or short the

EXHIBIT 3A
Positively Skewed Distribution of Returns

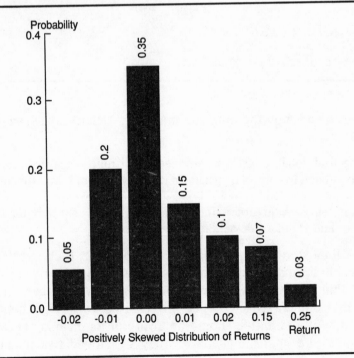

EXHIBIT 3B
Negatively Skewed Distribution of Returns

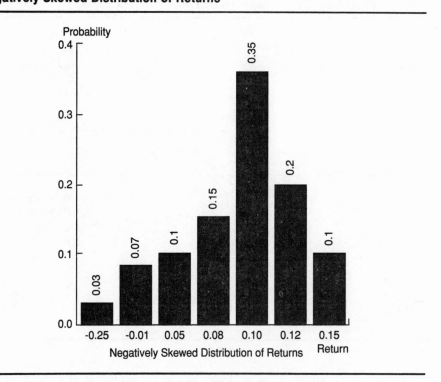

Negatively Skewed Distribution of Returns

option. Rick wanted to explore how different option strategies might change the expected returns of a portfolio to determine if the normality of returns would be affected. He thought the following information in the report would prove useful to the strategy committee.

Using Options in a Risk Management Context

To understand how options can be used in portfolio risk management, consider the payoff diagrams for two popular stock and option strategies: (1) covered call writing and (2) the purchase of protective puts. The profit/loss diagram for covered call writing (own stock and sell a call) is shown in Exhibit 4. Assume that XYZ stock is at $70 and the April 70 call, which expires in 2 1/4 months, can be sold for $5.25. The payoff for the stock is a 45-degree line through the current stock price of $70, indicating that the

EXHIBIT 4
Covered Call Writing (Sell the April 70 Call and Own XYZ Stock)

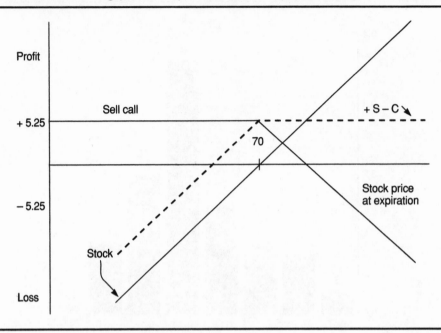

buyer of the stock gains or loses dollar for dollar as the stock price changes. The payoffs at expiration from selling a call are shown by the light solid line. If the stock is $70 or below at expiration, the call seller keeps the entire premium of $5.25. This represents the maximum profit that can be earned from the call. However, if the stock appreciates, the call seller loses dollar for dollar with the price increase.

The combined long stock plus short call position produces a payoff indicated by the dashed line. The most the covered writer will earn from selling an at-the-money call is the call premium. If the stock declines, the covered writer will participate in the loss, with some cushion provided by the call premium. The covered call-writing strategy appears to be most appropriate in a sideways market. It will produce real losses in a down-market and limited gains in a rising market. This is why the strategy performed so poorly for us after August 1982, when the bull market of the 80s began.

An alternative strategy is the purchase of protective puts on stocks held in the portfolio. Exhibit 5 shows the payoff diagram for the stock plus purchase of the April 70 put for $4.50. If the stock falls in price, the put becomes more valuable, while if the stock rises the put position will never

EXHIBIT 5
The Protective Put Portfolio (Buy the April 70 Put and Own XYZ Stock)

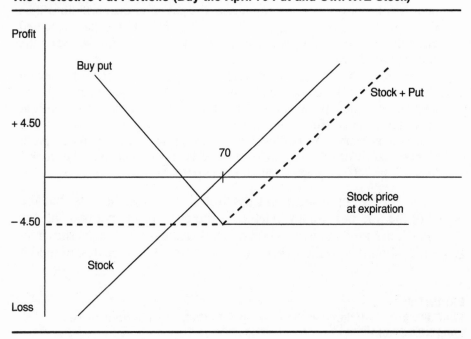

cost more than the purchase price of $4.50. Combining the put with the long stock position produces the dashed line shown in the exhibit. When the stock rises in price, the combined position produces a profit equal to the rise in the stock's price less the put premium. If the stock falls, the "stock plus put" portfolio will lose at most the $4.50 premium. For this reason, the purchase of a put against stock owned is called a *protective put* strategy, or *portfolio insurance*. The dynamic portfolio insurance program we used from 1986 to 1987 was an attempt to reproduce the payoffs of the stock-plus-put portfolio by synthetically creating the position with S&P 500 futures. If we can create the strategy using exchange-traded puts, rather than synthetic ones, the strategy should perform much better.

A final concept necessary to understand how options can be used in portfolio risk management is the *put-call parity* relationship. The put-call parity relationship holds precisely for European options on stocks that pay no dividends before option expiration. (European options can only be exercised at option expiration; American options can be exercised at any time.) The put-call parity concept still is appropriate for American options; however, the option prices are no longer exact values, but can be defined within upper and lower limits. Consider the covered call payoff diagram shown in Exhibit 4. If a European put is purchased for $4.50 with the identical expiration and strike as a European call, and the stock pays no dividends prior to option expiration, the payoff of the portfolio will be the horizontal dashed line shown in Exhibit 6, at $.70. It is the discounted value of the $.75 difference between the put purchased for $4.50 and the call sold for $5.25.

The graph in Exhibit 6 illustrates two important concepts for option strategies. First, by combining the positions of long stock, short call, and long put, a riskless position is produced. Regardless of the stock's price at expiration, the portfolio will be worth the exercise price of the options. This is demonstrated in Exhibit 7. If the stock price rises, the stock's profit will be exactly offset by the call's loss. If the stock price falls, the stock's loss will be offset by appreciation in the put.

The second important point illustrated from Exhibit 6 is that the prices of the put and call are related. If the price of the put and call are "correct", then the investor who creates a riskless position as shown in Exhibit 7, should earn the riskless rate of return. It can be determined if

EXHIBIT 6
Put-Call Parity Relationship (Sell the April 70 Call, Buy the April 70 Put, Long XYZ Stock)

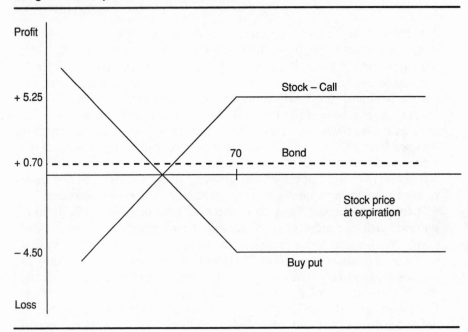

EXHIBIT 7
Payoff Diagram for Put-Call Parity—European Options, No Dividends*

		Payoff at Option Expiration	
	T_0 Value	(Cash Flows) $S < \$70$	(Cash Flows) $S \geq \$70$
Buy one share XYZ stock	$-S_0$	$+S$	$+S$
Buy 1 put	$-P_0$	$(E - S)$	0
Sell 1 call	$+C_0$	0	$-(S - E)$
Expiration value		$+E$	$+E$

* The relationship does not hold exactly if American options are used or if a dividend payment occurs before expiration. The underlying concept, however, remains valid, but the put and call prices can be defined only in terms of upper and lower limits rather than a single value.

the 75 cent difference between the put and call is appropriate by using the put-call parity equation as shown. There are 70 days until option expiration, and the yearly riskless rate is 6 percent. Let E represent the exercise price of the options; e^{-rT} is the symbol for continuous discounting over period T at rate r; thus Ee^{-rT} is the present value of the exercise price. The put-call parity relationship indicates:

$$Ee^{-rT} = S + P - C$$
$$\$70e^{-(.06/365 \text{ days})(70 \text{ days})} = \$70 - \$5.25 + \$4.50$$
$$\$69.20 \approx \$69.25$$

with the difference attributable to the 1/8 trading increments in option prices. If the call was underpriced, an arbitrageur could create a riskless position by buying the call, selling the put and shorting the stock. The riskless payoff would provide the exercise price of the option, but the arbitrageur would earn a return greater than the riskless rate. Existence of put-call parity helps keep option prices near their appropriate values.

The final topic of this part of Susan and Rick's analysis was to determine the effect of option strategies on portfolio return distributions. It appeared that a strategy such as covered call writing should skew the distribution in some fashion, because the upside potential was limited while losses were not. Conversely, the protective put strategy should have a different effect, because upside gains are unlimited while the maximum loss is defined. They also needed to determine how other option strategies such as buying calls combined with investment in

Treasury bills or selling puts over time would change the return distributions. For example, some outside consultants recently had recommended a strategy called a *collar*—the sale of an out-of-the-money call and purchase of an out-of-the-money put. What would the payoff diagram for this strategy look like, and what expected return distribution would it produce? Susan and Rick knew this would have to be determined before the Thursday strategy meeting.

Listed Option Contracts Useful for Institutional Investors

While Rick was working on the use of options to meet portfolio management objectives, Susan collected information about the different listed option products available that might be appropriate for risk management strategies. She decided to focus on index option products rather than individual equity options. A list of index option contracts along with their characteristics is shown in Exhibit 8. All index options are cash settled, usually based on the index value of the opening price on the Friday of the expiration week. For these options, trading in the contract will cease on the Thursday prior to expiration.

It is apparent that the variety of index options available should make it possible to construct a number of risk management strategies under various market scenarios. Susan liked the idea that maturities on the options varied from the near month for standard option contracts,

EXHIBIT 8
Selected Index Option Contracts

Contract	Multiplier	Style	Characteristics
S&P 100 (OEX)	$100 × index	American	The S&P 100 is a subset of the S&P 500 and is a capitalization-weighted index of 100 stocks.
S&P 100 LEAPS (OAX)	Reduced value	American	1/10 × $100 × S&P 100 Index. LEAPS are longer dated options with up to three years to expiration when first listed.

EXHIBIT 8 (*concluded*)

Contract	Multiplier	Style	Characteristics
S&P 500 (SPX)	$100 × index	European	The S&P 500 is a capitalization-weighted index of 500 stocks from a broad range of industries.
S&P 500 LEAPS (LSW)	Reduced value	European	1/10 × $100 × S&P 500 index
Russell 2000 (RUT)	$100 × index	European	The Russell 2000 is composed of the 2000 smallest companies in the Russell universe of 3000 stocks. It is considered one of the broadest measures of small-cap stock performance. It is a capitalization-weighted index of companies ranging in value from $40 million to $456 million.
Russell 2000 LEAPS (ZRU)	Reduced value	European	1/10 × $100 × Russell 2000 Index
Nasdaq-100 (NDX)	$100 × index	European	A capitalization-weighted index composed of 100 of the largest non-financial securities listed on the Nasdaq Stock Market
FT-SE 100 (FSX) Index	$100 × index	European	The accepted benchmark for large cap British equities.

EXHIBIT 9
Option Premiums from the Financial Press

Wednesday, January 19, 1994

Volume, last, net change and open interest for all contracts. Volume figures are unofficial. Open interest reflects previous trading day. p-Put c-Call

CHICAGO

RUSSELL 2000 (RUT)

Strike		Vol.	Last	Net Chg.	Open Int.
Feb	240p	60	1/4	- 11/8	211
Feb	245c	50	18	+ 7	200
Feb	245p	50	5/8	- 11/16	359
Jan	250c	106	115/8	+ 3/8	629
Jan	250c	470	1/16	- 1/8	9,480
Feb	250p	67	13/16	- 1/8	810
Jan	250p	287	71/4	+ 3/8	1,562
Feb	255c	20	9	+ 1/4	178
Feb	255p	165	13/8	- 3/16	2,676
Mar	255p	5	23/4	- 3/16	299
Jan	260c	125	27/16	+ 1/4	834
Jan	260p	143	5/16	...	638
Feb	260c	20	47/8	+ 1/8	177
Feb	260p	3	27/8	+ 1/16	1,173
Mar	260p	100	41/8	+ 1/4	4,763
Jan	265c	20	1/8	- 1/16	611
Feb	265c	5	13/4	...	662
Feb	265p	140	47/8	+ 1/8	1,431
Feb	270p	200	11/16	+ 1/8	1,295
Feb	270p	485	81/2	...	

Call vol......908 Open Int......28,031
Put vol......1,688 Open Int......47,892

RANGES FOR UNDERLYING INDEXES

Wednesday, January 19, 1994

	High	Low	Close	Net Chg.	From Dec. 31	% Chg.
S&P 100 (OEX)	439.90	436.74	439.90	+ 0.83	+ 10.44	+ 2.4
S&P 500 A.M. (SPX) .	474.70	472.21	474.30	+ 0.05	+ 7.85	+ 1.7
Russell 2000 (RUT) .	262.71	261.99	262.60	+ 0.20	+ 4.01	+ 1.6
Lps S&P 100 (OEX) .	43.99	43.67	43.99	+ 0.08	+ 1.04	+ 2.4
Lps S&P 500 (SPX) .	47.47	47.22	47.43	+ 0.01	+ 0.78	+ 1.7
S&P Midcap (MID) ..	180.39	179.27	179.74	- 0.65	+ 0.37	+ 0.2
Major Mkt (XMI)....	392.51	389.98	392.10	+ 0.81	+ 12.69	+ 3.3
Leaps MMkt (XLT)..	39.25	39.00	39.21	+ 0.08	+ 1.27	+ 3.3
Institut'l A.M. (XII) ..	472.90	469.44	472.29	- 0.10	+ 7.55	+ 1.6
Japan (JPN)			193.79	+ 5.20	+ 16.46	+ 9.3
MS Cyclical (CYC) ..	311.33	309.37	310.26	+ 0.01	+ 10.82	+ 3.6
MS Consumr (CMR) .	198.35	196.83	197.61	- 0.59	- 2.69	- 1.3
Pharma (DRG)	177.35	172.45	173.64	- 3.42	- 2.33	- 1.3
NYSE (NYA)	263.09	262.04	262.96	+ 0.20	+ 3.88	+ 1.5
Wilshire S-C (WSX) .	340.05	338.64	339.21	- 1.18	- 37.84	- 10.0
Gold/Silver (XAU) ..	144.66	142.59	142.59	- 1.47	+ 10.68	+ 8.1
OTC (XOC)....	602.53	594.18	596.65	- 5.56	+ 9.41	+ 1.6
Utility (UTY)	264.89	263.17	263.83	- 0.92	- 14.15	- 5.1
Value Line (VLE) ...	464.98	464.23	464.96	+ 0.42	+ 9.09	+ 2.0
Bank (BKX)	277.54	272.74	273.75	- 3.99	+ 1.08	+ 0.4

LEAPS-LONG TERM

MAJOR MARKET-AM

Dec 95	321/2p	60	7/8	+	3/16	1154
Dec 94	35p	2	5/8	-	1/4	11323
Dec 95	35p	2	13/16	-	1/8	1779
Dec 96	371/2p	21	23/4	-		41
Dec 95	40p	40	3	...		535
Dec 96	40p	5	33/16		5/16	56

Call vol.......0 Open Int.......9,463
Put vol.......130 Open Int.......43,928

S & P 500 INDEX-CB

Dec 94	321/2p	10	3/16	...		11644
Dec 94	35p	5	3/8	...		22220
Dec 94	371/2p	215	5/8		1/16	14716
Dec 94	40p	664	11/16		1/16	64232
Dec 94	421/2p	2053	13/4		1/16	15732
Dec 94	45p	240	27/8			2322

Call vol.......0 Open Int.......7,911
Put vol.......3,207 Open Int.......137,571

S & P 100 INDEX (OEX)

Exp	Option	Vol	Last	Chg	Open Int
Feb	380p	188	3/16	...	4,813
Mar	380p	50	1/2	+ 1/16	5,086
Apr	380p	5	13/16	+ 1/16	1,016
Feb	385p	240	5/16	+ 1/16	3,509
Mar	385p	470	9/16	−	1,164
Feb	390p	10	5/16	+ 1/16	3,481
Mar	390p	398	11/16	...	4,144
Apr	390p	19	13/16	...	1,120
Feb	395p	299	3/8	−	4,892
Mar	395p	31	7/8	− 1/16	1,074
Feb	400p	304	7/16	−	7,743
Mar	400p	734	1 1/8	− 1/16	5,815
Apr	400p	14	1 3/4	...	1,954
Feb	405p	6,572	9/16	...	8,000
Mar	405p	176	1 3/8	+ 1/16	2,815
Jan	410c	486	1/16	...	31,185
Feb	410c	1	29 1/2	−	220
Feb	410p	820	11/16	...	11,778
Mar	410p	1,258	1 3/4	− 1/8	5,552
Apr	410p	104	2 1/2	− 1/8	2,891
Jan	415c	2	24 3/8	+ 1/2	59
Jan	415p	2,053	1/16	...	32,415
Feb	415p	6,935	7/8	− 1/16	10,601
Feb	415c	430	2 1/4	+ 3/16	2,493
Jan	420c	130	18 1/2	− 1 7/8	2,456
Jan	420p	1,085	1/8	...	47,428
Feb	420p	121	1 3/4	− 1 1/2	1,092
Feb	420c	1,739	1 1/8	− 3/4	16,620
Mar	420c	25	21 1/4	− 1/4	422
Apr	420c	1,272	2 3/4	+ 1/4	8,237
Apr	420p	635	2 3/4	+ 1/4	92
Jan	425c	7,303	3 7/8	+ 1/4	5,273
Mar	425p	7,587	3/8	−	12,077
Feb	425c	170	15 3/4	− 1/8	52,723
Mar	425c	3,038	11 11/16	−	7,289
Feb	425c	8	16 1/2	−	27,226
Mar	425p	1,764	3 3/8	− 1/4	3,026
Jan	430c	18,022	10	− 1/4	8,600
Jan	430p	21,976	1/4	− 1/16	58,757
Feb	430c	2,013	11 3/8	+ 1/4	29,313
Feb	430p	8,293	2 9/16	− 1/8	34,041
Mar	430c	33	13	− 1/2	4,745
Mar	430p	1,370	4 3/8	− 1/2	8,876
Apr	430c	8	14 3/4	− 1/2	3,915
Apr	430p	3,823	6	− 1/4	10,096
Jan	435c	39,768	5	+ 1/4	43,968
Jan	435p	34,077	9/16	+ 1/8	44,002
Feb	435c	7,417	7 1/2	+ 1/4	24,958
Feb	435p	11,455	3 1/2	+ 1/4	30,450
Mar	435c	101	8 3/4	− 1 1/4	2,760
Mar	435p	555	5 7/8	+ 1 1/4	2,395
Jan	440c	43,065	1	− 9/16	64,727
Jan	440p	41,950	4 1/4	−	31,403
Feb	440c	8,269	5 5/8	+ 1/8	27,516
Feb	440p	7,829	6 1/2	+ 1/8	13,495
Mar	440c	2,521	7 3/4	−	1,634
Apr	440c	127	8 5/8	+ 3/8	19,136
Apr	440p	11	9 1/2	+ 1/8	515
Jan	445c	8,751	3/16	− 1/16	54,316
Feb	445p	5,681	6	− 1/2	3,739
Feb	445c	7,099	2 3/8	+ 1/16	26,758
Mar	445p	264	8 5/8	−	1,505
Mar	445c	158	3 5/8	− 3/8	6,961
Jan	450c	30	10 3/4	+ 1/4	166
Jan	450c	3,560	1/16	−	33,461
Feb	450p	12	12 1/2	+ 1 1/2	151
Feb	450c	9,024	15/16	− 1/4	38,183
Mar	450c	33	13	−	286
Mar	450p	994	2 1/8	+ 7/16	14,981
Apr	450c	827	3 7/8	+ 1/8	6,392
Feb	455c	3,602	3/8	− 1/16	13,234
Mar	455c	1,905	13 3/16	+ 1/8	8,180
Mar	455p	2	19 1/2	+ 1/4	84
Feb	460c	648	3/16	− 1/8	2,311
Mar	460c	1,062	9/16	+ 5/16	1,877
Apr	460p	1,010	13 3/16	−	1,621

Call vol. ....166,532 Open Int. 509,077
Put vol. .....178,598 Open Int. 632,728

S & P 500 INDEX-AM (SPX)

Exp	Option	Vol	Last	Chg	Open Int
Mar	390p	20	1/4	...	7,444
Jan	400c	436	73 7/8	− 3/4	508
Feb	400c	436	73 1/4	− 1/2	4
Feb	400p	230	1/8	− 1/16	1,088
Jan	415c	1,000	57 7/8	+ 3/4	1,500
Mar	415c	2,500	58 1/8	+ 7/8	...
Jan	420c	2,000	53	− 5	1,562
Mar	420c	3	53 3/4	+ 5/8	25
Mar	420p	9	11/16	− 1/16	11
Jan	425c	875	48	− 4 3/8	9,940
Mar	425c	550	48 5/8	+ 7/8	2,018
Jan	430c	600	43 3/8	− 6 1/4	3,470
Feb	430p	4	3/8	+	8,707
Mar	430c	3	43 3/4	+ 7/8	6,958
Jan	435c	5	39 1/4	− 1	610
Feb	435p	250	1/2	+ 1/8	200
Feb	440c	176	5/8	+ 1/16	7,049
Mar	440c	500	34 1/2	+ 5	10,417
Jan	445p	556	28 1/2	+ 1 1/8	608
Feb	445c	5	...	− 1/16	983
Mar	445p	340	3/4	+ 3/8	15,817
Jan	450c	590	2	− 1/8	17,009
Feb	450p	924	23	+ 1 1/2	12,613
Jan	450c	204	...	− 1	1,676
Feb	450p	714	25	− 1/16	14,434
Mar	450p	192	15 5/16	+ 2 1/8	399
Jan	455c	740	25 1/2	+ 7/16	18,620
Feb	455c	970	29 5/16	+ 2 7/8	10,115
Mar	455p	3	17 5/8	− 1/8	17,595
Jan	455p	681	1/16	−	2,848
Feb	455c	60	19 1/2	+ 4 3/4	10,777
Mar	455c	274	1 1/4	+	293
Jan	460p	7	21 1/8	+ 1 3/8	4,209
Feb	460c	592	13 5/8	− 3/8	1,659
Mar	460p	31	7/8	+ 7/8	7,090
Jan	460c	1,570	1/16	− 1/8	7,142
Feb	460c	74	15 1/2	− 1/4	12,170
					2,379
Feb	460p	3,627	1 3/4	...	6,555
Mar	460c	50	17 7/8	1 1/2	11,845
Mar	460p	555	4	− 1/2	28,146
Jan	465p	1,533	3 3/16	1 3/8	32,493
Mar	465p	3,699	7 7/8	− 1/8	42,862
Jan	465c	56	10 1/8	+ 2 3/8	15,649
Feb	465c	4,565	2 1/2	...	25,239
Mar	465c	275	13 7/8	+ 1/8	18,630
Feb	465p	1,487	5 3/8	+ 5/8	24,375
Jan	470p	6,017	4 1/2	− 1/2	12,014
Jan	470c	7,651	7 7/16	− 3/16	15,315
Mar	470c	3,393	7 3/4	− 1/2	10,915
Feb	470c	4,257	3 7/8	−	17,960
Feb	470p	1,677	10 3/8	+ 5/8	15,458
Mar	470p	1,805	6 1/4	+ 1/2	9,492
Jan	475c	12,295	1	+ 3/16	18,333
Jan	475p	1,293	2	− 1/4	7,250
Feb	475c	1,260	4 1/2	− 7/8	9,185
Feb	475p	446	6 1/4	+ 3/8	3,437
Mar	475c	1,500	7	− 5/8	22,463
Mar	475p	968	8 1/2	+ 5/8	15,977
Jan	480c	464	1/8	− 1/8	16,816
Feb	480p	167	5 1/2	+ 1/2	907
Feb	480c	4,371	2 1/2	− 1/4	12,078
Jan	480p	21	9 1/4	+ 3/4	334
Feb	480c	2,025	4 1/2	− 1/2	6,915
Mar	480p	16	11 1/8	+ 7/8	1,185
Jan	485c	11,080	1/16	− 3/16	25,372
Feb	485c	8,098	1 11/16	− 9/16	28,240
Mar	485p	1	13 7/8	− 1/8	10,253
Jan	490c	100	7/16	+ 3/8	13,584
Feb	490p	4,520	1/2	− 1/8	10,605
Feb	490c	6	17 3/4	+ 2	20,359
Mar	490c	157	1 1/2	− 5/16	10,323
Feb	495c	5,613	3/16	− 1/16	2,082
Mar	495c	1,322	7/8	− 1/8	6,123

out to three years for the LEAPS®. She was unsure, however, if it would be better to use the short-term options and roll forward positions as contracts expired, or to take a position in the long term using LEAPS and hold it until expiration. Susan also noted that only contracts on the S&P 100 were American-style options, while all the rest were European.

Susan also examined data on the premiums for the different options from the financial press that are shown in Exhibit 9. She noted that the American-style options seemed to be relatively more expensive than equivalent European-style options. Does the ability to exercise early (American) have value to Lincoln Trust's equity managers? Values for the various indices, plus several other indices that have options available, are shown in the box in Table 3 labeled "Ranges for Underlying Indices." For Thursday's meeting, Susan thought it would be useful to construct sample payoff diagrams for different strategies using the premiums shown in Exhibit 9. This should help the strategy committee better understand how option strategies can be used to modify the risk exposure of their equity portfolios.

The Issues of Small-Cap Stock Investment

In preparing for Thursday's meeting, Susan and Rick knew that they must be prepared to address the pros and cons of investing in small-cap stocks as an alternative strategy for the equity managers. It is apparent that interest in small-cap stocks has increased significantly over the past several years. Much of this interest is fueled by their performance compared to large-cap stocks, both in recent years and for extended market periods. For example, in 1992 the Russell 2000 small-cap index earned 16.36 percent while the S&P 500 rose 4.46 percent. The difference was even larger in 1991 when the Russell 2000 appreciated 43.68 percent compared to 26.31 percent for the S&P 500. Individual investors have become aware of the benefits of investing in small stocks as shown by the growth in small-cap mutual funds, whose capital under management has increased from $7 billion in 1985 to $20 billion in 1991 as reported by Morningstar, Inc.

On a long-term basis, small stocks earned a higher return than larger ones as shown in the data in Exhibit 10. Using the bottom quintile of stocks in the S&P 500 to represent small stocks, the data shows that small-cap stocks earned a higher average annual return over the 1926 to 1990 period, but had incurred greater risk as shown by the standard deviation of returns.

EXHIBIT 10
Summary Statistics of Annual Returns, 1926–1990

Series	Geometric Mean (%)	Arithmetic Mean (%)	Standard Deviation (%)
S&P 500 Index	10.1%	12.1%	20.8%
Small cap stocks	11.6	17.1	35.4
Long-term corp. bonds	5.2	5.5	8.4
U.S. T-bills	3.7	3.7	3.4
Inflation (CPI)	3.1	3.2	4.7

Source: *Stocks, Bonds, Bills and Inflation 1991 Yearbook* (Chicago: Ibbotson Associates, 1991), p 32.

Susan noted that the Russell 2000 Index has index options available, and she wanted to explore further the Index itself and how the options might be used to increase exposure to the small-cap market. According to Eric Weigel of the Frank Russell Company, the Russell 2000 Index was first published in 1984. However, data on the index have been calculated back to 1979. The Russell family of indices includes the Russell 1000, 2000, 3000, and others. All indices are market capitalization-weighted, and the market value of each company as of June each year determines its rank from 1 (largest) to 3000 (smallest). Shares outstanding of each company are adjusted for corporate cross-ownership and private holdings, so that the market value reflects only the "investable" portion of the stock.

To demonstrate how puts and calls on the Russell 2000 might be used to modify the risk and return from a small stock index, Susan obtained data from Eric to produce a simulation of a protective put option strategy using the Russell 2000 over the 1980 to 1992 period. Exhibit 11 shows the quarterly returns on the index itself, including dividends, and the returns for the protective put strategy, which assumes that three-month Russell 2000 index puts are purchased at the beginning of each quarter and held to expiration. Put premiums were calculated using the Black-Scholes Option Pricing Model, with the index volatility estimated from the index standard deviation during the quarter immediately preceding the pricing of the option. Quarterly dividends are assumed to be reinvested in the index. For comparison, quarterly data for the S&P 500 also are shown in Exhibit 11.

EXHIBIT 11
Quarterly Returns for Russell 2000 Index, Russell Index Insured with Puts, and S&P 500 Index

	Values for Russell Index				Values for Insured Port.			Values for S&P 500 Index			
Date	Index	Dividend	Quarterly Return (%)	Annual Return (%)	Put Prem.	Quarterly Return (%)	Annual Return (%)	Index	Dividend	Quarterly Return (%)	Annual Return (%)
79 4	137.97							107.94			
80 1	119.12	1.31	-12.71%		3.79	-1.75%		102.09	1.46	-4.10%	
80 2	141.84	1.30	20.16		7.53	13.02		114.24	1.56	13.40	
80 3	172.60	1.30	22.60		3.46	19.68		125.46	1.56	11.20	
80 4	184.58	1.52	7.82	38.65%	3.60	5.62	40.37%	135.76	1.58	9.50	32.40%
81 1	198.04	1.76	8.24		4.97	5.41		136.00	1.58	-1.30	
81 2	203.74	1.66	3.72		3.70	1.82		131.25	1.67	-2.30	
81 3	166.69	1.43	-17.49		1.87	-0.22		116.18	1.69	-10.20	
81 4	181.81	1.83	10.17	2.06	5.38	6.73	14.29	122.55	1.69	6.90	-4.90
82 1	163.38	1.49	-9.32		2.61	-0.61		111.91	1.67	-7.30	
82 2	159.60	1.49	-1.40		3.39	-1.14		109.61	1.76	-0.50	
82 3	174.81	1.52	10.48		3.05	8.41		120.42	1.73	11.40	
82 4	219.38	1.66	26.45	24.91	5.21	22.79	30.80	140.64	1.71	18.20	21.50
83 1	256.08	1.53	17.43		8.19	13.20		152.96	1.17	10.00	
83 2	306.42	1.55	20.26		6.58	17.25		168.11	1.79	11.10	
83 3	289.79	1.62	-4.90		5.33	-1.19		166.07	1.79	-10.00	
83 4	277.05	1.47	-3.89	29.08	5.03	-1.21	29.56	164.93	1.78	0.39	10.41
84 1	256.91	1.60	-6.69		3.03	-0.51		159.18	1.83	-2.38	
84 2	247.52	1.65	-3.01		4.53	-1.10		153.18	1.87	-2.60	
84 3	259.54	1.55	5.48		3.35	4.07		166.10	1.88	9.66	
84 4	250.47	1.56	-2.89	-7.30	5.10	-1.34	1.03	167.24	1.93	1.85	6.20
85 1	283.60	1.72	13.91		2.81	12.65		180.66	1.96	9.20	
85 2	292.15	1.49	3.54		4.41	1.95		191.85	1.99	7.30	
85 3	277.99	1.48	-4.34		2.40	-0.31		182.08	1.99	-4.50	
85 4	320.49	2.33	16.13	31.02	4.52	14.27	30.83	211.28	2.02	17.14	31.69

Year	Qtr	Index								Index Ann.			Insured Ann.
86	1	364.32	1.47	14.14	4.11	12.69	238.90	2.04	14.04				
86	2	380.61	1.36	4.85	5.41	3.31	250.84	2.07	5.86				
86	3	332.49	1.57	-12.23	5.23	-0.95	231.32	2.06	-6.96	5.68	12.74	18.61	
86	4	333.15	1.41	0.62	9.70	-2.23	242.17	2.10	5.60				
87	1	412.52	1.54	24.29	5.51	22.27	291.70	2.23	21.37				
87	2	407.87	1.71	-0.71	9.51	-1.85	304.00	2.20	4.97				
87	3	423.50	1.43	4.18	8.53	2.05	321.83	2.22	6.60	-8.82	21.50	5.23	
87	4	298.99	1.37	-29.08	4.75	-0.79	247.08	2.27	-22.52				
88	1	354.14	1.73	19.02	39.49	5.14	258.89	2.33	5.72				
88	2	375.91	1.48	6.57	10.94	3.37	273.50	2.44	6.59				
88	3	370.38	1.93	-0.96	6.70	-1.25	271.91	2.49	0.33	24.77	6.82	16.54	
88	4	366.03	1.83	-0.68	3.58	-0.47	277.72	2.56	3.08				
89	1	392.67	1.59	7.71	3.64	6.65	294.87	2.70	7.15				
89	2	415.96	1.71	6.37	4.67	5.12	317.98	2.77	8.78				
89	3	441.93	1.99	6.72	3.87	5.74	349.15	2.84	10.69	16.24	18.25	31.66	
89	4	418.09	2.04	-4.93	3.15	-0.25	353.40	2.90	2.05				
90	1	406.81	1.88	-2.25	8.42	-1.53	339.94	2.97	-2.97				
90	2	420.42	1.81	3.79	7.55	1.90	358.02	3.03	6.21				
90	3	315.61	2.10	-24.43	3.51	-0.33	306.05	3.07	-13.66	-19.47	0.94	-3.09	
90	4	329.05	2.46	5.04	12.85	0.93	330.22	3.09	8.91				
91	1	424.78	1.93	29.68	10.38	25.71	331.75	3.07	1.39				
91	2	416.31	1.77	-1.58	12.67	-2.49	371.16	3.04	12.80				
91	3	448.16	2.14	8.17	9.83	5.67	387.86	3.06	5.32	45.96	34.04	30.47	
91	4	471.70	2.12	5.73	9.71	3.48	417.09	3.03	8.32				
92	1	505.15	1.99	7.51	14.60	4.29	403.69	3.19	-2.45				
92	2	468.62	1.98	-6.84	10.95	-1.74	408.14	3.04	1.86				
92	3	480.05	1.97	2.86	11.77	0.34	417.80	3.36	3.19	18.39	15.84	7.67	
92	4	549.63	2.01	14.91	9.60	12.66	435.71	3.03	5.01				
Cumulative return '80 to '92										438.91	874.50	515.88	
Geometric average annual return										13.83	19.14	15.01	
Annual standard deviation										18.44	12.31	12.77	

For the Index, returns were calculated as ((P1 + Div)/P0) – 1.

For the Insured portfolio, it was assumed that at-the-money, 3-month puts were bought.

If the put was in-the-money at expiration, returns were calculated as ((Div/P0 + put)) – 1.

If the put was out-of-the-money, returns were calculated as ((P1 + Div)/(P0 + put)) – 1.

In addition to the performance data for the protective put strategy, Eric also provided Susan with quarterly put and call option premiums as shown in Exhibit 12. Susan thought they could be used to simulate alternative risk management strategies and evaluate their performance over this period. She surmised that the problem of high volatility in small-cap stocks could be addressed by risk management techniques using index options. However, at this point, she wasn't sure which strategies might be appropriate and which were not.

The Current Market Environment

Market conditions during January of 1994 motivated John's interest in applying portfolio risk management techniques to the equity portfolios managed by the fund. Since the Clinton election and subsequent budget legislation in Congress, the market had reached an all-time high above 4000 on January 31st 1994 as measured by the Dow Jones Industrial Average. The Nasdaq Index of over-the-counter securities also reached a record high of 803 in February 1994, as did the Russell 2000 Index at 271 (note the index was rebased in 1993, after the period covered by the data presented in Exhibit 11).

John Strong was sitting on a growing pool of cash and was trying to determine if he should commit additional funds to various equity expo-

EXHIBIT 12
Put and Call Premiums for the Russell 2000, 1979 to 1992

OBS	Year-Quarter	Russell 2000	Dividend Yield (%)	T-Bills	Put ($)	Call ($)
1	7903	115.83	0.66%	9.48%		
2	7906	122.45	1.54	9.06	$ 2.11	$ 4.38
3	7909	134.93	2.20	10.26	1.81	4.49
4	7912	137.97	3.08	12.04	1.72	4.75
5	8003	119.12	4.04	15.20	3.79	7.04
6	8006	141.84	3.51	7.07	7.52	8.77
7	8009	172.60	3.01	10.27	3.46	6.54
8	8012	184.58	2.94	15.49	3.60	9.26
9	8103	198.04	2.96	13.36	4.97	10.01
10	8106	203.74	3.06	14.73	3.70	9.51
11	8109	166.69	3.82	14.70	1.88	6.31
12	8112	181.81	3.67	10.85	5.38	8.58
13	8203	163.38	3.93	12.68	2.61	6.11

EXHIBIT 12 (concluded)

OBS	Year-Quarter	Russell 2000	Dividend Yield (%)	T-Bills	Put ($)	Call ($)
14	8206	159.60	3.91	12.47	3.39	6.73
15	8209	174.81	3.63	7.92	3.05	4.90
16	8212	219.38	2.81	7.94	5.21	7.98
17	8303	256.08	2.42	8.35	8.19	11.94
18	8306	306.42	2.04	8.79	6.58	11.67
19	8309	289.79	2.19	9.00	5.33	10.19
20	8312	277.05	2.22	9.00	5.03	9.66
21	8403	256.91	2.43	9.52	3.03	7.52
22	8406	247.52	2.56	9.87	4.53	8.99
23	8409	259.54	2.41	10.37	3.35	8.43
24	8412	250.47	2.54	8.06	5.10	8.51
25	8503	283.60	2.28	8.52	2.81	7.18
26	8506	292.15	2.16	6.95	4.41	7.87
27	8509	277.99	2.25	7.10	2.40	5.73
28	8512	320.49	2.19	7.10	4.52	8.41
29	8603	364.32	1.86	6.56	4.11	8.35
30	8606	380.61	1.75	6.21	5.41	9.62
31	8609	332.49	2.03	5.21	5.23	7.86
32	8612	333.15	1.74	5.53	9.70	12.83
33	8703	412.52	1.43	5.59	5.51	9.77
34	8706	407.87	1.53	5.67	9.51	13.70
35	8709	423.50	1.44	6.40	8.53	13.73
36	8712	298.99	2.03	5.77	4.75	7.52
37	8803	354.14	1.76	5.70	39.49	42.95
38	8806	375.91	1.60	6.46	10.94	15.47
39	8809	370.38	1.76	7.24	6.70	11.73
40	8812	366.03	1.90	8.07	3.58	9.15
41	8903	392.67	1.74	8.82	3.64	10.49
42	8906	415.96	1.70	8.15	4.67	11.30
43	8909	441.93	1.61	7.75	3.87	10.57
44	8912	418.09	1.75	7.63	3.15	9.22
45	9003	406.81	1.87	7.90	8.42	14.47
46	9006	420.42	1.83	7.73	7.55	13.67
47	9009	315.61	2.48	7.36	3.51	7.31
48	9012	329.05	2.51	6.74	12.85	16.29
49	9103	424.78	1.96	5.91	10.39	14.54
50	9106	416.31	1.99	5.57	12.67	16.36
51	9109	448.16	1.85	5.22	9.83	13.57
52	9112	471.70	1.69	4.07	9.71	12.50
53	9203	505.15	1.59	4.04	14.60	17.67
54	9206	468.62	1.76	3.66	10.95	13.16
55	9209	480.05	1.68	2.91	11.77	13.24
56	9212	549.63	1.46	3.22	9.60	12.01

sures or continue accruing cash while waiting for a market pull-back. From his own experience, he was aware of the difficulty in timing the market, and for this reason he favored a strategy that can best be described as "fully invested" at all times. However, the danger signals he noted about the market were (1) the falling dividend yield on stocks, which now was below 2.4 percent, (2) the apparent increase in interest rates, and (3) the Federal Reserve policy, which seemed to favor tighter money and higher, short-term rates. Offsetting these negatives were the large cash balances in the hands of professional investment managers, and the belief by many that stocks are the only investment that make sense in this market environment. As interest rates fell from 1990 to 1993, small investors cashed in bank CDs and corporations called higher-yielding debt issues, providing cash to investors for other uses. It was estimated that from January 1991 through April 1993, a net increase of $169 billion flowed into equity mutual funds. John believed that the market had good upside potential, but was concerned that a pullback from these levels could turn into a major market correction.

Late Wednesday Afternoon

As John Strong contemplated what investment strategy to pursue, he looked forward to the Thursday strategy meeting and the recommendations of Rick and Susan. John didn't like the way the market had behaved the past week, with implied volatility from the OEX options reaching a low of 8 percent, a level not seen since August of 1987, and some technical indicators suggesting that a market correction is imminent. He believed strongly that any major move in the market would be driven by interest rate changes rather than stock fundamentals. John received an E-mail message from Rick—"Boss, we would like to visit with you this afternoon about tomorrow's presentation. Thought you might like to see some of the ideas we have come up with."

PREPARING THE CASE ANALYSIS

As the case scenario ends, John Strong, Rick Bowlin, and Susan Jordan are preparing to review their presentation for Thursday's strategy meeting. Your objective is to outline the major concepts that they should include. To help you prepare your presentation, answers to the following points should be developed.

1. What is portfolio risk management? Compare traditional strategies for risk management to strategies based on options and futures. Why can options be used to create distributions of possible returns that are nonnormal.

2. Discuss the implications of put-call parity for portfolio risk management. Using the put-call parity relationship, show which put and call strategies should provide identical payoffs. How is this information valuable when developing strategies for different market environments?

3. Outline and evaluate various strategies involving options that can be used in different market environments. Be sure to include covered call writing, protective put buying, collars, and combining the purchase of calls or sale of puts with Treasury bills. Compare portfolio insurance strategies using listed options to the dynamic strategies that Lincoln Trust used in 1986.

4. Evaluate the advantages and disadvantages to Lincoln Trust of the different option contracts described in Exhibit 8. How important are such characteristics such as option maturity, style, and index composition. Should John consider individual equity options as well as index options?

5. List the advantages and disadvantages of increasing the fund's exposure to small capitalization stocks. Develop option-based strategies that can provide exposure to small-cap stocks while at the same time controlling for the additional risk inherent in these securities. Could similar strategies be used to gain exposure to foreign stocks?

6. What strategy would you recommend to John Strong in the current market environment?

Suggested Analysis for Lincoln Pension Trust Case

Objectives of the Case Analysis

This case provides you with a framework for exploring portfolio risk management and the opportunity for developing option-based strategies that can be used to control portfolio risk. It is assumed that you have read prior chapters in this book, with special attention given to Chapter

4, "Option Strategies: Analysis and Selection," and Chapter 7, "Institutional Uses of Options." The case should enhance your understanding of options by allowing you to express in your own words the concepts and ideas presented earlier. Your case analysis should focus on broad issues of portfolio strategies and risk management concepts rather than evaluation of detailed numerical data.

Portfolio Risk Management

As explained in the case, *risk management* means controlling the distribution of expected returns from an investment to achieve the objectives of the portfolio manager. Do not think of risk management only as risk reduction, but as the opportunity to control risk in order to achieve desired returns. The unique benefit of options with regard to risk management is that options enable the portfolio manager to construct return distributions that cannot be duplicated with any other security.

In the past, risk management tools were limited to changing the allocation between stocks and fixed income investments or cash. Risk could be reduced by lowering exposure to equities and could be increased by increasing equity exposure or by selecting more volatile stocks. As Exhibit 2 indicates, the distribution of returns using these techniques remains basically normal. Only the expected return and standard deviation of the distribution are altered.

The availability of derivative products such as options and futures provides a much richer set of tools for controlling portfolio returns. However, only options because of their asymmetric payoffs, enable the portfolio manager to create distinctively skewed distributions. To see this, compare the payoff from a position in a futures contract to an option.

The payoff from a futures contract is symmetrical. If the S&P 500 appreciates, S&P 500 futures will appreciate by a relative amount; if the S&P 500 Index declines, the futures value also will fall. However, the leverage available in futures magnifies both their positive and negative returns. Comparing futures to options, options have an asymmetric payoff that truncates upside or downside returns and thus can be used to produce return distributions that are decidedly non-normal. The skewed distributions available from using options can be illustrated with covered call writing and the purchase of protective puts as examples.

Portfolio Returns for Covered Call Writing

As shown in Exhibit 4, the sale of a call caps the portfolio's return at a value equal to the sum of the exercise price and the amount of the call premium received. On the downside, the covered call portfolio will mirror the decline in the underlying stock, cushioned by the amount of the call premium. During periods of low volatility, the covered call strategy may produce higher returns than the underlying portfolio. However, when the market appreciates, the covered call writer will not share in large gains because the stock will be called away at the exercise price. Consistently following a covered call strategy through time will produce portfolio returns characterized by no large positive returns, many small positive and negative returns near the mean, and a number of larger, negative returns incurred when the market declines. The mean or expected return will be lower than that of the underlying stock portfolio, standard deviation will be less, and skewness will be negative.

Exhibit 13 shows a stylized distribution of returns for a stock portfolio, A, a covered call portfolio using at-the-money calls, B, and 10 percent out-of-the-money calls, C. Note that the degree of undesirable negative skewness can be altered by varying either the exercise price of the written calls or the value of the portfolio that has options written against it.

Portfolio Returns for a Protective Put Strategy

Exhibit 14 in the case can be used to evaluate the impact on portfolio returns from purchasing protective puts. Contrary to covered calls, the protective put strategy provides no cap on the gains that can occur, but truncates the amount of the loss at the difference between the stock and the option's exercise price, less the cost of the put. Following this strategy over time and using at-the-money puts will produce a return distribution characterized by a maximum possible loss equal to the average put premium, a large number of small losses and gains caused by put premiums reducing profits in flat markets, and a limited number of large gains earned when stock prices appreciate. This strategy also is termed *static portfolio insurance* because no change in stock or option positions is required until the options expire. Alternatively, *dynamic portfolio insurance* is based on the use of futures contracts that require frequent trading to replicate the stock-plus-put portfolio payoffs.

Similar to the covered call strategy, the shape of the protective put return distribution can be controlled by varying the amount or exercise

EXHIBIT 13
Expected Return Distributions for Various Covered Call Portfolios

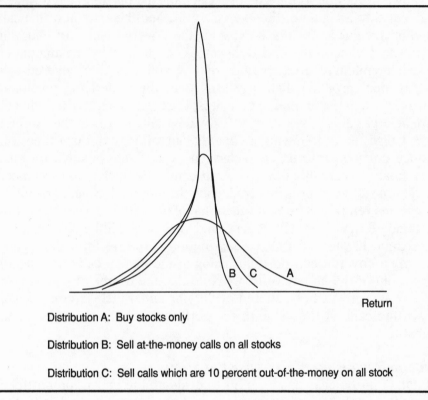

Distribution A: Buy stocks only

Distribution B: Sell at-the-money calls on all stocks

Distribution C: Sell calls which are 10 percent out-of-the-money on all stock

price of the purchased puts. For example, buying puts farther out-of-the-money will be less costly but will reduce the downside protection. Alternatively, protecting only half the portfolio's value by purchasing a reduced amount of puts will have a similar effect. Exhibit 14 shows stylized distributions for the stock portfolio only, A, buying at-the-money puts to cover the entire portfolio, B, and buying 10 percent out-of-the-money puts on the entire portfolio, C.

Because the volatility of the portfolio is reduced in a protective put portfolio, the expected return from such a strategy followed continuously through time typically lies below the stock-only portfolio. The lower return results from paying a premium for the insurance protection. The risk as measured by the standard deviation of returns also will be less for the protective put portfolios. Opposite from covered call writing, the protective put strategy has a return distribution with posi-

EXHIBIT 14
Expected Return Distributions for Various Protective Put Buying Portfolios

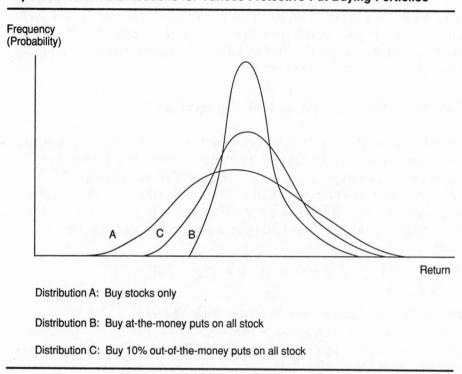

Distribution A: Buy stocks only

Distribution B: Buy at-the-money puts on all stock

Distribution C: Buy 10% out-of-the-money puts on all stock

tive skewness because of the limited losses coupled with potentially unlimited gains. Whether or not individual portfolio managers prefer return distribution A, B, or C in Exhibit 14 depends on their personal trade-offs of defined maximum losses in exchange for potential appreciation.

A protective put portfolio will appear most attractive if held when the market suffers a severe decline. For example, if the market index suffers a 15 to 20 percent decline, the put-protected portfolio should decline less than 5 percent. This has a two-fold advantage: (1) The current loss is much less, and (2) when the market rebounds, the protected portfolio begins at a much higher level. You don't have to recoup your loss first before you can start showing improvement. In sideways or appreciating markets, the strategy will underperform the market because the put premiums add cost with no tangible benefit.

Strategies using covered calls or protective puts are just two of a broad array of option-based strategies that can be used in portfolio risk management programs. They were chosen as illustrations because of their familiarity to institutional investors and because of the opposite results that they produce on the skewness of portfolio returns. The main purpose of this part of the presentation is to demonstrate that options are tools for managing risk in portfolios of financial assets. Additional strategies will be developed below.

Put-Call Parity and Portfolio Risk Management

Besides showing the relative prices of puts and calls, the put-call parity equation can be used to identify equivalent option-based strategies. By *equivalent* is meant strategies that produce identical payoffs. The put-call parity idea was presented earlier as a relationship that showed that a long stock, short call, long put portfolio was riskless, and if the options were properly priced, it should produce a payoff equal to the riskless rate:

$$Ee^{-rT} = \text{Stock} + \text{Put} - \text{Call}$$

The 90/10 Call Options and Treasury-Bills Strategy
If the put-call parity equation is rearranged to solve for the protective put strategy on the right side, the left side will be equal to a long call plus investment in the riskless bond:

$$Ee^{-rT} + \text{Call} = \text{Stock} + \text{Put}$$

For example, using the data from the case on XYZ stock, a payoff diagram shown in Exhibit 15 can be created for the call plus bond portfolio. If you buy the April 70 call for $5.25 and invest $69.20 in Treasury bills, the payoff will be the same as for the protective put strategy. If the stock falls below $70, the call is worthless, but the maximum loss you can incur is $4.45, the cost of the call, less the interest received from the Treasury bill (−$5.25 + $.80 = −$4.45) over the holding period of 70 days. If the stock appreciates above $70, the strategy will return the difference between $70 and the stock price (S − $70), plus the $.80 interest on the Treasury bill.

The label *90/10* was developed for the strategy because it often was implemented using six-month options whose premiums would average about 10 percent of the value of investable funds, leaving 90 percent for investment in Treasury bills. Similar to the protective put strategy, the 90/10 portfolio provides limited downside losses combined with unlim-

EXHIBIT 15
Profit/Loss Calculations for Calls plus Treasury Bills Strategy (Buy the April 70 Call for $5.25 Invest $69.20 in Treasury Bills)

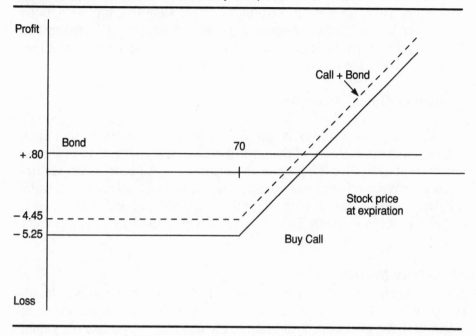

ited upside gains. The return distribution will have positive skewness and should look identical to the return distributions for protective puts shown in Exhibit 14.

Writing Puts and Buying Treasury Bills
If we rearrange the put-call parity equation to express covered call writing on the left side of the relationship, it is shown that covered writing is equivalent to selling puts and investing the discounted exercise price in Treasury bills:

$$\text{Stock} - \text{Call} = -\text{Put} + Ee^{-rT}$$

Again using the XYZ stock example from the case, the investor would sell the April 70 put for $4.50 and combine the proceeds plus other funds equal to $69.20 in Treasury bills. The return distribution from this strategy in an ideal world will exactly match the one shown in Exhibit 13 for the covered call position. Even though the payoff is identical to covered call writing, many institutional investors view it differently because when the market declines, it causes the fund to buy stock at prices above then-current market values.

In addition to the equivalence of strategies, the put-call parity relationship is useful to demonstrate that it is possible to combine options with other securities and produce a variety of payoffs. Understanding the put-call parity relationship is essential to grasping the potential that options provide for portfolio risk management.

Alternative Option Strategies

The advantage of options in portfolio risk management is that they enable the manager to mold the portfolio's expected returns to fit almost any market view. Building upon the analysis of the four strategies described above, and strategies described earlier in Chapters 4 and 7, the following option-based plans could be considered by John Strong and the Lincoln Pension Trust as they develop their risk management program.

Short-Term Bearish
If John Strong strongly believes that a short term correction is at hand, he could *buy short term, at-the-money puts,* with a face value equal to the underlying portfolio, thus completely insuring the portfolio's value. This *protective put strategy* would produce the truncated return distribution shown in Exhibit 14. If John is correct and the market declines, the gain in the value of the puts will offset the losses in the stock portfolio. The greatest loss he can incur is the cost of the puts. If John is wrong and the market appreciates, the equity portfolio will participate in the price rise, less the cost of the puts.

The relative "moneyness" and amount of options to buy will depend on John's degree of pessimism about the market. Exhibit 16 shows the impact on expected returns that is achieved by varying the relative exercise price of the puts. If he is extremely bearish, he could consider buying a portfolio multiple of puts, either at- or out-of-the-money, in which case he would profit from the market's decline. Buying a portfolio multiple means buying puts with a total contract value that is greater than the market value of the equity portfolio that is being insured.

It also could be argued that John should consider the use of *covered call strategies* under this market scenario. It should be recommended that Lincoln Pension Trust choose at-the-money calls, with relatively short maturities to get the greatest benefit from the written calls. The

EXHIBIT 16
Expected Return Distributions for Put, Purchased on 50% of the Stock

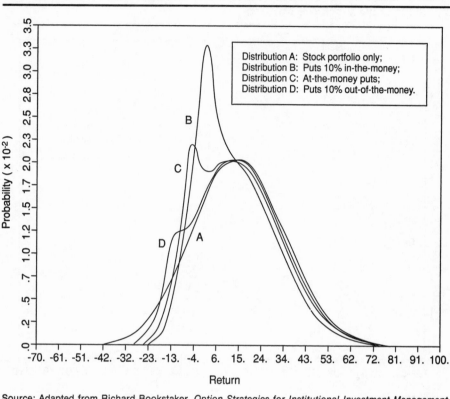

Distribution A: Stock portfolio only;
Distribution B: Puts 10% in-the-money;
Distribution C: At-the-money puts;
Distribution D: Puts 10% out-of-the-money.

Source: Adapted from Richard Bookstaker, *Option Strategies for Institutional Investment Management*
(Reading, MA: Addison-Wesley, 1983).

two disadvantages of writing calls compared with buying protective
puts are that (1) the call premium only cushions the losses if the market
falls, thus you still participate in the falling market. This effect can be
reduced if the Trust sells a portfolio multiple of calls to produce more
premium income. (2) If you are wrong and the market goes up, the calls
will have to be repurchased at a loss. Exhibit 17 shows hypothetical
return distributions when different amounts of the portfolio have calls
written against it.

A contrast between the use of options in risk management and the
use of index futures products is appropriate at this point. Under a bearish market view, the appropriate futures strategy is to sell index futures,
reducing the equity portfolio's exposure to market changes. If the market falls, the short futures position will appreciate, offsetting the loss in

EXHIBIT 17
Expected Return Distributions for Covered Call Strategy when Different Proportions of the Stock Are Covered

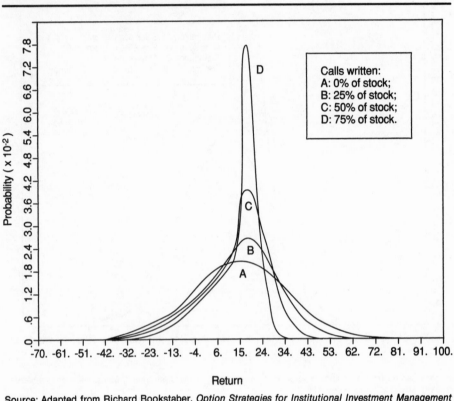

Source: Adapted from Richard Bookstaber, *Option Strategies for Institutional Investment Management* (Reading, MA: Addison-Wesley, 1983).

the equity portfolio. However, if the market rises, the short futures will become a liability, incurring a dollar-for-dollar loss with the rise in the market. As described earlier, futures do not provide an asymmetric payoff like options, and they will produce different effects on the portfolio's expected returns.

Long-Term Bearish
Under this market scenario, it should be recommended that John again choose a *protective put strategy* and extend the maturity on the purchased puts, possibly choosing puts with exercise prices out-of-the-

money. The *LEAPS* products listed in Exhibit 8 are appropriate vehicles to hedge this market view, because they can be purchased with maturities of up to three years.

Neutral, but Uncertain

An uncertain but negative view about the market calls for strategies that provide some downside protection for the portfolio, but at a reasonable cost. One appropriate strategy is the *purchase of protective puts,* but choosing those that are out-of-the-money to reduce the costs. Alternatively, the fund might consider the sale of out-of-the-money calls, *covered call writing,* which will generate current income that will offset losses in a market decline.

An alternative strategy mentioned in the case is the combination of a put and call to produce a *collar* or *fence* around the expected returns. To manage risk under this market expectation, the Trust would buy a short-term, out-of-the-money protective put and sell an equivalent call. The call premium received would offset most of the put's cost, enabling the strategy to be effected with little up-front cost. Exhibit 18 shows the payoff diagram for a fence strategy using XYZ stock from the previous example. It is assumed that XYZ stock is bought at $70, the April 75 call

EXHIBIT 18
Fence or Collar Strategy (Sell the April 75 Call, Buy the April 65 Put, Long XYZ Stock)

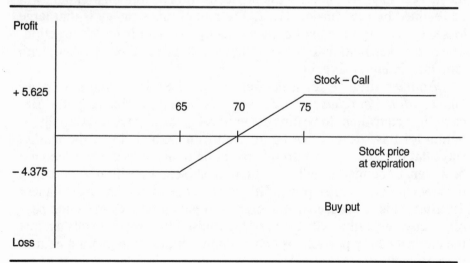

is sold for \$3.25, and the April 65 put is bought for \$2.625. The maximum gain for the position is capped at \$5.625 [i.e., (\$75 − \$70) + (\$3.25 − \$2.625)], which occurs if the stock appreciates above \$75. The maximum loss is \$4.375, which will happen if the stock falls below \$65. The expected return from this portfolio will be truncated beyond the exercise prices of the put and call.

It may be recognized that this strategy contains the same long-put, short-call option positions as used in put-call parity. The difference is that the strike prices are out-of-the-money rather than exactly at-the-money. With this in mind, it is possible to infer the shape of the expected return distribution from the *collar*. The written call will bring in the positive tail of the returns toward the center of the distribution, and the purchased puts will truncate the negative tail of returns. Exhibit 19 shows stylized distributions of returns when differing amounts of the stock portfolio are covered with the puts and calls.

Neutral Market View
Option strategies appropriate for the Pension Trust when they are entirely neutral about the market include those that generate current income, but may produce losses if the market moves strongly in either direction. The *sale of short term straddles,* that is, the sale of a put and call with the same strike and maturity, will produce this type of outcome. If the market moves strongly in either direction, the short put or call will become a liability and reduce the profits from the strategy. If the market stays flat, most of the proceeds from the option premium will be retained by the Pension Trust. The risk of this strategy is that large losses can occur if the market moves a large amount in either direction. The return distribution for this strategy would be relatively peaked, with long tails in either direction.

Another strategy for a neutral market view is *writing puts combined with the purchase of Treasury bills (writing escrowed puts).* Because it is equivalent to writing covered calls, the expected return distribution for this strategy can be inferred from Exhibit 13. If the market stays flat or rises, the put premium will be retained as current income; however, if the market falls, the fund must be in a position to purchase the stock at the exercise price. This can be done by liquidating sufficient Treasury bills. Because writing escrowed puts produces the same payoff as covered call writing, it can be surmised that writing calls against the current equity portfolio is another appropriate strategy for a neutral market view.

EXHIBIT 19

Expected Return Distributions from a Fence or Collar when Different Proportions of the Stock Are Covered (Put, 10% Out-of-the-money, Call, 20% Out-of-the-money)

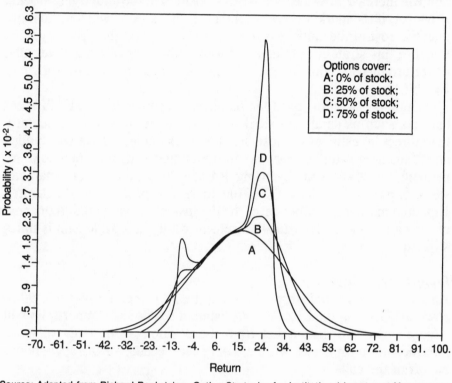

Options cover:
A: 0% of stock;
B: 25% of stock;
C: 50% of stock;
D: 75% of stock.

Source: Adapted from Richard Bookstaber, *Option Strategies for Institutional Investment Management* (Reading, MA: Addison-Wesley, 1983).

Short Term Bullish

Once the market outlook turns from bearish to bullish, it becomes appropriate to consider option strategies using index calls. For example, John Strong could increase his exposure to equities by using the *90/10 call options and Treasury bills* strategy, in addition to the exposure provided by the underlying equity portfolio. John could use a portion of his cash balances to buy short-term index calls and keep the remainder in cash. The moneyness and amount of calls to buy would be a function of John's bullish sentiment. If he is highly optimistic, he could buy out-of-the-money calls equivalent to the amount of equity exposure he wanted, or he could buy a multiple of the desired exposure using at-the-money calls. This strategy should be viewed only as a way to increase John's equity exposure because of his bullish view. It does not alter the returns from the underlying equity portfolio that John currently incurs.

If John is correct and the market appreciates, the index call position will increase in value, similar to a position in the underlying stocks. However, if the market stays neutral or declines, John will lose no more than the cost of the calls, less the interest earned on the Treasury bills. Because this strategy is equivalent to the purchase of protective puts, the return distributions for this strategy are identical to those shown in Exhibit 14.

Options also allow portfolio managers to gain exposure to different markets such as small-cap stocks or foreign markets more efficiently than direct investment in these areas. For example, if John was bullish about small-cap stocks or stocks in the United Kingdom, he could implement the 90/10 strategy using Russell 2000 options for small-cap stock exposure, or the FT-SE 100 to take a position in the United Kingdom market. In either case, the downside risk is limited to the cost of the calls less the Treasury-bill return, while the upside gain is unrestricted.

Long-Term Bullish
An extended-term bullish position can be implemented with the *90/10 strategy based on the LEAPS calls* listed in Exhibit 8. The portfolio will have exposure to the market from the position in the long calls and intermediate term losses will be dampened because of the asymmetric payoff of the calls.

Another strategy that pension fund managers are using in this scenario is the writing of at- or slightly out-of-the-money long-term puts while holding the underlying equity portfolio and cash balances. Those using this strategy rationalize their position because the long-term bias of the market is upward. Put premiums received today add to the current income of the portfolio. If the market retreats, cash balances are used to cover the puts when they expire, and new puts are written at lower strike prices. This is equivalent to buying stock at prices below those currently in the market.

A Comparison of Dynamic Insurance Using Futures to Static Insurance Using Listed Options
The term *portfolio insurance* has been used to describe the use of protective puts, or the 90/10 calls plus Treasury bills strategies. These are properly termed *static portfolio insurance* techniques. The dynamic

portfolio insurance Lincoln Pension Trust used in 1986 and 1987 was an alternative to static insurance based on listed options, and a comparison of these strategies may be useful.

Most fund managers who implemented dynamic insurance used the stock index futures markets to hedge the underlying equity portfolio, rather than trading in the stocks themselves. As John Strong noted in the case, when dynamic insurance is used, the portfolio insurer buys or sells sufficient futures contracts (each short futures contract has a delta of approximately -1.0, while the equity portfolio's delta[1] is $+1.0$) to create a delta on the equity portion of the portfolio equal to that specified by the option pricing model. The underlying portfolio combined with the short futures position and cash, will produce a payoff over the very short term, that is equivalent to the payoff from the stock plus a listed put option. The futures position has to be rebalanced every few days to meet the parameters specified by the option pricing model. The continual rebalancing produces an option-like payoff for the portfolio compared to an outright hedge that is created from maintaining a fixed short position in futures.

Dynamic rather than static portfolio insurance was used in the 1980s for a number of reasons:

1. Listed options were not available on indices that track a particular fund's portfolio.
2. Listed options may not have had the exercise price, maturity, or been of the type (American or European) that was desired. For example, insurers often used a one-year time horizon for the insurance, and until the S&P 500 contract was introduced, no listed contract was available with this maturity. Also, most insurers prefer a European contract because the early exercise feature of an American option is of no value to them. Option-like payoffs can be created with dynamic insurance having the exact characteristics desired by the fund manager.
3. The fund was so large that the listed options market did not have sufficient liquidity to meet their trading requirements.

John Strong's concern about the concept of portfolio insurance can be addressed by comparing the use of listed options versus the futures market to implement the strategy:

---

[1] The concept of delta is discussed and explained in Chapter 2.

1. The dynamic insurance strategy requires continual rebalancing of the positions, the use of listed options does not. Consequently dynamic insurance positions can get whipsawed in a volatile, nondirectional market.
2. Large jumps in stock prices can be disastrous for the dynamic insurer, as was evident in the market crash of October 1987. Static insurance strategies using listed options that require no trading in a volatile market performed well during the crash and are unaffected by large jumps in the market.
3. Transactions costs can be significant with the dynamic insurance strategy.
4. The cost of the protection under the dynamic insurance strategy is unknown when the insurance is implemented. The cost of static insurance is fixed when the put is purchased.

Two main points should emerge from the comparison of static and dynamic insurance strategies. First, a cost for the insurance exists for the dynamic strategy even though it is not as obvious as the put premium in the static strategy. The main difference is that the cost for the static strategy is known when the position is established, while the cost for the dynamic strategy is unknown until the insurance position is terminated. Second, because the static insurer does not have to trade in volatile markets, the protection afforded by listed puts is much greater than that of the dynamic insurance program. Because of the difficult market conditions during the market correction on October 19th and 20th in 1987, many dynamic insurers terminated trading, leaving their portfolios uninsured during that period.

By examining the listed option products shown in Exhibit 8 in the case (see below), it will become apparent that many of the reasons for using dynamic insurance no longer are relevant. John Strong is correct in suspecting that the concept of portfolio insurance is valid, and that the marketplace for options has evolved to allow listed contracts to be used to implement portfolio insurance strategies by institutional investors such as the Lincoln Pension Trust.

An Evaluation of Listed Option Contracts

Exhibit 8 presents a list of index option contracts traded on the CBOE. When considered along with the index option contracts traded on other exchanges in the United States and in other markets around the world, it is apparent that listed option products probably can be found to meet the risk management needs of most institutional investors. Some of the main considerations when selecting option contracts for risk management strategies include the option style (American or European), maturity, and index composition. In addition, the portfolio manager should be aware of the differences between individual equity and index options.

American versus European Options
According to Exhibit 8, only the S&P 100 options are American style, all others are European. When insuring a portfolio, which style option to use depends primarily on the fund manager's objectives. A European option will generally be cheaper than an American option on the same underlying security with identical attributes (e.g., time to expiration and strike). This happens because there is a cost associated with the privilege of early exercise afforded by the American option. If the objective is to insure a portfolio over some defined time horizon, say one year, and the ability to exercise the option has no value to the fund manager, then it is more cost effective to purchase European rather than American index options. Thus the S&P 500, Russell 2000, or FT-SE 100 options could be considered for *protective put* or *long calls and Treasury bills* strategies that involve the purchase of options. If the fund manager is using strategies involving the sale of options, such as escrowed puts or covered calls, and they will not be disturbed if the option is exercised early, then the higher premium income from American options such as the S&P 100 should be considered.

Option Maturity
Standard options such as the OEX, SPX, and RUT are available with maturities up to nine months. To implement option strategies of relatively short duration, these usually are the contracts that should be considered. Many option strategists select an option with expiration beyond the period they anticipate holding the contract and trade out of the position at least one month before option expiration. They believe that the market can become volatile for options as expiration approaches, and they wish to avoid trading in a volatile market.

For many risk management strategies, institutional investors often prefer options with maturities from one to three years. Consider a pension fund manager who wants to insure the value of an equity portfolio two years hence. The most effective way to do this is to use puts with a maturity at least as long as the insurance period desired. Once the stock and option positions are established, the manager knows that no further action will be required until the end of the period. Realize that this strategy will, in virtually all situations, produce a different terminal portfolio value than rolling over three-month options every quarter during the next two years. This occurs because realized profits or losses on the options every quarter will not match the profit or loss that the two-year option produces at the end of the insurance period. This phenomenon is called *path dependence*. It is impossible to know at the beginning of the period which strategy will be most costly; all that can be said is that the cost from rolling over three-month options over two years will differ from the cost of using an option with two years to expiration.

Index Composition

Besides the consideration of style and maturity, fund managers should analyze how their particular equity portfolio tracks the portfolio underlying the index option. The five indices underlying the index options listed in Exhibit 8 provides a range of alternatives for different types of equity portfolios. The broadly based S&P 500 should produce returns similar to many large equity portfolios held by institutional investors. Also, S&P 500 futures contracts are traded, which facilitates more sophisticated hedging strategies using options, futures, and the underlying equity portfolio. The S&P 100 is a subset of the S&P 500 selected from a broad range of industries. The Russell 2000 is a widely recognized index of small-cap stocks that can be used for risk management of small-cap equity positions. The Nasdaq 100 tracks over the counter stocks and includes both larger and smaller capitalization issues. The FT-SE 100 provides exposure to the United Kingdom equity market without the necessity of evaluating individual British companies.

Individual versus Index Options

Individual equity options differ in several ways from index options. While most institutional investors will favor the use of index options, it is useful to be aware of the differences in these products.

Differences in Payoffs. Payoffs will differ between the index and individual options depending on how the prices of individual securities change in the portfolio. It is not possible to predict which will produce the greatest payoff over a particular future period. The comparison in Chapter 7 between portfolios insured by index and individual puts showed little difference in profit between the two strategies. However, other examples could be constructed in which the results differ dramatically.

Differences in Premiums Caused by Differences in Risk.   The costs of index puts or calls will be lower than buying an equivalent portfolio of individual options. To understand why, recall that the case indicated total risk (price volatility) can be segmented into two sources. One source is general market factors that affect the prices of all stocks, this is called market risk. The other component is volatility caused by factors unique to each firm, called firm-specific risk. Between 40 and 60 percent of the price changes in the typical security are related to changes in the market, the remainder can be attributed to firm specific risk. The combination of market and firm specific risk represents total risk of the security. As securities are combined into portfolios, the firm-specific risk of each security tends to offset the firm-specific volatility in other stocks, and total risk in the portfolio declines as portfolio size increases. This is just a complex way to explain the common sense rule that investors should diversify their holdings.

The act of diversification quickly reduces the firm-specific risk in an equity portfolio toward the limiting value of market risk. Because the market portfolio is fully diversified, it contains only market risk. Considering the two risk components, the differential in pricing between individual and index options can be explained. Recall from Chapters 2 and 3 that the price of an option is directly affected by the volatility of its underlying security. The higher the volatility, the higher the option's price. The volatility estimate used to price options on individual securities will reflect the *security's* total risk, including the market and firm-specific components. The volatility estimate used to price options on an index, say the S&P 500, represents the total risk of the index, but it will contain only market risk because the firm-specific risk in the market portfolio has been removed by diversification. The lower relative volatility estimate means that it will cost less to purchase one S&P 500 Index put than individual puts on 500 securities. If the objective is to insure the portfolio, not each security, the purchase of index puts is the most cost-effective strategy. Buying individual equity options overinsures the portfolio because the total risk of each stock is protected.

Differences in Settlement.   The settlement procedure differs between individual and index options and may influence which options are selected. Index options when exercised are settled in cash, while individual options are exercised by delivery of the underlying stock. Obviously either index or individual options can be traded before expiration on the floor of the options exchange. Also, portfolio insurance strategies involving the purchase of puts or calls are not subject to unexpected exercise since the purchaser determines when the option is exercised. However, strategies involving the sale of options, such as covered writing or escrowed puts, expose the writer to potentially unexpected exercise of the call and sale of the underlying security with accompanying costs and tax consequences.

The Issue of Small-Capitalization Stocks and Foreign Investment

The interest in increasing exposure to small-cap stocks is a common one for institutional investors seeking additional diversification and greater potential returns. For many funds, direct investment in small-cap stocks is not feasible because of the small amount of stock outstanding, the infrequent trading of some issues, and the inability to get reliable information about the company's financial condition and economic prospects. These concerns can be reduced to some degree by the use of the Russell 2000 index options in risk management strategies described below.

Using Puts for Insurance
If a program of direct investment in small-cap companies is followed, the risk in the position can be reduced by purchasing an appropriate amount of Russell 2000 puts. This portfolio insurance strategy may be highly appropriate for investment in the volatile small-stock environment because significant losses can be avoided. The trust fund may elect to maintain the protection by using long-term LEAPS puts with exercise prices out-of-the-money to keep the insurance costs as reasonable as possible.

Gaining Exposure Using Calls and Treasury Bills
Instead of direct investment in selected small-cap stocks, Lincoln Pension Trust could gain exposure to them by following a 90/10 strategy using call options on the Russell 2000. As a long-term strategy, the fund could buy at- or out-of-the-money LEAPS calls, with a defined percentage of available cash, and hold the rest in Treasury bills. Like the protective put strategy, this plan will enable the fund to participate in price increases in small stocks while avoiding losses beyond the cost of the calls less the Treasury bill interest. If a shorter-term exposure to

small-cap stocks was desired, the fund could follow the same strategy using standard three- or six-month options on the Russell 2000.

Hedging Using Russell 2000 Futures and Index Options
While it is impossible to include a description of all derivative strategies in this book, it is useful to mention how futures and options can be combined to gain risk-controlled exposure to small capitalization stocks. Instead of buying individual small-cap stocks, Lincoln Pension Trust could buy futures on the Russell 2000 index that are traded on the Chicago Mercantile Exchange. Combining the long position in the Russell 2000 futures with a purchased Russell put option produces an insured portfolio with a payoff that would match direct investment in all 2000 stocks in the index. To protect the position against unanticipated losses, the portfolio manager could buy index puts to create an insured portfolio.

Evaluating the Data in Exhibits 11 and 12
Exhibits 11 and 12 provide insight about the impact of portfolio risk management strategies on actual data. It should be emphasized that the put and call premiums were determined by the Black-Scholes Option Pricing Model and do not necessarily reflect the option premiums that would be realized in actual trading. These results are influenced by the option pricing model, the input variables used to calculate the option premiums, the data period, and the assumption that transactions would have occurred at model prices. For example, if volatility estimates used to price the options were systematically lower than those used in actual trading, severe option underpricing would occur, and the insured strategy will appear better than it really could have been. With these caveats in mind, it is now useful to compare the returns over time for the three portfolios.

Using Exhibit 11, compare the quarterly performance of the unhedged Russell 2000 Index, the Russell 2000 Index insured with index puts, and the unhedged S&P 500 Index. Note that the insured portfolio shows a smaller gain when the market rises and a much smaller loss when the market declines dramatically. For example, in the fourth quarter of 1987, the insured Russell Index suffered a slight loss of .79 percent, while the unhedged index declined by 29.08 percent. For the year of 1987, the insured portfolio earned 21.5 percent compared with a loss of 8.82 percent for the index. When the index moves slightly in either direction, the insured portfolio will underperform the index portfolio because of the cost of the put.

The value of using the protective put to avoid a loss also can be illustrated in Exhibit 11. In quarter 3 of 1981 the Russell 2000 index suffered a loss of 17.49 percent, while the insured portfolio only lost .22 percent. Because the yearly returns represent the compound returns over four quarters, by avoiding the large loss the insured portfolio gained 14.29 percent for the year of 1981, while the index earned only 2.06 percent over the year.

Exhibit 20 uses the data in Exhibit 11 to produce a histogram of the quarterly returns for the two Russell strategies over the 1980 to 1992 period. The return on the axis represents the upper value of a 5 percent interval (e.g., −5 percent to 0 percent is shown in the "0.00" return interval). Note that over 40 percent of the quarterly returns for the hedged portfolio lie within the −5 percent to 0 percent interval, while 23 percent of the unhedged index returns are in this interval. Note also that the insured portfolio incurred no loss greater than −5 percent, and only

EXHIBIT 20
Russell 2000 Index and Insured Portfolio 1980 through 1992

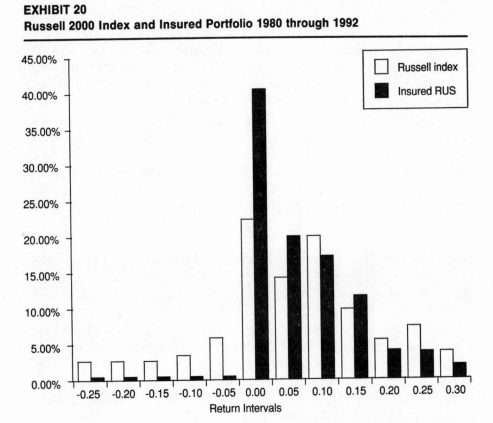

one gain in the 25–30 percent category. Both distributions have positive skewness, indicated by the larger tail of positive returns. Exhibit 20 represents the essence of portfolio risk management—the molding of the index returns to a new shape that may be preferred by management.

It also is useful to compare the summary statistics for the three portfolios shown at the end of Exhibit 11. The cumulative returns over the 13-year period is much greater for the insured portfolio, 874.50 percent, than either the Russell 2000, 438.91 percent, or S&P 500, 515.88 percent. In addition, risk as measured by the standard deviation of yearly returns is much lower for the insured portfolio. Note that the standard deviation of the insured portfolio, 12.31 percent, is slightly less than the S&P 500 index, 12.77 percent. This suggests that the problem of higher risk in the small-cap stock strategy can be reduced or eliminated through the purchase of protective puts on the small-cap index.

Exhibit 12, which presents put and call premiums and the Treasury bill yield, is provided to enable you to test other risk management strategies on the Russell 2000 Index. For example the 90/10 call and Treasury-bill strategy, covered call writing, the sale of escrowed puts, and the use of at-the-money fences all can be simulated using data in the table. These exercises will help you develop a better understanding of the way in which options modify returns of the underlying portfolio.

Gaining Exposure to Foreign Markets

The strategies described above also can be used to gain exposure and control risk of investing in United Kingdom equities. For example, the 90/10 call option Treasury-bill strategy could be implemented with FT-SE 100 LEAPS call options if the market view on the U.K. market was bullish. Downside losses are limited to the cost of the calls less the Treasury-bill interest. Alternatively, direct investment in a portfolio of U.K. securities could be insured with the purchase of FT-SE 100 LEAPS puts. Futures products also are available on the FT-SE 100 (traded on the London International Financial Futures Exchange, LIFFE) and can be combined with the LEAPS options instead of direct investment in securities.

Current Risk Management Strategies for John Strong

Factors in the Analysis

John Strong is interested in developing a risk management strategy to fit his view of the market and that is appropriate for the current status of the Pension Trust. Factors that should be considered include:

1. John is concerned about a market correction from recent highs but wants to participate in any market advance.

2. Implied volatility in the market is near the all-time low of 8 percent, a condition that occurred prior to the correction in 1987. Low implied volatility indicates that options will be relatively cheap compared to their prices in other market phases. This will favor strategies involving the purchase of options.

3. Interest rates seem to be holding steady, but the attitude is that they will increase in the future instead of falling further. This would be bearish for stocks.

4. The Pension Trust is sitting on a relatively large cash balance. Many other institutional investors also have a large amount of cash that they need to invest.

5. There is interest on the part of some members of the strategy committee to gain exposure to small-cap stocks or foreign stocks.

Recommendation

An appropriate strategy for the equity portfolio that the Pension Trust currently holds and that conforms to John Strong's market view of "neutral but uncertain," is to purchase out-of-the-money S&P 500 Index puts with a maturity of six months to a year. Considering the low volatility impounded into option premiums, an option-buying strategy is preferred. The out-of-the-money puts would be cheaper than at-the-money ones, yet provide protection if the market suffers a major pullback. He could consider creating a collar by selling out-of- the-money calls on the S&P 500 to help pay for the puts, but this would reduce his participation in a market advance. In addition, the low volatility means that call premiums would be relatively low.

With respect to his current cash balances, the difficulty of timing the market has been documented by many academic studies and John's own experience. Thus he is motivated to invest a majority of his cash to enable the fund to participate in any market advance. Three option-based strategies would enable him to achieve this objective.

1. Lincoln Pension Trust could buy selected small-cap stocks that fit his portfolio criteria and control their risk by purchasing LEAPS on the Russell 2000 Index. If small stocks enter a decline, the put LEAPS will truncate the losses at the put exercise price.

2. The Pension Trust could allocate 5 to 10 percent of the cash to the purchase of at-the-money, 6- to 12-month, S&P 500 index calls (remember the low volatility makes purchasing an option more attractive). The remainder should be retained cash. This would provide a similar return to direct investment in a diversified portfolio of larger capitalization stocks.

3. Lincoln Pension Trust could buy Russell 2000 index calls with 5 to 10 percent of the available cash, and again hold the remainder in Treasury bills. The calls would provide exposure to small-cap stocks, but the risk would be limited to the amount of the call premium.

The recommended strategies illustrate that portfolio risk management using options greatly enriches the portfolio manager's ability to design investment programs to fit individual needs and market perspectives. No other security possesses the asymmetric payoff pattern that makes it easy to mold expected returns to the needs of institutional fund managers. The purpose of this case was to enable you to review the principles of options explained earlier in the book and apply your knowledge to an actual investment situation.

Case Two, the Hampton Investment Fund, requires you focus on another dimension of derivative products in pension fund management. For many funds, the two biggest problems are first, gaining an understanding of options and how they can be used as risk management tools, and second, obtaining approval from their trustees to use derivative products as part of their investment strategy. The Hampton Fund case provides a setting for your analysis of the issues involved with gaining board approval for investment in derivatives.

CASE TWO

Hampton Pension Fund

Since the market correction of 1987, Ann Sawyer and her investment management team had been studying the feasibility of using options and futures in portfolio management strategies. They recently reached the decision that their pension plan, Hampton Pension Fund, should be using derivative products to manage risk and add value to their portfolios. Sawyer had 15 years experience in the money management business and had seen significant advancement in the tools available for investment management during her career. She and several members of her internal management team believed that derivative products could add value and enable them to manage risk in ways not possible with other financial products. The problem she faced was persuading the Trustee Committee for the Pension Plan that the plan documents should be amended to allow investment in derivative products.

Sawyer had scheduled a meeting for Thursday morning (tomorrow) to discuss a board presentation about derivatives with two trustees, Tom Jackson and Brenda Woods, who were very interested in this topic. Tom was 66 years old and a recently retired executive of the company who had spent his 38-year career with Hampton in plant operations. He had no formal training in finance or financial markets, but was respected by the Trustees for his common-sense approach to investment policy. Tom had the reputation of being very conservative in his views about investment strategies, to the extent that he often questioned why the Fund allocated so much to investment in "those risky common stocks." Brenda Woods represented a much different viewpoint. She was 40 years old, had an MBA from the University of Chicago, and was an executive vice president for a large manufacturing firm headquartered in New York City. Brenda was the youngest board member and was considered by the other board members as "very, very bright." Other board members often turned to her for explanations about the technical details of presentations that they received. Ann thought the meeting with Tom Jackson and Brenda Woods would be helpful to her as she developed her proposal to the full committee, which meets in one week.

The Hampton Electronics Company

The Hampton Pension Fund is a $12.5 billion pension fund that was established for employees of the Hampton Electronics Company headquartered in New York City. Hampton Electronics has been in business since 1922 and is considered one of the premier manufacturers worldwide of commercial electrical and electronic products. Sales are split between commercial and industrial products, which accounts for 58 percent of sales and 52 percent of pretax income, and the appliance and construction division, which provides 42 percent of sales and 48 percent of income. Primary products include process control systems, industrial motors and drives, fractional horsepower motors, and appliance components. Since the 1960s, Hampton has followed a deliberate strategy of worldwide expansion, both in sales and manufacturing. In 1991, foreign sales revenues amounted to 40 percent of total sales, a figure that has been gradually increasing every year. Most of its low-technology manufacturing operations have been moved to low-cost facilities in China and India, enabling Hampton to keep costs down and prices competitive in the global market. Company prospects are excellent, and the pension company benefits have traditionally been among the most generous in the industry.

The Hampton Pension Plan

Hampton's pension plan includes both defined-benefit and defined-contribution programs, with the larger portion being the defined-benefit program containing three-fourths of the fund's value, $9.1 billion. The defined-benefit fund is the older plan, and it is funded with common stocks and long-term fixed-income investments. Most of the bonds and GICs (guaranteed investment contracts) in this plan were purchased in the 1980s when interest rates were much higher than today. Sawyer's plan is to use option and futures strategies for the defined-benefit component of the plan.

The fund's assets are divided between nine internal managers and eight external management firms. Ann's internal staff manages $7.1 billion of the fund's assets. The internal management team includes three equity managers who invest primarily in large-capitalization U.S. stocks, and one manager who invests in foreign equities; two domestic fixed-income managers and one manager of foreign fixed-income securities; one real estate manager; two managers of private investments; and one manager of direct placements. The managers' experience ranges from 25 to 4 years, and they all consider themselves "students of the market" who are interested in new ideas and ways to add value to their portfolios.

The other $5.4 billion of pension fund assets are managed by eight external managers who follow a variety of strategies. About one-third of the assets are passively managed as an index fund, having the objective of replicating returns from the S&P 500 each quarter. Last year, they requested permission from Sawyer to "equitize" cash balances by using

S&P 500 futures, thus remaining fully invested at all times, but she has been unable to authorize this strategy because of plan restrictions. The rest of the assets are placed with smaller managers who specialize in what can best be called active management styles. Most use a bottom-up approach and attempt to identify stocks or sectors that they believe are undervalued.

Ann Sawyer reports to the fund's general manager, Bill Cochran, who is responsible for administration of the entire pension plan. She views her role as director of investment planning as one of setting overall investment strategy for the plan, and being closely involved in the day-to-day investment decisions. Ann follows a strategy of tactical asset allocation, under a base guideline of 60 percent equity/40 percent fixed-income investments. Fund documents, as shown below, provide guidelines for different asset classes allowed by the plan. In addition to the tactical asset allocation decision, Ann determines the allocation of fund assets between internal and external managers for equity and fixed-income investments. Ann is familiar with the academic studies about market efficiency and the apparent inability of many institutional investors to consistently outperform market indices like the S&P 500. Her attitude is that, while it is difficult to beat the market, the market is not strictly efficient. She believes that good investment decisions can be made that will produce risk-adjusted returns above the long-term market averages.

Sawyer's Study of Derivatives

The market correction in 1987 probably was the catalyst that motivated Hampton's managers to examine portfolio risk management. If losses such as those that occurred during the market crash of '87 were to be avoided, it appeared that derivative products like puts, calls, and futures offered the best means to do it. In 1988, internal managers at the Hampton Plan began studying how options and futures could be used to manage portfolio risk. They had considered the technique of dynamic portfolio insurance, but the bad press it received relating to the '87 market crash made them wary. Ann then explored strategies using listed puts and calls. Particularly appealing were the strategies of covered call writing, protective put buying, the purchase or sale of straddles, and the sale of escrowed puts.

Like most pension fund managers, Ann Sawyer receives numerous investment ideas from money managers. One manager designed a system that purchases futures as a *cash-overlay* strategy—buying futures to gain market exposure for cash held in the fund's cash management accounts. This is an extension of the cash equitization idea noted above. Two other investment managers proposed strategies based on options. One suggested a technique called *cash equivalent alternatives* and the other suggested a risk control strategy called a *fence* or *collar*.

Cash-Equivalent Alternatives

A fund manager in California, Hunter Green Investments, specializes in arbitrage using options. The concept is that a riskless position can be created using the underlying asset and its options, or even just the options themselves. Brief periods of mispricing in options may occur around periods of market movements, and they provide opportunities to create a riskless position that will yield a return above the riskless rate.

The Forward Conversion. Hunter Green provided two examples, forward conversions, and box spreads, to illustrate cash-equivalent strategies. Shown in Exhibit 1 is an example of a *forward conversion* that uses a long position in UAL stock combined with a short call and long put. He explained that "it is based on the put-call parity equation" (which was described in the previous case).

The Box Spread. A box spread is another riskless arbitrage strategy that combines a call (bull) spread with a put (bear) spread. The position value at expiration is totally independent of the price of the underlying instrument. By creating the position for less than the expiring value, a profit will be realized at expiration, as shown in Exhibit 2.

EXHIBIT 1
Forward Conversion Example (UAL Equity Options with 32 Days to Expiration)

Bought UAL stock	−$282.500
Bought UAL 280 put (T = 32 days)	−5.875
Sold UAL 280 call (T = 32 days)	10.750
Net investment	−$277.625
Receive at expiration	+$280.000
Net return	$ 2.375 for 32 days
Annualized return (2.375/277.625) × (365 days/32 days)	9.76%
versus Treasury-bill rate of	6.49%

EXHIBIT 2
Box Spread Example (S&P 500 Index Options with 210 Days to Expiration)

	Bull Call Spread Portion	
Purchased:	June 365 S&P 500 Call	−$14.500
Sold:	June 370 S&P 500 Call	11.625
Cost		−$ 2.875
	Bear Put Spread Portion	
Sold:	June 365 S&P 500 Put	$12.750
Purchased:	June 370 S&P 500 Put	−14.625
Cost		−$ 1.875
Total cost		−$ 4.750
Value at expiration (370 − 365)		5.000
Net profit		$ .250
Annualized return (.25/4.75) × (365 days/210 days) = 9.15%		
versus Treasury-bill yield of		6.49%

The riskless arbitrage idea was attractive to Ann because there was virtually no probability of loss and the return would be higher than Treasury securities. It was a way to add value to the portfolio for no increase in risk. If the plan would have permitted, she would have liked to place $50 million with Hunter Green on an experimental basis. However, approval would have to be given by the trustees before this could happen.

The Fence or Collar

Bob Strong of Newark Trust Company, the master custodian for Hampton Pension Fund, recently suggested to Ann a risk control strategy using options. The strategy is called a *fence* or *collar* and is created with a put and call on the S&P 500 Index. It can be implemented using listed options traded on exchanges such as the CBOE, or using customized option contracts traded in the over-the-counter market. Exhibit 3 shows the details of the Newark Trust proposal.

Bob explained that the fence should be considered a risk control position against the underlying equity portfolio. For example, if Hampton would buy the 90 put and sell the 110 call, the fund would actually receive a credit of .75 percent of the notional amount when the transaction was initiated. If the S&P 500 is between 90 and 110 percent of its

EXHIBIT 3
Example of a Fence or Collar Using S&P 500 Index Options

Option seller:	Hampton Pension Fund
Option buyer:	Newark Financial
Notional amount:	$10 million to $500 million
Underlying index:	S&P 500 Index
Option maturity:	1 Year
Option type:	European (OTC)
Settlement:	Cash

Strike and Premiums

	Strike (% of Spot)	Premium (% of Notional)
Put	90	1.30
Put	80	.35
Call	110	2.05
Call	120	.53

current value at the end of the year, both options will expire worthless. However, the long 90 put will protect the fund against losses if the index falls below 90 percent of its present value. Alternatively, if the S&P 500 appreciates, the 110 call will cap-off or collar the gain at 10 percent above the current level. The profit/loss diagram for this strategy, assuming that the fund holds a portfolio that behaves exactly like the S&P 500, is shown in Exhibit 4.

Ann liked the idea of limiting losses, but was not sure that it was beneficial to cap the gain at 10 percent. She also had questions about doing the trade directly with Newark instead of using listed options to effect the same strategy. Ann told Bob Strong that she would consider his suggestion and present the idea to the board members later in the month.

The Plan Document

The original pension plan was written in the late 1940s and has been amended over time to adapt to changes in the investment environment. As mentioned above, the original pension plan was a defined-benefit program that was popular at the time. The original intent of offering a pension plan was to attract the best workers in the tight labor market after World War II. The defined contribution program was added in the

EXHIBIT 4
Fence or Collar Strategy (Sell the 1-Year 110 Call, Buy the 1-Year 90 Put, Long S&P 500 Index)

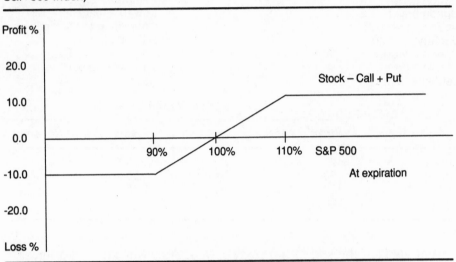

late 1970s and is the only plan available to new employees. Under the defined-contribution plan, employees contribute 7.5 percent of salary to the Fund, and Hampton Electronics contributes 8.5 percent. Vesting occurs in two years.

The plan documents provide specific guidelines relating to investment policy and the type of assets that may be purchased. It states that the fund's objective is *to maximize expected returns subject to the following constraints* designed to control risk:

1. Investment in corporate bonds is limited to those rated AA (S&P) or Aa (Moodys). No junk or high-yield bonds may be purchased. Corporate bonds must be traded on the NYSE Bond Market or widely traded by market makers (more than 4).

2. Investment in foreign corporate and government bonds is permitted. These bonds must meet equivalent quality standards as specified for U.S. corporate bonds.

3. Investment in U.S. equities is limited to securities traded on the NYSE, AMEX, or the top 500 in capitalization, traded in the over-the-counter market.

4. Investment in foreign equities is limited to those traded on the

country's primary stock exchange, and must be among the top 250 companies in capitalization in the country. [The plan was amended in 1985 to allow for the purchase of foreign securities.]

5. The fund may not invest more than 5 percent of its assets in any individual asset.

6. The fund may invest in equity private investments or new ventures, but such investment is limited to 5 percent of the fund's assets.

7. The fund may invest in real estate, but real estate holdings cannot exceed 10 percent of the fund's assets.

8. The fund will diversify its investments according to the following guidelines:

	Target %	Minimum %	Maximum %
Domestic equities	55.0%	35.0%	80.0%
Foreign equities	5.0%	0.0%	10.0%
Domestic bonds	25.0%	10.0%	40.0%
Foreign bonds	7.0%	0.0%	10.0%
Real estate	3.0%	1.0%	5.0%
Private investments	2.0%	2.0%	8.0%
Cash	3.0%	1.0%	10.0%

Fund management should invest toward the target percentages, with discretion allowed for their expectations about performance of the different market sectors. Each asset class will be rebalanced at the end of every quarter. Under no instance, will the amount invested in any category rise above or fall below the minimum or maximum amounts.

The performance of both internal and external managers will be evaluated each quarter using rates of return and risk measures (volatility and beta) calculated by an external consultant. These performance measures will be compared to customized benchmarks agreed to by negotiation between the specific fund manager and the plan director. If performance over a three-year period averages more than 200 basis points below the agreed-upon benchmark, the fund manager will be carefully evaluated before reappointment.

It is specified in the plan document that any changes to the plan must be approved by a majority vote of the fund's trustees. The plan is silent about options and futures because they were not available in the 1940s when the original plan document was written. No one has taken the initiative to change the plan document to include or prohibit investment in options or futures.

The Trustees

The fund's trustee committee consists of eight people who meet four times a year, in the month following each calendar quarter. Their main business at each meeting is reviewing quarterly performance of different fund managers, analyzing current market conditions, and evaluating the internal director's expectations about the market over the next 3 to 12 months. Each meeting, Ann makes a presentation about the current asset allocations and the strategy she expects to use over the next quarter.

Ann believes that the trustees understand their role as one of setting overall investment policy and insuring that the fund is being managed to the greatest possible benefit of the stakeholders. However, she has expressed concern from time to time that the trustees are overly conservative in their investment policies and the strategies they allow. Concern with their fiduciary responsibilities under ERISA (Employee Retirement Income Security Act of 1974) seems to make them resistant to change. She is fortunate that they have not tried to "micro-manage" the fund and have avoided involvement in the day-to-day investment management process.

The eight members have served on the board for at least six years, and one person has been a member for 12 years. The level of sophistication about investments is varied, and most board members are not in financially related occupations. The most knowledgeable member probably is Jack Miller, the 50-year-old CFO of Hampton. Jack has a Ph.D. in finance from New York University and is quite familiar with portfolio theory and the academic literature about portfolio management and options. The other five board members are executives or managers of companies. Ann frequently uses time during the quarterly meetings to educate them about the latest developments in the field and important issues on the horizon. Over the past two years she has made three or four presentations about options and futures, covering basic terminology, definitions, and strategies. The board has some curiosity in the opportunities provided by these instruments.

Ann's Meeting with Bill Cochran, Tom Jackson, and Brenda Woods

SAWYER

Tom and Brenda, I appreciate your willingness to meet with me and Bill to discuss our interest in trading in options and futures. I'm aware that these instruments are relatively new to some board members and that they will be concerned about how these securities will be used to meet overall objectives of the fund. I also would like your evaluation of the proposals I sent you about cash-equivalent alternatives and the use of fences and collars.

JACKSON

I'm glad you asked me to come. I know you are working hard to make money for the fund in a difficult market environment, but I'm concerned about using these securities. They are really risky; why do you want to use them?

COCHRAN

Tom, we've talked about this several times before. Considered alone, the leverage available in options and futures makes their prices more volatile than the underlying stocks—what you refer to as more risky—but we are not going to speculate on the market with these securities. We are talking about using them to control market risk by combining them with positions in other options and the underlying asset.

JACKSON

It seems to me that we can do the same thing by changing our tactical asset allocations. If Ann thinks that stocks are going to decline, she can sell stock and go to cash. Why would I want to fool with options if the market is going down?

SAWYER

Tom, I understand your concerns. I'll develop for the trustees an explanation of portfolio risk management and provide some illustrations about the ways options and futures are used in risk management strategies.

WOODS

Ann, I agree that would be useful. I think most members feel pretty comfortable with the concept of portfolio risk management, but they could use some clarification as to why using options differs from the strategy of tactical asset allocation.

JACKSON

Another thing, I'm concerned about the legal issues involved. Does ERISA restrict us from trading options or futures? Have you received any opinion from legal on making these type of investments?

COCHRAN

Tom, we've also had this discussion before. To my knowledge, ERISA doesn't prohibit investment in options or futures, but it views investment decisions in a portfolio context. Its not the investment tool that's right or wrong, but how the security fits into the entire portfolio.

SAWYER

Before we went very far with our study of these products, we asked our legal department for an opinion. I'm sure that every pension program is unique with respect to its plan and legal documents, so we cannot make a statement about anyone else, but for us, legal came back with no substantive issues. The only requirement is that the board must give its approval for us to trade derivative instruments on a routine basis. Our lawyers could find nothing in ERISA that prohibits the use of options. It is not the instrument, but the manner in which any investment is used that can be inappropriate. For example, buying puts while holding an underlying stock portfolio is a means of reducing risk and insuring a portfolio's value. This is a perfectly reasonable and prudent investment strategy. However, buying puts merely to speculate on a market decline is a strategy that may be open to criticism.

JACKSON

Ann, it seems to me that we are taking enough of a prudent risk by investing in stocks. I think we are open to criticism if we take on more risk with these options and futures just to speculate on the market. For example, I think the board will want to know why you would buy a six-month or one-year option and hold it to expiration?

SAWYER

Tom, the markets in listed options and futures are very liquid, so we don't have to hold a position until the option expires. In fact, in most cases we probably would close the position before the expiration month. It appears I will need to describe to the trustees again how these markets work and the participants in them.

WOODS

Ann, another thing that will require more explanation is the cash-equivalent strategies. Are you absolutely sure that there is no risk in these positions? I'm not sure that everyone on the board will understand why this is true.

JACKSON

Brenda, for once we agree on something. Even if it appears that no risk is incurred, is this an appropriate investment strategy for a pension fund to use. We generally are considered long-term investors, not traders. It sure seems that this strategy will lead to a lot of trading costs that we normally would not incur.

COCHRAN

Tom, I know this is a different type of strategy than we have used in the past, but we are projecting a positive return above Treasury bills after commissions and all other costs of trading. This strategy should be viewed as an alternative to holding cash.

WOODS

I'd like to talk about the other strategy presented by Newark Trust called a collar or fence trade. What do you see as the advantages and disadvantages of this transaction?

SAWYER

Brenda, as you probably already know, the fence is one of many strategies that can be used to control the fund's risk exposure. The advantage of the position is that income from the call more than offsets the cost of the put. Thus we can create a position in which losses are defined to the put's striking price, while giving up gains above the striking price of the call. An alternative strategy is purchasing only the puts. This will cost more, but we retain all the upside potential.

WOODS

You know the Newark Trust proposal indicates that they will be the buyer of the put and call we are selling. I believe this is called an over-the-counter trade. How does this differ from implementing the strategy using options traded in the listed options market such as the CBOE? Is there any difference in risk or cost?

COCHRAN

The over-the-counter market in options has developed dramatically over the past years. The ability to tailor the options to our particular needs looks attractive, but I have some concerns about entering a position that involves only our fund and the trust company. It sure seems riskier than using market-traded options, but I don't have all the information to answer that question.

SAWYER

I agree, Bill. I'll get more information ready on this question prior to the trustee meeting next week.

WOODS

You know that I support your proposal to implement strategies using options and futures for the fund. While several trustees share my view, I think that it will be necessary to demonstrate why these strategies should be used. It also will be necessary to overcome some of the biases about the risk of derivatives that have been created by the popular press.

JACKSON

I still think this derivatives business is all hocus-pocus. It seems to me that we should just get out of equities or bonds if we think the market is going to decline. Why should we fool around selling calls or buying puts or trading futures to manage our risk. Going to Treasury bills when the market looks weak is what I think we should do. You'll have a difficult time making me change my mind.

PREPARING THE CASE ANALYSIS

1. Outline the steps in a strategic plan for implementing the trading of options in a pension fund. In your analysis, be sure to explain the benefits to the plan of using options and futures strategies. Are options as risky as Tom Jackson believes? Create examples to show how pension funds can use options and futures to reduce risk in their portfolios.

2. Explain the underlying concepts of the cash-equivalent alternatives. How is an investment's terminal value locked-in when the positions are first created? Would you support the index fund manager's suggestion to use S&P 500 futures to equitize cash balances?

3. How does the trading of options listed on organized exchanges differ from trading option contracts over-the-counter. What differences in risks exist between the two?

4. Assume it is the end of the trustee's meeting and they have found Ann Sawyer's arguments persuasive. Before giving final approval, they would like you to draft an amendment to the plan document that would permit the use of derivatives. Please prepare this amendment, which should be no longer than two or three paragraphs.

Suggested Analysis for Hampton Pension Fund Case

Objectives of the Case

In your case analysis, you should develop a plan that will result in approval from the pension fund's trustee committee for implementing strategies using options and futures. It may first be helpful to outline a series of strategic steps that can be implemented over time. It should be expected that the approval process will be incremental, with increasing discretion for option and futures strategies being given as the committee gains confidence in these instruments. Questions raised during the meeting with Jackson and Woods should be answered in that presentation.

The solution for this case builds on the material presented in Chapter 7, "Institutional Uses of Options," and the suggested solution to the preceding case, "Lincoln Pension Trust." Where appropriate, reference will be made to information presented earlier in this chapter. Keep in mind that the information presented below represents only a suggested solution to the case scenario. Different circumstances and personalities may call for a different approach. Study of this material should better prepare you for the process of implementing derivative strategies in your particular situation.

Devising a Strategic Plan

The two fundamental reasons for using options and futures in pension fund strategies are (1) to control risk in ways not possible with other instruments and (2) to add value to the portfolio. Once a decision-maker in the fund has determined that derivative strategies provide these benefits to the pension fund, the following steps may be helpful to gain approval for using these instruments.

Education of Internal Managers and Trustees
It is necessary to understand that derivative products can be used to control risk in portfolios in ways that cannot be achieved with any other strategy. Managers must become familiar with *specific* strategies and their appropriate applications. Trustees must understand the concept of risk management and realize a *general* understanding of strategies and applications.

In the Lincoln Pension Trust case, risk management was defined as controlling the distribution of expected returns from an investment to achieve the objectives of the portfolio manager. Options, because of their asymmetric payoff, can skew the distribution of expected returns either negatively, as shown earlier in Exhibit 13 for a covered call portfolio, or positively, as shown in Exhibit 14 for a protective put strategy. Numerous strategies using options can be devised that will mold the return distribution to the shape desired by the portfolio manager.

When explaining the idea of portfolio risk management, it is imperative that options be considered as part of a total portfolio. Not placing options in a portfolio context is causing Tom Jackson a great deal of difficulty in understanding that derivatives are *not* speculative gambles, but represent important tools for implementing risk control procedures. Easy examples to use in explaining this concept are the protective put portfolio, long stock + long put, whose profit and loss diagram is shown in the Lincoln Trust case, Exhibit 5, and the put-call parity relationship, long stock + short call + long put, shown in Exhibit 6.

Once the asymmetric payoff property of an option is understood, it can be shown how risk management using options differs from asset allocation between stocks, bonds, and cash instruments. As shown in the Lincoln Trust case, Exhibit 2, changing the allocation between stocks and bonds, or stocks and cash as suggested by Jackson, does not change the normality of the return distribution, it merely reduces its spread. As an extreme example, consider moving completely out of stocks into cash when the market is expected to fall. The fund manager has locked-in the risk-free rate of return, but if the market goes up, the fund will not participate.

Numerous studies have documented the difficulty of timing the market, and the opportunity losses incurred from being out of the market when it appreciates. For example, William Droms examined the differential forecasting accuracy required for bull and bear markets using an annual timing strategy and noted that it is much more important to correctly forecast a bull market than a bear market. Exhibit 5 shows the combinations of forecast accuracy needed under annual timing to outperform the buy-and-hold portfolio.

If investors are right on 70 percent of the bull markets, they must correctly call 80 percent of the bear markets to beat the buy-and-hold. However, if they call every bull market, 100 percent bull, they need to call only one bear market correctly. Droms suggests that these results

EXHIBIT 5
Bull and Bear Market
Forecasting Accuracy
Required to Outperform
a Buy-and Hold
Portfolio, 1926 to 1986

70% bull and 80% bear
80% bull and 50% bear
90% bull and 30% bear
100% bull and any bear

Source: William Droms, "Market Timing as an Investment Policy," *Financial Analyst Journal*,
45, January–February 1989, pp.
73–77.

probably are beyond the forecasting ability of most market timers. For
additional information about market timing, see Robert Jeffrey's article,
"The Folly of Stock Market Timing," *Harvard Business Review*, 62,
July–August 1984, pp. 102–10. These studies suggest that Jackson's
strategy of "just get out of equities or bonds if we think the market is
going to decline," and "going to Treasury bills when the market looks
weak," is virtually impossible to execute profitably through time.

However, using an option strategy such as the purchase of protective puts gives the portfolio manager the ability to protect against losses
if the market should decline, while still participating in the market if it
should rise. This is the great benefit of options compared to other investment techniques.

Trial Trading of Options and Futures Products
Trial trading gives managers the confidence in using the instruments and
uncovers glitches in internal accounting and trading procedures. Besides gaining familiarity with trading procedures for options and futures,
it enables fund managers to determine if their accounting department
can develop procedures to book the trades, and if their custodian has
the ability to properly account for short and long positions in options
and futures.

It may be possible to obtain trustee permission to execute experimental trades of futures and options in what can be defined as risk
management positions. Example trades include: (1) Buying S&P 500

futures to maintain market exposure while transitioning between equity managers, (2) buying S&P 500 Index puts to hedge an expected market decline, and (3) selling individual call options on stock that the plan desires to sell.

The experimental trades can help identify a variety of problems that need to be solved before derivative strategies can be implemented. For example, the accounting department may have no idea of what options or futures are or why they were being traded. Consequently, they may not have the necessary perspective to relate long stock positions with a hedge created by long positions in index puts. A loss on the puts is viewed as a dumb decision instead of a premium paid to insure the portfolio from a loss. Short positions in puts and calls also may be baffling to the fund's accounting department. The accounting system may be set up only for purchases of financial assets, not anticipating that a pension fund would want to short sell anything.

Trial trading can be extremely useful because the problems it identifies usually are not insurmountable. They can be solved with proper education, patience, and modifications in the accounting procedures.

Place Emphasis on Strategies Rather than Tools

By putting the emphasis on the strategy, two things are accomplished: (1) the focus is kept on the portfolio context of options and futures rather than considering them as individual positions, and (2) it will not be necessary to go to the trustees for approval when a new tool is brought to market. Trustees seem more comfortable in approving strategies rather than giving a broad brush approval to the use of derivative instruments.

Dynamic changes in the listed options market over the past 20 years underscore the wisdom of emphasizing strategy approval. When listed options were introduced by the CBOE in 1973, only calls were available, and only on 16 stocks. Trading of individual equity puts started in 1977, and index puts and calls began trading in 1983. LEAPS®, options with expirations up to three years on both individual equities and indices, were introduced in late 1990. If the approval had been granted only for the tool, each time a new product is introduced the fund manager would have to request the trustee's approval to use it. However, if the trustees are requested to approve a strategy, then the fund manager can use the tool for the strategy that is most appropriate at the time. New tools may make strategy implementation easier.

Pay Attention to External Considerations

These will include the trustees' concerns about ERISA, the impact on fund beneficiaries, and the impact on the sponsor's income. Trustees may become overly conservative because of their obligations under the prudent man rule of ERISA. However, court rulings have upheld the notion that it is diversification and the portfolio of assets that are critical to demonstrate prudent investment behavior.

Realize that the Process Will Be Lengthy

It may take more than two or three years before the committee fully endorses all aspects of derivative trading. As noted above, it often is better to request approval of strategies, rather than individual tools for trading. As the trustees become more comfortable with basic strategies, such as using portfolio insurance using listed puts, more complex strategies can be suggested and implemented.

The Concept Underlying Cash-Equivalent Alternatives

The cash-equivalent alternative, which may be called interest arbitrage, is often an appropriate way to introduce option trading in a fund. Risk is minimal, but not zero, and the average return should exceed Treasury bills. The trustees must understand that funds invested in interest arbitrage represent an alternative to investment in cash assets.

The concept underlying cash equivalent investments is that a pricing relationship exists between different options on the same underlying asset. For a put and call, it can be expressed as the put-call parity equation introduced earlier. In the Lincoln Pension Trust case, Exhibit 6 shows that the put, call, and underlying stock must be priced correctly, or an arbitrage position can be created that will earn a return greater than the riskless rate. In equation form, put-call parity is given as

$$Discounted\ Bond = Stock + Put - Call$$

If the put and call are properly priced, the right-hand side of the equation is equivalent to an investment in a discounted bond paying interest rate r over period T. At expiration the Stock + Put − Call portfolio will be worth the exercise price of the options.

In a forward conversion as shown in Exhibit 1, the UAL options both have a strike of 280 and 32 days to expiration. Either the call is overpriced or the put is underpriced (we can't tell from put-call parity). Regardless, the combined Stock − Call + Put portfolio will pay 280 at option expiration. This is a return of 9.76 percent annualized from the 32-day holding period, and much higher than the 6.49 percent available from Treasury bills.

An arbitrage profit can be earned from a box spread as shown in Exhibit 2, because of mispricing between pairs of puts and calls with different striking prices. To prove that the value of the portfolio at maturity is the difference in the two option striking prices, consider the following. If the S&P 500 is above 370 at expiration, say 380, the short 370 call will cost 10 to cover, but the long 365 call will be worth 15. A net profit of $5 is the most the position will pay for any index price above 370. If the S&P 500 is between 365 and 370, the 365 call will have a value of (Index value − 365), and the 370 call will be worthless. At an index value below 365, both calls will be worthless.

Now add the payoff from the put positions. If the S&P 500 is above 370, both the 365 and 370 puts will be worthless. In this case, the value of the calls will be $5, and the entire portfolio will be worth $5. If the index is between 370 and 365, the 370 put will have a value of (370 − Index). Adding the call portion gives a value for the entire box spread position of (370 − Index) + (Index − 365), which equals $5. Finally, if the index is below 365, the long 370 put will be worth (370 − Index), and the short 365 put will cost −(365 − Index). Again, this value is (370 − Index) − (365 − Index), which equals $5. If the box spread can be created with a cost below $5e^{-rT}$, then a riskless arbitrage profit can be earned. As shown in Exhibit 2, the box spread position can be put on with a cost of $4.75 and will be worth $5.00 at option expiration. This is a rate of return of 9.15 percent compared to 6.49% available on Treasury bills.

Describing the interest arbitrage examples to the trustees accomplishes two things. First, it emphasizes that portfolio dimension of options. To evaluate the risk of a position, it is necessary to consider the entire investment portfolio rather than an individual component. Second, interest arbitrage is a means to add value to the pension fund at virtually no risk.[1]

Jackson asks the question, "Is this investment activity appropriate for the pension fund to pursue?" It seems quite different from their

---

[1] The risks of these positions are discussed in greater details in Chapter 8, pp. 255–57.

long-term investment philosophy. The answer to his question is that interest arbitrage is important to make the marketplace work. Fund managers who engage in this strategy will bid down the prices of expensive options and bid up the price of cheap ones, until both converge to their appropriate economic value.

The idea of equitizing cash balances using futures, suggested by one of Hampton's external managers, is a popular technique used by many funds. It enables the fund to maintain a fully invested equity position without having to make decisions on individual securities every day. As noted above, it is difficult to time the market. To meet equity performance objectives, it is necessary to participate in market advances. Maintaining a fully invested position by the use of futures is one way to insure participation in the market at all times.

It should be noted that options can also be used to maintain a fully exposed position to market appreciation without exposure to market declines. These strategies were discussed in the Lincoln Pension Trust case. For example, the 90/10 strategy of buying calls and Treasury bills will appreciate in value if the market rises, but will not lose value if the market declines. This may be a more appealing strategy than the purchase of futures.

Trading Listed Options on the Exchanges versus Over-the-Counter Option Contracts

The over-the-counter options market is controlled by a few large Wall Street firms who offer customized options to large institutional investors. The size of the market in early 1993 was estimated at $50 billion. The primary advantage of the market is that the option's characteristics can be tailored precisely to meet the requirements of the institution regarding strike price, maturity, exercise price, underlying asset, and face amount. Rather complex positions can be constructed to meet whatever conditions are required. Exhibit 3 describes a straightforward over-the-counter options arrangement.

The primary disadvantages of using the over-the-counter market are cost, lack of liquidity, and counterparty risk. Remember that prices for exchange-traded options are determined on the exchange floor through interaction between buyers and sellers. Academic studies of these markets indicate that option prices closely track the economic value of the options. In an over-the-counter trade such as proposed in Exhibit 3, the prices of the put and call must be negotiated between

Hampton and Newark Financial. It takes a sophisticated investor to determine the correct price of each option. To complicate the issue, institutional investors frequently are offered packages of derivatives rather than a single position. For example, Newark offered a fence strategy to Ann Sawyer instead of just a protective put position. The package provides more negotiating room in the trade because the price of both the put and call must be determined. The institution must determine if the price it must pay for the customized product is worth the potentially extra cost.

With regard to liquidity, there is no secondary market for over-the-counter options. If the institution desires to sell the option position before expiration, the Wall Street firm usually will take the other side. However, the institution is at a severe disadvantage in determining the price, because no other buyers would be available.

The third disadvantage of the over-the-counter market is counterparty credit risk. The institution buying the customized options is relying on the creditworthiness of the firm that sells them. If the seller goes bankrupt, the options' protection becomes worthless.

In contrast, creditworthiness for exchange traded options is provided by the Option Clearing Corporation (OCC). The OCC, as described in Chapter 1, is an indispensable participant in all listed option trading because it provides liquidity and guarantee of performance for all options. The OCC becomes the buyer for every option seller and the seller for every option buyer. This arrangement effectively "delinks" individual buyers and sellers, making possible the secondary trading of the contracts. If an option buyer chooses to sell the option before expiration, the position is closed by selling the contract to another buyer on the floor of the exchange. The original buyer's name is replaced on OCC records by the person who bought the option. The original option seller still holds the position and is not involved with the second transaction because the contract is with the OCC rather than an individual. The OCC is only concerned that an equal number of buyers and sellers exists for each contract.

The OCC also performs the function of guaranteeing performance on each contract. As noted above, if the option is exercised, the buyer's brokerage firm delivers the exercise notice to the OCC. The OCC then randomly selects an option seller to receive the assignment notice. In the rare instance when the seller does not comply, the OCC steps in to honor the contract to the buyer, in effect guaranteeing performance of the contract. The two primary problems of the OTC options market are thus avoided—illiquidity and uncertainty about the seller complying with an exercise notice.

Because of the need for customized option products, the CBOE launched *FLexible EXchange*™ options in 1993. Institutions with special requirements that cannot be met with available listed options can tailor the contract with respect to underlying stock index, strike price, expiration date, and American or European style. The CBOE's objective is to provide the specialized products more cheaply and with greater liquidity than those available in the over-the-counter market. (See *The Wall Street Journal* article, "CBOE Will Let Investors Tailor Options," Jeffrey Taylor, January 29, 1993, p. C–1.; see also above, Chapter 5, pp. 160–161.)

Suggested Amendment to the Plan Documents

Any amendment to a pension trust document must be tailored to fit the objectives of the particular pension plan. The question regarding a draft to change the plan document is to make you consider how to develop a broad statement about using derivatives in a pension fund. We offer an example of one way Hampton may consider changing their plan document to permit investment in derivatives. Below are (1) stylized minutes of the trustee's meeting in which a resolution was passed to permit the use of derivative products, and (2) a proposed amendment to the pension trust.

1. Stylized Minutes—Investments/Derivatives

The Chairman called upon the Hampton Pension Plan Administrator to discuss the Trust's use of derivative financial instruments. The Plan Administrator stated that derivatives are financial instruments whose value is based upon, or derived from, another security or asset. He further stated that puts and calls on common stock and common stock indices, and futures on stock indices, all of which are traded on exchanges, are popular examples of derivatives. However the advent of the computer has enabled the investment industry to abstract individual features from stock or a debt instrument, such as an income stream, and sell that feature as a separate financial instrument. He then noted that there are times and situations when it would be advantageous for the trust to purchase only certain features of a security, rather than the security as a whole.

After discussion, on motion duly made and seconded, it was unanimously

RESOLVED, That the Investment Committee has the authority, and may permit Investment Managers of the Hampton Pension Trust, to invest on behalf of the Trust in derivative or abstracted features or indices of securities, financial futures, obligations, or properties (real or personal), referred to herein collectively as "derivatives," including, but not limited to, financial and commodity index funds, financial swaps, streams of income, or gain or loss abstracted from an asset or whose value is based upon or derived from a feature of another asset, and

FURTHER RESOLVED, That the Hampton Pension Plan Administrator may take all such actions as are necessary to effect any Investment Committee decision to invest, or permit an Investment Manager to invest in derivatives, his action in such respect to be conclusive evidence of the Investment Committee's approval.

2. Proposed Amendment to Pension Trust

Article VI
INVESTMENT OF FUNDS

The first sentence of Article VI is proposed to be amended as follows (italics are additions to the original document):

The Trustees shall have the power to invest and reinvest all funds received by them in such securities, *financial options and futures,* obligations or properties (real or personal), or participations or interests therein, *or derivatives or abstracted features or indices thereof,* referred to herein collectively as *"assets"* including, without limitation, shares of stock (whether common or preferred), trustees' or receivers' obligations, equipment trust certificates, conditional sale agreements, *financial and commodity index funds, financial swaps, streams of income or gain or loss abstracted from assets or whose value is based upon or derived from a feature of other assets,* lease and purchase agreements, insurance company group annuity investment contracts and agreements, as they may deem advisable in their discretion as though they were the beneficial owners thereof, excluding securities issued or to be issued by any of the Companies, *and futures and options on tangible commodities other than currencies;* provided, however, that investments shall be so diversified as to minimize the risk of large losses unless under the circumstances it is clearly prudent not to do so.

Conclusions

Development of the listed options market has provided pension fund managers with powerful new tools to manage risk in stock and bond portfolios. The suggested issues and solutions to this case and the preceding one should provide you with a greater understanding of option strategies that are appropriate for use by institutional investors. However, many pension fund managers, who now realize how useful options can be to implement their investment strategies, face the next challenge—obtaining approval from their trustees to implement option strategies within the pension fund.

This case has explored typical questions raised by trustees who are being asked to change their plan document to permit the use of derivative strategies by the fund managers. While no strategy for gaining approval will be best for every situation, we have observed that most successful plans include the following steps:

1. Educate trustees on the reasons for using options in the portfolio—to control risk and to add value.
2. Emphasize that options must be considered in the context of the entire pension fund portfolio, and from this perspective, they control, rather than add risk, to the fund.
3. Obtain approval for a period of trial trading in derivatives. Your investment managers will become more comfortable with the products, and problems can be uncovered and solved in the accounting and custodial operations.
4. Emphasize strategies rather than tools. This will preclude the necessity of obtaining approval for each new option product that is introduced.
5. Be sensitive to the trustee's concerns about ERISA, the fund sponsor, and the fund beneficiaries.
6. Finally, recognize that the process will be a lengthy one but is well worth the effort.

The purpose of this case was twofold. First, to make you consider how to address the approval process in your organization, and second, to further your understanding of the appropriate use of options by institutional investors. If you can articulate why and how options should be used by pension fund managers, you can feel comfortable about your knowledge of options and the concepts presented in this book.

GLOSSARY

adjusting A dynamic trading process by which a floor trader with a spread position buys or sells options or stock to maintain the delta neutrality of the position. See **delta.**

adjusted strike price Strike price of an option, created as the result of a special event such as a stock split or a stock dividend. The adjusted strike price can differ from the regular intervals prescribed for strike prices. See **strike price interval.**

aggregate exercise price The total dollar value transferred in settlement of an exercised option.

American option An option that can be exercised at any time prior to expiration. See **European option.**

arbitrage A trading technique that involves the simultaneous purchase and sale of identical assets or of equivalent assets in two different markets with the intent of profiting by the price discrepancy.

ask price The price at which a seller is offering to sell an option or stock.

assignment Notification by the Options Clearing Corporation to the writer of an option that a holder of the option has exercised and that the terms of settlement must be met. Assignments are made on a random basis by the Options Clearing Corporation. See **delivery** and **exercise.**

at-the-money A term that describes an option with an exercise price that is equal to the current market price of the underlying stock.

automatic exercise Same as **exercise by exception.**

averaging down Buying more of a stock or an option at a lower price than the original purchase so as to reduce the average cost.

backspread A delta-neutral spread composed of more long options than short options on the same underlying stock. This position generally profits from a large movement in either direction in the underlying stock.

barrier options Various options that cease to exist or are automatically exercised once a stated level is reached by the underlying. Mostly traded over-the-counter. CAPS are exchange-traded barrier options.

bearish An adjective describing the belief that a stock or the market in general will decline in price.

bear spread One of a variety of strategies involving two or more options (or options combined with a position in the underlying stock) that will profit from a fall in price in the underlying stock.

bear spread (call) The simultaneous sale of one call option with a lower strike price and the purchase of another call option with a higher strike price.

bear spread (put) The simultaneous purchase of one put option with a higher strike price and the sale of another put option with a lower strike price.

beta A measure of how closely the movement of an individual stock tracks the movement of the entire stock market.

bid price The price at which a buyer is willing to buy an option or stock.

Black-Scholes model A mathematical formula used to calculate an option's theoretical value from the following inputs: stock price, strike price, interest rates, dividends, time to expiration, and volatility.

book Same as **public order book.**

box spread A four-sided option spread that involves a long call and short put at one strike price as well as a short call and long put at another strike price. In other words, this is a synthetic long stock position at one strike price and a synthetic short stock position at another strike price.

break-even point A stock price at option expiration at which an option strategy results in neither a profit nor a loss.

broker A person acting as an agent for making securities transactions. An "account executive" or a "broker" at a brokerage firm deals with customers. A "floor broker" on the trading floor of an exchange actually executes someone else's trading orders.

bullish An adjective describing the belief that a stock or the market in general will rise in price.

bull spread One of a variety of strategies involving two or more options (or options combined with a stock position) that will profit from a rise in price in the underlying.

bull spread (call) The simultaneous purchase of one call option with a lower strike price and the sale of another call option with a higher strike price.

bull spread (put) The simultaneous sale of one put option with a higher strike price and the purchase of another put option with a lower strike price.

butterfly spread A strategy involving four options and three strike prices that has both limited risk and limited profit potential. A long call butterfly is established by: buying one call at the lowest strike price, selling two calls at the middle strike price, and buying one call at the highest strike price. A long put butterfly is established by: buying one put at the highest strike price, selling two puts at the middle strike price, and buying one put at the lowest strike price.

buy-write Same as **covered call.**

CBOE The Chicago Board Options Exchange. CBOE opened in April 1973, and is the oldest and largest listed options exchange.

CFTC The Commodity Futures Trading Commission. The CFTC is the agency of the federal government that regulates commodity futures trading.

calendar spread Same as **time spread.**

call option. A contract that gives the holder the right (but not the obligation) to purchase the underlying stock at some predetermined price. In the case of American call options, this right can be exercised at any time until the expiration date. In the case of European call options, this right can only be exercised on the expiration date. For the writer (or grantor) of a call option, the contract represents an obligation to sell stock to the holder if the option is exercised.

carrying cost The interest expense on money borrowed to finance a stock or option position.

cash settlement The process by which the terms of an option contract are fulfilled through the payment or receipt in dollars of the amount by which the option is in-the-money as opposed to delivering or receiving the underlying stock.

Christmas tree spread A strategy involving six options and four strike prices that has both limited risk and limited profit potential. For example, a long call Christmas tree spread is established by buying one call at the lowest strike, skipping the second strike, selling three calls at the third strike, and buying two calls at the fourth strike.

class of options A term referring to all options of the same security type— either calls or puts—covering the same underlying security.

closing price The final price at which a transaction was made, but not necessarily the settlement price. See **settlement price.**

closing transaction A reduction or an elimination of an open position by the appropriate offsetting purchase or sale. An existing long option position is closed out by a selling transaction. An existing short option position is closed out by a purchase transaction.

closing rotation See **trading rotation.**

collateral Securities against which loans are made. If the value of the securities (relative to the loan) declines to an unacceptable level, this triggers a *margin call*. As such, the investor is asked to post additional collateral or the securities are sold to repay the loan.

combination spread An option technique involving a long call and a short put, or a short call and a long put. Such strategies do not fall into clearly defined categories, and the term *combination* is often used very loosely. This tactic is also called a *fence strategy*. See **fence.**

commodities See **futures contract.**

condor spread   A strategy involving four options and four strike prices that has both limited risk and limited profit potential. A long call condor spread is established by buying one call at the lowest strike, selling one call at the second strike, selling another call at the third strike, and buying one call at the fourth strike. This spread is also referred to as a *flat-top butterfly* or a *top hat spread*.

consecutive expiration cycle   See **cycle.**

contingency order   An order to conduct one transaction in one security that depends on the price of another instrument. An example might be, "Sell the XYZ Jan 50 call at 2, contingent upon XYZ being at or below $49 1/2."

contract size   The amount of the underlying asset covered by the option contract. This is 100 shares for one equity option unless adjusted for a special event, such as a stock split or a stock dividend. For index options, the contract size is the index level times the index multiplier.

conversion   An investment strategy in which a long put and a short call with the same strike price and expiration are combined with long stock to lock in a nearly riskless profit. The process of executing these three-sided trades is sometimes called *conversion arbitrage*. See **reverse conversion.**

cover   To close out an option position. This term is used most frequently to describe the purchase of an option to close out an existing short position for either a profit or loss.

covered call   An option strategy in which a call option is written against long stock on a share-for-share basis.

covered combination   Same as **covered strangle.**

covered option   An open short option position that is fully collateralized. If the holder of the option exercises, the writer of the option will not have a problem fulfilling the delivery requirements. See **uncovered option.**

covered put   An option strategy in which a put option is written against a sufficient amount of cash (or T-bills) to pay for the stock purchase if the short option is assigned.

covered straddle   An option strategy in which one call and one put with the same strike price and expiration are written against 100 shares of the underlying stock. In actuality, this is not a "covered" strategy because assignment on the short put would require purchase of stock on margin.

covered strangle   A strategy in which one call and one put with the same expiration—but different strike prices—are written against 100 shares of the underlying stock. In actuality, this is not a "covered" strategy because assignment on the short put would require purchase of stock on margin. This method is also known as a *covered combination*.

credit   Money received in an account either from a deposit or a transaction that results in increasing the account's cash balance.

credit spread   A spread strategy that increases the account's cash balance when it is established. A bull spread with puts and a bear spread with calls are examples of credit spreads.

curvature   Same as **gamma.**

cycle   The expiration dates applicable to the different series of options. Traditionally, there are three cycles: January/April/July/October, February/May/August/November, and March/June/September/December. Today, equity options expire on a sequential cycle that involves a total of four option series: two near-term months and two far-term months. For example, on January 1, a stock traditionally in the January cycle will be trading options expiring in these months: January, February, April, and July. Index options, however, expire on a consecutive cycle that involves the four near-term months. For example, on January 1, index options will be trading options expiring in these months: January, February, March, and April.

day trade   A position that is opened and closed on the same day.

debit   Money paid out from an account either from a withdrawal or a transaction that results in decreasing the cash balance.

debit spread   A spread strategy that decreases the account's cash balance when it is established. A bull spread with calls and a bear spread with puts are examples of debit spreads.

decay   See **time decay.**

delivery   The process of meeting the terms of a written option when notification of assignment has been received. In the case of a short call, the writer must deliver stock and in return receives cash for the stock sold. In the case of a short put, the writer pays cash and in return receives the stock purchased.

delta   A measure of the rate of change in an option's theoretical value for a one-unit change in the price of the underlying security.

delta-neutral spread   A trading strategy, sometimes used by professional market makers, that matches the total long deltas of a position (long stock, long calls, short puts) with the total short deltas (short stock, short calls, long puts).

diagonal spread   A strategy involving the simultaneous purchase and sale of two options of the same type that have different strike prices and different expiration dates. Example: Buy 1 May 45 call and sell 1 March 50 call.

discount   An adjective used to describe an option that is trading below its intrinsic value.

discretion   Freedom given to the floor broker by an investor to use his judgment regarding the execution of an order: Discretion can be limited, as in the case of a limit order that gives the floor broker 1/8 or 1/4 point from the stated limit price to use his judgment in executing the order. Discretion can also be unlimited, as in the case of a market-not-held order. See **market-not-held order.**

dynamic hedging A short-term trading strategy generally using futures contracts to replicate some of the characteristics of option contracts. The strategy takes into account the replicated option's delta and often requires adjusting.

early exercise A feature of American options that allows the holder to exercise an option at any time prior to the expiration date.

edge (1) The spread between the bid and ask price. This is called the *trader's edge*. (2) The difference between the market price of an option and its theoretical value using an option pricing model. This is called the *theoretical edge*.

equity In a margin account, this is the difference between the securities owned and the margin loans owed. It is the amount the investor would keep if all positions were closed out and all margin loans paid off.

equity option An option on a common stock.

equivalent positions Same as **synthetic positions.**

European option An option that can be exercised only on the expiration date. See **American option.**

ex-dividend date The day before which an investor must have purchased the stock in order to receive the dividend. On the ex-dividend date, the previous day's closing price is reduced by the amount of the dividend because purchasers of the stock on the ex-dividend date will not receive the dividend payment.

exercise To invoke the rights granted to the holder of an option contract. In the case of a call, the option holder buys the underlying stock from the option writer. In the case of a put, the option holder sells the underlying stock to the option writer.

exercise by exception A procedure used by the Options Clearing Corporation to exercise in-the-money options, unless specifically instructed by the holder of the option not to do so. This procedure protects the holder from losing the intrinsic value of the option because of failure to exercise. Unless instructed not to do so, the Options Clearing Corporation will exercise all equity options of 75 cents or more in-the-money in customer accounts, and 25 cents or more in firm and market-maker accounts. For index options subject to cash settlements, the Options Clearing Corporation, unless instructed not to do so, will exercise all index options 25 cents or more in-the-money in customer accounts, and a penny or more in firm and market-maker accounts.

exercise cycle   See **cycle.**

exercise limits   The total number of puts and/or calls that a holder is allowed to exercise during any five consecutive trading days.

exercise price   The price at which the holder of an option can purchase (call) or sell (put) the underlying stock from or to the option writer.

exotic options   Various over-the-counter options whose terms are very specific, and sometimes unique. Examples include Bermuda options (somewhere between American and European type, this option can be exercised only on certain dates) and Look-back options (whose strike price is set at the option's expiration date and varies depending on the level reached by the underlying security).

expiration date   The date on which an option and the right to exercise it cease to exist.

extrinsic value   Same as **time value.**

fair value   A price that favors neither buyer nor seller. In the case of options, this term is often used to describe the theoretical price of an option derived from a mathematical formula.

fence   A strategy involving a long call and a short put, or a short call and long put at different strike prices with the same expiration date. When this strategy is established in conjunction with the underlying stock, the three-sided tactic is called a *risk conversion* (long stock) or a *risk reversal* (short stock). This strategy is also called a *combination*. See **conversion** and **reverse conversion.**

FLexible EXchange options (FLEX)   Exchange traded index options. The user can specify, within certain limits, the terms of the options, such as exercise price, expiration date, exercise type, and settlement calculation. Can only be traded in a minimum size, which makes FLEX an institutional product.

floor broker   A trader on an exchange floor who executes trading orders for other people.

floor trader   An exchange member on the trading floor who buys and sells for his own account and therefore functions as a market maker.

frontrunning   An illegal securities transaction based on prior nonpublic knowledge of a forthcoming transaction that will affect the price of a stock.

fundamental analysis   A method of determining stock prices based on the study of earnings, sales, dividends, and accounting information.

fungibility   Interchangeability resulting from standardization. Options listed on national exchanges are fungible, while over-the-counter options generally are not.

futures contract   A contract calling for the delivery of a specific quantity of a physical good or a financial instrument (or its cash value) at some specific date in the future. There are exchange-traded futures contracts with standardized terms, and there are over-the-counter futures contracts with negotiated terms.

gamma   A measure of the rate of change in an option's delta for a one-unit change in the price of the underlying security. See **delta.**

good-until-cancelled (GTC) order   A type of limit trading order that remains in effect until it is either executed (filled) or cancelled, as opposed to a day order, which expires if not executed by the end of the trading day.

grantor   Same as **writer.**

guts   The purchase (or sale) of both an in-the-money call and an in-the-money put. A box spread can be viewed as the combination of an in-the-money strangle and an out-of-the-money strangle. To differentiate between these two strangles, the term *guts* refers to the in-the-money strangle. See **box spread** and **strangle.**

haircut   Similar to margin required of public customers, this term refers to the equity required to floor traders on equity option exchanges. Generally, one of the advantages of being a floor trader is that the haircut is less than margin requirements for public customers.

hedge   A position established with the specific intent of protecting an existing position. Example: an owner of common stock buys a put option to hedge against a possible stock price decline.

hedge ratio   Same as **delta.**

historical volatility   A measure of how volatile a stock has been over a given period of time. Usually defined as the annualized standard deviation of a stock's daily returns.

holder   The owner of a long stock or option.

horizontal spread   Same as **time spread.**

implied volatility   The volatility percentage that justifies an option's price. Calculated from the options current price, the price of the underlying, the exercise price, time to expiration and interest rate and dividends, and "backing out" the volatility estimate.

index   A compilation of several stock prices into a single number. Example: the S&P 100 Index.

index option   An option whose underlying entity is an index. Generally, index options are cash-settled.

institution   A professional investment management company. Typically, this term is used to describe large money managers such as banks, pension funds, mutual funds, and insurance companies.

intermarket spread   A strategy involving opposing positions in securities related to two different underlying entities. Example: long OEX calls and short SPX calls.

in-the-money   An adjective used to describe an option with intrinsic value. A call option is in-the-money if the stock price is above the strike price. A put option is in-the-money if the stock price is below the strike price.

intrinsic value   The in-the-money portion of an option's price. See **in-the-money.**

iron butterfly   An option strategy with limited risk and limited profit potential that involves both a long (or short) straddle, and a short (or long) strangle.

jelly roll spread   A long call and short put with the same strike price in one month, and a short call and long put with the identical strike in another month. This is the combination of synthetic long and short positions in different months. Generally only floor traders used this spread.

kappa   Same as **vega.**

lambda   A measure of leverage. The expected percent change in the value of an option for a 1 percent change in the value of the underlying.

last trading day   The last business day prior to expiration during which purchases and sales of an option can be made. For equity options, this is generally the third Friday of expiration month. For other types of options, the specification of the last trading day varies greatly.

leg   A term describing one side of a position with two or more sides. When a trader *legs into* a spread, he establishes one side first, hoping for a favorable price movement so the other side can be executed at a better price. This is, of course, a risk-oriented method of establishing a spread position.

leverage   A term describing the greater percentage of profit or loss potential when a given amount of money controls a security with a much larger face value. For example, a call option enables the holder to assume the upside potential of 100 shares of stock by investing a much smaller amount than that required to buy the stock. If the stock increases by 10 percent, for example, the option can double in value. Conversely, a 10 percent stock price decline can result in the total loss of the purchase price of the option.

limit order   A trading order placed with a broker to buy or sell a security at a specific price.

liquid market   A trading environment characterized by high trading volume, a narrow spread between the bid and ask, and the ability to trade larger sized orders without significant price changes.

listed option   A put or call traded on a national option exchange with standardized terms. In contrast, over-the-counter options usually have nonstandardized or negotiated terms. See **FLexible EXchange options.**

local A floor trader on a futures exchange who buys and sells for his own account, thus fulfilling the same role as a market maker on an options exchange.

long position A term used to describe either (1) an open position that is expected to benefit from a rise in the price of the underlying stock such as long call, short put, or long stock; or (2) an open position resulting from an opening purchase transaction such as *long call, long put,* or *long stock.*

Long-term Equity AnticiPation Securities (LEAPS) Long-term equity and index options. There are no differences between equity LEAPS and equity options except the longer exercise term of the LEAPS.

margin The minimum equity required to support an investment position. To buy *on margin* refers to borrowing part of the purchase price of a security from a brokerage firm.

market basket A group of common stocks whose price movement is expected to closely correlate with an index.

market maker An exchange member on the trading floor who buys and sells for his own account and who has the responsibility of making bids and offers and maintaining a fair and orderly market.

market-maker system A method of supplying liquidity in options markets by having market makers in competition with one another.

mark-to-market An accounting process by which the price of securities held in an account are valued each day to reflect the last sale price or market quote if the last sale is outside of the market quote. The result of this process is that the equity in an account is updated daily to properly reflect current security prices.

market-not-held order A type of market order which allows the investor to give discretion to the floor broker regarding the time and price at which a trade is executed.

market order A trading instruction from an investor to a broker to immediately buy or sell a security at the best available price.

married put strategy The simultaneous purchase of stock and the corresponding number of put options. This is a limited risk strategy during the life of the puts because the stock can be sold at the strike price of the puts.

mixed spread A term used loosely to describe a trading position that does not fit neatly into a standard spread category.

multiple listed options Options (most often equity options) that are traded on two or more security exchanges.

naked option Same as **uncovered option.**

net margin requirement The equity required in a margin account to support an option position after deducting the premium received from sold options.

net order Same as **contingency order.**

neutral An adjective describing the belief that a stock or the market in general will neither rise nor decline significantly.

90/10 strategy An option strategy in which an investor buys Treasury bills (or other liquid assets) with 90 percent of his funds—and buys call options with the balance.

nonequity option Any option that does not have common stock as the underlying asset. Nonequity options include options on futures, indexes, interest rate composites, physicals, and so on.

nonsystematic risk The portion of total risk that can be attributed to the particular firm. See **systematic risk.**

not-held order A type of order that allows the investor to release the floor broker from the normal obligations implied by the other terms of the order. For example, a limit order designated as "not-held" allows the floor broker to use his discretion in filling the order when the market trades at the limit price of the order. In this case, the floor broker is not obligated to provide the customer with an execution if the market trades through the limit price on the order. See **discretion.** See **market-not-held order.**

OTC option An over-the-counter option is one that is traded in the over-the-counter market. OTC options are not usually listed on an options exchange and generally do not have standardized terms.

omega Same as **vega.**

opening rotation See **trading rotation.**

opening transaction An addition to or creation of a trading position. An opening purchase transaction adds long options (or long securities) to an investor's total position, and an opening sell transaction adds short options (or short securities).

open interest The total number of existing option contracts.

open outcry The trading method by which competing market makers make bids and offers on the trading floor.

option A contract that gives the buyer the right, but not the obligation, to buy or sell a particular asset (the underlying security) at a fixed price for a specific period of time. The contract also obligates the seller to meet the terms of delivery if the contract right is exercised by the buyer.

optionable stock A stock on which options are traded.

option period The time from when an option contract is created to the expiration date.

option pricing curve A graphical representation of the estimated theoretical value of an option at one point in time, at various prices of the underlying asset.

option pricing model   A mathematical formula used to calculate the theoretical value of an option. See **Black-Scholes model.**

Options Clearing Corporation (OCC)   A corporation owned by the exchanges that trade listed stock options, OCC is an intermediary between option buyers and sellers. OCC issues and guarantees all option contracts.

option valuation model   See **option pricing model.**

option writer   The seller of an option contract who is obligated to meet the terms of delivery if the option holder exercises his right.

order book official   An exchange employee in charge of keeping the public order book and executing the orders therein.

out-of-the-money   An adjective used to describe an option that has no intrinsic value, i.e., all of its value consists of time value. A call option is out-of-the-money if the stock price is below the strike price. A put option is out-of-the-money if the stock price is above the strike price. See **intrinsic value** and **time value.**

over-the-counter-option   Same as **OTC option.**

overvalued   An adjective used to describe an option that is trading at a price higher than its theoretical value. It must be remembered that this is a subjective evaluation, because theoretical value depends on one subjective input—the volatility estimate.

overwrite   An option strategy involving the sale of a call option against an existing long stock position. This is different from the covered-write strategy, which involves the simultaneous purchase of stock and sale of a call.

parity   An adjective used to describe the difference between the stock price and the strike price of an in-the-money option. When an option is trading at its intrinsic value, it is said to be *trading at parity.*

physical option   An option whose underlying entity is a physical good or commodity. For example, currency options traded at the Philadelphia Exchange and many OTC currency options are options on the currency itself, rather than on futures contracts.

pin risk   The risk to a floor trader with a conversion or reversal position that the stock price will exactly equal the strike price at option expiration. The trader will not know how many of his long options to exercise because he will not know how many of his short options will be assigned. The risk is that on the following Monday he will have a long or short stock position and thus be subject to the risk of an adverse price move.

pit   Same as **trading pit.**

position   The combined total of an investor's open option contracts and long or short stock.

position limits The maximum number of open option contracts that an investor can hold in one account or a group of related accounts. Some exchanges express the limit in terms of option contracts on the same side of the market, and others express it in terms of total long or short delta.

position trading An investing strategy in which open positions are held for an extended period of time.

premium (1) Total price of an option: intrinsic value plus time value. (2) Often this word is used to mean the same as **time value.**

primary market (1) For securities that are traded in more than one market, the primary market is usually the exchange where the most volume is traded. (2) The initial sale of securities to public investors. See **secondary market.**

profit graph A graphical presentation of the profit and loss possibilities of an investment strategy at one point in time (usually option expiration), at various stock prices.

profit profile Same as **profit graph.**

public order book The limit buy and limit sell orders from public customers that are away from the current market price and are managed by the order book official or specialist. If the market price moves so that an order in the public order book is the best bid or offer, that order has priority and must be the first one filled at that price.

put option A contract that gives the buyer the right (but not the obligation) to sell the underlying stock at some predetermined price. For the writer (or grantor) of a put option, the contract represents an obligation to buy stock from the buyer if the option is assigned.

ratio calendar combination A term used loosely to describe any variation on an investment strategy that involves both puts and calls in unequal quantities and at least two different strike prices and two different expirations.

ratio calendar spread An investment strategy in which more short-term options are sold than longer-term options are purchased.

ratio spread (1) Most commonly used to describe the purchase of near-the-money options and the sale of a greater number of farther out-of-the-money options, with all options having the same expiration date. (2) Generally used to describe any investment strategy in which options are bought and sold in unequal numbers or on a greater than one-for-one basis with the underlying stock.

ratio write An investment strategy in which stock is purchased and call options are sold on a greater than one-for-one basis.

realized gain and losses The net amount received or paid when a closing transaction is made and matched together with an opening transaction.

repair strategy An investment strategy in which an existing long stock position is supplemented by buying one in-the-money call (or one at-the-money call) and selling two out-of-the-money calls, all calls having the same expiration. The effect of this strategy is to lower the break-even point of stock ownership without significantly increasing the risk of the total position.

resistance A term used in technical analysis to describe a price area at which rising price action is expected to stop or meet increased selling activity. This analysis is based on historic price behavior of the stock.

reversal Same as **reverse conversion.**

reverse conversion An investment strategy used by professional option traders in which a short put and long call with the same strike price and expiration are combined with short stock to lock in a nearly riskless profit. The process of executing these three-sided trades is sometimes called reversal arbitrage.

rho A measure of the expected change in an option's theoretical value for a 1 percent change in interest rates.

risk arbitrage Commonly used terms to describe the purchase of a stock subject to takeover rumors with the hope of selling at a significant profit to a company effecting the takeover. The risk is present because there is never any guarantee that a takeover will materialize.

risk conversion/reversal See **fence.**

rolling A trading action in which the trader simultaneously closes an open option position and creates a new option position at a different strike price, different expiration, or both. Variations of this include roll up, roll down, and roll out.

rotation See **trading rotation.**

SEC The Securities and Exchange Commission. The SEC is the federal government agency that regulates the security industry.

scalper A trader on the floor of an exchange who hopes to buy on the bid price, sell on the ask price, and profit from moment to moment price movements. Risk is limited by the very short time duration (usually 10 seconds to 3 minutes) of maintaining any one position.

secondary market A market where securities are bought and sold after their initial purchase by public investors.

sector indices Indices that measure the performance of a narrow market segment, such as biotechnology or small capitalization stocks.

sequential expiration cycle See **cycle.**

series of options Option contracts on the same underlying stock having the same strike price and expiration month.

settlement price   The official price at the end of a trading session. This price is established by the Options Clearing Corporation and is used to determine changes in account equity, margin requirements, and for other purposes. See **mark-to-market.**

short option position   The position of an option writer which represents an obligation to meet the terms of the option if it is assigned.

short position   Any open position that is expected to benefit from a decline in the price of the underlying stock such as long put, short call or short stock.

short stock position   A strategy that profits from a stock price decline. It is initiated by borrowing stock from a broker-dealer and selling it in the open market. This strategy is closed out at a later date by buying back the stock.

specialist   An exchange member who manages the limit order book and makes bids and offers for his own account in the absence of opposite market side orders. See **market maker.**

speculator   A trader with an expectation of a particular market price behavior.

spread   A position consisting of two parts, each of which alone would profit from opposite directional price moves. These opposite parts are entered simultaneously in the hope of (1) limiting risk, or (2) benefiting in a change of price relationship between the two.

spread order   Trading order to simultaneously make two transactions, each of which would benefit from opposite directional price moves.

standard deviation   A statistical measure of variability in a data series. Used as an estimate of volatility.

stock index futures   A futures contract that has as its underlying entity a stock market index. Such futures contracts are generally subject to cash settlement.

stop-limit order   A type of contingency order placed with a broker that becomes a limit order when the security trades, or is bid or offered at a specific price.

stop order   A type of contingency order placed with a broker that becomes a market order when the security trades, or is bid or offered at a specific price.

straddle   A trading position involving puts and calls on a one-to-one basis in which the puts and calls have the same strike price, expiration, and underlying entity. A long straddle is when both options are owned and a short straddle is when both options are written.

strangle   A trading position involving out-of-the-money puts and calls on a one-to-one basis. The puts and calls have different strike prices, but the same expiration and underlying stock. A long strangle is when both options are owned, and a short strangle is when both options are written.

strap A strategy involving two calls and one put. All options have the same strike price, expiration, and underlying stock.

strike price Same as **exercise price.**

strike price interval The normal price difference between option exercise prices. Equity options generally have $2.50 strike price intervals (if the underlying security price ranges from $5 to $25), $5.00 intervals (from $25 to $200), and $10 intervals above $200. Index options generally have $5 strike price intervals at all price levels. See **adjusted strike price.**

strip A strategy involving two puts and one call. All options have the same strike price, expiration, and underlying stock.

suitability A requirement that any investing strategy fall within the financial means and investment objectives of an investor.

support A term used in technical analysis to describe a price area at which falling price action is expected to stop or meet increased buying activity. This analysis is based on previous price behavior of the stock.

synthetic position A strategy involving two or more instruments that has the same risk-reward profile as a strategy involving only one instrument. The following list summarizes the six primary synthetic positions.

synthetic long call A long stock position combined with a long put.

synthetic long put A short stock position combined with a long call.

synthetic long stock A long call position combined with a short put.

synthetic short call A short stock position combined with a short put.

synthetic short put A long stock position combined with a short call.

synthetic short stock A short call position combined with a long put.

systematic risk The portion of total risk that can be attributed to the overall market. See **nonsystematic risk.**

tau Same as **vega.**

technical analysis A method of predicting future stock price movements based on the study of historical market data such as the prices themselves, trading volume, open interest, the relation of advancing issues to declining issues, and short selling volume.

theoretical value An estimated fair value of an option derived from a mathematical model.

theta A measure of the rate of change in an option's theoretical value for a one-unit change in time to the option's expiration date. See **time decay.**

tick (1) The smallest unit price change allowed in trading a security. For a common stock, this is generally 1/8th point. For an option under $3 in price, this is generally 1/16th point. For an option over $3, this is generally 1/8th point. (2) The net number of stocks upticking or down ticking. For example, if there are 10 stocks total with 7 having traded on upticks and 3 having traded on downticks, then the tick is +4.

time decay   A term used to describe how the theoretical value of an option "erodes" or reduces with the passage of time. Time decay is specifically quantified by theta. See **theta.**

time spread   An option strategy most commonly used by floor traders which involves options with the same strike price, but different expiration dates.

time value   The part of an option's total price that exceeds intrinsic value. The price of an out-of-the-money option consists entirely of time value. See **intrinsic value** and **out-of-the-money.**

trader   (1) Any investor who makes frequent purchases and sales. (2) A member of an exchange who conducts his buying and selling on the trading floor of the exchange.

trading pit   A specific location on the trading floor of an exchange designated for the trading of a specific security.

trading rotation   A trading procedure on exchange floors in which bids and offers are made on specific options in a sequential order. Opening trading rotations are conducted to guarantee all entitled public orders an execution. At times of extreme market activity, a closing trading rotation can also be conducted.

traditional expiration cycle   See **cycle.**

transaction costs   All of the charges associated with executing a trade and maintaining a position. These include brokerage commissions, exchange fees, and margin interest. The spread between bid and ask is sometimes taken into account as a transaction cost.

Treasury bill/call option strategy   Same as **90/10 strategy.**

type of options   The classification of an option contract as either a put or call.

uncovered option   A short option position that is not fully collateralized if notification of assignment is received. A short call position is uncovered if the writer does not have a long stock position to deliver. A short put position is uncovered if the writer does not have the financial resources in his account to buy the stock.

underlying security   The asset that can be purchased or sold according to the terms of the option contract.

undervalued   An adjective used to describe an option that is trading at a price lower than its theoretical value. It must be remembered that this is a subjective evaluation because theoretical value depends on one subjective input—the volatility estimate.

unit of trading   The minimum quantity or amount allowed when trading a security. The normal minimum for common stock is 1 round lot or 100 shares. The normal minimum for options is one contract (which covers 100 shares of stock).

unsystematic risk   Same as **nonsystematic risk.**

upstairs trader   A professional trader who makes trading decisions away from the exchange floor and communicates his instructions to the floor for execution by the floor broker.

vega   A measure of the rate of change in an option's theoretical value for a one-unit change in the volatility assumption.

vertical spread   (1) Most commonly used to describe the purchase of one option and sale of another where both are of the same type and same expiration, but have different strike prices. (2) It is also used to describe a delta-neutral spread in which more options are sold than are purchased.

volatility   A measure of stock price fluctuation. Mathematically, volatility is the annualized standard deviation of daily returns.

volatility test   A procedure in which a multisided options position is evaluated, assuming several different volatilities for the purpose of judging the risk of the position.

wasting asset   An investment with a finite life, the value of which decreases over time if there is no price fluctuation in the underlying asset.

write   To sell an option. An investor who sells an option is called the writer, regardless of whether the option is covered or uncovered.

INDEX